Environmental Anthropology Engaging Ecotopia

Environmental Anthropology and Ethnobiology

General Editor: **Roy Ellen**, FBA
Professor of Anthropology and Human Ecology, University of Kent at Canterbury

Interest in environmental anthropology has grown steadily in recent years, reflecting national and international concern about the environment and developing research priorities. 'Environmental Anthropology and Ethnobiology' is an international series based at the University of Kent at Canterbury. It is a vehicle for publishing up-to-date monographs and edited works on particular issues, themes, places or peoples which focus on the interrelationship between society, culture and the environment.

Volume 1
The Logic of Environmentalism: Anthropology, Ecology and Postcoloniality
Vassos Argyrou

Volume 2
Conversations on the Beach: Fishermen's Knowledge, Metaphor and Environmental Change in South India
Götz Hoeppe

Volume 3
Green Encounters: Shaping and Contesting Environmentalism in Rural Costa Rica
Luis A. Vivanco

Volume 4
Local Science vs. Global Science: Approaches to Indigenous Knowledge in International Development
Edited by Paul Sillitoe

Volume 5
Sustainability and Communities of Place
Edited by Carl A. Maida

Volume 6
Modern Crises and Traditional Strategies: Local Ecological Knowledge in Island Southeast Asia
Edited by Roy Ellen

Volume 7
Traveling Cultures and Plants: The Ethnobiology and Ethnopharmacy of Human Migrations
Edited by Andrea Pieroni and Ina Vandebroek

Volume 8
Fishers And Scientists In Modern Turkey: The Management of Natural Resources, Knowledge and Identity on the Eastern Black Sea Coast
Ståle Knudsen

Volume 9
Landscape Ethnoecology: Concepts of Biotic and Physical Space
Edited by Leslie Main Johnson and Eugene Hunn

Volume 10
Landscape, Process and Power: Re-Evaluating Traditional Environmental Knowledge
Edited by Sabrina Heckler

Volume 11
Mobility and Migration In Indigenous Amazonia: Contemporary Ethnoecological Perspectives
Edited by Miguel N. Alexiades

Volume 12
Unveiling the Whale: Discourses on Whales and Whaling
Arne Kalland

Volume 13
Virtualism, Governance and Practice: Vision and Execution in Environmental Conservation
Edited by James G. Carrier and Paige West

Volume 14
Ethnobotany in the New Europe: People, Health and Wild Plant Resources
Edited by Manuel Pardo-de-Santayana, Andrea Pieroni and Rajindra K. Puri

Volume 15
Urban Pollution: Cultural Meanings, Social Practices
Edited by Eveline Dürr and Rivke Jaffe

Volume 16
Weathering the World: Recovery in the Wake of the Tsunami in a Tamil Fishing Village
Frida Hastrup

Volume 17
Environmental Anthropology Engaging Ecotopia: Bioregionalism, Permaculture, and Ecovillages
Edited by Joshua Lockyer and James R. Veteto

Volume 18
Things Fall Apart? The Political Ecology of Forest Governance in Southern Nigeria
Pauline von Hellermann

Volume 19
Sustainable Development: An Appraisal from the Gulf Region
Edited by Paul Sillitoe

Volume 20
Beyond the Lens of Conservation: Malagasy and Swiss Imaginations of One Another
Eva Keller

Environmental Anthropology Engaging Ecotopia

Bioregionalism, Permaculture, and Ecovillages

Edited by
Joshua Lockyer and James R. Veteto

berghahn
NEW YORK • OXFORD
www.berghahnbooks.com

First edition published in 2013 by

Berghahn Books

www.berghahnbooks.com

First paperback edition published in 2015

Library of Congress Cataloging-in-Publication Data

Environmental anthropology engaging ecotopia : bioregionalism, permaculture, and ecovillages / edited by Joshua Lockyer and James R. Veteto.
p. cm. — (Studies in environmental anthropology and ethnobiology ; v. 17)
ISBN 978-0-85745-879-7 (hardback : alk. paper) -- ISBN 978-1-78238-905-7 (paperback : alk. paper) – ISBN 978-0-85745-880-3 (ebook)
1. Human ecology. 2. Ethnobiology. I. Lockyer, Joshua. II. Veteto, James R.
GF41.E418 2013
304.2—dc23

2012032900

British Library Cataloguing in Publication Data

A catalogue record for this book is available from the British Library

Printed on acid-free paper.

ISBN: 978-0-85745-879-7 hardback
ISBN: 978-1-78238-905-7 paperback
ISBN: 978-0-85745-880-3 ebook

Joshua Lockyer would like to dedicate this book to all the people in Celo Community, Earthaven Ecovillage, Dancing Rabbit Ecovillage, and other intentional communities who have inspired him with their true commitment to finding a way to live more sustainably.

James R. Veteto would like to dedicate this book to his first permaculture mentor and good friend Joe Hollis and to the wonderful plant sanctuary, Mountain Gardens, that he and his lively band of co-conspirators and apprentices have created over the past forty years in Katuah bioregion, USA.

Contents

Illustrations

Figures

Tables

Maps

Acknowledgments

I would like to acknowledge the Department of Anthropology and the Environmental Studies Program at Washington University in St. Louis, where a postdoctoral fellowship provided time and resources to envision and germinate this volume. My colleagues in the Department of Behavioral Sciences at Arkansas Tech University provided a supportive environment in which to bring the book to fruition and continue to incorporate the bioregional vision into teaching, learning, and research. Some of the chapters were presented at a panel at the 2010 American Anthropological Association annual meetings in New Orleans entitled "Circulating Ecotopian Imaginaries." Three anonymous reviewers provided valuable and encouraging feedback on the manuscript. Brian Burke and Geoff Kelley assisted with especially insightful comments on a draft of the introduction. Last but certainly not least, my friend and colleague Jim Veteto was, once again, a superlative co-conspirator.

—Joshua Lockyer

I would like to thank all of the daring cultural revolutionaries of the 1960s (and before) who set ecotopian thinking into motion. My life and thinking in the domains that are the subject of this book have been enriched by the work of Tim Ingold, Arturo Escobar, David Graeber, Robert Rhoades, Harold Conklin, Virginia Nazarea, Gary Paul Nabhan, Julian Steward, E. N. Anderson, Robert Netting, Gary Snyder, Roy Rappaport, Keith Basso, Peggy Barlett, Wendell Berry, Roy Ellen, Eugene Hunn, Darrell Posey, Bill Mollison, Peter Kropotkin, Simon Ortiz, James Mooney, Julie Cruikshank, Peter Berg, James Scott, Carl Sauer, Vandana Shiva, and John Bennett, among others. I would especially like to thank Katuah bioregion, the Eastern Band of Cherokee Indians, and Celo Community for educating me in the ways of place-based Appalachian mountain living. My collaboration with Josh Lockyer continues to be much like the emergent bioregional mead-making movement—it just gets better the more it ferments.

—James R. Veteto

Foreword

E.N. Anderson

My father grew up on a small, struggling cotton farm in a remote part of east Texas. The farm was sold long ago, and the land is now neglected, growing back to brush and small trees. Worldwide, millions of acres of such land—fine soil, easily recultivated—are unused today, waiting for better farming regimes that can use them to advantage.

Meanwhile, in spite of Rachel Carson's classic (1962), the "silent spring" advances. Throughout much of rural America, pesticides and fence-to-fence cultivation have virtually wiped out all forms of life other than the one or two crop species grown. No birds sing, no rabbits run across the road, scarcely a weed raises its head. The same is now true in China, and increasingly so from Mexico to Indonesia. The resulting increase in expenses, problems, and government activity has led to a decline of small farms and a rise in large agribusiness enterprises. Conservationists have succeeded in saving many wild lands, and urban environmentalism has cleaned up some cities, but the decline of the world's rural landscapes gets worse all the time.

A natural reaction began long ago with the organic farming movement. In the 1960s and 1970s, this was joined by several new movements, based on more comprehensive knowledge of science and technology. Bill Mollison's permaculture, which drew considerably on Chinese and Southeast Asian traditional practices, has been the most successful and lasting. Meanwhile, the back-to-the-land movement, always a strong one in America and parts of Europe, has survived and flourished.

I started using the term "ecotopia" in 1969. Ernest Callenbach, who of course deserves all the credit for making it famous, tells me (by email, 2010) the term was in the air; apparently, a European group independently coined it about the same time. At the time, I was involved with a wonderful group called the New Alchemists, who brought to alternative agriculture many of the new methods and ideas of the 1960s; some are mentioned in the present book. I somewhat lost touch when the leaders moved from California to Massachusetts, but the excitement never died. I had a tiny farm at the time, producing much of our family food and extra avocadoes for sale. Like other small orchards in the Riverside area of California, it did not survive the "energy shock" of the mid-1970s. Since then, I have devoted my life to observing traditional societies that have managed to live sustainably on their lands. I try to figure out how they do it. The authors of the studies within this volume have addressed the question of sustainability in several communities around the world. Studies vary from urban garden projects to truly utopian—ecotopian—communities in remote mountain refugia. All these experiments, in one way or another, point the way to alternatives to modern industrial agriculture—alternatives to monocropping, to pesticides, to dependence on fossil fuels, and to a system that wastes fantastic amounts of fuel, water, and food in a world where over a billion people are hungry.

Many of the experiments are based on concepts from bioregionalism, permaculture, and ecovillage design. They explain these concepts and principles far better than I can. Suffice it to say that bioregionalism and permaculture since the 1970s have been critical in a broad rethinking of agriculture around the world. They have grown and spread widely, in spite of competition from industrial agriculture. Bioregionalism has much wider implications, having the goal and real potential to reform urban planning, education, water management, and indeed all aspects of human communal existence. It rather plays against the current tendency toward "globalization," but its time will come. Various tests of bioregional knowledge have emerged from the movement—tests that ask students to state where their water comes from, where their milk comes from, what the local plant communities are, and so on—and should be more widely used to challenge today's students, so expert with electronics yet so widely ignorant of local environments.

This brings us to the teaching function of the present book, and of the communities and projects described herein. Richard Louv, in his excellent and widely known book *Last Child in the Woods* (2005), has pointed out that American environmental education is in desperate shape. Children increasingly grow up with no contact with nature; their parents are afraid to let them play outside (snakes!), schools have dropped natural history, and almost all children now live in cities or in rural areas so transformed by industrial agriculture that they are actually more barren and unnatural than the cities. The world of sixty years ago, when most of us grew up familiar with wild plants and animals and with traditional mixed farming, is gone. Aldo Leopold's model farm in *A Sand County Almanac* (1949), on which kids grow up trapping muskrats from the family pond and selling the fur for pocket money, seems like something from ancient Mesopotamia or Classical Greece. The first need today is to get the kids to have *some* contact with nature—any contact, so long as it is in a peaceful environment without too much to scare their parents. However, the children need to be able to relate to it. Merely exposing an urban kid—or, increasingly, even a rural kid—to the wild may simply lead to incomprehension and inability to form any connection. The alternative farms and gardens in this book provide ideal environments. If nothing else, children can relate to the food and to any domestic animals present.

Science education in the United States has been sacrificed to endless drills in reading and math for standardized testing, and there is virtually no field science taught in American schools today (see education postings on my website, www.krazykioti.com, which review the problem). Some authors in the present book address this directly; more deal with cultural transmission, demonstration projects, outreach, and the simple and direct value of successful ecotopian communities, projects, and farms as teaching opportunities. No one can visit them without being influenced.

Traditional cultures, broadly speaking, teach through a process of guided performance. Children learning a skill learn by doing, with varying degrees of verbal instruction (often very little). Stories and similar verbal traditions are learned more passively, but often in ritual or ceremonial settings where the importance of the stories comes through clearly from the importance of the occasion. Managing salience is a major key to traditional, and indeed to all, education. Clearly, we need all these things in modern education. We have to escape the mindless drills, and the devotion to empty, decontextualized "facts" that such drills reflect and encourage.

Several authors herein address Karl Marx's contrast between utopian socialism and what Marx called "scientific" socialism. The former rested on experimental communities, the latter on developing mass movements. The former transforms the world one community at a time—hopefully with a snowball effect; the latter transforms the world one step at a time. The former runs the risk of gradualism. The latter runs the risk of transforming the world only to find out too late that the plan was badly flawed (as happened, indeed, with Marxism).

We need to try both approaches. Time is short; peak oil is expected any day now. Ecotopian projects and communities not only provide the world with alternatives, but also show that they are practicable. They are working in real time and in the real world. They have faced the problems of developing new systems; they have dealt with the bugs—real ones as well as metaphoric ones.

The history of alternative communities in the United States goes back to earliest settlement. Many of the original European colonies were founded by religious dissidents fleeing persecution: Puritans in New England, Quakers in Pennsylvania and North Carolina, Mennonites and other German and Dutch Anabaptist groups in the same two states, Catholics in Maryland, Huguenots in New York, Calvinists almost everywhere. The Anabaptists in particular formed intentional communities, many of which survive today (the Amish, Hutterite, and Mennonite communities). Later sects, notably the Mormons, set up their own worlds. More radical and less religious communities emerged in the nineteenth century, and inspired, indirectly, our present eco-communities; classic histories by Charles Nordhoff (1875) and John Noyes (1870) are still well worth reading.

Countless later communities began and occasionally flourished, though two familiar to me in the southern California desert—the socialist Llano and anarchist Palm Desert—succumbed to shaky organization and a lack of water (they survive in more ordinary forms; Palm Desert is now a mere suburb of Palm Springs, but Llano retains a remote, free-spirited ethos). The rise of both religious and secular communes and alternative communities since 1960 has not found a definitive chronicler, but the present book details some of the most hopeful, well-planned, and successful of the efforts from this time.

This has taken me to the question raised by the chapters in the book at hand: what are the wider contexts and constraints—cultural, political, and economic—that surround alternative agriculture and alternative eco-communities?

Much of the answer lies in the motivation of the actors.

The authors in this volume are aware that alternative farming is not mere technology. It is done as a labor of love and as a passionate ethical commitment. No one does it to get rich. No one does it out of the economists' "rational individual self-interest." Environmental anthropologists are now aware of the importance of emotion, passion, and spirituality in human-environment relationships. Traditional societies often use religion as the social force for teaching and motivating moral and pro-environmental action (Anderson 1996; Berkes 2008; Milton 2002). Others, less explicitly religious, still have strongly conservationist and holistic worldviews. "Religion," a broad term, here implies—among other things—a reverent, respectful, caring, and responsible attitude toward the environment.

Even in the modern secular world, where religion is often an empty shell or is narrow and unconcerned with environment, ecological and environmental concerns are passionately held and deeply felt. Many, if not most, farmers and ranchers, even big agribusiness operators, are kept in business by love of the lifestyle more than profit (see, e.g., Hedrick 2007). Religion remains surprisingly common as a base. Secular values systems can work also, but with difficulty. Getting a really large number of people to internalize a values system is difficult, especially if it is a system that privileges the future over the present. Humans tend to discount the future; a dollar today is better than a hundred dollars a year down the line. Prioritizing long-term and wide-flung considerations over short-term and narrow ones is the heart and soul of conservation and sustainability, but it requires religion or some equivalently passionate personal commitment to a moral program. Religion also gives people the excuse to feel the awe, reverence, and devotion that most people feel toward wild and semi-wild nature (however defined!); in our society, many people feel compelled to think of worries and work unless directed to "higher things."

The urban bioregionalists, ecovillagers, and permaculturists described in this volume are driven by such commitments. They are dedicated, often to the point of living with poverty, backbreaking toil, cold, heat, and heartbreaking setbacks. Many have dealt successfully with the emotional tensions that are inevitable when strong-souled idealists form communities. They are driven by a complex dream: creating a world that is not only ecologically sustainable but is also personally rewarding through community, richness, beauty, pride, and the real joys of self-sacrifice for a good cause. These immediate benefits may make it possible to prioritize, successfully, the long-term, just as the beauty and richness of ceremony and ritual helps religion prioritize moral claims.

The environmental movement depends on such passionate commitments. This was often seen by our forefathers better than by current writers. Here is William Hornaday writing in 1913, in *Our Vanishing Wild Life:*

> To-day, the thing that stares me in the face every waking hour, like a grisly spectre with bloody fang and claw, is *the extermination of species*. To me, that is a horrible thing. It is wholesale murder, no less. It is a capital crime, and a black disgrace to the race of civilized mankind. I say "civilized mankind," because savages don't do it! (Hornaday 1913: 8)

His use of the word "savages" is ironic here; he goes on to provide a very modern-sounding account of good management by Native Americans as compared to the terrible management by white Americans in the early twentieth century.

Hornaday was not a wild-eyed countercultural; he was a pillar of the New York establishment and head of the New York Zoo. His rhetoric was typical of that period. We need more like it today. Perhaps most interesting, though, was that this rhetoric—and a great deal more like it—was in a book that also buried the opponents to conservation in literally thousands of meticulous, carefully gathered statistics and other factual data. People in the age of Hornaday, Muir, and Leopold knew that humans think and act by combining emotion and cognition. This once-evident fact of life was only recently rediscovered by psychology and anthropology (Anderson 1996, 2010).

We should not be afraid of moral passion, of openly loving our lifestyles and environments, or of maintaining that good food, good land use, and good care for the future are not just matters of opinion or of "discourse." It is so easy to get bogged down in the details of toilet design, raised bed maintenance, and arguments about road building, and forget to remind the world that beauty and health are, in the end, better than ugliness and sickness—even if the latter pay, under an outrageously corrupted economic regime. Only passion and enthusiasm, coupled with solid evidence, will engage the rest of the world.

We also need deep humility before the complexities of nature and of human society. As Hippocrates said 2,500 years ago, "the art is long, life is short."

Since permaculture and related small-farming methods are clearly superior to standard, contemporary, high throughput agriculture, why have they not triumphed long ago? Why do the intensive methods that inspired them—Chinese rice agriculture, Southeast Asian vegetable and tree culture, European mixed farming, and the rest—go to the wall in the face of "modern" agribusiness?

There are several reasons, but the most critical one faced by modern permaculturists and other alternative cultivators is the subsidy economy. Governments today pour fantastic amounts of direct and indirect subsidies into agriculture, and the money goes almost entirely to support large-scale farming that uses maximal amounts of fossil fuels—not only as fuel, but also as feedstocks for fertilizers and pesticides. The subsidy structure is the result of power politics. Large landowners, fossil fuel corporations, and chemical corporations have set the agenda, often with the direct intention of destroying small farms and organic farmers. It is no accident that politically conservative periods in American history—such as the 1920s and 1980s—were periods of unprecedented and extreme abandonment of small farms and expansion of large-scale agribusiness enterprises.

The result is not even remotely like the "free market," and is "capitalist" only by stretching definitions. In fact, the most extreme forms of government-funded chemical and heavy equipment farming have been in Communist countries, China being probably the worst case. The United States is strikingly similar; American agriculture is more socialist than capitalist, and it is a socialism devised by and for giant agribusiness. Thus, many trenchant and scathing critiques have come from genuine free marketeers (e.g., Baden 1997; Bovard 1991; Myers 1998; for a different, anthropological view, see Barlett 1993). The three hundred thousand largest farm enterprises in the United States produce 89 percent of the product and receive 76 percent of the direct subsidies to agriculture (Conkin 2008), and probably at least that much of the indirect ones. Most of the subsidies go to major commodity producers: staple grains and cotton. No smaller enterprise can really compete in today's political-economic framework.

The resulting landscapes are ugly. Our aesthetic sense, often disregarded in the (post)modern world as a frill or an arbitrary afterthought, is actually an evolved guide to good land and landscapes. The decline in aesthetic appeal of rural landscapes is an indicator too often ignored.

Subsidized production of monocropped "commodities," heavily subsidized oil, government-built highways, government-subsidized railways and shipping, public university research on chemicals and crops, and a whole host of other agendas dominate the rural economy. World development agencies have spread this gospel abroad. The Global South copies the Global North. The World Bank, World Trade Organization, and other bodies actively propagate an economic order dominated by large firms and their interests, unresponsive to local alternatives (on development, see Dichter 2003; Easterly 2006; Ellerman 2005; Escobar 2008; Hancock 1991; Stiglitz 2003; Yos 2003, 2008). To this must be added outright corruption, and the thuggish behavior of many governments supported by big oil and big agribusiness (cf. Anderson 2010; Ascher 1999; Bunker and Ciccantell 2005; Juhasz 2008).

It has been pointed out repeatedly that the real price of a gallon of gasoline is much higher than the pump price; various estimates of the real price vary from $20 to $200 or more. The low pump price reflects passing on the real costs of production and consumption to the suffering citizens of the producing countries, who are often murdered outright by oil extraction interests (Juhasz 2008), and the suffering citizens of consuming countries, who endure pollution and pay exorbitant taxes to build roads and subsidize oil firms. Obviously, if the real costs of fossil fuels were factored into its purchase price, agriculture would look very different—and much more like what is described in the present volume. On a level playing field, with any kind of reasonable discounting, alternative farmers would out-compete the wasteful, throughput-maximizing mechanical agriculture of today. But without altering the policies of virtually every nation today, the future of alternative farming is not assured.

Meanwhile, alternative farmers—permaculturists, organic farmers, or plain old small farmers—deal with economic and social realities. They are constructing new worlds within the shell of the old, in city lots, in mountain valleys, in abandoned small farm landscapes. They are creating models that everyone can actually see, and can thus learn how much beauty and value a rural landscape can have. They deserve our full respect as well as worldwide emulation.

References

Anderson, E. N. 1996. *Ecologies of the Heart*. New York: Oxford University Press.

———. 2010. *The Pursuit of Ecotopia*. Santa Barbara, CA: Praeger.

Ascher, William. 1999. *Why Governments Waste Natural Resources*. Baltimore: Johns Hopkins University Press.

Baden, John, ed. 1997. *The Next West: Public Lands, Community, and Economy in the American West.* Washington DC: Island Press.

Barlett, Peggy. 1993. *American Dreams, Rural Realities: Family Farms in Crisis.* Chapel Hill: University of North Carolina Press.

Berkes, Fikret. 2008. *Sacred Ecology.* 2nd ed. New York: Routledge.

Bovard, James. 1991. *The Farm Fiasco.* San Francisco: Institute for Contemporary Studies.

Bunker, Stephen, and Paul Ciccantell. 2005. *Globalization and the Race for Resources.* Baltimore: Johns Hopkins University Press.

Carson, Rachel. 1962. *Silent Spring.* Boston: Houghton Mifflin.

Conkin, Paul Keith. 2008. *A Revolution Down on the Farm: The Transformation of American Agriculture Since 1929.* Lexington: University Press of Kentucky.

Dichter, Thomas W. 2003. *Despite Good Intentions: Why Development Assistance to the Third World Has Failed.* Amherst: University of Massachusetts Press.

Easterly, William. 2006. *The White Man's Burden: Why the West's Efforts to Aid the Rest Have Done So Much Ill and So Little Good.* New York: Penguin Press.

Ellerman, David. 2005. *Helping People Help Themselves: From the World Bank to an Alternative Philosophy of Development Assistance.* Ann Arbor: University of Michigan Press.

Escobar, Arturo. 2008. *Territories of Difference: Place, Movements, Life,* Redes. Durham, NC: Duke University Press.

Hancock, Graham. 1991. *Lords of Poverty.* London: MacMillan.

Hedrick, Kimberly. 2007. "Our Way of Life: Identity, Landscape, and Conflict" (PhD diss., University of California, Riverside).

Hornaday, William. 1913. *Our Vanishing Wild Life.* New York: Charles Scribner's Sons.

Juhasz, Antonia. 2008. *The Tyranny of Oil: The World's Most Powerful Industry and What We Must Do to Stop It.* New York: William Morrow.

Louv, Richard. 2005. *Last Child in the Woods: Saving Children from Nature-Deficit Disorder.* Chapel Hill, NC: Algonquin Books of Chapel Hill.

Leopold, Aldo. 1949. *A Sand County Almanac.* New York: Oxford University Press.

Milton, Kay. 2002. *Loving Nature: Towards an Ecology of Emotion.* London: Routledge.

Myers, Norman. 1998. *Perverse Subsidies: Tax $s Undercutting Our Economies and Environments Alike.* With Jennifer Kent. Winnipeg, Canada: International Institute for Sustainable Development.

Nordhoff, Charles. 1875. *The Communistic Societies of the United States, from Personal Visit and Observation.* New York: Harper and Brothers.

Noyes, John Humphrey. 1870. *History of American Socialisms.* Philadelphia: J. B. Lippincott.

Stiglitz, Joseph. 2003. *Globalization and Its Discontents.* New York: W. W. Norton.

Yos Santasombat. 2003. *Biodiversity, Local Knowledge and Sustainable Development.* Chiang Mai, Thailand: Regional Center for Social Science and Sustainable Development.

———. 2008. *Flexible Peasants: Reconceptualizing the Third World's Rural Types.* Chiang Mai, Thailand: Regional Center for Social Science and Sustainable Development.

Environmental Anthropology Engaging Ecotopia

An Introduction

Joshua Lockyer and James R. Veteto

We are living in a utopian moment. The majority of humans are already being negatively affected by a number of coupled social and environmental crises. These conditions are created in large part by hegemony of thought and practice that ontologically separates humans from nature, rationalizes the externalization of the social and environmental costs of production and consumption, justifies extreme inequality, and sees solutions only in a continuation of the same systems that generated the problems in the first place. Together these and other problems constitute a crisis that demands imaginative responses and viable alternatives. We contend that anthropology must find ways to engage with such existing possibilities.

The present crises are not new; the fundamental idea that the current situation cannot continue was recognized decades ago with the rise of international discourse on the topic of sustainable development (Brundtland 1987). The widely promoted concept of sustainability is ultimately utopian in nature; it is the good state that we must strive for but may not actually exist except in theory. Despite our best efforts, we do not know exactly what a sustainable society looks like. This has been the paradox of utopianism since Sir Thomas More ([1516] 1906) coined the term "utopia" in 1516, and it is the paradox of sustainability today.

The premise underlying this volume is the basic belief that, at its best, anthropology has always been about exploring real possibilities for a more just and sustainable world. From the early work of Lewis Henry Morgan on indigenous rights (Eriksen and Nielson 2001) and Franz Boas on dispelling popular misconceptions surrounding the concept of race (Boas 1928); to the mid-twentieth-century work of Laura Thompson and her interdisciplinary participatory efforts to improve social and environmental conditions within the Hopi tribe (Thompson 1950); to more contemporary examples such as Nancy Sheper-Hughes (2006) working to protect the basic human rights of her informants, Robert Rhoades promoting the inclusion of mountain people's perspectives in sustainable development and planning (Rhoades 2000, 2007), and Eugene Hunn's (1999) legal testimony and advocacy work protecting the traditional subsistence rights of Native American tribes in the Pacific Northwest, anthropology has a long and perhaps underutilized tradition in providing solutions to socioenvironmental problems. With this volume, we seek to bring environmental anthropology into more productive engagement with the active pursuit of real ecotopian possibilities in our capacity as theorists, applied social scientists, and concerned citizens. In order to do this and in the spirit of engagement, we reach beyond the confines of academic environmental anthropology to connect with academics from other disciplines and, perhaps more importantly, with some of the leaders in the diverse social movements that are engaged in active pursuit of more just and sustainable lifeways and livelihoods.

This volume brings together anthropologists, environmental social scientists from other fields, and citizen activists who are engaged with three interrelated and often overlapping ecotopian social movements: bioregionalism, permaculture, and ecovillages. All of the contributors share a belief that in the current global context of increasingly negative news about interrelated social and environmental conditions, it is time to put forward work that is solution-focused rather than problem-oriented. As issues related to climate change, environmental degradation, and socioenvironmental injustices have increasingly become major areas of concern for communities around the world, people have begun asking themselves more frequently, "How can we create sustainable communities and livelihoods?" We share a belief that the bioregionalism, permaculture, and ecovillage movements offer potential and partial answers to this question and that engaging with them is one way to improve the relevance of anthropology to the wider world.

Our effort to bring together solution-focused instead of problem-oriented work does not suggest a move away from critical analysis. Rather, it reflects an acceptance of the severity of social and environmental problems, a recognition that solutions are already being developed from the bottom up, and a realization that these grassroots solutions can potentially be strengthened and made more viable through academic analysis. What we are suggesting is a strategic decision to engage with citizen-activists around the world who share understandings of the nature of social and environmental problems and the forces that create them, and who build collective commitments to pursue more just and sustainable possibilities. Our collaborative work in this domain may be characterized by what E. N. Anderson called "ethnoanthropology of the ecological community" (1969:

275) or, following a similar line of thinking in participatory international agricultural development (e.g., Rhoades and Booth 1982), solutions-back-to-solutions. This work is grounded in the premise that anthropologists must engage across disciplines and with practitioners around the world to pose, analyze, and refine viable possibilities, and in doing so, move beyond disengaged cultural critique. In fact—in going beyond our usual roles of recognizing, describing, analyzing, and deconstructing culture—such work suggests that anthropologists can be co-creators, with engaged practitioners of our research projects, in the cultural process. To borrow and modify a concept from permaculture and ecology, we are proposing that an important avenue for environmental anthropologists is engaging in *ecocultural edgework* that moves beyond nature-culture dualisms and strengthens ongoing efforts to build a sustainable world.

Ecotopian Possibilities

The idea that anthropology is well positioned to contribute to an ecotopian future is not new. Indeed, this goal was expressed quite clearly in 1969 by Anderson in the well-known volume *Reinventing Anthropology,* edited by Dell Hymes. In his essay "The Life and Culture of Ecotopia," Anderson laid out a prescient picture of emerging socioenvironmental crises and proposed that anthropologists prepare themselves to participate in "restructuring the world as an 'ecotopia'" (275).

Along these lines, Anderson envisioned two general strategies. First, citing the work of Marvin Harris and Roy Rappaport, he promoted the use of an emergent cultural ecology framework for documenting the energy flow and resource use patterns of non-Western societies in the belief that these societies manifested more sustainable patterns of human-environmental relationships. Although cultural ecology has been critiqued for being overly functionalist and teleological in its treatment of traditional and indigenous cultures (e.g., Orlove 1980), we believe that the proliferation of self-identified "living laboratories" in the form of ecovillages grounded in a bioregional worldview and permaculture design principles opens up unique opportunities for applying the lens of cultural ecology. Another critique of cultural ecology and ecological anthropology has centered on their overuse of ecological analogies in describing human communities; yet bioregionalists, permaculturalists, and ecovillagers are explicitly trying to redesign their real-world communities according to the principles of ecology. How well are groups of people who use ecology as their primary navigational compass in constructing communities of place doing at achieving their goals? Despite the rapid proliferation of such groups, there is very little research aimed at assessing their endeavors. Such research, especially where it is ethnographically informed, promises to be revealing—both for the successes and shortcomings it may uncover—and has the potential to expand the analysis of both cultural ecology and ecological anthropology while simultaneously engaging questions of interest to political ecologists and other theorists (Veteto and Lockyer 2008; Chapter 5, this volume).

Second, building in part on empirical case studies, Anderson suggested that "anthropologists should concern themselves with planning for the world" (1969: 276). Invoking a reinvigoration of applied anthropology, Anderson's suggestion was that anthropologists could help formulate and test "organizational structures" that might lead us toward ecotopia by focusing in part on "how the balance of power can be redressed" (278). How, exactly, this was to be achieved remains unclear in Anderson's essay, although he mentions that "organizational strategies can be formulated and computer-simulated" (278) and enters into a long description of what an ecotopian society might look like. Anderson alluded to the fact that some countercultural groups were actively trying to model such a society, but believed that their vision was simultaneously shortsighted and overly idealistic.

For a variety of good reasons, many anthropologists would balk at such a utopian project as planning for the world. Anthropological interventions in the world have, at times, had regrettable outcomes. However, we see an alternative possibility, one alluded to but not pursued by Anderson when he references countercultural groups as people who were potentially moving in the right direction. While the failure and collapse of the 1960s countercultural projects have been widely remarked upon, a closer examination indicates that emerging social movements—bioregionalism, permaculture, and ecovillages among them—are building on the successes and failures of the 1960s counterculture in an attempt to develop more effective strategies for moving toward ecotopia. Indeed, bioregionalists, permaculturalists, and ecovillagers are in effect "planning for the world" through active experiments in their own communities and the development of ecotopian models that may be altered, refined, and expanded as appropriate for other local biocultural contexts. This "bioregional planning" does not employ the totalizing meta-utopianism characteristic of industrial capitalism or socialism, but rather builds on Wendell Berry's insight that "[t]here is, as maybe we have all noticed, a conspicuous shortage of large-scale corrections for problems that have large-scale causes. Our damages to watersheds and ecosystems will have to be corrected one farm, one forest, one acre at a time" (2008: 45). Nor do these groups succumb to the escapist and oppositional mentalities that have often marginalized countercultural groups in the past. In fact, these movements today typically seek to build bridges across a number of divides—ivory tower from village, Global North from Global South, and nature from culture.

While important and insightful work ensued in the years after 1969 and many of Anderson's suggestions were at least nominally taken up in the fields of ecological and environmental anthropology, his essay is still relevant today. The patterns of inequality, injustice, and ecological degradation that he referred to have only become more manifest in the world and are increasingly acknowledged and studied by environmental anthropologists. From early synchronic approaches in cultural ecology that used culture as the unit of analysis and answered fundamental questions about how groups made their living through subsistence strategies, the social structures that resulted from local adaptations, and the ways in which they rationalized that living ideologically (Steward 1955); to approaches in ecological anthropology that shifted the unit of analysis to the scale of population and measured human energy flows through ecological systems (Rappaport 1968); to more processual approaches that incorporated actor-based theory, history, and political economy (Orlove 1980) or contemporary environmental anthropology, with its blend of theory, political awareness, and applied policy concerns (Townsend 2009), environmental anthropologists have always been concerned with sustainability and human societies. It is only appropriate that anthropologists would take an increasingly active role in the transition to a post-carbon world.

Anderson's (2010) more recent volume, *The Pursuit of Ecotopia,* nominally an exposition on what traditional and indigenous societies can teach the world about the pursuit of ecotopia, is as much a lament of the fact that ecotopia still seems as far (or farther) away today than it did in 1969. We believe that the idea of anthropologists contributing to a more ecotopian society remains an important goal, and strategically choosing to engage with ecotopian movements is one valuable avenue for pursuing it. We also believe our efforts may shed light on some of the most fundamental questions in environmental anthropology, such as: What does a sustainable community look like in the twenty-first century? How can we transition to a world of socially just sustainable communities? What are effective political, personal, and social actions for achieving a sustainable world? What strategies can be undertaken to lessen the impact that highly extractive areas of the world have on less consumptive regions? How can we combine traditional ecological knowledge with appropriate technology in creating more sustainable communities?

In the following section of this introduction we provide a selective overview of the ideological and practical strategies of the bioregional, permaculture, and ecovillage movements and how they interrelate with approaches and concerns in environmental anthropology. We will then link these movements with contemporary thought in radical, solutions-based environmental anthropology. We conclude this introduction with an overview of each chapter in the book and some common themes that run throughout the volume.

Bioregionalism, Permaculture, and Ecovillages

Our conceptualization of this book is rooted in many years of research in ecological and environmental anthropology and an even longer engagement with activism in the environmental and social justice arenas. In our academic work and activism, each of us engaged with bodies of ideas and groups of people who are attempting to enact just and sustainable alternatives to existing political and economic hegemonies. We sought, in part, to move beyond a politics of protest to engaging active utopian pursuits of just and sustainable futures. In the course of these explorations, we repeatedly returned to three movements, each of whose vision is global in scope, but with activities that are typically local in scale. These movements articulate and enact alternative development strategies that foreground moral concerns with justice and sustainability and attempt to contend with the complexities of biocultural diversity, power inequalities, and structural violence. In addition, each movement aims to build global networks that bridge diverse contexts while simultaneously maintaining focus on sustainable local livelihoods. These three movements, bioregionalism, permaculture, and ecovillages, have been largely ignored by mainstream development practitioners and anthropologists alike, while being employed extensively on a grassroots level. With this volume, we aim to provide at least a partial foundation for greater engagement with these socioecological movements.

Each of these three movements and their respective philosophies and practices represent essential components for transformation to a more just and sustainable world. Bioregionalism represents the worldview and resulting politics—a basic understanding that humans and human activities are fundamental components of ecosystems, not separate or even "coupled," and that human organization should be guided by natural systems instead of arbitrary political boundaries. Permaculture represents an ethically grounded methodological toolkit for putting the bioregional worldview into practice; it provides guidelines for developing sustainable human ecosystems wherein humans live simply, so that all may simply live. Typically, ecovillages are the incomplete and ever imperfect results of using permaculture to enact the bioregional worldview; each ecovillage is a unique "socionature" that actively attempts to model just and sustainable human lifeworlds in a particular places.

While bioregionalism, permaculture, and ecovillages are simultaneously diffuse and interrelated, it is possible, at the risk of reification, to identify them individually. Each is to some degree rooted in countercultural currents of the late 1960s, although they burst onto the scene somewhat later and are in a constant state of dynamism. All three simultaneously incorporate a global-scale critique of industrial capitalism and a vision of locally based forms of sustainable development. Each of the movements has at its heart a fundamentally ecotopian imaginary; however, each movement also seeks to put those imaginaries into practice. Below, we provide a brief introduction to bioregionalism, permaculture, and ecovillages, and suggest areas where they intersect with environmental anthropology.

Bioregionalism

Bioregionalism emerged in the 1970s with the writings of Raymond Dasmann, Peter Berg, Gary Snyder, and Stephanie Mills, to name several of the more prominent bioregional thinkers. It is a philosophy that resonates with, and draws directly on, early theory and ethnography in ecological and environmental anthropology. Bioregionalists have built their theory and praxis in part by directly citing the works of A. L. Kroeber, Ruth Underhill, Marshall Sahlins, Karl Polanyi, Roy Rappaport, Robert Netting, and Gregory Bateson, among others, indicating that environmental anthropology has fundamentally contributed to the construction of ecotopian possibilities. It also suggests that we would be remiss not to engage with those who use anthropological theory and knowledge to effect sociocultural transformation.

A prominent precursor to, and influence on, bioregional thought is evidenced in the work of nineteenth-century geologist and anthropologist John Wesley Powell. Powell's contributions to early American anthropology are too often written out of the history of the discipline, despite the fact that he was founder and director of the Bureau of American Ethnology from 1879 until his death in 1902. In addition, his approaches toward classifying and organizing Native American cultures and languages still serve as a foundation for anthropological knowledge today. Yet, Powell was more than an anthropologist, and his attempt to bring together geological, geographic, and ethnographic knowledge in the interest of sustainable development in the American West is where the closest articulation of bioregionalism in the history of American anthropology can likely be found.

In his *Report on the Lands of the Arid Region of the United States* (1879), Powell recognized that sustainable human settlement and development of the West depended on topography, surface water sources, and cooperation grounded in the knowledge of these features. Based on this inherently bioregional perspective, he proposed a radically different plan for the settlement of the American West than the imperialist vision of Manifest Destiny. In Powell's articulation, land in the arid West would not be divided into rectangular quadrants, but rather into irregularly shaped parcels dictated by the undulations of watersheds. Cooperative communities of freeholders—modeled in part on Mormon customs and New Mexican acequia associations—would develop small- to medium-scale irrigation, timbering, and pasture systems appropriate to each specific locale. Such place-based cooperative organizations would prevent the exploitation of local resources by outside interests and ensure sustainable human settlements.

Needless to say, Powell's recommendations did not become the basis for policy and the West was divided and settled according to more familiar models grounded in the misguided meta-utopianism of Manifest Destiny—denoted by rectangular land parcels and more amenable to manipulation by powerful special interests. In retrospect, Powell's vision was prescient if imperfect. While today's anthropologists would certainly balk at his cultural evolutionism, bioregionalists and anthropologists alike can recognize the fundamental wisdom in his recognition of the human-nature dialectic in the American West. Had his policy recommendations been adopted, the western part of the United States might have developed more along the lines that future bioregionalists later envisioned. Indeed, had his proposals been fully implemented, they may have negated the need for the bioregional movement to arise some seventy years after Powell's death.

Fundamentally, bioregionalism suggests, following Gary Paul Nabhan (1997), that human groups are "cultures of habitat." Bioregionalism roots human cultures in particular places. Bioregionalists seek to organize cultural, economic, and political life according to the criteria presented by vaguely defined eco-regions and more empirically identifiable watersheds. Bioregionalism proposes that economic activities should be dictated by ecological boundaries rather than arbitrary political divisions. It envisions a re-grounding of culture and community within particular watersheds and ecosystems.

The fundamental program of the bioregional approach is "reinhabitation." Reinhabitation entails a process whereby individuals and communities decide to commit themselves to a particular bioregion and live "as if" their descendents will be living there thousands of years into the future. The antithesis of the current global economic system, which rewards hypermobility and jumping at the chance for quick profit, reinhabitation means doing what is best for the long-term health and viability of the socioecological community (Snyder 1995). Bioregionalists often take the indigenous societies of their bioregions as models of long-term inhabitation and sustainability, but work within their own cultural traditions, with a sense of dynamism that does not reify or essentialize traditional place-based cultures. Reinabitation does not mean that people cannot travel or network with others at different scales within the global community; in fact, reinhabitatory bioregionalists are more properly understood as practicing a place-based form of what Escobar (2001) has described as a fully networked "localization."

> Bioregionalism calls for commitment to this continent place by place, in terms of biogeographical regions and watersheds. It calls us to see our country in terms of its landforms, plant life, weather patterns, and seasonal changes—its whole natural history before the net of political jurisdictions was cast over it. People are challenged to become reinhabitory—that is, to become people who are learning to live and think "as if" they were totally engaged with their place for the long future. (Snyder 1995: 246–47)

Bioregionalists are also focused on experimenting with watershed-level forms of direct democracy and consensus decision making. The basic proposal is to create cultures that are informed by local ecological dynamics and empower citizens to govern their own bioregions based on a more ecological worldview. Nation-states and international governing agencies are viewed as power-hungry entities that make decisions in faraway places and impose arbitrary political boundaries (often based on profit motives) that are usually harmful to local people. States can be worked with when it is necessary and beneficial to local bioregional interests, but local governance is the political ideal. Bioregionalism can thus be properly viewed as a pacifist eco-anarchist formulation.

A risk familiar to environmental anthropologists posed by the bioregional movement is that of suggesting that environmental determinism be the guiding philosophy for future human organization. Bioregional thought does tend toward a watershed-level environmental determinism, and as anthropologists we suggest that bioregional conceptualizations remain fluid, dynamic, and negotiable to diverse groups of local people. This is, in fact, the reality that bioregionalists have experienced as they have sought to enact their imaginaries. In the current global context, bioregions and watersheds are crosscut by diverse groups of people from widely divergent ethnicities, languages, socioeconomic statuses, occupations, and worldviews. In fact, human groups have organized themselves throughout history in ways that do not always correspond exactly to constructed bioregion or watershed formulations. For example, in Ecuador, Rhoades (1999) found that when international development researchers tried to implement watershed-level management programs, local indigenous groups were spread out across multiple watersheds. This led to a situation where scientific watershed management, which has a lot in common with ecological bioregional thinking, became a top-down bureaucratic formulation being imposed on local people. Snyder, in recognizing the pitfalls of the scientizing tendencies of institutional ecological bioregionalism in California, has identified a parallel "cultural bioregionalism" that is more attuned to the nuances of local social constructions and human organization. Cultural bioregionalism is an excellent entry point for collaboration between cultural anthropologists and the bioregional movement:

> Here is perhaps the most delicious turn that comes out of thinking about politics from the standpoint of place: anyone of any race, any religion, or origin is welcome, as long as they live well on the land ... [This] sort of future culture is available to whoever makes the choice, regardless of background. It need not require that a person drop his or her Buddhist, Jewish, Christian, animist, atheist, or Muslim beliefs but simply add to that faith or philosophy a sincere nod in the direction of the deep value of the natural world and the subjecthood of nonhuman beings. A culture of place will be created that will include the "United States," and go beyond that to an affirmation of the continent itself, the land itself, Turtle Island. (Snyder 1995: 234)

Figure 0.1. Ninth Continental Bioregional Congress, Earthaven Ecovillage, Katuah bioregion, summer 2005. Photo by Joshua Lockyer.

In ongoing efforts to enact this proposal, bioregionalists have since the early 1980s come together in bioregional congresses to share stories and strategies and to cooperate with neighbors to build bioregional communities. As Peter Berg says in his opening chapter in this volume, "There's a tremendous diversity among bioregions … but the schema for growing native life-place politics starting with socialsheds of neighbors, joining these in watershed councils, and proceeding to the creation of bioregional federations or congresses can fit them all."

Thus, bioregionalism provides a potential model for human reinhabitation and a language for organizing processes that will unite people in enacting that model. The oldest bioregional group—the Ozark Area Community Congress—has been in existence since 1980 (see Campbell, Chapter 3, this volume) and the Continental Bioregional Congress, after an initial meeting in 1984, continues to meet every four or five years at sites in the United States, Canada, and Mexico.

Permaculture

Permaculture aims to create

> consciously designed landscapes which mimic patterns and relationships found in nature, while yielding an abundance of food, fibre, and energy for provision of local needs.… I see permaculture as the use of systems thinking and design principles that provide the organising framework for implementing the above vision. It draws together the diverse ideas, skills and ways of living which need to be rediscovered and developed in order to empower us to move from being dependent consumers to becoming responsible and productive citizens. (David Holmgren 2002: xix)

If bioregionalism is an ecotopian philosophy/worldview and political ecology that is actively redefining socio-politico-ecological boundaries, then permaculture is an ecotopian methodology. Permaculture is an ecological design science grounded in a fundamental recognition that economic viability and social justice are interrelated with functioning ecological systems. Permaculture guides the redesign of systems for production, consumption, and inhabitation according to this foundational viewpoint.

The emergence of permaculture can be traced directly to the 1970s, when Australian bio-agronomist Bill Mollison and his student David Holmgren began experimenting with regional perennial polycrop food systems. They developed a framework for applying this system of design in various contexts and at various scales (from garden bed to entire landscape) and started traveling the world to teach people how to apply the framework in their home regions. Thousands of permaculture practitioners have since been trained and most can trace their genealogy back to

Mollison and Holmgren. While permaculture maintains a primary focus on agricultural systems, this design science has been applied to all dimensions of human-environment interaction in rural and urban, overdeveloped and underdeveloped contexts:

> [Permaculture] is about designing sustainable human communities, and preserving and extending natural systems. It covers aspects of designing and maintaining a cultivated ecology in any climate: the principle of design; design methods; understanding patterns in nature; climatic factors; water; soils; earthworks; techniques and strategies in the different climatic types; aquaculture; and in the social, legal, and economic design of human settlement ... Strategies for the necessary changes in social investment policy, politics itself, and towards regional or village self-reliance are now desperately needed. (Mollison 1988: i)

The permaculture paradigm encompasses a set of ethical principles and design guidelines and techniques for creating sustainable, permanent culture and agriculture. Guided by permaculture's three ethical principles—earth care, people care, and fair share—and its twelve ecological design principles (see below), permaculturalists around the world come together for gatherings, convergences, and trainings to share examples of permaculture design projects from their yards, gardens, farms, and broader communities. Permaculturalists have moved beyond an initial conceptualization of permanent agriculture to a vision of permanent, bioregionally rooted culture.

Permaculturalists worldwide have been involved in the type of ecological planning that Anderson (1969) recommended be undertaken by environmental anthropologists decades ago. Anthropologists have generally not answered the call, but citizen activists and planners in the permaculture movement have been contributing to building more sustainable communities, one garden at a time, across the entire globe for the past thirty-five years. As we have suggested elsewhere—with issues of ecological destruction, climate change, and peak oil looming before us—cross-fertilization between permaculture and environmental anthropology is a timely and vital project (Veteto and Lockyer 2008; Chapter 5, this volume). In this volume, contributions by Aistara, Haluza-DeLay and Berezan, Randall, Fox, and Pickerill (see summaries below) give compelling examples of collaborations between anthropologists and permaculturalists; and in several cases, of projects where environmental anthropologists have been certified in permaculture design and are using skills from both domains to improve sustainability in communities where they both live and work. Permaculture provides these anthropologists with a methodology for challenging dominant paradigms and constructing alternative bioregional possibilities, both within anthropology and the world at large.

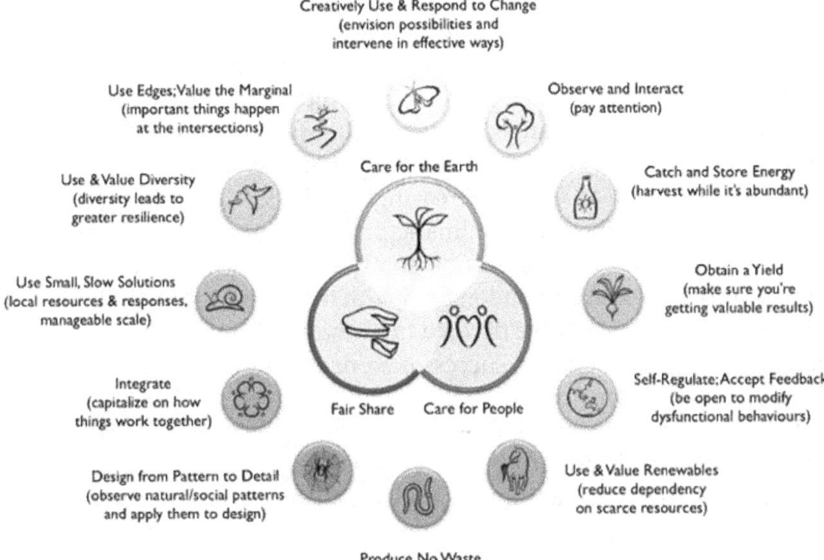

Figure 0.2. Permaculture ethical and design principles. Image courtesy of http://www.permacultureprinciples.com.

Permaculture also stands to benefit from collaborative interaction with environmental anthropology, as its leading practitioners have taken notice of critique from the academy that permaculture is relatively weak on theory (Holmgren 2002). Although permaculture was initially conceptualized within an academic setting, its subsequent development has taken part largely as applications in real-world settings. This has been both a strength and weakness of the permaculture approach. While sustainable living systems have been developed in thousands of sites across the globe, the ecological theory that informed permaculture's theoretical foundations has not been updated to reflect developments in the field. Permaculture was and is heavily influenced by the ecological systems theory of both Howard T. (especially) and Eugene Odum (Holmgren 2002; Odum 1971). Since permaculture was developed by Mollison and Holmgren in the 1970s, it is not surprising that they were heavily influenced by the ecological approach of the time. However, theory and modeling in ecology have generally moved past system approaches that focused on negative feedback loops, homeostasis, climax, and equilibrium to more dynamic and diachronic approaches that incorporate the ecological realities of non-equilibrium, disturbance, chaos, complexity, and patchwork dynamics over deep time (Scoones 1999). Permaculture has not only failed to keep up with such changes in ecological theory, it has also failed to engage the more contemporary functionalist systems-based ecological theories of resilience and panarchy (e.g., Folke 2006; Gunderson and Holling 2002). This is somewhat surprising. Given permaculture's evolving concern with peak oil and climate change, resilience theory would seem like an appropriate model for understanding how permaculture design systems can withstand and adapt to increasingly volatile environmental conditions. In addition, the erratic climatic patterns caused by anthropogenic climate change and other environmental factors can themselves be more successfully modeled and understood with non-equilibrium modern ecology. Permaculture's relative divorce from the academy over the past forty years has resulted in many successes in praxis, but has left it behind in theoretical development.

Environmental anthropology has much to contribute to theory and praxis in permaculture through its wealth of conceptual work in appraising human-environmental interactions in all times and all places across the planet and its accumulation of thousands of case studies in communities that have been or are living relatively sustainably—exactly the type of communities that permaculture seeks to design. Unlike bioregionalism, permaculture has incorporated almost nothing from environmental anthropology into either its conceptual or practical toolkit. Holmgren (2002) mentions ethnobiology as one of the most important intellectual disciplines that has contributed concepts to permaculture design, but both his book *Permaculture: Principles and Pathways Beyond Sustainability* and Mollison's *Permaculture: A Designers Manual* (1988) (arguably the two most foundational texts in the permaculture canon) do not include any works by ethnobiologists or other environmental anthropologists in their bibliographies. This is a situation that could be remedied through further engagement, as we have argued elsewhere (Veteto and Lockyer 2008; Chapter 5, this volume). For example, the subdisciplines of cultural ecology and political ecology are well positioned to inform permaculture. Cultural ecology's focus on environmental adaptations of groups of people in different areas of the world has produced a large amount of empirical data on sustainable livelihoods. This materialist data (particularly smallholder agriculture case studies) is the type of information that permaculturalists can use in sustainable design. A cultural ecology database that was made available for anthropologists engaged in permaculture research and application as well as to permaculture practitioners would be a robust sustainability tool.

Political ecology is another subfield that can productively collaborate with permaculture. Political ecology has brought political economy and power to the forefront of an ecological analysis that had been apolitical in its more traditional approach, highlighting how limited access to and control over resources has disempowered individuals and communities in local environments on multiple scales. A significant body of work in political ecology has focused on the relationship of power hegemonies in the Global North to nations and communities in the Global South. The political ecology approach to cultural critique articulates well with permaculture ethics, which encourage modern individuals to live a more simple and ecological lifestyle, thereby enacting a more democratic division of and access to global environmental resources. Both permaculture and prominent strains of political ecology are engaged in resistance to current globalization trends orchestrated by a capitalism whose political power is centered in the Global North. Permaculture offers political ecology the opportunity to study how citizens—particularly in the Global North—are experimenting with lifestyle and social changes to meet the sustainability challenge. Political ecology, among its other theoretical tools, offers permaculture the opportunity for practitioners to contextualize their own positions in global society, which are often privileged to various degrees (see Veteto and Lockyer, Chapter 5, this volume, for more suggestions on how permaculture can be usefully cross-fertilized with ethnoecology, historical ecology, and agricultural anthropology). Taken as a whole, environmental anthropology has much to add, particularly from a cultural perspective, to a permaculture framework that has been dominated by a biological gaze to date and has been less adept at studying human ecology despite its explicit aim of designing sustainable human communities.

Ecovillages

Ecovillages are "human-scale, full-featured settlements in which human activities are harmlessly integrated into the natural world in a way that is supportive of healthy human development and can be successfully continued into the indefinite future" (Gilman 1991: 10). Building on that foundational definition, ecovillages are intentional human communities that use integrative design, local economic networking, cooperative and common property structures, and participatory decision making to minimize ecological footprints and provide as many of life's basic necessities as possible in a sustainable manner. Ecovillages put bioregional thought and permaculture methodology into practice at the community level in service of the fundamentally ecotopian goal of sustainability. Permaculture, agroecology and organic agriculture, alternative energy systems such as solar, wind, and microhydro, and natural and green building methods are common features of these communities. Ecovillages are the most recent manifestation of a long historical phenomenon of intentional community building. For thousands of years, intentional communitarians have actively sought to enact the vision of small, cooperative, commons-based community living in response to experienced hegemonies of church, state, corporation, and market.

Some ecovillages have their roots in the communes and intentional communities of the 1960s, but most came into being during and after the 1990s as the ecovillage model became a worldwide phenomenon and collective effort emerged to reformulate intentional community building based on more comprehensive ecotopian thinking. The Global Ecovillage Network (GEN) is currently tracking 522 ecovillages around the world, including 234 in the Americas (Global Ecovillage Network n.d.). Hundreds of other ecovillages are either forming or exist that are not documented by GEN. The ecovillage movement is largely centered in the United States and western Europe, but has spread to seventy-two countries around the world (Global Ecovillage Network n.d.). The government of Senegal, for example, has recently created a National Ecovillage Agency in cooperation with the GEN, its Senegalese affiliate GENSEN, the Global Environment Facility, and the United Nations Development Programme (see Dawson, Chapter 12, this volume).

Kasper (2008) has pointed out that ecovillages represent an on-the-ground attempt to overcome the nature-culture dualism identified by diverse disciplines such as anthropology, sociology, environmental history, environmental philosophy, and environmental economics as being at the root of the ecological crisis. Scholars have conceptualized multiple ways past this Western dualism: Latour's (1993) "nature-culture," Haraway's (1991) "cyborgs," and Swyngedouw's (1999) "socionature" are a few prominent examples. Ecovillagers, however, operate more in the realm of physical reality than academic discourse. They attempt to live in ways that reduce the patterns of social and environmental injustice resulting from uneven distribution of resources and resource use among rich and poor on both local and global levels. Ecovillagers essentially are attempting to internalize what economists refer to as externalities; they recognize that the global economy creates far-flung consequences that are not accounted for in the cost of what they consume. They are attempting to make these costs more visible by bringing production and consumption processes within a more local sphere. At a fundamental level, ecovillagers are trying to put environmental and social justice ethics into action by creating communities that are more locally self-reliant and premised on the notion that each person and community must take responsibility for the socioecological impacts of fulfilling their economic and subsistence needs. Ecovillagers attempt to realize their visions for sustainable and just communities by building them in various locales around the world. From the

1990s on they have been increasingly successful in working out sustainable solutions in communities that range from a few families to villages of several thousand people, such as the well-known ecovillage Auroville in southern India.

One example of an established ecovillage is Dancing Rabbit, a community of approximately fifty members located on 280 acres of farmland in northeastern Missouri. Their stated goal is to live ecologically sustainable and socially rewarding lives, and to share the skills and ideas behind that lifestyle with broader publics. The members of Dancing Rabbit have agreed to organize their lives around defined lists of ecological covenants and sustainability guidelines. Because they recognize the impacts of fossil fuel extraction on ecosystems and communities and the implications of high levels of fossil fuel use for global climate change, they have agreed not to use fossil fuels to power vehicles, heat or cool homes, provide refrigeration, or heat domestic water supplies. The members of Dancing Rabbit have put in place renewable energy systems that use locally produced biofuels, passive solar building design, renewable and community-scale energy sources, and decreased energy demand in order to lessen their dependence on fossil fuels and, by extension, their contributions to further ecological degradation and social injustice.

In addition to addressing energy use, Dancing Rabbit has policies in place that specify the sourcing of lumber used in constructing their buildings. Ecovillage members agree to only use lumber harvested within their own bioregion for building projects. Recognizing that this is difficult in the rolling prairies of northeastern Missouri (where wood resources are scarce), they allow exceptions for recycled lumber. As a result, Dancing Rabbit members frequently participate in building demolitions in their local area and harvest the reclaimed lumber for use in the growing number of residential and community buildings in their village. In addition to seeking more sustainable patterns of energy and material consumption, the members of Dancing Rabbit address ways to deal with waste as well. One of their ecological covenants states that all organic and recyclable material used in the village will be reclaimed for use by the community. One manifestation of this is the extensive food waste composting Dancing Rabbit practices. They use compost to build soils, thus contributing to their goal of becoming more food self-reliant while simultaneously restoring the fertility of the degraded farmland that they inherited from previous generations.

Numerous opportunities exist for anthropologists to collaborate with ecovillagers. We (Lockyer and Veteto) have recently initiated an exploratory comparative project with both Dancing Rabbit and Earthaven Ecovillage (located in North Carolina) to help identify and assess sus-

Figure 0.3. Dancing Rabbit Ecovillage (northeastern Missouri) community building. Photo by James R. Veteto.

tainability goals and projects, educational and outreach programs, and future aspirations that guide each ecovillage and their resident members. This information will be used in a longer-term project of developing and implementing a set of methods, tools, and indicators aimed at assessing and comparing each community's progress toward their goals of sustainable living and effective educational outreach. Neither community has been satisfied with existing sustainability measurement tools, such as ecological footprinting, which is geared toward individuals who live more mainstream modern lives. Dancing Rabbit has been measuring their fossil fuel and other energy use since the founding of the community, but otherwise lacks the ability to effectively communicate (outside of on-site living demonstrations) to the outside world how their lifestyle compares with mainstream Americans. Our project will help them better evaluate the effectiveness of their environmental lifestyles in comparative contexts.

Although anthropological involvement with intentional communities has been relatively minimal (for notable exceptions, see Brown [2002] and Bennett [1967]), there are four interdisciplinary societies that promote and engage in scholarly research on historical and contemporary intentional communities (with many members both living within and conducting participatory action research in collaboration with extant communities)—the US-based Communal Studies Association, the International Communal Studies Association, the Society for Utopian Studies, and the Utopian Studies Society in Europe. Ecovillages have been an increasing subject of study in each of these academic societies, which provide established platforms by which environmental anthropologists can both engage with ecovillagers and share their research with other scholars.

As noted by Dawson (Chapter 12, this volume), in recent years the ecovillage movement has moved from an inward focus on self-sufficiency to an outward focus on building alliances with neighbors, citizen groups, and educational organizations. The difficulties of buying land, developing village infrastructure, and maintaining viable and healthy consensus-based decision-making processes have slowed down ecovillage development in recent years after initial excitement in the 1990s and early 2000s. Those ecovillages that have survived the test of time are now serving as educational models and living laboratories of sustainability. The Findhorn Foundation, based in Scotland and one of the oldest and most prominent ecovillages in the world, has ongoing collaborative projects with the United Nations and was named a UN "best practice" community. Ecovillages around the world are partnering with nearby cities and towns in the Transition movement, a worldwide phenomenon initiated by Rob Hopkins in Ireland that is helping communities move toward sustainability in a post peak oil world increasingly threatened by unpredictable climate change. Elsewhere, schools such as Berea College in Kentucky and Pacific Union College in California are developing partnerships with or constructing on-campus ecovillages for students to learn about and experiment with sustainable living. Living Routes, an ecovillage study abroad program that places college students in ecovillages worldwide, is detailed by Daniel Greenberg in his contribution to this volume (Chapter 15). The increase of partnerships between ecovillages and the academy are an excellent opportunity for applied environmental anthropologists to engage in socially relevant and meaningful work.

Environmental Anthropology Engaging Ecotopian Possibilities

> Anthropology ... can contribute to the critique of current hegemonies as a question of the utopian imagination: can the world be reconceived and reconstructed from the perspective of the multiplicity of place-based practices of culture, nature, and economy?
>
> —Arturo Escobar, "Culture Sits in Places"

> We could start with a kind of sociology of micro-utopias.
>
> —David Graeber, *Fragments of an Anarchist Anthropology*

In his Distinguished Lecture in General Anthropology at the 1992 meeting of the American Anthropological Association, Roy Rappaport noted the paradox that Western economic rationality was both a main cause of growing social and environmental problems and the dominant discourse being used to frame their potential solutions. Rappaport asserted that solutions to such problems demanded a more holistic view, informed by ecological thinking and social justice. In response, he called on anthropologists to engage our research in pursuit of solutions to the world's problems, specifically calling for renewed commitment to cultural critique and applying anthropological knowledge to the empowerment of local solutions (Rappaport 1993).

Returning to the theme with which we began this introduction, some may object to the idea of anthropology engaging in such a romantic and subjective undertaking as the pursuit of ecotopia. Indeed, words like utopia and ecotopia carry largely negative connotations. Utopia is often associated either with naïve idealism or with hegemonic metaprojects such as nationalism, state-based socialism, and global neoliberalism. However, it could also be argued that utopian striving for a better world is a fundamentally human condition and that anthropology would be remiss not to engage with it.

Some of anthropology's most productive scholarship has focused on utopian endeavors. Richard Fox's cultural history of Gandhian utopianism in twentieth-century India is but one prominent example (1989). In this work, Fox portrays Gandhi and other Gandhians as utopian experimentalists struggling against hegemonies of modernization and British colonialism, a struggle that was essentially cultural in nature: "[T]hey were social experimentalists, struggling with new visions of culture" (Fox 1989: 6). They also shared a grand vision of a better India: "The Gandhian utopian vision asserted that India, given its traditions, could develop a more humane and rewarding future society than either Western socialism or Western capitalism had accomplished" (Fox 1989: 7).

Fox acknowledges that his cultural history is an account of a utopian vision that was never fully realized. Nonetheless, the pursuit of the vision was quite real; it constituted the daily struggle of Gandhian utopians engaged in spiritual public service, home rule, and civil disobedience over many decades. Their experiments took at least some hold in the wider world: "As the experiments accumulated over time … this utopia became a complex culture trait. That is, it became a set of cultural meanings … constituting social identity and practice in twentieth-century India" and laying the groundwork for future utopian experiments (Fox 1989: 8).

Gandhian utopian experimentalists confronted the structures of the world system and the hegemonies that system generated. Fox used such confrontations to address the question of what role individuals or groups and their utopian visions may play in cultural change. Ultimately, Fox concluded that "an effective cultural resistance, such as Gandhian utopia, can arise from confrontations with an existing cultural hegemony, even though the resistance never fully escapes that hegemony" (Fox 1989: 14). In this view, the pursuit of utopia (or ecotopia) is significant as a process in itself, and the focus shifts from an unachievable endpoint toward the effort to get there, and ideas and practices guiding the journey (Lockyer 2009).

While the bioregionalism, permaculture, and ecovillage movements have been little explored in anthropology, they resonate with both Rappaport's and Fox's analyses. Each movement builds moral economies grounded in forms of discourse other than dominant Western economic rationality and guided by the compass of justice and sustainability. James Scott (1976) has shown that Southeast Asian peasants organize social life and economic livelihood activities around a fundamental belief that everyone has a right to adequate subsistence and react strongly when colonial modernization projects impinge on this right. Bioregionalists, permaculturalists, and ecovillagers in the Global North hold to this same belief, but they expand outward to a global scale and turn it on its head. They recognize that their own lifestyle practices obstruct the ability of less affluent people in faraway places to obtain adequate subsistence and continue their traditional customs. Consequent lifestyle changes represent an attempt to decrease consumption and increase simplicity at home in order to take pressure off individuals in the Global South and provide space and support for subaltern movements for cultural rights and economic justice. Like Fox's Gandhian utopians, these ecotopians struggle against a hegemony of thought and practice from which they can scarcely break free—but within which they create real, if partial, alternative possibilities. They are building on the foundation of 1960s countercultural experimentation and are broadening the possibilities of dynamic ecotopian imaginaries and practices.

Our engagement with bioregionalism, permaculture, and ecovillages also resonates with some of the best contemporary anthropological theory building and activist work. Arturo Escobar's engagement with groups constructing alternative political ecologies and subaltern strategies of localization in the Colombian Pacific region and David Graeber's work with the praxis of direct democracy in the Global Justice movement are two prominent examples. Both Escobar and Graeber engage with these movements not only as social scientists, but also as citizen activists who desire, paraphrasing Graeber (2004), to develop social theories that can be actively applied to assisting projects of social transformation toward a more just and sustainable world. Escobar and Graeber's contributions are representative of broader themes in anthropology to which we hope to contribute modestly with this volume.

Escobar's work with social movements in the Colombian Pacific region brings together concepts of place, networks, and social movements in an effort to engage with, analyze, and further processes of economic and cultural localization (2001, 2008). By pointing to "the continued vitality of place and place-making for culture, nature, and economy" in existing communities (Escobar 2001: 141), Escobar provides a counternarrative to real processes in globalization that disembed cultures and economies from places and to accompanying trends in sociocultural theory that claim an end to local cultural ecologies. Although he does not use the same terminology, Escobar engages with many of the same ecotopian themes that we and our bioregionalist, permaculturalist, and ecovillage interlocutors do when he asks "to what extent can we reinvent both thought and the world according to the logic of a multiplicity of place-based cultures?" (2001: 142). His engagement with networked social movements who share dual commitments to preserving ecological diversity and integrity as well as renewing local economies and communities leads him to recognize that such a transformation is a real possibility. The bioregionalism, permaculture, and ecovillage movements share similar commitments and manifest similar possibilities.

While defending the importance of place for both activist communities and in the realm of social theory, Escobar notes that place-based movements are simultaneously connected to transnational networks even as they are primarily focused on the defense of home territories. Paradoxically, in the era of globalization, these transnational networking strategies prove especially important to the viability of reinhabitation. Simultaneous attention to global networks and local projects enable reinhabitory movements—and the scholars who engage them—to combine an understanding of larger political economic forces that impinge on local places with a phenomenological understanding of how local communities experience place and assign meaning and value to it. Perhaps even more significantly, global networks of place-based movements provide unique opportunities to share strategies and lessons for the defense of place and to build collective strengths.

Following Escobar's logic further, a focus on local, reinhabitory, and restorative movements enables both scholars and citizen activists to shift emphasis away from global political economic forces as the dominant problematique and to reorient their gaze onto what Harvey (2000) might call "spaces of hope." As Escobar suggests, "to construct place as a project, to turn place-based imaginaries into a radical critique of power, and to align social theory with a critique of power by place requires that we venture into other terrains" (2001: 157). This argument reflects our desire to shift scholarly engagement from a problem-oriented trope to one that is more solution-focused, a move that we believe—following Graeber—builds upon the fundamental anthropological project of providing real, alternative possibilities to dominant hegemonies. Indeed, this exploration of alternative possibilities is exactly the kind of work that reinhabitory movements are engaged in: "For the most farsighted social movements, whether the situation is read in an ecological or a cultural register or a combination of both, the basic idea is the same: overcoming the model of modern liberal capitalist society has become a must for survival, and perhaps a real possibility" (Escobar 2008: 303).

Both Escobar and Graeber pay particular attention to the relationship between theory and practice and between activism and scholarship. They recognize that the participants in the movements they focus on are, along with scholars, social analysts as well, and that the forms of theory and practice engaged by both activists and scholars have potential for cross-fertilization. In this line of thinking, the constituent members of social movements are recognized as political ecologists in their own right and active producers of knowledge (Escobar 2008). As exemplified in the use of environmental anthropology by bioregionalists, these social movement actors draw on critical social knowledge produced by academics as they construct and refine their ecotopian visions and practices. In such situations, "one obvious role for a radical intellectual is … to look at those who are creating viable alternatives, try to figure out what might be the larger implications of what they are (already) doing, and then offer those ideas back, not as prescriptions, but as contributions, possibilities—as gifts.… such a project would actually have two aspects, or moments if you like: one ethnographic, one utopian, suspended in a constant dialogue" (Graeber 2004: 12).

Conclusion

> Someone has to do something that is consistent with the vision of fitting into ongoing natural processes before any reasonable person will support that vision.
>
> —Peter Berg, *Envisioning Sustainability*

> Active bioregionalists don't merely raise their hands to vote on issues but also find ways to interact positively with the life-web around them. They work with neighbors to carry out projects and build a bioregional culture together. Put another way, they are the working practitioners of what academics and others term "a paradigm shift."
>
> —Peter Berg, *Envisioning Sustainability*

We hope the selections contained in this volume illustrate Berg's comments by showing how diverse groups of people are actively modeling real ecotopian possibilities. We also hope they demonstrate the value of engaging with those constructing such possibilities. Former Association of American Geographers President James J. Parsons expressed a similar sentiment in 1985 when he commented on the emergence of bioregionalism:

> Recently a whole new subculture of bright, energetic and dedicated amateurs has emerged, especially in the western U.S. and Canada, that is reasking in new ways questions that have long been fundamental concerns of geography about the human use and abuse of natural systems. They have been dressing up old ideas and concepts about the interrelationships between nature and human culture and responsible stewardship of the earth with refreshing originality and vitality. They are potential allies and they have things to say to us that are deserving of our attention. (Parsons 1985: 1; see also Chapter 2, this volume)

Just as Parsons recognized affinities between bioregionalists and geographers, we note a similar affinity among bioregionalists, permaculturalists, ecovillagers, and ecological/environmental anthropologists and multidisciplinary political ecologists.

While these citizen activists may appear at first glance as romantic idealists, a closer examination reveals endeavors that are simultaneously ecotopian and practical. Such individuals may have grand visions, but they recognize those visions are not within immediate reach and are engaged in a constant iterative process of critical analysis, reassessment, and consequent adjustment of their projects. They share some of our fundamental ideals regarding justice and sustainability, incorporate anthropological knowledge into their projects, provide living laboratories of cultural change, and represent opportunities to make environmental anthropology more relevant to immediate concerns.

Just as Rappaport (1993) suggested two decades ago that ecological health has been subverted by the discourse of short-term economic growth in the fields of development and sustainability, so too have hope and idealism been subverted by practical (and supposedly objective) as well as overly critical postmodern and Marxist approaches in mainstream anthropology. Yet, it remains true that much of anthropology is fundamentally guided by a moral compass: a utopian impulse to contribute to positive change in the world guided by our accumulated knowledge of the forces and factors that create human suffering or flourishing. What we are suggesting is an ecotopian anthropology that engages with movements for environmental justice and sustainability and applies its knowledge, methods, and forms of critical analysis toward ultimate goals and values we share with those groups. We hope this effort will help lead us simultaneously toward a deeper understanding of the processes of cultural change and toward a more sustainable future.

Ecotopian Possibilities for a Sustainable Future: The Contributions

This volume contains sixteen contributions from scholars and citizen-activists of diverse backgrounds. We divided the book into three sections focused on bioregionalism, permaculture, and ecovillages, but readers will notice that overlaps among the sections reflect integration among these movements in both theory and practice. Collectively, the contributions enhance our knowledge and understanding of these three movements while also posing important nodes for critical analysis aimed at advancing the goals of justice and sustainability and addressing broader theoretical issues.

We begin the first section on bioregionalism with a classic piece of activist literature first published by Peter Berg in the bioregional journal *Raise the Stakes* in 1986. This chapter builds the foundational framework and vision for bioregionalism and is appropriately rooted in the specific experiences of activists in a particular place—the Shasta bioregion of northern California. Moving beyond an ecotopian vision, Berg explores the possibilities and practicalities of expanding bioregional governance across various contexts—including urban areas, continental bioregional networking, and coalition building with other movements.

Berg's chapter is followed by one by former Association of American Geographers President James J. Parsons, originally published in *The Professional Geographer* (1985), wherein he notes a distinct affinity between bioregional thought and action on the one hand and academic theory building in geography on the other. While no distinct and persistent engagement between academic geographers and bioregional activists emerged in response to this call for collaboration (for exceptions, see Carr [2004], Frenkel [1994], and McTaggart [1993]), Parsons's chapter foregrounds one of the main aims of this book—to bring scholarship and activism together in pursuit of shared goals of social justice and environmental sustainability.

In Chapter 3, Brian C. Campbell presents an overview of the longest-standing bioregional network in the United States, the Ozark Area Community Congress (OACC). Grounded in collaborative ethnographic fieldwork, it is a cultural history of the network, focusing on the challenges these bioregionalists have faced and the significant accomplishments they can claim. Campbell's research demonstrates the role of place, in this case the Ozark landscape, and symbolism in constructing sustainable intentional communities and the importance of learning from established agrarian populations. Through the integration of traditional and modern ecological knowledge and praxis, OACC serves as an example for contemporary post-industrial society's necessary venture into sustainable community building.

The bioregionalism section ends with Steve Alexander and Baylor Johnson's account of a unique educational program, the Adirondack Semester at St. Lawrence University in New York, which uses bioregional thinking and experience as a foundational pedagogical tool. This semester-long, off-campus, residential program integrates academic coursework, direct and deliberate experiences, and a purposeful living and learning community to generate a bioregional ethos in the program's operations and participants. Were such approaches more widely available to younger generations through education programs, reorganizing society along more bioregional lines, or at least according to "cosmopolitan" bioregional ethics, might be a more distinct possibility.

Section II, on permaculture, begins with a reprint of our 2008 article in the anthropological journal *Culture and Agriculture,* "Environmental Anthropology Engaging Permaculture: Moving Theory and Practice Toward Sustainability." In this chapter, we identify the historical development of the permaculture paradigm, show how permaculture is being employed at Earthaven Ecovillage in the Katuah bioregion in the United States, and identify fruitful theoretical and practical areas of collaboration between permaculturalists and environmental anthropologists. We close with a suggestive vignette on what the future of environmental anthropology might look like from the vantage point of situated ecovillage life and research.

In Chapter 6, Guntra A. Aistara examines the reception of permaculture practices among Latvian eco-farmers. The chapter builds on ethnographic research Aistara conducted with the Eco-Health Farm Network and the Latvian Organic Agriculture Association from 2003 to 2010, and includes farmers' reflections on the potential for a locally adapted permaculture to further enhance on-farm resilience and long-term sustainability. Aistara builds bridges between permaculture concepts and theoretical ideas within environmental anthropology from a range of thinkers including Tim Ingold, Bruno Latour, and Anna Tsing.

Randolph Haluza-DeLay and Ron Berezan, in Chapter 7, focus on the development of a permaculture network in Edmonton, Alberta, Canada. This network serves, they argue, as a "distributed ecovillage" and a social field productive of ecological habitus. A Bourdieuian theory of practice is applied to the permaculture network, asking to what degree it contributes to ecological habitus. The authors trace the processes of social learning and the development of hybridized and complicated socio-natures in the Edmonton urban permaculture movement. The dialogical structure of the chapter has each author commenting on key themes from their respective vantage points of reflective practitioner and activist-scholar.

In Chapter 8, Bob Randall details the process of how he, as an environmental anthropologist, used lessons learned from a sixteen-year research period in the southern Philippines (1971–1986) to design a sustainable agriculture organization called Urban Harvest that has partially transformed the Houston metropolitan foodshed. Key to Randall's efforts were his training in permaculture design with Bill Mollison and the use of permaculture as an organizational design tool to unite diverse Houston groups in a collective endeavor to transform the city's foodways.

Katy Fox compares the conceptualizations and processes of progress, hope, and commons thinking among rural Romanian farmers and United Kingdom permaculturalists in Chapter 9. Her chapter elucidates the issue of how these different social groups engage with change in times of ecological, economic, and social crisis. Two central questions frame her ethnography. First, what is the model of progress underlying how people imagine their life projects? Second, how is hope reimagined and practiced in the two groups? For permaculturalists in the UK, permaculture principles provided a pragmatic and dynamic framework for situated action that made it possible to envision the future differently in practice. For Romanian peasants, a discrepancy existed between their narratives about the future and the way in which their practices unfolded. This, Fox argues, is related to two different notions of transition at work in the two groups, and the effects of implicitly and explicitly envisioning better futures.

In Chapter 10, Jenny Pickerill analyzes Low Impact Developments (LIDs) in Britain. This chapter uses the LID example to explore the practices and implications of the permaculture approach when put into holistic practice. LID is a radical approach to housing, livelihoods, and everyday living that began in Britain in the 1990s as a grassroots response to the overlapping crises of sustainability. It is also a direct response to social needs for housing, an anti-capitalist strategy forging alternative economic possibilities, and a holistic approach to living that pays attention to the personal and political simultaneously. As such, it is shaped by the three ethical foundations of permaculture (earth care, people care, fair share) and explicitly aims to put these into practice. Pickerell uses results from ethnographic studies of four British LIDs to critically explore the practices of permaculture and its use within solution-orientated approaches to environmental problems. Moreover, she identifies key lessons from such projects—both practical and academic—that can inform ongoing attempts to shape a more sustainable future.

In the concluding chapter of the permaculture section, Aili Pyhälä looks at how permaculture can, on the one hand, inform development policy and practitioners working on community development and disaster relief and, on the other hand, reframe the whole development policy agenda through a closer look at ethics. Using recent case studies from across the world, combined with theoretical analyses, Pyhälä examines how the principles and ethics of permaculture can be applied in the field of development cooperation to resolve current challenges facing both donors and recipients.

The final section of the book—focused on ecovillages—begins with a contribution by Jonathan Dawson, the former president of The Global Ecovillage Network (GEN), who gives a historical overview of the ecovillage movement and a summary of current developments in ecovillage thinking. Dawson charts how ecovillages—most recently rooted in the intentional community building of the 1960s and 1970s and reaching their apex in the 1990s and early 2000s as "grown-up" endeavors focused on ecological sustainability—have recently made a strategic shift from an inward emphasis on self-sufficiency toward more outward concentration on educational efforts and making cross-linkages with citizen initiatives such as the Transition movement.

In Chapter 13, Brian J. Burke and Beatriz Arjona examine two Columbian ecovillage experiences. The authors assert that ecovillages are alternative political ecologies in the making and that their construction requires transformations at both personal and community scales. Arjona's personal story exemplifies the most common ecovillage experience in Columbia—that of disaffected middle or upper class urbanites seeking a more fulfilling life through a connection with nature and community—and the range of motivations and challenges such ecovillages face. The authors then examine the exceptional case of Nashira, an ecovillage of low-income single mothers—many of whom are victims of violence and displacement—to consider possibilities for developing ecovillages among structurally disadvantaged populations. By placing these two examples in comparative context, Burke and Arjona aim to combat stereotypes of both the Global North and the Global South that impede clearer analyses of the actual social conditions that give rise to and constrain ecovillage projects worldwide.

Todd LeVasseur, in Chapter 14, documents the challenges that five members of an ecovillage training program held in 2000 at the Findhorn Foundation community in Scotland have faced in subsequently implementing the ecovillage vision in diverse locales around the world. Oral history interviews with five individuals—all of whom were co-participants with LeVasseur in the training—show on-the-ground obstacles and successes in implementing ecovillage-inspired development plans in the Philippines, El Salvador, Brazil, and Austria. Comparing experiences in the Global North and the Global South, LeVasseur shows how local structural relationships contextualize the ecovillage endeavor.

In Chapter 15, Daniel Greenberg uses Living Routes—a semester-long study abroad program that he directs—to explore the pedagogical possibilities that exist for developing stronger linkages between the academy and ecovillages. He identifies ecovillages as an excellent platform for breaking down barriers between ivory tower and village, as well as between thought and praxis. Greenberg calls for increased collaboration between academia and ecovillages as we strive to create sustainable solutions to global environmental problems.

Ted Baker, in the final chapter of the book, makes interconnections between anti-capitalist literature and increasing interest in ecovillages. His chapter asks some critical questions: How are we to conceive of the relationship between intentional communities and the capitalist context they exist within? More specifically, what are the tensions and contradictions engendered by the attempt to construct sustainable communities (ecovillages) within an unsustainable context (capitalism)? Baker grounds his analysis in an ethnographic examination of an ecovillage in southwestern Ontario, Canada, and then proceeds to a more theoretical examination of the relationship between ecovillages and capitalism. Drawing mostly from thinkers in autonomist Marxist and anarchist traditions, he then suggests an anti-capitalist approach that not only provides us with valuable ways to conceptualize this relationship, but can also be enriched and further developed by being brought into contact with the concrete realities of ecovillages.

References

Anderson, E. N. 1969. "The Life and Culture of Ecotopia." In *Reinventing Anthropology,* ed. Dell Hymes. New York: Vintage Books.

———. 2010. *The Pursuit of Ecotopia: Lessons from Indigenous and Traditional Societies for the Human Ecology of Our Modern World.* Santa Barbara, CA: Praeger.

Berg, Peter. 2009. *Envisioning Sustainability.* USA: Subculture Books.

Bennett, John W. 1967. *The Hutterian Brethren: The Agricultural Economy of a Communal People.* Palo Alto, CA: Stanford University Press.

Berry, Wendell. 2008. "The Way of Ignorance." In *The Virtues of Ignorance: Complexity, Sustainability and the Limits of Knowledge,* ed. B. Vitek and W. Jackson. Lexington: University Press of Kentucky.

Boas, Franz. 1928. *Anthropology and Modern Life.* New York: W.W. Norton & Company.

Brown, Susan Love. 2002. *Intentional Community: An Anthropological Perspective.* Albany: State University of New York Press.

Brundtland, Gro Harlem. 1987. *Our Common Future: The World Commission on Environment and Development.* Oxford: Oxford University Press.

Carr, Mike. 2004. *Bioregionalism and Civil Society: Democratic Challenges to Corporate Globalism.* Vancouver: University of British Columbia Press.

Eriksen, Thomas Hylland, and Finn Sivert Nielson. 2001. *A History of Anthropology.* London: Pluto Press.

Escobar, Arturo. 2001. "Culture Sits in Places: Reflections on Globalism and Subaltern Strategies of Localization." *Political Geography* 20: 139–74.

———. 2008. *Territories of Difference: Place, Movements, Life,* Redes. Durham, NC: Duke University Press.

Folke, Carl. 2006. "Resilience: The Emergence of a Perspective for Social-Ecological Systems Analysis." *Global Environmental Change* 16: 253–67.

Fox, Richard G. 1989. *Gandhian Utopia: Experiments with Culture.* Boston: Beacon Press.

Frenkel, Stephen. 1994. "Old Theories in New Places? Environmental Determinism and Bioregionalism." *Professional Geographer* 46 (3): 289–95.

Gilman, Robert. 1991. "The Eco-village Challenge." *In Context* 29. http://www.context.org/ICLIB/IC29/Gilman1.thm (accessed 6 August 2010).

Global Ecovillage Network. n.d. "Homepage." http://gen.ecovillage.org/ (accessed 22 October 2011).

Graeber, David. 2004. *Fragments of an Anarchist Anthropology.* Chicago: Prickly Paradigm Press.

Gunderson, Lance H., and C. S. Holling. 2002. *Panarchy: Understanding Transformations in Human and Natural Systems.* Washington DC: Island Press.

Harraway, Donna. 1991. *Simians, Cyborgs, and Women: The Reinvention of Nature.* London: Routledge.

Harvey, David. 2000. *Spaces of Hope.* Berkeley: University of California Press.

Holmgren, David. 2002. *Permaculture: Principles and Pathways Beyond Sustainability.* Hepburn, Australia: Holmgren Design Services.

Hunn, Eugene S. 1999. "The Value of Subsistence for the Future of the World." In *Ethnoecology: Situated Knowledge/Located Lives,* ed. V. D. Nazarea. Tucson: University of Arizona Press.

Hymes, Dell, ed. 1969. *Reinventing Anthropology.* New York: Vintage Books.

Kasper, Debbie Van Schyndel. 2008. "Redefining Community in the Ecovillage." *Human Ecology Review* 15 (1): 12–24.

Latour, Bruno. 1993. *We Have Never Been Modern.* Cambridge, MA: Harvard University Press.

Lockyer, Joshua. 2009. "From Developmental Communalism to Transformative Utopianism: An Imagined Conversation with Donald Pitzer." *Communal Societies* 29 (1): 1–14.

McTaggart, W. Donald. 1993. "Bioregionalism and Regional Geography: Place, People, and Networks." *Canadian Geographer* 37 (Winter): 307–19.

Mollison, Bill. 1988. *Permaculture: A Designer's Manual.* Tylagum, Australia: Tagari Publications.

More, Sir Thomas. [1516] 1906. *Utopia*. London: A Constable and Co.
Nabhan, Gary Paul. 1997. *Cultures of Habitat: On Nature, Culture, and Story*. Washington DC: Counterpoint.
Odum, H. T. 1971. *Environment, Power, and Society*. New York: John Wiley and Sons.
Orlove, Ben. 1980. "Ecological Anthropology." *Annual Review of Anthropology* 9: 235–73.
Parsons, James J. 1985. "On 'Bioregionalism' and 'Watershed Consciousness.'" *The Professional Geographer* 37 (1): 1–6.
Powell, J. W. 1879. *Report on the Lands of the Arid Region of the United States*. Washington DC: Government Printing Office.
Rappaport, Roy A. 1968. *Pigs for the Ancestors: Ritual in the Ecology of a New Guinea People*. New Haven, CT: Yale University Press.
———. 1993. "Distinguished Lecture in General Anthropology: The Anthropology of Trouble." *American Anthropologist* 95 (2): 295–303.
Rhoades, Robert E. 1999. *Participatory Watershed Research and Management: Where the Shadow Falls*. Gatekeeper Series 81. London: International Institute for Environment and Development.
———. 2000. "Integrating Local Voices and Visions into the Global Mountain Agenda." *Mountain Research and Development* 20 (1): 4–9.
———. 2007. *Listening to the Mountains*. Dubuque, IA: Kendall/Hunt.
Rhoades, Robert E., and Robert Booth. 1982. "Farmer-Back-to-Farmer: A Model for Generating Acceptable Agricultural Technology." *Agricultural Administration* 11: 127–37.
Scoones, I. 1999. "New Ecology and the Social Sciences: What Prospects for a Fruitful Engagement?" *Annual Review of Anthropology* 28: 479–507.
Scott, James. 1976. *The Moral Economy of the Peasant: Rebellion and Subsistence in Southeast Asia*. New Haven, CT: Yale University Press.
Sheper-Hughes, Nancy. 2006. "The Primacy of the Ethical: Propositions for a Militant Anthropology." In *Anthropology in Theory: Issues in Epistemology*, ed. H. Moore and T. Sanders. Malden, MA: Blackwell.
Snyder, Gary. 1995. *A Place in Space: Ethics, Aesthetics, and Watersheds*. Washington DC: Counterpoint.
Steward, Julian. 1955. *Theory of Culture Change: The Methodology of Multilinear Evolution*. Urbana: University of Illinois Press.
Swyngedouw, Erik. 1999. "Modernity and Hybridity: Nature, Regeneracionismo, and the Production of the Spanish Waterscape, 1890–1930." *Annals of the Association of American Geographers* 89: 443–65.
Thompson, Laura. 1950. *Culture in Crisis: A Study of the Hopi Indians*. New York: Harper & Brothers.
Townsend, Patricia K. 2009. *Environmental Anthropology: From Pigs to Policies*. 2nd ed. Long Grove, IL: Waveland Press.
Veteto, James R., and Joshua Lockyer. 2008. "Environmental Anthropology Engaging Permaculture: Moving Theory and Practice Toward Sustainability." *Culture and Agriculture* 30 (1–2): 47–58.

I

Bioregionalism

Chapter One

Growing a Life-Place Politics

Peter Berg

The most obvious conclusions sometimes disguise the most mysterious situations. Ask city dwellers where their water comes from, for instance. Most will answer with something like, "The faucet, of course. Want water? Turn the tap handle. Got another timeless puzzler you need help with?" So it seems, especially if your life has been spent mastering survival in apartment buildings. But the faucet is only the last place water was, not where it came from. Before that it was in the plumbing, and before that in the mains. It got there from a reservoir, and from an aqueduct connected to a storage lake. "So tell me the name of the lake and I'll know where the water really comes from." Finding out the name and, even better, walking on the shore of that lake is definitely a start toward acquiring a sense of care and gratitude. But even that lake is just another place where water was. It got there as runoff from rain or snow that fell from clouds. Where do clouds come from? Evaporated ocean water? Two weather systems meeting? Whatever forces are involved in making a particular cloud, the source of every particle of water within it remains a deep mystery. If anything can be said about the ultimate state of water, it is probably that it does not begin or end anywhere but is constantly cycled through one form and location to another.

Here is another easy observation: we all live in some geographic place. And here is the accompanying mysterious and very critical situation: the places where we live are alive. They are bioregions, unique life-places with their own soils and landforms, watersheds and climates, native plants and animals, and many other distinct natural characteristics. Each characteristic affects the others and is affected by them, as in any other living system or body. And bioregions are all different from each other. Not just "mountains," but Appalachian Mountains or Rockies. Not just "river valleys," but Hudson or Sacramento.

People are also an integral part of life-places. What we do affects them and we are in turn affected by them. The lives of bioregions ultimately support our own lives, and the way we live is becoming crucial to their ability to continue to do so.

Knowing that water is always cycling has a lot of practical value (regardless of how frail our sense of every station in the cycle may be). It means, for example, that simply dumping water that is dirty with sewage or chemicals will not really get rid of those pollutants. They will just be carried along to the next stream, wherever it happens to be, to the water intake of a town downstream, perhaps, or through the ground to later seep into a well. Some water that we've used has a good chance of quickly becoming someone else's—limiting what goes into it and treating it before sending it along becomes a realm of social responsibility and reciprocity. That is the basis of what could be termed "water cycle politics," and it is serious business. Most town, city, and county governments have official departments to oversee water supplies and sewage, and questions of water quality and use can arouse some of the most serious public debates.

What is the practical response to knowing what we share in the lives of bioregions? If what we do degrades them, how does that fit with our concepts of social responsibility and reciprocity? What is a life-place politics?

Rootstock

It is probably best to begin by looking at the actual conditions that exist where some people live. Doing this may run the risk of overparticularizing, but at least it will not deliver the kind of overgeneralization and abstraction that can turn political thinking sour with ideology.

Right now I am in a clearly defined sixty-mile-long watershed that empties into the Pacific Ocean on a fairly remote stretch of the northern California coast. I have been teaching Shakespeare's sonnets ("When I consider everything that grows …") at the small high school my daughter attends here, work-learning about fruit trees from a local master pruner, and helping with community projects. A borrowed cabin provides heat by woodstove and light by kerosene lamps. Water comes from the same creek that later flows through salmon-rearing tanks tended by self-taught homesteaders who are trying to bring native fish back up to their historical levels of population in the river.

Living here has never been especially prosperous. Fifth-generation families still cut and haul firewood, maintain excellent gardens, and home-can everything from cherries to salmon. So do many of the new settlers. Much of the work that requires more than one person's labor is carried out on an informal exchange or volunteer basis that is held together with good-willed neighborliness (people's skills and the services they can make available are wide-ranging and sometimes astonishing). A volunteer fire department garage is the most visible municipal institution in the nearest town, a small post office is the only sign of a distant national government.

If police cars are ever called, they will come from the county sheriff's office by mountain ridges and an hour and a half away. "Folk anarchism" would not be a bad term for the social ethos that guides generally respectful relations between this valley's residents. Most of them are here because they like it that way.

"You make it sound too idyllic," remarks my pruner friend. "I live here but I'd move there, the way you're describing this place. You've left out the mentality about doing anything you want to your own land even if it means destroying it. How about bickering over water rights or the personal grudges that can go on for years?"

There is all that—but a visitor who has any interest in reversing the degradation of life-places could not help but be struck by seeing the rootstock that exists here for sustainable future inhabitation. Plentiful local renewable wood for heating fuel, good water from springs and creeks, natural building material, varying but workable soil, and some natural provision of food from fish and native resources. Human resources include broad skills, a spirit of informal mutualism, serious work on natural preservation and fishery enhancement projects, and a growing ecologically centered culture.

Actually achieving a workable harmony with natural systems in this valley is another matter, however, and much more difficult than it would appear to be to a casual visitor. For one thing, it would require the acceptance of a political perspective that is different from anything most people here (or elsewhere) have known.

Let us start with the place itself, which has not been treated very well over the last century since settlers arrived and native inhabitants suffered extermination or removal. Cattle and sheep overgrazing (with forest-burning to create larger pastures) and brutal logging have scarred most of the hills. Subsequent erosion carried away vast amounts of soil, caused huge landslides, and filled the formerly pristine river with gravel bars. A sustainable future would first of all have to be based on a local commitment to restore and maintain the river, soil, forests, and wildlife that ultimately support inhabitation here.

Next would come developing the means for meeting human needs in ways that are both sustainable and self-reliant. Current food production, although more evident than in some other places, is really only minimal.

Even hay for animals often comes from outside the valley. Energy needs, now partially met with local wood, could be completely filled by using alternative techniques and other renewable sources such as solar and microhydro power. Gasoline is presently one-fifth more expensive here than it is just outside the valley. Nearly all manufactured goods are carried or shipped in from outside. There are a few health practitioners, but complicated cases (or even ones requiring eye glasses or dentistry) have to travel outside the watershed limits for care. And public transportation is nonexistent.

Finally, there is the problem of earning a living in a place where there is little regular employment. Income from the present boom in marijuana cultivation (which also exists in many other deeply rural areas) is in perpetual jeopardy from law enforcement zealots. Even if marijuana became legalized, the most effective long-term economic solution would be to build on other existing activities that are more boom-and-bust proof and compatible with restoring rather than further depleting natural systems—natural enhancement projects, education (especially in sustainable fishing, forestry, grazing, and farming practices), visitor services, and local crafts and culture. The internal need for cash can simultaneously be reduced through community undertakings that "make money by not using money"—some large commonly held farms, tool and machinery sharing co-ops, labor exchanges for new improvements like refitting homes for energy efficiency, a local currency or system of credits for trading goods and services, a transportation-sharing system, and other formal ways to heighten social interdependence.

Restore natural systems, satisfy basic human needs, and develop support for individuals: those are the most fundamental requirements for sustainability and should be the goals of watershed-scaled bioregional politics in the valley. Achieving these is already the concern among some of the people, and their numbers could easily grow in the future. Even so, those who have been involved the longest feel that they will not see full fruition in their lifetimes. How many generations might it take to restore the valley (for that matter, has it really happened anywhere else before)? How self-reliant in regard to food, energy, manufacturing, education, and health can this place ever become? How much continuing outside support is needed, and under what terms should extra watershed support be secured? As for increasing social interdependence, what political means can enable all the individualistic and differing personal beliefs that exist here to coalesce in formal cooperation without losing the free-souled spirit that the valley nurtures now?

Closer to hand, there are plenty of issues that need immediate attention. There should be a moratorium on logging the few stands of first-growth trees that still remain. A full recycling program should replace hauling away unsorted garbage from the local dump. A valley-wide alternative energy plan should be mapped out and put into action. Watershed education, although featured at the small high school, should be a concern of the larger elementary and junior high schools and should be offered to adults as well. There is a lot to keep everyone busy before politics can be largely framed by the principles of restoring natural systems, filling human needs, and developing support for individuals.

Evolving Watershed-Scaled Governments

Growing the politics for a life-place has to be based on the reality of living there, and it is necessary to remind ourselves that no facts are established without evidence. Someone has to do something that is consistent with the vision of fitting into ongoing natural processes before any reasonable person will support that vision.

No outside agency proclaimed that salmon enhancement should begin in the valley, for instance. A desire to see past numbers of salmon running in the river again led a few people to investigate how this might be accomplished and inspired them to commit time-consuming labor (with frustratingly numerous false starts and mistakes) that eventually led to some small successes. They communicated their vision to other people, involved them in the project, and consequently increased their chances for success. Now that more neighbors are involved, the threats to restoring salmon, such as loss of fish habitat through further logging, overgrazing, overfishing, and stream destruction, are becoming more widely exposed and understood issues. If it becomes a generally shared ethic, "Don't do anything that could hurt the spawning cycle" could lead to profound changes here.

A bioregional politics originates with individuals who identify with real places and find ways to interact positively with the life-web around them. Involving close by watershed neighbors creates a "socialshed." This seed group is and will remain the most important unit of bioregional political interaction. Several socialsheds of neighbors working on a wide variety of different projects (co-ops, community gardens, renewable energy, bioregional education, recycling, and many others) can easily join together to form an organization for the broader local community. In effect, it would be a watershed council, rightfully claiming representation for the closely shared place itself.

A watershed council is the appropriate forum for directly addressing inhabitory issues and also for stating new objectives that are based on the principles of restoring natural systems, meeting human needs, and supporting individuals. It can effectively contend with the closest institutions of government (town, city, and county) to secure positions. These established governments may be arbitrary units in bioregional terms, with unnatural straight-lined borders or control over a patchwork of different natural geographies, but their policies hold for parts of real life-places and must be dealt with while the council presses for eventual self-determination in the watershed.

Whole bioregions are usually larger than one watershed and are overlaid with equally arbitrary and even more powerful governments: several counties, state(s), national departments, and agencies—too many, in fact, to serve as practical institutions for resolving bioregion-wide problems. Rather than seeking to influence anything higher than local governments, watershed councils must band together to form an independent body in order to represent their entire bioregion. A council from the valley, for instance, while holding positions on town and county issues, would also join with similar northern California (Shasta bioregion) groups in a federation or congress.

Watershed councils and bioregional congresses have, in fact, sprung up in parts of North America, reaching from Cascadia in the Pacific Northwest to the lower Hudson estuary in New York. One might ask (as even the environmentalist establishment does) whether these new groups are really necessary. Could the goal of sustainability be reached through existing forms, and would it not be better if those forms were made to work rather than cranking up something that is probably going to be seen as unacceptably radical anyway? And how about places other than remote valleys, areas that are more populated or nearer to metropolitan centers?

It goes without saying that creating a new political framework is difficult and that it will inevitably be seen at first as too radical (with some justification, considering the snaggy frustrates and boilingly ambitious types it may attract). The only reason to bother is to gain something that is absolutely necessary but cannot be achieved through existing means. The question becomes: is there any other way to preserve life-places? Aside from immediately local ones, governments and dominant political parties are not generally open to accepting sustainability as a serious goal. They seem barely able to hear outcries against obviously large-scale destruction of the planetary biosphere from merely reform-minded environmentalists, and are not likely to take bioregionalists seriously until the District of Columbia itself becomes totally uninhabitable. Government has forfeited defense of life-places to the people who live in them. Watershed councils and bioregional groups are necessary to secure inhabitory rights.

Is sustainability really necessary? Rather than reviewing all of the colonialist, resource-depleting environmental horror stories of the twentieth century that continue in the present and that, without opposition, will definitely extend in a compounded form into the next century, let us simply look at who we want to be. Do we want to degrade ourselves by participating in the degradation of humanity and the planet? And don't both of these processes begin where we live? Unsustainability simply is not a lifesome alternative. With sustainability, as with freedom, struggle is necessary if we want to achieve it.

As for abstracting from the situation in a northern California valley to other places, will that be committing the same error that earlier was said to turn political thinking sour with ideology? Frankly, yes. No two life-places are the same, for one thing, and the differences between back-country, rural, suburban, and city environs are enormous. Are there any similarities? Yes to that, too. Every site of human inhabitation is part of some watershed or other and exists within a distinct bioregion. The goals that are appropriate in this valley—of restoring natural systems, meeting human needs, and supporting individuals—apply wherever else people are living. The problem in any life-place lies in searching out how human activities are ultimately rooted in its natural processes and discovering how to fit into them.

A more populated rural area, for instance, may share the same watershed as a nearby urban center. This is the case for most of the agricultural country near cities on the Atlantic seaboard stretching from Boston to Atlanta, although the population-dense coastal edge is commonly seen as one long megalopolis and the connection between each city (usually sited at a river or at its mouth) and its watershed of support is virtually ignored. This natural continuity must be restored to consciousness, and recognizing the differences between whole bioregions that lie within the territory separating the Atlantic Coast and Appalachian Mountains is an important initial step toward developing sustainability in that part of the continent.

In the Great Plains, however, cities are much smaller and often already identify with the country surrounding them. The problem there is that agricultural use of the land has supplanted native features nearly completely. Mammoth farming operations exhaustively mine soil and water to export it in the form of grain and meat to places as far away as Japan. The Great Plains region (like the great valleys of California) is a resource colony for global monoculture and is rapidly being stripped of the basic components of sustainability. Watershed councils and bioregional groups in this increasingly endangered part of the continent advocate restoring native prairies, nonabusive farming methods, and greater diversification to relieve dependency on monocrop agriculture.

There is tremendous diversity among bioregions, from the Sonoran Desert to the Gulf of Maine, from the Great Lakes to the Ozarks, but the schema for growing native life-place politics starting with socialsheds of neighbors, joining these in watershed councils, and proceeding to the creation of bioregional federations or congresses can fit them all.

Green Cities

Cities do not hover on space platforms. They are all within bioregions and can be surprisingly dependent on fairly close sources for food and water. All of them can become more responsible for sustainability by lessening their strain on the bioregions where they are situated. Urban life-place politics can be expressed through Green City programs for whatever aspects of restoring natural places, meeting human needs, and supporting human individuals are realistically possible. And there are more ways to do this than a typical city dweller might think.

Processing urban sewage into fertilizer that can be returned to farmland would reciprocate directly with provision of food, for example. Establishing neighborhood common gardens and orchards would partially relieve the outlying countryside while helping to make a city more self-reliant. Energy demands could be sharply reduced by public projects to retrofit buildings and homes for alternative sources and heat efficiency. City governments can help facilitate starting new neighborhood food cooperatives, and establish centers for lending tools and equipment (public libraries for books are an impressive precedent). Neighborhood-scaled recycling programs could be established. Cities can sponsor urban-rural exchanges to trade labor for agricultural produce. They can create wild corridor parks so that native creeks, vegetation, birds, and other animals can pass through and provide a natural presence. Bioregional arts programs and citywide celebration of totem lifeforms are projects easily begun.

Some of the points in a Green City program may seem similar to current environmentalist proposals, but there is a fundamental difference between them. From a bioregionalist perspective, people are part of a life-space, as dependent on natural systems as native plants and animals. Green City proposals are not based on simply cleaning up the environment, but rather on securing reciprocity between the urban way of life and the natural life-web that supports it.

On the surface there seem to be few ways to demonstrate bioregional connectedness to city people. They do not see the actual sources for their food, for example, and often do not know where they are. But that doesn't make the life-place link any less real; it just confirms the need to expose it. Since cities are educational, cultural, and media centers, the means for exposure are already there. Green City programs can emphasize natural underpinnings by proposing curricula and art that communicate with everyone from school children to theater audiences. They can promote appearances by speakers and cultural groups from outside the city to bring a sense of bioregional partnership. Green City "bioregional reports" could readily become an aspect of daily news. When these and all other urban informational possibilities are considered, developing life-place consciousness in cities may not be so difficult after all.

Continental Congresses

What makes sense after the watershed council and bioregional group (now including a Green City program) levels of life-place politics? Representation of these larger, naturally scaled assemblies seem to follow, and just as there are currently dozens of watershed-bioregion groups, there was, in May 1984, the first North American Bioregional Congress (NABC). But the air becomes thinner at this level, and it is good to take a deep breath before climbing up.

The intent of such an assembly should be to extend whatever links that have been previously made between groups, make new ones, prepare mutually felt statements on continent-wide concerns, and decide on an effective course of action that all of the different groups can take in common. Some of this was accomplished at the first congress. Representatives met each other, information was exchanged, there were statements on some positions, and a few working committees were established.

The continental air is thin because it is difficult enough to understand one's own watershed and then fit it into a larger bioregion, but much more so to "think like a continent." For one reason or other, many attendees at the NABC were basically unfamiliar with bioregional ideas and activities. Some had come to learn what these are. Others came to represent their own different movements. North America as a living entity in the planetary biosphere was eventually understood and celebrated, but how bioregions interact with each other, what neighboring relationships might be, how groups can assist with real projects in different places, and other matters that presumably should have been covered were hardly touched on.

To overcome the thin air, future continental congresses will have to be more definite about their identity and intent. Crucial discussions and decisions should be framed in terms of their usefulness to active representatives of life-places, and there should be more addresses by those who can assist in "thinking like a continent," an array extending from geographers and water basin specialists to storytellers and poets. A North American Bioregional Congress is an important new political forum, and there is much needed work that it can do. National and state governments persistently maintain destructive policies toward the continent's life-places. A congress that authentically represents North America can claim authority to initiate beneficial ones. It can confront the problem of arbitrary (and multiple) government powers over bioregions. It can select priority issues to bring attention to situations in particular life-places (such as ruinous diversion of rivers in desert Sun Belt areas) and organize exchanges of expertise, work parties, and cultural events to support member groups. It can eventually stand as the main voice for a large continent-wide movement.

We have come a long distance from a remote northern California valley to the North American Bioregional Congress, and have picked up new long-term struggles at every level along the way. Restoring the valley will take several generations—the Shasta bioregion several more. How many for the continent? Meeting the basic human needs of all its people? Creating means of support for all of them? These are very challenging goals, but undoubtedly worthwhile, since they are ways to retrieve the future and offer a definite vision for what is vaguely termed "postindustrial society." Achieving them is the work, *the doing*, of bioregionalism.

A Basis for Alliances

There are opportunities for life-place political alliances at all these levels, from local watershed to continental congress (and eventually with other continents' assemblies). Only a fanatical mind-set would dictate that the basis for these should be to convert everyone else into a bioregionalist, and that would make a travesty of the terms for coalitions. Let us go back to the work of fitting into real natural processes to find more legitimate terms.

Active bioregionalists do not merely raise their hands to vote on issues, but also find ways to interact positively with the life-web around them. They work with neighbors to carry out projects and build a bioregional culture together. Put another way, they are the working practitioners of what academics and others term a "paradigm shift." There is a wide range of ways to express life-place consciousness and no need to exclude anyone's creativity in doing so, but bioregionalists do share a common interest in actually applying their convictions to local situations (in addition to having opinions about more distant ones). Their political activity is an extension of the work they do. They have a hands-on identity that is compatible with the goals of restoring natural systems, meeting basic human needs, and creating support for individuals.

Some other groups have a natural affinity for these same goals. Native Americans are an obvious example. Renewable energy, alternative technology, and permaculture (sustainable agriculture) proponents can easily share support on many issues. Earth-spirit women's groups, radical conservationalists, natural living advocates, and deep ecology adherents envision a similar ecocentric future. It would not be too difficult for many current environmentalists to also fit their causes into a longer-range bioregional perspective.

Less apparent, perhaps, is the basis for alliances with progressive movements that are aimed at affecting policies of existing large government structures and political parties. Disarmament, nonintervention, antinuclear, and other movements with a more distant focus than on the immediate local level leave little room for sharing direct support. Bioregionalists do not want nuclear arms or power facilities where they live, of course, and would certainly join with specifically antinuclear groups. Whether or not a watershed council or North American Bioregional Congress should endorse positions of every group or movement that each representative at those assemblies finds deserving is another matter. Some positions will be found in common, but the bioregional movement has its own character and its own concerns. Without these it would not be worth much as an ally anyway.

There has been some confusion about the relationship between life-place concerns and "green politics" ever since the first North American Bioregional Congress. A few participants at that event have even stated since that there is no difference between the two. The distinctions are very clear, however, and should be understood so that genuine bioregional goals can be realized.

First of all, "green politics" attempts to cover a more extensive range of areas, but where there are similarities, bioregional directions are much more definite and specific. This is obvious in a statement of definition from the initial Green Organizing Planning Meeting:

> Green politics interweaves ecological wisdom, decentralization of economic and political power whenever practical, personal and social responsibility, global security, and community self-determination within the context of respect for diversity of heritage and religion. It advocates non-violent action, cooperative world order, and self-reliance.

Some of the words are the same, but the sense of them is very different. Bioregionalists have a specific direction for "ecological wisdom": they want to restore and maintain watersheds and bioregions. Those are the places to which they want to decentralize and where they wish to practice self-determination. Their "personal and social responsibility" is to meet basic human needs and create ways to support individuals in life-places. As for extending their goals to "global security … cooperative world order," bioregionalists may well choose to ally with groups and movements that develop effective ways to apply that sentiment, but their own primary effort is to solve problems where they live (and that may be the best locale for rooting a planetary perspective, after all).

The first North American Bioregional Congress recognized this distinction by declaring, "If the emerging Green political organization does indeed reflect these bioregional concerns, we urge support from these bioregional groups and individuals from around the continent." *If* it does—and at this point no unified acceptance of bioregional goals by "greens" has been stated.

Another distinction is evident in the way "green politics" is developing structurally. At the Green Organizing Planning Meeting in August 1984, committees were formed to represent megaregions based on the compass points in the United States: Northeast, South, Midwest, West, and Northwest. Isn't this the old centralized way of describing territory? All of these areas have several bioregions within them. People have been identifying and seeking to fit into these unique life-places for some time. Do they really need another arbitrarily defined political district? The "green" structure seems to be oriented from the top down. Bioregional movement groups originate on the watershed level and move up to join in naturally scaled continental assemblies.

The most critical difference between the movements may lie with their actual ecological orientation. How much "ecological wisdom" are they really prepared to accept? Bioregionalists answer, "All we can get!" They see their lives as intertwined with ongoing natural processes, part of the life of a place. From their ecocentric viewpoint, human society is ultimately based on interdependence with other forms of life. They follow that conviction to make choices about which kinds of work to undertake and to oppose late industrial era depredations.

It is not established that "green politics" followers are similarly committed, and questionable as to whether they will become so. Theirs is a multiplicity of concerns (ecological wisdom is only one of ten key values listed), and among many "greens," ecological awareness is limited to an older environmentalist perspective, attempting to reform industrialism instead of aiming to replace it. Some bioregionalists who are also active in "green politics" feel that they can reach members of that movement and change its direction. No doubt some will be persuaded, but wishful evangelism isn't a good foundation for building coalitions. Truly relevant life-place politics will originate from watershed councils, bioregional groups, and the North American Bioregional Congress. When support for the positions of these naturally scaled groups is sought, "greens" may yet prove to be very strong allies regardless of their different emphasis and direction.

Leaving No One Out

Is it realistic to assume that anyone, the next person you meet, for instance, will be able to understand and sympathize with bioregional goals? Would most people be able to suspend conventional political ideas long enough, or be able to see past labels like "environment," "natural resources," and so on?

Admittedly, many people are likely to have only slight awareness of day-to-day contact with nonhuman forms of life and to view natural systems as something to be insulated from. The best ground for introducing life-place consciousness may lie further forward in their minds and involve feeling about the course of present society. Try asking if society hasn't lost its ethical basis by subjecting human and natural life to continuous threats and damage.

Most people feel that a disaster will occur before they are actually told that one is even possible, that human-induced natural disasters occur more and more frequently, and that the next one will be more horrendous than the last. Usually they will agree that industrial society has been and continues to be irresponsible about endangering both nature and people.

How about the promise of the future? Can present society ever right the balance of its demands on nature? It may come as a surprise, but many people are reluctant to discuss the future. They may even fear it, and when they don't, unguarded optimism is rarely offered.

On the positive side, encourage remembering that we really are part of all life, that we are born as mammalian creatures and continue to survive, sense the seasons, and experience weather as mammals—that life is always looping through us: food, water, energy, and materials sustain us before moving on as wastes and refuse. Point out that although our skillful mobility permits changing locations more quickly than we can become familiar with a new place, we always end up in some bioregion or other and are part of it no matter how briefly. Suggest that nature is not a remotely distant entity but actually exists everywhere and can be experienced by simply recognizing the unique characteristics of the places where we live. Invite imagining how deeply we could feel and in how many ways we could celebrate, restore, defend, and identify with those places.

The Mystery Remains and We No Longer Deny It

There were no unsolvable physical mysteries during the industrial era, and nature was thought to be merely physical. Physics, chemistry, and engineering could unravel any puzzle for what was thought to be the inevitable betterment of humankind: produce anything imaginable, restructure any environment, remove any amount of wanted resource, and exterminate or discard anything unwanted. If it came to the point that doing these things created new problems (considered a doubtful outcome for the greatest part of the period), there were still ways that were believed capable of restoring a human upper hand: (a) just be thankful for what progress has been made and accept living with whatever negative consequences come with it; (b) stop doing something that is known to be disastrous and start doing some new thing whose effects are completely unknown; and (c) apply more industrial techniques to solve problems brought through industrialism in the first place. The result of all this self-deception? We live with poisons up to the waist in a junkyard of breaking machines.

Most environmental agencies will not ultimately relieve our situation. They would only be further appendages of a political core that is welded to industrialism itself. We need a core based on the design of nature instead, from watershed to bioregion and continent to planetary biosphere. Is it self-defeating to avoid established governments other than immediately local ones? Not if we want to anticipate a society whose direction already lies outside those institutions. We need to uncover and follow a natural design that lies beneath industrial asphalt.

What about world spheres of influence, global economies, and other international considerations? The whole planet is undergoing the severe strains of the late industrial period now: chemical plagues, wholesale mechanical removal of landscapes, disruption of the largest river courses, accelerated destruction of ecosystems, and overnight disappearance of habitats. Humanity is suffering the consequences of these suicidal, devouring attacks on the biosphere as late industrial society begins to eat itself. Could we tame the suicidal appetite by adopting sustainability as a goal? If we become bioregionally self-reliant, that would be a large step toward taking the strain off the rest of the planet's life-places.

On a farm in the country or in a city apartment, we are all completely enmeshed in the web of life. We cannot know all of the details of all the connections. Bioregional politics does not try to overcome the mystery; it is aimed toward making a social transition so that we can live with that mystery. Can we stop tearing the web apart, and consciously build a role as partners in all life? We better, and we can by beginning where we live.

Notes

Reprinted with permission from *Raise the Stakes* 11 (1986): 5–8.

Chapter Two

On Bioregionalism and Watershed Consciousness

James J. Parsons

There are strong indications of a reawakening of interest in the character and functioning of regions and microregions in most of the social sciences. Within geography it is a theme that is probably most congenial to those with historical or humanistic bents. Among the lay public this revival is reflected in many ways, as in the strength of the environmental movement, the resurgence of interest in local history, and the deepening attachment to place and to one's ancestral roots.

Recently a whole new subculture of bright, energetic, and dedicated amateurs has emerged, especially in the western United States and Canada, that is re-asking in new ways questions that have long been fundamental concerns of geography about the human use and abuse of natural systems. They have been dressing up old ideas and concepts about the interrelationships between nature and human culture and responsible stewardship of the earth with refreshing originality and vitality. They are potential allies and they have things to say to us that are deserving of our attention.

"Bioregion" and "bioregionalism" are not words that can be found in your dictionary. They are neologisms not more than ten years old that are rapidly being absorbed into popular usage (Callenbach 1980; Foster 1984; Hunter-Wiles 1982). They have taken on deep meaning for the above-mentioned group, who see them as defining, however loosely, a new international (they would say "planetary") environmental movement. Their users are talking the language of geography even when they use different words; their convictions are often intensified by the belief that they have discovered something new. They call themselves "bioregionalists."

A "bioregion," says Peter Berg of the San Francisco–based Planet Drum Foundation, is a geographical province of marked ecological and often cultural unity, its subdivisions, at least ideally, often delimited by watersheds (water divides) of major streams. "Watersheds," a term much employed by bioregionalists, are seen as delimiting local natural communities, providing the operational basis for organizing and managing the relations between humans and their local environment. Berg writes:

> The term bioregion refers both to a geographical terrain and to a "terrain of consciousness"—to a place and the ideas that have developed about how to live in that place. A bioregion can be determined initially by use of climatology, physiography, animal and plant geography, natural history, and other descriptive natural sciences, [but] the final boundaries are best described by people who have lived within it. Bioregionalism and bioregional perspective involve learning to live-in-place, a kind of spiritual identification with a particular kind of country and its wild nature [that is] the basis for the kind of land care the world so definitely needs. (Berg 1977: 2)

Ecological Models

These new bioregionalists are for the most part a spiritually motivated, back-to-the-land, do-it-yourself group only marginally derivative of the communitarian counterculture tradition of the 1960s (Dasmann 1974; Vance 1972). Ecological concerns are writ large among them, inevitably underscored by the awesome nuclear threat. Self-reliance, appropriate technology, local control, and responsible stewardship of the land are critical props to their philosophy. Small is beautiful. The doctrine of human dominance over nature is seen as the root of most of our troubles. They frequently look to the ecological wisdom, the values, the land ethic of the American Indians, living in Rousseau-like harmony with nature before the arrival of "the invaders," as a model. The movement has attracted a remarkably sensitive, literate group of adherents who feel an almost mystical reciprocity between people and place. And they want to learn. They are obsessed with the importance of knowing one's own area, often defined in terms of a drainage basin and seen as a miniature biosphere in which the connection is direct between what is going on in the valleys and on the hillslopes. "Watershed consciousness" is their term for it. Restoration of logged-off or overgrazed slopes or debris-clogged salmon streams has a high priority. Leaving a river wild and free is a blow struck for God's original plan. They are of, but not in, the organized conservation movement and have no ties with such groups as the Sierra Club, Friends of the Earth, or the Audubon Society.

Bioregionalism is spawning a considerable literature. The underground press of the 1960s and 1970s, observes the editor of *Siskiyou Country,* is becoming the bioregional press of the 1980s (Helm 1983). Its leaders and theoreticians have included poets, novelists, and philosophers—names like Peter Berg, Jim Dodge, Peter Marshall, Michael Helm, Stephanie Mills, Gary Snyder, Ernest Callenbach—but academics have contributed little to it. Callenbach's future-fiction novels *Ecotopia* (1975) and *Ecotopia Emerging* (1981) talk of the bioregional distinctiveness of the forested fringe of the Pacific coast from Monterey Bay to Puget Sound in which a right-thinking society secedes from the rest of the materialistic, wasteful United States and sets out on its own ecologically rational course. Stewart Brand's *Co-Evolution Quarterly*, with special issues on "Bioregions" and "Watersheds," has been a quiet voice in support. More important has been Peter Berg's Planet Drum Foundation (P.O. Box 31251, San Francisco CA 94131) and its tabloid-form triannual review *Raise the Stakes*, dedicated to communicating "the concept of bioregions" through books, "bundles" (of loose-leaf materials), and workshops and fostering exchange "among bioregional groups and projects and the growing number of people exploring cultural, environmental and ecologic forms appropriate to the places where they live" (Planet Drum Foundation 1986:1).

A similarly oriented journal published in Arizona, *Coyote*, recently had this to say about the Sonoran bioregion:

> *Coyote* is talking about what it means to really live here like you intend to stay and love it for a while. That means learning who your neighbors are, too, especially when they have lived here a generation or more. They have stories to tell about what has happened and what is happening, here, in this place like no other. So *Coyote* is enchanted with this place, its animals, its plants and its people. *Coyote* also has a way of looking at them all together, kind of like they were all part of an ecology. Environmentalism doesn't say all this. A new term, "bioregionalism," better expresses the message. A "bioregion" is a place on earth that has developed plant, animal and human cultures that are deeply intertwined with each other and distinctly different from the regions that surround it. The Sonoran Desert is a bioregion. Within it you find a plant, animal and human dimension that has been shaped by the nature of the place. Its common character is inescapable. When you travel beyond the boundaries of this bioregion you know it from the disappearance of the sahuaros and the mesquite. Within a few miles you are looking at yucca and tall grass, or scrub oak and junipers, and you are not in the "desert" any more. (Ray 1983: 1–2)

"Bioregionalism is not an easy movement to see," it goes on, "because it is not a particularly flashy undertaking in the first place, and being local is not as important to some as the state or national scene. The politics of bioregionalism turns [the] 'bigger is better' notion on its head. The politics of bioregionalism are the politics of place" (Ray 1983: 2).

Reinhabitation

At a critical time a few years ago, liberal, ecologically oriented state governors in California and Oregon (Jerry Brown and Tom McColl, respectively) gave something akin to official recognition to "bioregionalism." The Resources Agency of California, through its Office of Appropriate Technology, gave support to Peter Berg's work on bioregions as a context for renewable energy policy (Berg and Turkel 1980). At the same time, the California Arts Council, reorganized administratively on a "bioregional" basis, sponsored publication of the provocative collection of essays and poetry *Reinhabiting a Separate Country: A Bioregional Anthology of Northern California* (Berg 1978), which included an essay by Berg and wildlife ecologist Ray Dasmann entitled "Reinhabiting California" (reprinted from *The Ecologist*, vol. 7, December 1977) in which they wrote:

> Once all California was inhabited by people who used the land lightly and seldom did lasting harm to its life-sustaining capacity. Most of them have gone. But if the life-destructive path of technological society is to be diverted into life-sustaining directions, the land must be reinhabited. "Reinhabitation" means developing a bioregional identity. It means learning to live-in-place in an area that has been disrupted and injured through past exploitation. It involves becoming native to a place through becoming aware of the particular ecologic relationships that operate within it. Simply stated it involves becoming fully alive in and with such a place. It involves applying for membership in a biotic community and ceasing to be its exploiter. (Berg and Dasmann 1977: 399)

Concerned for the increasingly defensive stance of the environmental movement in the face of a deepening crisis of civilization, Berg has recently argued that "it's time to shift from just saving what's left and begin to assert bioregional programs for reinhabitation. Our greatest threats no longer come from natural disasters but from the means we use to subdue nature" (Berg 1983: 2).

Bioregionalists distrust central authority. They emphasize community action and local community control, frowning on hierarchical structures of all types, whether in government or in personal relations. They lobby for regulation of natural resource use and for legislation directed toward the retention of native cultures and values. Although they have on occasion supported sympathetic candidates for local public office, their political activities up to the present have been of much more modest dimension than, for example, the German *Grünen.* They are not conspicuously religious, yet they recognize that religious practice and social custom are intrinsic parts of the close relationship between many cultures and their surrounding nature. Their historical concerns are limited to a recognition of what local history may contribute to identification with the spirit of a place, what Yi-Fu Tuan has taught us to call *topophilia.* They seem ready to accept the world as they find it, without crimination or censure.

They have a special sympathy for separatist, home-rule movements (Quebec, the Basques, the Lapps, the Celtic fringe of Europe, Australian aborigines, American Indians) and for minorities, at least in developed countries. Cultural diversity is prized. Michael Helm writes: "People are realizing that it is only when they bring an identity rooted in specific places that they have anything genuine to share. After all, the whole point of being international and cosmopolitan in perspective is to go somewhere (or receive a visitor) and say, 'This is my culture, my place, and I share it with you. And what is your culture?'" (Helm 1981: 3).

They have difficulties with cities, although there is some optimism in their literature that even a Los Angeles could reorganize itself into something approaching a self-sufficient, ecologically rational community if it would only try.

Controversy over Origins

The term "bioregion" has a nice ring to it. How does it happen that we geographers seem never to have thought of it? Carl Sauer used to speculate as to how different it all might have been had geography grown out of biology rather than geology as it did. The aspect of "Man's Role in Changing the Face of the Earth" that most interested him was the impact of human activity on biotic communities through the long corridors of time. It is sometimes called "cultural biogeography." The bioregionalists seem to be reinventing it with some added twists.

It may have been Allen Van Newkirk, a Canadian poet and biogeographer without formal academic credentials, who first used the term. He sought to define the study of "bioregion" both as a linked study of cultural and biotic regions and as a point of view. This was in the form of a brief statement of limited distribution in the summer of 1974 that was published the next year in *Environmental Conservation* (Udvardy 1975) and later in the lively and innovative *CoEvolution Quarterly.* In these he announced the establishment of an Institute for Bioregional Research at Heatherton, Nova Scotia, and sought contacts with like-minded persons. The institute seems not to have materialized and its protagonist appears to have had no contact with any of the leaders in the bioregional "movement" that since has taken form.

Van Newkirk saw bioregional research as "the study of culturally induced changes in the distribution of wild plants and animals [and] how the different natural regions of the earth have been successively inhabited and deformed by various cultures" (Van Newkirk 1975: 108). "Bioregions," he insisted, were to be distinguished from biotic provinces. To him they were biogeographically determined culture areas whose study, he wrote, might be called "regional human biogeography." He spoke of "bioregional strategies" for cultural adaptation and the restoration of the earth's natural plant and animal diversity within a "bioregional framework." Language, poetry, and myth were among the research tools he saw as appropriate for the study of bioregional cognition, bioregional history, habitat perception, and the restoration of altered habitats.

But it was Peter Berg, one of the central figures in the movement, who may have done the most to popularize the term and the concept. He seems first to have used the words "bioregion" and "bioregionalism," without attribution, in a paper in an ephemeral Bay Area "ecotopian" journal entitled "Strategies for Reinhabiting the Northern California Bioregion" (Berg 1977). He elaborated further upon the theme, with Ray Dasmann, in "Reinhabiting California" in *The Ecologist* (Berg and Dasmann 1977).

The publication of Miklos Udvardy's colored world map of biogeographical provinces (instigated by Dasmann and designed by geographer Ted Oberlander) in the *CoEvolution Quarterly* (1976) and later as frontispiece to the *Next Whole Earth Catalog* (Brand 1980) has been heralded as an important further contribution to increasing "bioregional awareness," a significant step toward defining the earth's "bioregions," although Udvardy does not use the term. This handsome cartographic representation, delineating areas or life zones of similar vegetation and wildlife associations, had been commissioned originally by IUCN and UNESCO for conservation planning purposes (Udvardy 1975).

A New Way of Thinking?

The original bioregional notion, then, was seen as a kind of unifying principle, a way of thinking about land and life within a regional framework. It has come to represent what might be termed an action-oriented cultural geography, partially disguised in a new vocabulary and bolstered by an intensely practical idealism (Berg 1976). No surveyor's lines demark the bioregion. Rather, it is defined by people's feelings about an area, the way it has been used through human time. Bioregionalism is a moral philosophy, sometimes romanticized as a "system of thought," a framework for action that celebrates geographic and cultural diversity, the sacredness of the Earth, and the responsibilities of local communities to it. Its literature is characterized by a positive, upbeat attitude that guards effectively against the arrogance that can naturally stem from conviction and enthusiasm (Helm 1983). It is "an idea whose time has come," says Stewart Brand

(Brand 1981). To others it is still just an interesting concept that largely ignores the troublesome matter of scale and does not sufficiently recognize the extralocal origin of many ecological and cultural problems.

An impressive number of local bioregional groups have been emerging, especially in the cutover regions of coastal northern California and the Pacific Northwest (Dileo and Smith 1983; Dodge 1981; Garreau 1981). Their names commonly locate them: the Frisco Bay Mussel Group, the North Coast Area Council, the Redwood Alliance, the Cascade Holistic Ecologic Council, the Mogollon Highland Watershed Association, the High Plains Alliance, the Driftless Area Bioregional Network, Wabash Landschaft, the Creosote Collective in Tucson, RAIN in Oregon. Organizations like the New Alchemy Institute on Cape Cod and Tilth in the Pacific Northwest, seeking new, productive ways to provide food, energy, and shelter for self-sustaining communities, often have closely related goals. Many are affiliated with the Movement for a New Society, a Philadelphia-based umbrella organization of alternative lifestyle groups committed to a decentralized participatory democracy. In May 1984, the first North American Bioregional Congress was hosted by the Ozark Area Community Congress near Kansas City, Missouri, with the attendance of representatives of a wide range of groups "relating to bioregionalism" (Nelson 1984; North American Bioregional Congress 1984; Sale 1984). The symbol of Turtle Island, based on the Seneca tribe's myth of the continent's formation, was used throughout to convey the spirit of "ecological inhabitation" (Hughes 1983). The participation of indigenous peoples of North America was conspicuous. A second such conference has been scheduled tentatively for the fall of 1986.[1]

Bioregionalism clearly does not mean any one thing. It's not so much a fixed ideology as a diverse set of notions informed above all by a sense of place (Helm 1983). Most often it seems to fall somewhere between the reformist "shallow ecology" of the conventional environmentalists and the long-range "deep ecology" movement represented by the new breed of eco-philosophers who, following the Norwegian philosopher Arne Naess, emphasize the compelling need for revolutionary changes in the behavior and value system that pervades the modern worldview (Devall 1979; Devall and Sessions 1984; Naess 1973, 1984; Sessions and Devall 1984). Its adherents may at times appear as misty-eyed visionaries caught up in New Age semantics, but these are kindred folk who need no convincing as to the importance of geography and a sense of place. They are groping, self-critically, for alternatives to the dominant social paradigm of modern mass culture and the destructive exploitation that has characterized it. The rule of thumb is to "maintain diversity, save all the parts." They may be the unwitting architects of a new popular geography, a grassroots geography with "heart," a different kind of activist, radical geography that should be uniquely compatible with the environmental concerns we traditionally have shared.

Notes

The original version of this chapter was presented at the annual meeting of the Association of Pacific Coast Geographers at Eureka, California, in September 1983. The author is grateful to Margaret and David Hooson for constructive comments. The current version is reprinted with permission from *The Professional Geographer* 37 (1) (1985): 1–6.

1. [eds. The 1986 North American Bioregional Congress did take place on the shores of Lake Michigan in the Leelanan Province of the Great Lakes Macroregion.]

References

Berg, Peter. 1976. "Amble Towards Continent Congress." Planet Drum Bundle 4. San Francisco: Planet Drum. Reprinted in *Earth Journal* 6 (4).

———. 1977. "Strategies for Reinhabiting the Northern California Bioregion." *Senatum: The Journal of Ecotopia* 1 (3): 2–8.

———. 1983. "More Than Just Saving What's Left." *Raise the Stakes* 8 (Fall): 1–2.

———, ed. 1978. *Reinhabiting a Separate Country: A Bioregional Anthology of Northern California.* San Francisco: Planet Drum.

Berg, Peter, and Ray Dasmann. 1977. "Reinhabiting California." *The Ecologist* 7 (December): 399–401. Reprinted in *Reinhabiting a Separate Country: A Bioregional Anthology of Northern California,* ed. Peter Berg. San Francisco: Planet Drum.

Berg, Peter, and George Turkel. 1980. *Renewable Energy and Bioregions: A New Context for Public Policy.* Sacramento: State of California Solar Business Office.

Brand, Stewart. 1981. "Presenting Peter Berg." *CoEvolution Quarterly,* 32 (Winter): 5.

———, ed. 1980. *The Next Whole Earth Catalog.* Sausalito, CA: POINT.

Callenbach, Ernest. 1975. *Ecotopia, the Journal of Edward Weston.* Berkeley, CA: Banyan Tree Books.

———. 1980. *The Ecotopian Encyclopedia for the 80s: A Survival Guide for the Age of Inflation.* Berkeley, CA: And/Or Press.

———. 1981. *Ecotopia Emerging.* Berkeley, CA: Banyan Tree Books.

Dasmann, Ray. 1974. "Conservation, Counter-culture and Separate Realities." *Environmental Conservation* 1 (Summer): 133–37.

Devall, Bill. 1979. "Reformist Environmentalism." *Humboldt Journal of Social Relations* 6: 129–58.

Devall, Bill, and George Sessions. 1984. "The Development of Natural Resources and the Integrity of Nature: Contrasting Views of Management." *Environmental Ethics* 6 (44): 293–322.

Dileo, Michael, and Eleanor Smith. 1983. *Two Californias: The Truth About the Split-State Movement.* Covelo, CA: Island Press.

Dodge, Jim. 1981. "Living by Life: Some Bioregional Theory and Practice." *CoEvolution Quarterly* 32 (Winter): 6–12.

Foster, C. H. W. 1984. *Experiments in Bioregionalism: The New England River Basin Story.* Hanover, NH: University Press of New England.

Garreau, Joel. 1981. *The Nine Nations of North America.* Boston: Houghton-Mifflin.

Helm, Michael. 1981. "Planet vs. Global Mind." *Raise the Stakes* 3 (Summer).

———. 1983. "Bioregional Planning." *RAIN* 9 (6) and 10 (3): 22–23.

Hughes, J. Donald. 1983. *American Indian Ecology.* El Paso: Texas Western University Press.

Hunter-Wiles, Sara. 1982. "Indian Bioregions." *High Country News,* 24 December, 24.

Naess, Arne. 1973. "The Shallow and the Deep, Long Range Ecology Movement: A Summary." *Inquiry* 16: 95–100.

———. 1984. "A Defense of the Deep Ecology Movement." *Environmental Ethics* 6 (3): 265–70.

Nelson, Kris. 1984. "Bioregions Congress Unites Movement." *RAIN* 10 (6): 31–32.

North American Bioregional Congress. 1984. *Proceedings, First North American Bioregional Congress.* Drury, MO. San Francisco: Planet Drum Foundation.

Planet Drum Foundation. 1986. "Front Matter." *Raise the Stakes* 12: 1. San Francisco: Planet Drum Foundation.

Ray, Michael. 1983. "The Power of Place." *Coyote* 2: 1–2.

Sale, Kirkpatrick. 1984. "Bioregional Green." *The Nation,* 16 June, 724–25.

Sessions, George, and Bill Devall. 1984. *Deep Ecology: Living as if Nature Mattered.* Layton, UT: Peregrine-Smith Books.

Udvardy, Miklos. 1975. *A Classification of the Bioregional Provinces of the World.* Occasional Paper 18. Morges, Switzerland: International Union for Conservation of Nature.

Van Newkirk, Allen. 1975. "Bioregions: Towards Bioregional Strategy for Human Cultures." *Environmental Conservation* 2: 108.

Vance, James E., Jr. 1972. "California and the Search for the Ideal." *Annals, Association of American Geographers* 62: 185–210.

Chapter Three

Growing an Oak

An Ethnography of Ozark Bioregionalism

Brian C. Campbell

The Ozark region has been referred to as hills, mountains, and highlands, but it began as a plateau and was slowly and methodically weathered by precipitation to create a vertical topography. The Ozarks represent the only extensive elevated area in the United States between the Appalachian and Rocky Mountains, encompassing southern Missouri, northern Arkansas, and a small fraction of northeastern Oklahoma. Geographers distinguish the Ozarks by the general ruggedness of the landscape, a karst topography characterized by sinkholes, springs, losing streams, and caves, with a thin layer of topsoil (Rafferty 2001). The verticality of the landscape and the inferiority of most Ozark soils have prevented large-scale industrial crop production (Aley 1992; Blevins 2002). Before the mid-twentieth century, however, the Ozarks was "the domain of the small farmer," with communities and isolated homesteads of self-reliant forager/farmers scattered throughout (Blevins 2002: 4; Campbell 2009; Otto and Burns 1981). As more isolated sectors became integrated into modern transportation and media routes, farming as a livelihood began to disappear, resulting in out-migration (Blevins 2002; Gallaher 1961).

The people who remained in the more secluded Ozark "hollers" continued traditional lifeways, which Ozarks folklorists and travel writers promote—some exaggerating with their arcadian evocations (Blevins 2002). This literature attracted "urban refugees" who sought beautiful wilderness and traditional culture away from the mainstream rat race. Blevins characterizes them as "counterculture proponents (hippies), urban escapists, and disenchanted young people" and emphasizes that the "vast majority stayed only a short time before being driven back to civilization by snakes, chiggers, heat, cold, and starvation" (2002: 200). But Harington astutely notes the similarities between distinct generations of Ozark homesteaders: "Elsewhere in Arkansas the latest blooming hippies have all cleaned up and moved back to the suburbs. Those who persist and endure in Newton County, are the strong ones, fit survivors, like the real pioneers in the nineteenth century, who came as a kind of spillover of the mountain settlement to the east" (1986: 98–99).

These distinct generations of Ozark homesteaders share an understanding of the species and landscape of the Ozark bioregion. Traditional Ozarkers engaged in necessary conservatism, simple living, and innovation, and their culture stressed reliance on local resources and ecological knowledge. Contemporary homesteaders reflect similar traits by choice, as a retort to mainstream society's conspicuous consumption. They demonstrate uncanny innovation, like their predecessors, but with contemporary networking opportunities they share and receive ideas throughout the region and even the world. Back-to-the-landers who remained in the Ozarks and developed and sustained the bioregional movement were no run-of-the-mill hippies; they share values and ideals and are inspired, to a certain degree, by that movement, but stand out as some of the most intelligent, thoughtful, innovative, and driven people one will encounter. Some are (inter)nationally recognized figures in their fields. The range and scope of innovative technologies and ideas that have emerged from Ozark bioregionalism are remarkable. A full treatment of their practical successes would require volumes; this chapter presents a brief overview of Ozark bioregionalism's origins, a review of participants' shared ethos, and a summary of key achievements and political obstacles.

Origins of Ozark Bioregionalism

Ozark bioregionalism, as a conscious, purposeful movement, has its roots in 1970s back-to-the-landers' fledgling experimental farms, communes, and intentional communities scattered around the Missouri and Arkansas Ozarks. As these predominantly urban, college-educated young people in their twenties and thirties met at swimming holes and gatherings, a palpable energy grew through discussions of freedom from mainstream excess and dependency. A few key players with excessive energy and passion invigorated others to move beyond parties and pipe dreams to seize the opportunity to create an "Ozark Free State: an unofficial, undeclared, ecological Ozark nation! A nation that would bring all good and ethical things together, and run on solar energy, appropriate technology, and co-operative economics, while defending the Ozarks' ecological integrity." These are the words of the recognized founder of Ozark bioregionalism, who acknowledged that at this point in their organizing they had not heard the word "bioregion." Yet he perceived "the Ozarks as a distinct bio-political, as well as bioregional entity" with "ancient ecological principles that guided and developed life … for millions of years before humanity arrived, and that they … constituted an imminent, unacknowledged, and untranslated body of law and design principles for developing sustainable new political and physical support systems for human communities." In 1977 he called a meeting for Ozarkers who felt a similar need to "get eco-political" that resulted in an activist group with the preliminary title "acorn," referencing "the totem and power tree of the Ozarks," which soon after changed to OAK (OACC)—Ozark Area Community Congress.[1]

New Life Farm (NLF)

In 1972 a young back-to-the-lander with degrees in business and engineering acquired a 240-acre farm in the Missouri Ozarks and constructed a methane digester and solar air and water heaters. This "New Life Farm" attracted other back-to-the-landers who wanted to learn and develop sustainable energy and food production technologies. In 1978 the New Life Farmers connected with eco-activists envisioning OACC and their ecologically political discussions moved into community development through appropriate technology outreach (Fischer and Swack 1979). New Life Farm was incorporated in the spring of 1978 as a tax-exempt, nonprofit educational and research organization with the following stated goals:

> [P]ursuing R&D techniques that could be used by local farmers to improve the productivity of their land while maintaining the natural balance of the ecosystem; acting as an educational center for training in these technologies and assistance in implementing them; providing periodic employment for laborers, researchers, and managers from the community; and serving as a focal point for community services like day-care and for activities such as theater groups and crafts collectives. (Fischer and Swack 1978)

New Life Farm's objectives meshed perfectly with the goals of the politically minded Ozark bioregionalists. By 1979 New Life Farm had forty members, and they constituted the majority of the planning committee for the inaugural gathering of the Ozark Area Community Congress. Between 130 and 150 participants gathered at New Life Farm for OACC I in October 1980. They conceptualized the Ozarks as a "free state" and tasked themselves with organizing it according to ecological laws and principles. They asked themselves:

> Within this free state, if you were in charge, how would you run things? How would you change things? How would you try to orient the culture of the people who live here towards sustainability and bioregional self-reliance? … There were brainstorming sessions with charts and butcher paper and magic markers, and … copious amounts of butcher paper produced [written on] and then we started tearing them in pieces, … organizing ideas,

> and from that we created committees: the agriculture committee, the forestry committee, water quality committee, education committee, and people self-selected as to what committee they wanted to work on. Then we separated to different parts of the house, or corners of the barn, or circles outside.[2]

Before its conclusion, they developed by consensus "the first bioregional resolutions" and a "constitution for the Ozarks." OACC I has been described as "a festival of ecological ideas and celebration with a big group of peers meeting as empowered equals to chart the course of a new ecological nation."[3] Interviewees comment on the "bio-electric charge" radiating through OACC I and describe it as an incident like nothing they had experienced before or since.

In many cultural movements, key individuals exude such charisma, wisdom, and/or healing/magical ability that people cannot help but follow their lead. In many such cases the leader desires and exploits their power; however, in the sustainability movement, these "servant leaders" oftentimes remain humble, "acting in the background, doing what needs doing, not directly calling attention to themselves" (Gilman 1990: 12). Ozark bioregionalism has such an individual in the aforementioned organizer; in one interview after another participants related his fundamental role in energizing and bringing together groups and individuals with diverse interests and expertise related to sustainable living. I refrain from identifying him or other participants by name in this chapter because some interviewees requested anonymity, but also by design, because it fits the spirit of the movement. The OACC founder notes that

> those who truly work primarily for the Earth and humanity and not their own personal agendas will come to know themselves to be of one family. ...The words "Bioregionalism," "Deep Ecology," "Social Ecology," "Green," and the ideologies that go with them are not at all important in the face of the need of serious healing of the Earth and the human species' relation to the Earth and one another. Nor is who did what and when. I don't care who does it and what they call themselves, as long as it is done.[4]

The selfless, altruistic approach of foundational Ozark bioregionalists relates directly to their desire to create a congress—a space where all participants are equal and have equal voice, where decision making occurs through consensus and considers future generations. A central OACC figure explains:

> [I]t should be the people who were there who were talking, who were presenting, and nobody should come in as an authority, or the big speaker, or something like that.... Same thing with the press, because you wonder, "why hasn't bioregionalism spread a little more?" But he [OACC founder] never wanted the publicity to be a certain way, or I don't think he wanted publicity.[5]

The egalitarianism of OACC creates a sense of empowerment, and in the early years, inspired the activists to dream big. As a member relates: "the word Congress at that time had some meaning because it was … conceptual, a process, of how would you do it if you were in charge. Like I said, it was exhilarating to really try that. And at that time we were idealistic enough to think we could really do it."[6]

Ethos of Ozark Bioregionalism

Sustainability

OACC culture mirrors the basic tenets of the sustainability field. When I visited homes and villages I saw immediately that they practice what they preach. In their everyday lives they engage the ecological principles that sustainability-oriented social scientists and biologists may teach and write about in an abstract fashion. The sustainability movement necessarily begins with a critique of the neoclassical economic model of unlimited growth, citing its violation of the second law of thermodynamics, the law of entropy, as evidence for its unsustainability (Wessels 2006). An OACC member passionately observed:

> I hesitate to say it, you know? But, we're just basically removing ourselves from the picture. And it's happened over and over again with rogue species. If you don't follow the rules, you have to leave … We think we're so smart, but we're not.… I believe intelligence is ecologically defined, sanity is ecologically defined, ethics are ecologically defined. When you look at those things from the perspective and you look at what we're doing, you think, "Whoa!" There's just not intelligence. It's terminal cleverness. We're so clever in that everything we're doing to multiply our advantage against the natural world is basically undermining our own capacity to stay here as a species. And it's just absolutely amazing how really precise that is. Nature takes care of every little atom and every little molecule. You put them out of place and it all starts working back as entropy. If you're talking thermodynamics, we're creating so much entropy and ecosystems are naturally anti-entropic. They create order in the most astounding ways, again unexplicably, and what we do is make entropy. We're entropy-incorporated![7]

The sustainability movement focuses on criticism as a "tool, not an end," and rather than destroying an imperfect world, strives to improve it through realistic, empirical approaches (Gilman 1990). Similarly, OACC participants articulate ecological threats, but they formulate pragmatic strategies to ameliorate such problems and work within the system to achieve results. In many cases, Ozark bioregionalists are dissatisfied with actions by government agencies, such as the US Forest Service's use of herbicides and clear-cutting in national forests, but they recognize their limitations in these instances. They encourage participation in the public comment process, but also develop their own strategies for protecting Ozark lands, such as regional and community land trusts. While OACC members disagree with government agencies and some industrial corporations' actions, they work diplomatically to find points of agreement and collaboration. OACC collaborates with a wide range of businesses each year and frequently invites representatives from the US Forest Service, Missouri Department of Conservation, and Missouri Department of Natural Resources, who give speeches and participate in workshops.

Like sustainability theorists, OACC members advocate an ecologically grounded pedagogy as a necessary precondition for future sustainability. Ozark bioregionalists recognize the inadequacies of the mainstream educational system and counter it by creating hands-on learning opportunities for children and adults. David Orr (1991), a founder of the experimental research village in the Arkansas Ozarks that hosted OACC XIV, proposes that educators consciously focus on process, context, and engagement with local ecology and avoid the anthropocentric, reductionist tendencies of Western science.

Traditional Ecological Knowledge

While the bioregionalists share much with the sustainability field, they distinguish themselves in their devotion to place, their watershed. This knowledge of place goes beyond contemporary soil analyses or casual living and observation. It constitutes a thorough empirical approach to understanding the sociocultural precedents and agroecological patterns that increase the chances of coexisting with the landscape. A foundational OACC member wrote:

> Everyone lives somewhere. Most people will eventually, or at least hope to, settle down in one spot on this earth, in a place where their physical and mental needs are met. Bioregional consciousness is acquiring the knowledge of and connecting to that life-place, or the bioregion where you landed and live. It begins with understanding both … its ancient and modern biological and social history. This consciousness also involves physically experiencing your life-place by leaving the house or apartment and car and proceeding to walk, swim, lay, smell, taste, listen, or simply, just be, in it. Once that connectivity occurs, chances are a rootedness will result, in turn manifesting a territorial sensibility. When humans become territorial, they tend to protect and cherish that territory with which they are identified.[8]

OACC members engage in anthropological and ethnohistorical research on their own, to learn about and from the previous inhabitants of their bioregion. They experiment with traditional land use practices of their Ozarkian predecessors and modify and/or employ them accordingly to ensure they provide a well-adapted, sustainable strategy for their time and watershed. OACC gatherings and related publications consistently extol the traditional uses of wild plants as medicine, food, and fiber. At many OACC gatherings midwives give workshops and talks about the history of Ozark midwifery; they now carry on a legacy that has been a cherished, respected tradition in the region (Allured 1992). A locally renowned traditional midwife and preacher in northwest Arkansas received a huge contingent of soaked, exhausted hippies from a rained-out folk festival in the early 1970s and went on to share much of her traditional medical knowledge with an OACC member, who later published a biography about her. OACC material culture reveals the important role of traditional ecological knowledge and originality in bioregional value systems. In each of the original OACC members' homes hangs an emblematic drawing titled *Ozark Seasons* that depicts an astrological calendar filled with the Ozarks' key ecological occurrences according to their seasonal timing and concomitant subsistence practices. An oak tree holds the center; elderberries and pawpaws ripen alongside seed ticks hatching during the "Dog Days" of Leo; hens get broody, yarrow flowers, copperheads leave dens, and white bass run while Ozarkers gather slippery elm bark during the bullish days of Taurus. At OACC IV they distributed a sampler pack with a drawing of a prototypical Ozark homestead on the cover and the title, "Home Sweet Home, an Ozark Sampler." It included "The Green Pages, An Ozark Bioregional Directory," an incredibly comprehensive alphabetical phone book/guide to as many alternative, sustainable activities you could imagine in the Ozarks; a diagram and description of karst topography, "geo-hydrology of the Ozarks"; an ethnohistorical summary of Native American occupation and use of the bioregion; a record by The Hot Mulch Band; a "regional seasonal eating plan"; an Ozarks water guide; and a few other pamphlets and artistic pieces. The music celebrates a shared value of both traditional and bioregional Ozark cultures—self-reliance: "We'll get our eggs from chickens and milk from a cow, a horse that plows and a book that tells how, an organic garden growin' comfrey and peas, get honey from our bees and fruit from our trees. Self-sufficient, that's the name of the game, gonna get myself a system self-contained, a wind mill to give me my electricity no phone in my dome I'll use ESP."

Influences

OACC members initially came to the Ozarks to get "far enough away from the mainstream and into the woods to get away from the social and ecological mess of the overdeveloped places we had lived in." But they

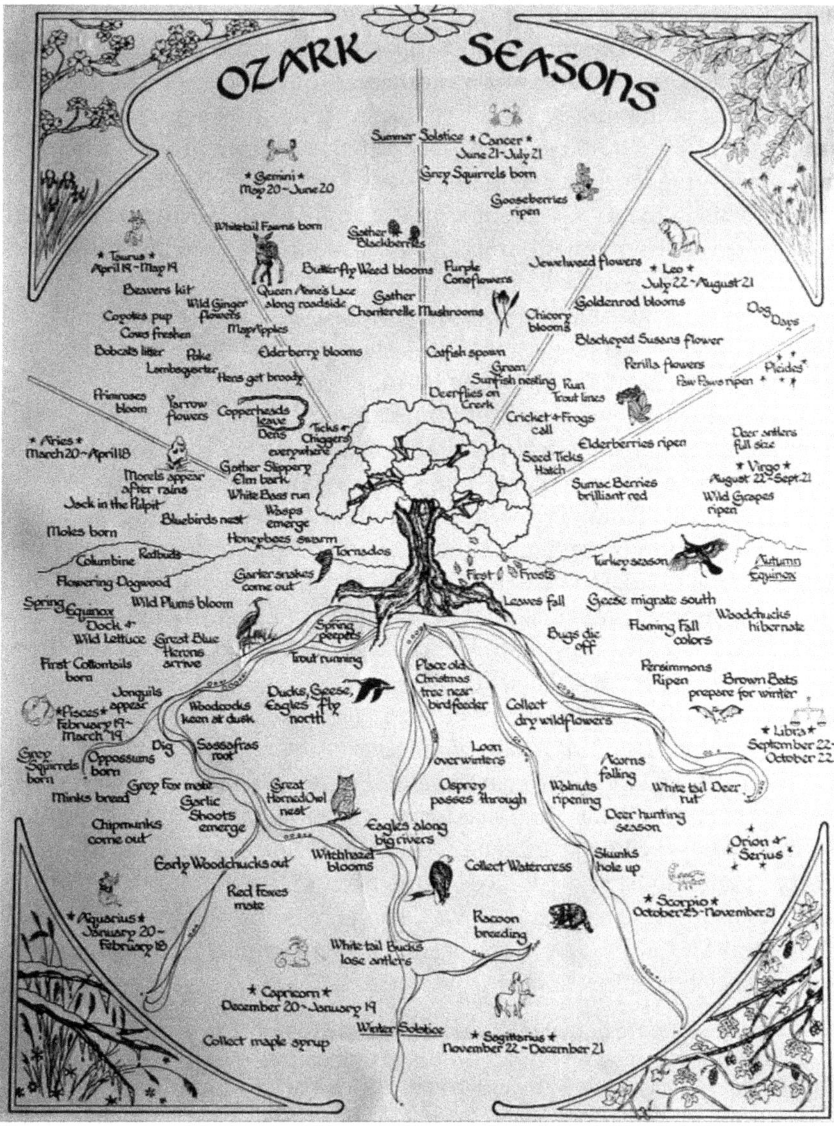

Figure 3.1. *Ozark Seasons* drawing. Image courtesy of Denise Vaughn, Ozark Area Community Congress.

quickly came to the realization that "the Ozarks was being trashed and polluted just like everywhere else. One of our naive notions was that the so-called system was going to fall apart before it could ruin the Ozarks."[9] They believed that a "collapse" of mainstream society loomed because of sociopolitical events, personal experiences, and academic and lay publications. Evidence for imminent collapse ranged from "the fact that the Soviet Union had 3000 armed intercontinental ballistic missiles and we had 7000 aimed at each other" to "oil shortages" to "climate change. We were the canaries in the mines. We knew the superstorms were coming. I was sure by 2010 we would be completely untethered from the petrochemical industry." A high school girl in the 1970s experienced the effects of an ice storm: "City came to a screeching halt. People were moving out of their houses to motels, to other parts of the city or state, where there was electricity. A simple bit of ice made people freak out for electricity … [it] paralyzed my entire world and I was just like: 'this is stupid, this dependence on technology—was just stupid.'"[10] A short time later she was living off the grid in the Ozarks at New Life Farm.

Personal experiences with environmental destruction and/or pollution, ranging from chemical pollutants in local rivers to deforestation to lead mining to nuclear power plant construction, affected many of the OACC participants in traumatic and influential ways, pushing them into their roles in the bioregional movement. Literary influences that instigated Ozark bioregionalists to evaluate their impact on the planet and engage in more sustainable livelihoods include: Ernest Callenbach's *Ecotopia* (1975), Paul R. Ehrlich's *The Population Bomb* (1968), Frances Moore Lappé's *Diet for a Small Planet* (1971), Aldo Leopold's *A Sand County Almanac* (1949), James Lovelock's *Gaia: A New Look at Life on Earth* (1979), E. F. Schumacher's *Small Is Beautiful: Economics as if People Mattered* (1973), Laura Ingalls Wilder's *Little House on the Prairie* (1935), *Mother Earth News*, the *Whole Earth Catalog*, and academic writers like ecological economist Herman Daly, ecologist Eugene Odum, and cultural historian Thomas Berry. As previously noted, most of the back-to-the-landers obtained college degrees before retreating to the Ozarks; therefore, in many cases their ecological and sociological studies encouraged them to reassess mainstream society's anthropocentric tendencies:

> I remember sitting in that [ecology] class, and we were having a discussion, … the situation was: if you had a piece of virgin forest, and you also needed to put a highway through there, … what do you do? And to me that was a no-brainer. I was really, absolutely shocked to find out that I was in the minority. I mean, I just had no clue that most of the people, at least most of the vocal people there, absolutely thought that you would put the highway through.[11]

Activities, Organizations, Obstacles

> We saw everything that was wrong and we knew we had the template to fix it. We knew exactly what needed to be done and we all adopted those

> practices in our own homes. We would go home [from OACC meetings] and apply all the things we discussed as models in our particular watershed area, either politically, personally, or teaching others in whatever fashion we could.[12]

OACC's achievements emerge in response to obstacles. The Ozarks landscape and infrastructure provide minimal economic opportunities. The resources available to mainstream businesspeople who engage in status quo political-economic procedures, such as loans or agricultural extension, are either useless or unavailable to back-to-the-landers because they opt for sustainable methods that do not receive consideration by conventional agencies. Ozark bioregionalists create their own opportunities through networks that OACC both creates and maintains. OACC directly inspired and informed the development of a range of organizations, cottage industries, and cooperative endeavors that allow participants to return to their respective watersheds and engage in community organization and mobilization and sustainable occupations.

The National Water Center, Eureka Springs, Arkansas

The establishment of the National Water Center in Eureka Springs, Arkansas emerged as a direct result of the proposed construction of a sewage treatment plant. In the late 1970s a young chemist and mother, who would later become the research director for Greenpeace International and an OACC member, returned to her home state of Arkansas and purchased land in the Ozarks, where she intended to live a relatively anonymous, self-sufficient life. Despite her best intentions, she could not avoid the good fight:

> One day I was driving home, and someone … stopped me and said, "You know there's this water issue here. They're gonna build this big water treatment plant at the base of Lake Leatherwood," which was not very far from where my place was; "We're having a meeting on that tonight and we'd like for you to come." In the interim, I had also established, in another part of the state, an analytical lab that did water and wastewater analysis for small cities and industries, so people around Eureka … knew that I did this, so they wanted me to come to this meeting.… I just looked at him and I said; "You know, I don't go to meetings." And I got in my truck and drove home. Then they brought me the engineer's facility plans … for the city's [Eureka Springs] wastewater and water system. First, both documents were internally inconsistent to a great degree, and between the two, they totally cancelled each other out. So I did what I knew to do on these things … a critique of the documents and effectively [I] was able to strangle the engineers with their own numbers and words and … establish that the cheapest thing, the most energy-efficient way forward, was just simply to make a few improvements to the existing gravity-fed trickling filter.[13]

She then began collaboration with a local organizer and water activist to establish the National Water Center to study and disseminate findings on the inadequacies of current wastewater treatment strategies and sustainable alternatives. They connected with the New Life Farmers in the Missouri Ozarks who shared their passion for protecting Ozark waters. She recollects:

> They had information on other methods of waste management, including composting toilets and ... we finally decided that the dumbest thing that humans ever did was start pooping in the water. What we really wanted to do was re-train, re-toilet-train people, that water-borne waste systems simply are the most mentally flawed concept that modern civilization has come up with. It teaches you two things, ... that water is a waste vehicle, ... [and] that your feces and urine are not only repugnant, but have no use; when actually, your feces and urine are what you give back to the environment.... We're running out of the mined fertilizer, phosphates, and excreta is an especially good source of such; the same thing for nitrogen. And it turns out that for an average adult on an average Western diet, the amount of nitrogen and phosphorous that a person excretes in a year is almost exactly the amount of nitrogen and phosphorous that's needed to grow that person's annual needs for whole grain.[14]

A foundational OACC member fondly recollects her first encounter with a New Life Farmer: "One of the first the things he said to me ... was: 'The flush toilet is the curse of mankind.' And I was a seventeen-year-old girl from suburban Kansas City and I went: 'Huh?' But you know what; I have a composting toilet right now."[15] Each interviewee had either an outhouse or composting toilet at their residence.

New Life Farm (NLF)/Ozarks Resource Center (ORC)

The lyrics from Hot Mulch's song about New Life Farm present some of the innovative, sustainable technologies and the ideology underlying the Ozark bioregional movement: "Get a Solar Air Heater from New Life Farm, in the Wintertime it will keep me warm. My methane digester's a great big hit. It makes methane gas out of Chicken manure. If I keep my faith in the Organic way, maybe some day my tomb stone might say, 'we shredded his body, turned to compost in a week he was an Ozark Mountain Mother Earth News Freak'" (*Ozark Mountain Mother Earth News Freak*).

New Life Farm (NLF) served as the hub for Ozark bioregionalism through financial management, technological innovation, and a physical location for congregation and brainstorming tangibility. The energy crisis of the 1970s spurred unprecedented economic support for alternative energy technologies, which funded diverse research at NLF. A 1979 study by Fischer and Swack documents four funded projects, two of which relate to methane or biogas digesters, which convert organic material "into a high-quality liquid fertilizer and a burnable gas that can be used in place of propane or natural gas for heating and cooking" (95). The Rural Gasification Project (which received a $155,000 grant from the Community Services Administration) resulted in the design and construction of twenty digesters for low-income farmers, and a collaboration with the University of Missouri at Rolla (three-year, $230,000 grant from the Department of Energy) tested and evaluated different crops' fertilizer and gas production capacities. The Why Flush? Water Quality Conservation Project ($3,750 grant from the Rockefeller Foundation, $500 grant from the National Demonstration Water Project) educated the public on alternatives to conventional sewage handling, and Solar Heating Made Easy, (funded by the US Office of Education with Southwest Missouri State University) resulted in workshops that demonstrated how to install a simple, low-cost solar space or water heater in the home. NLF technologies work well in the marginal Ozarks landscape because they mimic ecology; they transform by-products from one stage (energy and/or materials) into inputs for the next stage, thereby creating an efficient, productive cyclic process (Fischer and Swack 1979).

Without external funds to facilitate unconventional economic strategies, Ozark bioregionalists would never have realized their many successes. By establishing a legitimate research station that received grants, NLF allowed an alternative economy and lifestyle to flourish. In July 1982, NLF approved start-up funding for the Bioregional Project, which made full-time bioregional planning possible. Ozark bioregionalists then worked fervently with groups like the Kansas Area Watershed (KAW) Council to establish a "congress of congresses," the North American Bioregional Congress (NABC; Mirriam-Goldberg n.d.). OACC has been credited as the original inspiration for KAW, NABC (now Continental Bioregional Congress), and "more than a dozen bioregional congresses and councils."

The transition from the Carter to the Reagan administration and the symbolic removal of White House solar panels represents a formidable event in this timeline. The "trickle-down" effects of Reagan's termination of financial support for alternative energy development included a drought for external funding for Ozark bioregionalism. The general public lost interest in alternative energy "when Reagan came … there were just lots of years where there was no support, and the SUVs went wild and all the gas guzzling."[16] While mainstream society abandoned the "environmental" ship with Reagan, Ozark bioregionalism remained afloat through the philanthropy of the kind and wealthy bioregional supporter, Ella (Macdonald) Alford. As a now famous author and photographer recalls:

> There was a woman there, Ella Macdonald, who was instrumental in funding a lot of bioregional work, both at the local level, and nationally in the early 1980s. She talked … about her funding during an OACC session and I was a young, naïve, 23 year old, … naïve enough to write her a letter the next week, saying "I want to write a book," and "will you give me a grant to do it" … and she did.[17]

She funded the Ozark Beneficial Plant Project through NLF, which resulted in publications on *Echinacea* and "comparisons of medicinal plants disjunct between eastern Asia and eastern North America."[18] Ozark species constitute a key component of both of these works; the former stimulated the global *Echinacea* market, promoted conservation-oriented production by emphasizing the domesticated species, *Echinacea purpurea,* and encouraged international research on "the plant's biology, … chemistry and pharmacology, and now clinical applications." The latter research reveals ethnobotanical similarities between plants in the southeastern United States and in Japan and eastern China, such as the fact that "the closest genetic relative of the vernal Witchhazel from the Ozarks is not the other North American species, it's an east Asian species."[19]

Ozark Regional Land Trust (ORLT)

Ella Alford fulfilled a needed role in Ozark bioregionalism, funding myriad sustainable, bioregional endeavors. Part of her legacy includes Alford Forest, a 4,300-acre oak-pine-hickory stand in the Missouri Ozarks; 3,200 acres belong to the Ozark Regional Land Trust (ORLT) and 1,100 acres reside in private ownership with ORLT conservation easements. Ecological forestry methods determine the management of these lands, including an "uneven-aged," "single-tree selection" strategy that increases "both the health and the value of the forest."[20] The ORLT emerged shortly after Robert Swann, the E. F. Schumacher Society president who developed the community land trust concept, spoke at OACC (Witt and Swann 1992). He especially inspired one key attendee, who founded the ORLT in 1984. An interviewee recalled his reaction to Swann's talk: "[He] got really excited, and said, 'I think we can do this in the Ozarks' and I was there when that all happened."[21] ORLT, a nonprofit 501(c)(3) conservation land trust, has projects totaling 21,570 acres of Ozark land, including unique ecological, geological, and historic features, and employs diverse methods, such as community land trusts, conservation easements, nature preserves, and partnerships, to protect Ozark lands.

Organizations for an Alternative Ozarks Economy

Ozark Organic Growers Association (OOGA)

The founder of OOGA characterizes the significance of a cooperative approach to market gardening in the Ozarks: "It enabled us … to ship our products into markets that would pay a fair price, and that we would not otherwise have been able to do. You name it; we sold every vegetable crop that could be grown in the Ozarks, everything from watercress to potatoes, to green onions, bell peppers, tomatoes, apples, grapes, raspberries, strawberries … the whole gamut."[22]

Organic farmers in the Ozarks face myriad challenges: poor soils and transportation routes, inadequate research and extension assistance, and inaccessible markets and monies. Through OACC collaborations, member-farmers overcame these obstacles. In 1985, in response to a lack of local markets, they formed the Ozark Organic Growers Association (OOGA), a nonprofit growers' cooperative, to facilitate group marketing to grocery chains. The absence of uniform organic standards, however, confounded farmers, who wanted to receive just compensation for the intensive labor that goes into the production of a premium product. OOGA members worked diligently and collaboratively to help create present-day "organic" legislation:

> For a long time certification was confusing to consumers, confusing to growers, because as you went from state to state, different organizations had different rules, different definitions of what organic production meant, and there was no single standard for organic production. So it became important as markets matured, as industries matured, consumers wanted more assurances about the quality of the products and they wanted to know that they were in fact organically grown. So it became important to have a single national standard and that was created initially through the 1985 farm bill. It took 10 more years before we actually had a certification program that was really in effect, but [we] were instrumental in the language of that initial bill that made it possible, along with some people from OACC.[23]

Massive amounts of money pass through land-grant universities for agricultural research that will benefit industrial agriculture, yet organic farmers remain at a loss for where to turn for advice for their operations. Over two hundred growers in three states marketed through OOGA, and this glaring need prompted them to create the Ozark Small Farm Viability Project (OSFVP), a 501(c)(3) educational nonprofit: "Just as we couldn't go to the banks to get funds to plant our crops, nor could we go to our county extension agent and get info on how to grow our crops organically. We could get all kinds of info on how to use herbicides, fungicides, pesticides … and chemical fertilizers to put on our crops but we got blank stares when we asked for non-chemical methods of production."[24]

OSFVP hosted annual conferences, established an organic agriculture library (presently housed at the Boone County Library in Harrison, Arkansas), published a newsletter, held workshops on integrated greenhousing, and maintained a staff of "alternative extension agents who would go make farm visits, and consult with farmers about particular problems they might be having or ways they could increase their income by diversifying their crops, or how to integrate livestock into crop production, those sorts of things."[25]

Financing Ozarks Rural Growth & Economy (FORGE)

Many Ozark bioregionalists engaged in organic farming and encountered obstacles in their attempts to convert such practices into innovative entrepreneurial ventures: "We could not go to our local bank and take out a loan for a thousand dollars to buy raspberry plants for example, or to buy drip irrigation lines, because organic farming was considered such an unknown and therefore risky investment for banks that they would not touch those sorts of loans."[26]

Lack of capital hindered organic farmers who wanted to incorporate innovative sustainable practices into their operations. OOGA overcame this challenge by establishing Financing Ozarks Rural Growth & Economy (FORGE), a community loan fund to make small loans available to organic farmers. FORGE, modeled after the Grameen Bank (a community development bank and microfinance organization started in 1976 in Bangladesh by Muhammad Yunus, who won the Nobel Peace Prize for the effort), began in 1989 as a specific response to farmers' needs, but has expanded to assist diverse businesses that support rural communities. It has a peer-based review system, a very low default rate, and makes loans as small as a few hundred to a few thousand dollars, for projects ranging from start-up creameries and bakeries to home improvements. FORGE's loan program includes energy saving, credit establishment, and emergency loans. In 1998 FORGE became a US Small Business Administration (SBA) Microlender and offers technical assistance to start-up businesses. FORGE's primary goal remains "to link borrowers with investors to create healthy sustainable communities through[out] the Ozarks" (FORGE n.d.).

As local businesses, funding sources, and markets emerged, the need to ship produce out of the region disappeared; OOGA created its own demise. OOGA's objective all along was the establishment of local markets, because direct economic relationships sustain the community. The funding that NLF attracted, and Ms. Alford provided, can now come through the sustainable, locally run FORGE, which fosters an alternative sustainable economy.

Conclusion

OACC illustrates the capacity of generous, thoughtful, inspired people to overcome sociopolitical obstacles through ingenuity and cooperation. While Ozark bioregionalists themselves have made headway in their local watersheds, the potential of these innovative OACC members to improve the larger society has not been completely realized. The sad fact is that the "cutting-edge" alternative technologies that New Life Farmers developed and disseminated three decades ago remain "cutting edge" today because of institutionalized stagnation and collusion. Contemporary society, despite being behind the curve, now realizes that the status quo cannot be sustained. OACC's true contribution is by example. Ozark bioregionalists' ability to develop sustainable communities through cooperative organizations, hard work, and ecological respect in the face of innumerable political barriers deserves emulation. Their egalitarian principles allow them to identify the strengths of each of their members, use them strategically, maintain productivity and motivation, and coordinate alliances, organizations, and work projects. Their empirical understanding of and respect for ecology combined with their pragmatic approach results in technologies and land management that efficiently and safely improve life and sustain resources. Most notably, they have established a real foundation for an ecologically inspired local economy, simultaneously within the system and without it. That economy, like an oak, has dropped many acorns in receptive Ozark soil.

Notes

1. The quotations in this paragraph come from unpublished manuscripts and documents obtained through ethnographic research and will not be cited in this chapter in the interest of anonymity.
2. Interview near West Plains, Missouri, in February 2010.
3. This quotation comes from an unpublished manuscript obtained through ethnographic research and will not be cited in this chapter in the interest of anonymity.
4. This quote comes from an unpublished manuscript obtained through ethnographic research and will not be cited in this chapter in the interest of anonymity.
5. Interview near Eureka Springs, Arkansas, in January 2010.
6. Interview near West Plains, Missouri, in February 2010.
7. Interview near Brixey, Missouri, in May 2010.
8. This quote comes from a published source obtained through archival research and will not be cited in this chapter in the interest of anonymity.

9. Interview near West Plains, Missouri, in February 2010.
10. Interview near West Plains, Missouri, in February 2010.
11. Interview near Doniphan, Missouri, in February 2010.
12. Interview near West Plains, Missouri, in February 2010.
13. Interview near Eureka Springs, Arkansas, in April 2010.
14. Interview near Eureka Springs, Arkansas, in April 2010.
15. Interview near West Plains, Missouri, in February 2010.
16. Interview near West Plains, Missouri, in February 2010.
17. Interview in Eureka Springs, Arkansas, in June 2010.
18. Interview in Eureka Springs, Arkansas, in June 2010.
19. Interview in Eureka Springs, Arkansas, in June 2010.
20. Interview near Brixey, Missouri, in May 2010.
21. Interview near West Plains, Missouri, in February 2010.
22. Interview near Red Star, Arkansas, in April 2010.
23. Interview near Red Star, Arkansas, in April 2010.
24. Interview near Red Star, Arkansas, in April 2010.
25. Interview near Red Star, Arkansas, in April 2010.
26. Interview near Red Star, Arkansas, in April 2010.

References

Aley, Tom. 1992. "Karst Topography and Rural Poverty." *Ozarkswatch* 5 (3): 19–21.

Allured, Janet L. *1992.* "Women's Healing Art: Domestic Medicine in the Turn-of-the-Century Ozarks." *Gateway Heritage* 12 (4): 20-31.

Blevins, Brooks. 2002. *Hill Folks: A History of Arkansas Ozarkers and Their Image.* Chapel Hill: University of North Carolina Press.

Callenbach, Earnest. 1975. *Ecotopia.* San Francisco: Banyan Tree Books.

Campbell, Brian. 2009. "'A Gentle Work Horse Would Come in Right Handy': Animals in Ozark Agroecology." *Anthrozoös* 22 (3): 239–53.

Ehrlich, Paul R. 1968. *The Population Bomb.* New York: Ballantine Books.

Fischer, Michael, and Swack, Michael. 1979. "New Life Farm, Drury, Missouri." Harvard Workshop on Appropriate Technology for Community Development, Department of City and Regional Planning, Harvard University, Boston.

FORGE. n.d. "FORGE: Financing Ozarks Rural Growth & Economy." http://www.forgeonline.com/ (accessed 14 August 2010).

Gallaher, Art, Jr. 1961. *Plainville Fifteen Years Later.* New York: Columbia University Press.

Gilman, Robert. 1990. "Sustainability: The State Of The Movement." *In Context* 25 (Spring): 10.

Harington, Donald. 1986. *Let Us Build Us a City: Eleven Lost Towns.* New Milford, CT: Toby Press.

Lappé, Frances Moore. 1971. *Diet for a Small Planet.* New York: Ballantine Books.

Leopold, Aldo. 1949. *A Sand County Almanac.* Oxford: Oxford University Press.

Lovelock, James. 1979. *Gaia: A New Look at Life on Earth.* Oxford: Oxford University Press.

Mirriam-Goldberg, Caryn. n.d. "The Last Ten Years of the U.S. Bioregional Movement and One Small Kansas Group Got Things Going Again." http://biocongress.org/history/history1998-2009/ (accessed 10 May 2010).

Orr, David. 1991. "What Is Education For?" *In Context* 27 (Winter): 52.

Otto, John Solomon, and Augustus Marion Burns III. 1981. "Traditional Agricultural Practices in the Arkansas Highlands." *Journal of American Folklore* 94 (372): 166–87.

Rafferty, Milton. 2001. *The Ozarks: Land and Life.* Norman: University of Oklahoma Press.

Schumacher, E. F. 1973. *Small Is Beautiful: Economics as if People Mattered.* London: Blond & Briggs.

Wessels, Tom. 2006. *The Myth of Progress: Toward a Sustainable Future.* Lebanon, New Hampshire: University of Vermont Press.

Wilder, Laura Ingalls. 1935. *Little House on the Prairie.* New York: Harper Collins.

Witt, Susan, and Robert Swann. 1992. *Land: The Challenge and Opportunity.* Great Barrington, MA: E. F. Schumacher Society.

CHAPTER FOUR

The Adirondack Semester

An Integrated Approach to Cultivating Bioregional Knowledge and Consciousness

Steven M. Alexander and Baylor Johnson

In academic and educational circles we often find ourselves speaking of the necessary knowledge we must equip students with. Proponents of bioregionalism also speak frequently of such essential knowledge. However, we believe such discussions fall short, as this is only half the story. In a seminal essay from 1977, Peter Berg provides the following definition and description of bioregionalism:

> The term bioregion refers both to a geographical terrain and to a "terrain of consciousness"—to a place and the ideas that have developed about how to live in that place. A bioregion can be determined initially by use of climatology, physiography, animal and plant geography, natural history, and other descriptive natural sciences, [but] the final boundaries are best described by people who have lived within it. Bioregionalism and bioregional perspective involve learning to live-in-place, a kind of spiritual identification with a particular kind of country and its wild nature [that is] the basis for the kind of land care the world so definitely needs. (Berg 1977: 2)

Based on Berg's definition and description of a bioregion, we believe it is necessary to speak not only of bioregional knowledge but also of bioregional consciousness. Bioregional knowledge is extensive, characterized by both depth and breadth. Along with ecological, geological, and geographical knowledge of place, it requires cultural and political knowledge as well. It also necessitates knowledge of both the past and the present. Bioregional consciousness, on the other hand—or "watershed consciousness" (Parsons 1985)—is a way of thinking about one's bioregion and one's way of living in it. It is a way of being, perceiving, and moving through the day-to-day. Bioregional consciousness includes the necessary knowledge, as well as the values, attitudes, habits, and imagination that foster a sustainable way of life.

Berg nowhere defines the boundaries of a bioregion. It might reasonably be construed as defined by flora, fauna, and all the resources necessary to sustain life in that region. However, nearly everyone is involved as producer, consumer, or both, in the global economy, so that what is done locally is affected by and affects other bioregions. Climate change and pollutants that transcend national and even continental boundaries are examples of effects that span multiple bioregions. For some, the ideal of bioregionalism is that people will return to the days when their ecological footprint was almost entirely local; when living sustainably within one's bioregion guaranteed that one lived sustainably on the globe. Whether this is desirable or possible is a question that lies beyond the scope of the present chapter. It does not, however, describe the way most people, and especially most of us in the affluent, developed world, live today. Whatever the future may bring, today we need global consciousness and carefully fashioned, globally sustainable ways of life in addition to modes of life that permit us to live sustainably within our own bioregions.

As explained below, some people have more than one local bioregion (e.g., the one they inhabit as a student and the one they call home, or a primary residence and a much-used second home). To the extent that this is true, an individual will need to cultivate more than one kind of bioregional knowledge; at minimum, an understanding of what is globally sustainable, as well as how to live sustainably within one's local bioregion. One program that seeks to explore just such an understanding with students is the Adirondack Semester at St. Lawrence University.

St. Lawrence University, a small liberal arts college, is located at the northern edge of the Adirondack foothills in upstate New York, only twenty miles from the Canadian border. Its Adirondack Semester is an off-campus, residential program situated an hour south of the main campus that engages undergraduate students in the study of nature and human relationships with nature. In this chapter we propose that the Adirondack Semester provides a useful programmatic and pedagogical framework for cultivating bioregional knowledge and consciousness. In the first section, we offer three vignettes describing typical experiences that students might have during their time in the Adirondack Semester. Just as the Adirondack Semester enriches academic study with complementary experiences for the students, so we hope that these descriptive vignettes provide imaginative detail for the reader, detail that brings to life the elements of the program described in the second section. This second portion unravels the tightly knit fabric that is the Adirondack Semester to reveal the key elements that make possible the experiences described in the vignettes. The third section goes on to explore how those key elements come together and interact, offering a whole greater than the sum of its parts. The chapter then concludes with an examination and discussion concerning bioregional pedagogy for undergraduate education.

Semester Sketches

Observing

Their paddles dip rhythmically, driving their canoe across the lake. The two young paddlers are silent, lost in their own thoughts, feeling their paddle strokes and watching. Watching sun light play on the water, watching where the lake meets the forested shore. They live here, and so the landscape is almost as familiar as the suburban streets where they grew up. But they listen and look with quiet attention. They are learning to inhabit their home. They are learning appreciation for the subtle changes that occur at every moment. Some are important and practical: three days of cloud are ending, or the wind is kicking up and the lake crossing will be tricky. Some mean nothing of consequence, but delight the senses and make boredom unthinkable.

The student in the bow of the boat grunts softly. The sound is barely audible, but the one in the stern looks up, then follows the line of her companion's pointing hand. Two tiny dots cleave the water a quarter mile away. Looking closely, the students can see the wake trailing behind the two dark shapes, fanning out in a pair of overlapping Vs. Without speaking, the paddlers turn their canoe toward these other travelers on the lake. They could be Canada geese, passing through on their ancient migration route from the far north. But they are too low in the water for geese. They might be loons, annual residents of the lake. Ducks are possible too. But these travelers aren't drifting and diving as ducks and loons probably would. They are crossing with intention. They might be beavers. A pair lives nearby, with a dam on the lake outlet, and they come across some evenings to browse in an aspen grove near the shore. But the time of day is wrong.

A hundred yards away, the students are sure of what they are seeing. They stop paddling, letting their boat slow. These are otters. They are a rare sight, because an otter's territory is big, and these two will visit here only occasionally, and mostly without being observed. As the boat slows, the paddlers dip in and stop forward motion. It would be rude to come too close to these sleek neighbors. To do so would frighten the otters, unaccustomed as they are to human approach. Instead the boat follows slowly, at a distance, until the otters reach the shore and splash up onto the bank, disappearing instantly into the woods. Then the paddlers turn again and head home to their tiny village down the shore, excited to tell the others about what they have seen, and feeling the near-magic of sharing their world so intimately with these more-than-human beings.

Canoe Dreams

Allison wakes from a crazy dream in which she paddled a canoe home through Greenwich Village as the clanging bell of a fire truck chased her. When her eyes open she is lying in her sleeping bag, on a pad in the yurt where she lives. Manhattan is four hundred miles away, her canoe a hundred yards, but the clanging bell persists. The ringing of an iron triangle, calling everyone to breakfast, echoes through the yurt village. The morning is chilly, and she pulls a fleece jacket on top of her sweat pants and sweater, because to walk from her bedroom to the kitchen/dining room will mean going out under the canopy of towering pines and hemlocks. She slips into her boots, laces loosely tucked in for the fifteen yards to breakfast. After stopping briefly to wash her hands under the drip of a plastic barrel filled with water, she slips inside the kitchen. A woodstove, heat from the propane cook stove, and the bodies of her thirteen companions have already made the building warm.

Two nights ago it was unseasonably warm, the moon was nearly full, and the sky clear. That night, she finished homework by nine, and had a late night snack together with her study group. Then she wrote her plans on a dry-erase board in the corner of the dining room so others would know where she had gone, gathered her sleeping bag, a camping mattress, and a plastic tarp just in case, and walked fifty yards down a path illuminated by moonlight and headlamp to where the canoes are kept. Alone, she piled her gear into the boat and paddled out onto the lake. She looked up at the moon and stars, felt the stillness of the night, and asked herself once more if she was confident there would be no rain. Deciding, she pushed her pad out onto the floor of the canoe, arranged her bag on top, and wiggled down under the canoe yoke stretching side to side across the middle of the boat. Lying on her back, she looked up at the moonlit sky, and drifted slowly to sleep, while her canoe drifted even more slowly down the lake, riding the gentle currents as cooling air fell down the hills. She had no way of knowing just where she would wake, but it would be home. The lake—and also the eskers, ponds, forest, and hills around it—have all become a second home in the last few weeks.

Blacksmithing

Eben looks carefully at the color of the bar of iron he holds with tongs. It glows yellow, tinged with red around the edges. Judging that the temperature is right, he lays one end of the bar on the big anvil and begins to flatten it with hammer strokes. The iron clangs loudly, but he scarcely notices as he carefully guides the hammer to carry force to the right spot. He tries also to keep his grip as light as possible. He will pound this iron, heat it, then pound again over and over for at least twenty minutes, and he must waste no strength by gripping too hard. As each blow hits, he lets his wrist go a little limp, breaking the tie between hammer and arm so that the weight of the head flattens the iron while his wrist shakes off the blow like a shock absorber.

He takes his work to his practicum mentor, David, an Adirondack blacksmith. David's ancestors migrated into the Adirondacks from French Canada generations back, and David knows the Adirondacks like he knows his own house, like he knows his own family. He has been a park ranger, a logger, a woodworker, and is now a blacksmith, doing mostly decorative work for gift shops. He knows half the people in his hometown, and if there is someone he does not know, he most likely does know one of their relatives. The Adirondack community is so small and intertwined that he could not spend half a day in any town in the ten thousand square miles of the park without being recognized, most likely by a friend.

David gives Eben's product a quick inspection and says it is good enough. He sees a couple of small things he could comment on, but since Eben is living at David's during his practicum, he decides it will make good dinner conversation to wait until then. Living with David, Eben is learning the beginning skills of a blacksmith, but he is also learning about life in the Adirondacks. He is learning about the life of people making a living from half a dozen different skills, building boats by day and playing in a band by night, or logging in season, guiding fishermen in the summer, and making duck decoys late into the night. He is learning that locals can tell you whose gates can be safely crossed, who expects a request, and who guards his land like a bank vault. They can tell you where to buy rough-cut lumber at a fraction of lumber yard prices, what to do with each species and grade, and what season to log it if you want the best quality. Eben is getting a glimpse. He would have to settle here and spend his life to have a chance of catching up even halfway to what David knows. But at least he's getting that glimpse, seeing that it is possible to live in a place so that the place is unique and true to its history, climate, and ecology, and not just another space readily interchangeable with any other space. Not just real estate flattened by the same chain stores, brand names, and pastimes that have covered the North American continent.

Program Elements

The Adirondack Semester is an off-campus residential program whose mission is to engage students in the study of nature and human relationships with nature through academic classes enriched by direct experience.[1] Twelve students live through the change of seasons from late summer to early winter in a village of yurts[2] nestled among a towering canopy of white pines and hemlocks on the shore of Lake Massawepie. Modeled on programs abroad, it embraces an ethos of immersion, though in this case, it is immersion in nature.

The students come and go by driving two miles down a dirt road, walking half a mile to the lakeshore, and then canoeing across to their secluded "campus." Known as Arcadia, a name suggesting the perfect bal-

Figure 4.1. Arcadia. Photo by Allan Alexander.

ance between wilderness and civilization, the "campus" is composed of a cluster of eight yurts—large, round tents with wooden floors—that house the students and staff along with a classroom and community space.[3] A small timber-framed kitchen, composting toilet, wood-fired sauna, and solar array round out the facility. Meanwhile, faculty commute from the main university campus to offer a full load of academic courses. In this next section we will unravel the tightly knit fabric of the Adirondack Semester to reveal and describe the key elements of the program: academic coursework, direct and deliberate experiences, and a purposeful living and learning community. Those elements together make possible the experiences described in the vignettes above.

Academic study is at the heart of the program's mission. Thus, the students are enrolled in a full course load taught by a team of faculty and staff. The five carefully chosen and complementary courses include: Natural History and Ecology of the Adirondacks; Land Use Change in the Adirondacks; Philosophy and the Environment; Creative Expressions of Nature; and Cultivating Place: Bioregionalism and Community Engagement. Each course brings its own disciplinary/interdisciplinary perspective, providing students a suite of lenses to examine the essential question of the program, yet numerous threads run between them all.

The Natural History and Ecology of the Adirondacks course introduces students to the ecological and geological processes that have both shaped and continue to shape the landscape. Weekly field trips and field studies find the students hiking to over four thousand feet to examine the delicate alpine environment, taking core samples from a sphagnum bog to age the more than five-thousand-year-old soil, and exploring the glaciated landscape immediately surrounding Arcadia. As part of the course, students are required to identify and record one hundred species by the end of the semester—approximately one species per day—noting where they observed it and in what conditions, describing it in detail, and using field guides to classify it. As the semester progresses, they are able to draw upon their readings and class notes to add general information about those species already identified. Because the students are immersed in the natural landscape that is the focus of this course, there is little separation between their daily life and the subject of the course. It is common, and natural, for them to chat about the species they are passing as they go on an afternoon run or to recognize and identify the otters described in the first vignette.

Land use has been the key controversy in the Adirondack Mountains almost since the area's penetration by Europeans in the early nineteenth century. These mountains became a nursery for the idea of wilderness conservation. Conservation, however, soon came into conflict with rapacious logging practices. The ultimate result—still evolving—is the immense

Adirondack (State) Park formed from a patchwork of public and private lands. Encompassing six million acres, it is larger than the Grand Canyon, Yellowstone, Yosemite, and Olympic National Parks combined. Developers, local residents, recreationists, environmentalists, and others still fight ceaselessly over what will become of this wild landscape. In the Land Use Change in the Adirondacks course, students learn about these battles and their importance in environmental history. Students begin to understand that what looks to the casual tourist like a great, tranquil forest is in fact the result of strenuous human efforts, past and present. They see also that the Adirondacks are home to thousands of people whose differing visions could have immense implications for the immediate region and beyond. The course also enables them to see that environmental problems are not simply due to pollution, but have roots deep in our attitude to land and its uses. Conversely, they see how land use policy can play an important role in addressing seemingly unrelated environmental problems.

The Philosophy and the Environment course analyzes social causes and solutions to environmental problems, especially consumption. It presents a theory of happiness to explain how we can live well while consuming less and reducing our environmental footprint. The theory also explains why we find it so difficult to consume less. Though the course promotes voluntary simplicity, it also explores limits to individual reductions in consumption, as well as the importance of public policy that steers everyone toward environmental protection. More than any other, this course explains the rationale for the material simplicity of life at Arcadia. It also provides a forum for students to understand the joy they inevitably derive from their simple life there, expanding their understanding, their care (practically as well as emotionally) for one another, and why they find pleasure in their senses and physical activity. In short, the course provides a theoretical framework for understanding why happening upon otters or exercising the hand-eye-brain-body skills of blacksmithing is so deeply satisfying.

The Creative Expressions of Nature course asks the students to look at our interaction with the natural world through an individual and artistic eye. It encourages students to slow down, observe, and reflect on the personal relationship they have with the natural world. Through studying the work of other writers and artists they examine the purpose of art in general, and the multitude of ways to engage with and represent *both* the internal and external landscapes. It provides an opportunity for digging deep into the students' experience of the program—as do the other courses—and it opens the boundaries for the form that reflection can take, and thereby encourages new forms of reflection. Students who saw otters would certainly add them, and a biological description, to their species list for Natural History of the Adirondacks; but they could also describe the sensuous details and what the experience meant to them personally for Creative Expressions of Nature.

The fifth and final course that makes up the academic element of the program is Cultivating Place: Bioregionalism and Community Engagement. It explores the foundations of bioregionalism and how as individuals and communities we connect to and identify with place. Largely, the course provides a framework for the students to more explicitly integrate their other courses and deliberate experiences in a very pragmatic way. This same framework assists in facilitating and cultivating bioregional knowledge and consciousness. In addition, this course serves as the academic and administrative home for the Adirondack Practicum, a three-week experiential capstone highlighted through Eben's experience in the third vignette and discussed further below.

Though the academic courses reinforce one another, direct and deliberate experiences unite the elements of the program. This experiential curriculum is composed of several components, including extended backcountry trips, weekend excursions, weekly woodworking, regular class field trips, a daily practice of material simplicity, and the Adirondack Practicum. Despite the variation in magnitude, length, and regularity of the experiences, each contributes in a significant way. Taken together, they provide numerous threads with which to tie the program together, in turn creating a stronger fabric. Two of these experiential components serve as bookends to the semester.

After a two-day off-site group orientation and initial round of classes, the semester is kicked off with the *orientation expedition,* an eight- to ten-day backcountry trip either backpacking or canoeing in the heart of the Adirondacks. This trip provides students with their first intimate experience with the landscape, and the opportunity and time to begin cultivating community within the group. It also serves as a warehouse of experiences that the academic courses draw upon in discussions and assignments. The semester then culminates with the Adirondack Practicum, a three-week experiential capstone involving independent study, work with a local person or organization, and a homestay. The practicum encourages students to reflect on the lessons of the semester, synthesize the elements into a personal whole, and form a vision of how to transfer these elements into their future lives. The practicum also serves in bridging theory and practice. After a semester of reading and writing about nature and human relationships with nature, students are provided the opportunity to gain firsthand experience with individuals and organizations connected to the land and/or community in various capacities.

Between these two experiential bookends, one finds many deliberate experiences that are just as significant. Weekend excursions take the students rock climbing, whitewater canoeing, hiking in the high peaks, apple picking, or visiting the farms that provide their produce, eggs, and meat for the semester through a community supported agriculture partnership. These excursions develop students' skills, introduce them to new people and places, and provide experiences that enrich their academic courses. The students also learn woodworking from master craftsmen in two different noncredit courses. In the first six-week course they build a canoe paddle, and in the second they design and build one or more objects of their own design. Just as the weekend excursions serve multiple purposes, so too does the woodworking. It introduces students to a new skill, the joy and simple pleasures that come from working with your hands and with individuals deeply connected to their landscapes and communities, all the while providing experiences that can be drawn upon in their academic courses. Regular class field trips make their way into the course syllabi, providing yet another set of rich, deliberate, and integrated experiences.

The last experiential component, the daily practice of material simplicity, is perhaps the most easily overlooked, hardest to convey (most abstract), and/or toughest to appreciate. Personal electronics are limited to MP3 players. Accommodations in yurts are spartan. A small trunk and a backpack full of clothes and gear is all most students bring. The material simplicity of Arcadian life, however, offers a chance both to practice and to test the premise that a sustainable society is one in which we satisfy our fundamental human needs—for food, drink, comforts, social relationships, and interesting activities—more directly and with less extraneous possessions as intermediaries. Daily and weekly chores such as chopping wood and carrying water provide an added avenue for mindfulness in daily living.

The third key element of the program, in addition to the academic and the experiential elements, is an emphasis on community. Faculty and staff guide the development of a purposeful living and learning community. This process starts during the first extended backcountry trip. It continues after arriving at Arcadia, as the students cook for one another and share responsibility in the cleaning and maintenance of the village. The intimacy of the small group, shared chores, service to one another, adventure, fun, and intellectual exploration are together the foundation for an extraordinary living and learning community.

Bioregional Knowledge and Consciousness through Integration

Immanuel Kant wrote that "thoughts without content are empty; intuitions without concepts are blind" (Kant 1929: A51-B75). Academic coursework is "empty" only in the worst cases, but too often it is impoverished compared to its theoretical potential because students do not grasp the riches inherent in the concepts presented. Lacking "percepts," i.e., experiences that bring out the implications of the concepts in ways that students can understand and remember, the concepts remain abstract formulas with little concrete content, easily ignored and forgotten.

Conversely, we all have experiences that are intensely memorable and meaningful to us. But when we lack an adequate conceptual framework through which to connect these experiences to others—other experiences of our own and also the experiences of other people differently situated—we fail to grasp the full significance of them. The power of feeling tells us that the experiences are significant, but it takes appropriate concepts to understand what they signify.

The ideal, then—one sought, if not always achieved, in the lecture and laboratory format of many science courses—is to provide concepts and percepts in a rich and integrated array. This is the inspiration for the Adirondack Semester. It is an attempt to integrate concepts and percepts in a way that makes the whole greater than the sum of its parts. In what follows we make no attempt to give a complete tally of the outcomes of the Adirondack Semester. Instead we provide limited examples to suggest how the program develops bioregional knowledge and consciousness.

As put forth in the introduction to this chapter, bioregional knowledge is best characterized by depth and breadth, necessitating knowledge of both the past and present for matters ranging from the ecology and geology to the culture and politics of place. While any one of the key elements of the program—academic work, experiential curriculum, community—on its own would go quite a ways in developing bioregional knowledge, together they result in a much richer and more robust outcome.

Take, for example, ecology, geology, and geography. Those facets of bioregional knowledge were illustrated during the first vignette as the two students, while paddling on the lake and making observations, worked through the process to properly identify the figures in the distance. The Natural History and Ecology of the Adirondacks course provides students a strong foundation and contributes immensely to the cultivation of their bioregional knowledge. Through the semester-long assignment, which requires them to identify and record a new species every day, they become incredibly familiar with the common flora and fauna of the region. Not least, since students live in this immediate landscape, seldom leaving it for the whole semester, their academic study of its plants, animals, and geological forms and extensive observational time, facilitated by the daily practice of material simplicity, constantly enriches and reinforces the readings, lectures, discussions, and field studies of the course. Moreover, just as learning a first foreign language makes it easier to learn a second because it provides a model for how that is done, so this course provides a model of the concepts and skills needed to read and interpret whatever landscape students will inhabit in the future.

Additionally, as the students travel through the landscape during the orientation expedition, they get their first introduction to numerous biotic communities, begin identifying species, and start learning the geography of the Adirondacks—the rivers and ranges, the lakes and lowlands. Weekend excursions and course field trips not only provide more opportunities for observation and identification, they also contribute immensely to students' geographic knowledge. Operating in a manner akin to a GPS and GIS program, each trip and stop provides new waypoints, allowing the students to catalogue place names and terrain features while constructing their own mental maps of the region.

Another example we could look at is the cultivation of cultural knowledge, both past and present—that facet of bioregional knowledge illustrated during the third vignette, which found a student working with a blacksmith during his practicum. The Land Use Change in the Adirondacks course introduces students to those inhabitants who came before, including European settlers and Native Americans. It explores the story of a landscape that has been described by one environmental historian as that of a "contested terrain" (Terrie 1997). At the same time, the course examines the history of people, place, and politics, which continue to define the Adirondack region. Weekend excursions and field trips reinforce discussions while providing firsthand experiences and illustrative examples.

Beyond the academic classes, the woodworking classes introduce students to another, more experiential form of cultural bioregional knowledge. It is as much about the weekly, informal conversations had with the two master craftsmen as it is about the paddles and projects the students walk away with or the new skills acquired. Serving as texts in and of themselves, the individuals whose lives are so intimately connected to place and the ensuing conversations are invaluable in regards to students' understanding of the culture and politics of both the present and the past. Just as the conversations during woodworking provide a window into individual lives and place-based experiences, so too does the practicum. As illustrated through Eben's experience working and living with a blacksmith in the third vignette, both the homestay and placement during the practicum contribute to the cultivation of cultural knowledge.

The second outcome from this integrated programmatic and pedagogical approach is the cultivation of bioregional consciousness. As described in the introduction, bioregional consciousness is a way of being, thinking, perceiving, and moving through the day-to-day. While bioregional knowledge and awareness are both prerequisites, bioregional consciousness is much more. To best illustrate how the integrated approach of the Adirondack Semester contributes to the cultivation of bioregional consciousness, we will focus on three specific elements: concreteness of residency, mindfulness to community, and a bioregional ethos that guides the program's operation.

The concreteness of residency present within the Adirondack Semester is central to the program's power.[4] Such concreteness is that which is imagined when speaking of the conditions necessary for *reinhabitation* or the process of "becoming fully alive in and with a place" (Berg and Dasmann 1990: 35). Reinhabitation, or becoming "native to a place," requires not only an ecological and cultural understanding of a locale or region but a reconnecting to the ecological and cultural communities that define them (Berg and Dasmann 1990). Here, the concreteness of residency emerges from the cultivation of bioregional knowledge coupled with the daily practice of material simplicity. The material simplicity of life at Arcadia as described above may sound painfully ascetic, yet this is not its effect on the students. The richness of their social community, the stimulation provided by their learning, the sensuous pleasures of life in close proximity with nature, and their growing awareness of the wildlife and natural processes around them more than make up for the absence of the things they lack. Nature is everywhere around them, all the time. Any trip outside a yurt means passing under the canopy of towering hemlocks and white pines, feeling the weather—even the subtlest changes—hearing the wind overhead or the lamenting of the loons. It is easy to forget the planet in urban or suburban settings, but at Arcadia, Gaia is ever present—as the soft morning mist, as the staccato call of a woodpecker, as the moment-to-moment change of the face of the lake. This is not nature in the abstract or the sublime nature that overpowers. This is an enveloping, ever-present, whispered reminder of the mystery of existence and of our co-occupation of the planet with other wondrous forms of life.

Just as important to bioregional consciousness is mindfulness of community. As Daniel Kemmis states, "[T]o in*habit* a place is to dwell there in a practiced way, in a way that relies upon certain regular, trusted habits of behavior" (1990: 79). Kemmis goes on to speak of *inhabitory practices* necessary for a thriving community-like cooperation (1990: 80). In the Adirondack Semester, the intimacy of the small group, shared chores, service to one another, adventure, fun, and intellectual exploration are together the foundation for the cultivation of such inhabitory practices.

This mindfulness of community is by no means limited in scope to the most immediate and direct living and learning community composed of faculty, staff, and students. Rather, it is composed of several concentric circles, slowly casting themselves farther across the landscape. This extended community is cultivated through such connections as woodworking with the two master craftsmen, participation in community-supported agriculture, and the homestays and placements of the practicum. Just as the immediate community of students, faculty, and staff grows in strength throughout the entirety of the semester, so too does the extended community.

The third and final element we wish to highlight, albeit briefly, that contributes to the cultivation of bioregional consciousness in the Adirondack Semester is the bioregional ethos that guides the program's operation. Because of this ethos, the program's food is, as much as possible, locally grown. This ethos also influences decisions made concerning the sourcing and purchasing of supplies and materials in general. The bioregional ethos reinforces and models all that is discussed and explored throughout the rest of the program.

Bioregional Pedagogy

Since its origin in the late 1960s and 1970s (Aberley 1999), bioregionalism has encountered several critiques. It has been indicted for being utopian, overly regional, and for its supposed inability to address large-scale issues such as acid rain and climate change. Especially in the wake of a globalized economy, there is a significant division of thought concerning bioregionalism. Some firmly believe that a bioregional vision is imperative to counter the current trajectory, while others are left wondering if such thoughts are futile. Thomashow (1999) grapples with these questions and adds significantly to this discourse through an exploration of the by-products of globalization. He begins by asking several pertinent and critical questions: "How does a bioregional vision accommodate the bifurcation of economic globalization and political decentralization, the instability and dislocation of ecological and cultural diasporas, the elusiveness of pluralistic identities and multiple personas?" (Thomashow 1999: 121). Exploring these contemporary issues, Thomashow illustrates the challenges that globalization presents to the current and predominant conceptualization of bioregionalism in preparation for offering an alternative.

Bioregional pedagogy and place-based education have faced equal criticism and questioning. For example, with place often associated with the local context, one might ask whether students are equipped to address the complex issues and wicked problems of today, such as global environmental change.[5] Along with such criticism, bioregional pedagogy—particularly at the undergraduate level—is faced with several challenges. There are those challenges affiliated with the changing nature of the conceptual and perceptual skills necessary for addressing such wicked problems. There are also the inherent challenges accompanying the emerging and predominant culture, where placelessness is pervasive. Landscapes are increasingly homogenized. Current and future generations will travel more, have more jobs and careers, relocate more often, and join more groups, communities, and social networks. These are features of an emerging globalized culture, especially—but not exclusively—for global elites such as American undergraduates. Finally, there are the challenges presented by a transient student body. The undergraduate students whom we teach are in a particularly transient stage, taking temporary residence in a university or college town for four years. And these four years are partial years at that, with many students studying abroad and taking summer jobs or internships elsewhere. Taken together, the changing nature of what skills we must equip students with, the pervasive placelessness, and a transient student body all imply that bioregional pedagogy must be shaped to deal with these new realities.

In response both to the above critiques and his own criticisms, Thomashow introduces the concept of a *cosmopolitan bioregionalism,* one that would and should "speak to the transient as well as the rooted" and that accommodates pluralistic identities (1999: 124–25). In this same piece, Thomashow also writes of what he terms a *bioregional sensibility:*

> Bioregional sensibility should develop ways of exploring spatial and temporal relationships that show the connections between place-based knowledge and global environmental change, the interdependence of local ecology and global economies, and the matrix of affiliations and networks that constitute ecological biodiversity and multicultural and multispecies tolerance—allowing different people to understand all the different places that may be considered home. (Thomashow 1999: 121)

Such a bioregional sensibility not only provides a useful framework for reconceptualizing bioregionalism as a cosmopolitan bioregionalism, it also offers an effective framework for bioregional pedagogy, particularly regarding undergraduate education. It serves as a constructive reminder for programs and courses such as the Adirondack Semester. It reminds us that a bioregional pedagogy for undergraduate students must focus on transference, and on the underlying skills necessary for developing bioregional knowledge and bioregional consciousness with a local/global dialectic. As Thomashow states, it should be focused upon "developing the observational skills to patiently observe bioregional history, the conceptual skills to juxtapose scales, the imaginative faculties to play with multiple landscapes, and the compassion to empathize with local and global neighbors" (1999: 130).

Notes

1. This section of the chapter borrows extensively from a description the authors gave in an article published in *Liberal Education* 95 (3) (2009).
2. A yurt is a circular, wood-latticed structure commonly used by the nomadic people of central Asia traditionally covered in felt. Yurt in the English language is derived from the Russian term *yurta,* and in North America they are most commonly covered with canvas or vinyl.
3. Our use of the name Arcadia is derived most directly from *The Ecology of Eden* (Eisenberg 1999). Use of this name is limited mostly to current and former participants. Otherwise, the program and location are generally referred to simply as The Adirondack semester.
4. By the phrase "concreteness of residency" we mean to call attention to the way residence at Arcadia fosters awareness of concrete details of one's life.
5. "Wicked" is a term used by environmental scientists to describe problems that are unique, often evolving, and unlikely to have any final resolution.

References

Aberley, Doug. 1999. "Interpreting Bioregionalism: A Story from many Voices." In *Bioregionalism,* ed. Michael V. McGinnis, 13–42. New York: Routledge.

Berg, Peter. 1977. "Strategies for Reinhabiting the Northern California Bioregion." *Seriatim: Journal of Ecotopia* 1 (3): 2–8.

Berg, Peter, and Raymond F. Dasmann. 1990. "Reinhabiting California." In *Home! A Bioregional Reader,* ed. Van Andruss, Christopher Plant, Judith Plant, and Eleanor Wright, 35–38. Philadelphia: New Society.

Eisenberg, Evan. 1999. *The Ecology of Eden: An Inquiry into the Dream of Paradise and a New Vision of Our Role in Nature.* New York: Vintage.

Johnson, Baylor, and Steve Alexander. 2009. "The St. Lawrence University Adirondack Semester." *Liberal Education* 95 (3): 44–49.

Kant, Immanuel. 1929. *Critique of Pure Reason* (Translated by Norman Kemp Smith) New York: St. Martin's Press: (93) [A51-B75].

Kemmis, Daniel. 1990. *Community and the Politics of Place.* Norman: University of Oklahoma Press.

Parsons, James J. 1985. "On 'Bioregionalism' and 'Watershed Consciousness.'" *The Professional Geographer* 37 (1): 1–6.

Terrie, Philip G. 1997. *Contested Terrain: A New History of Nature and People in the Adirondacks.* 1st ed. Blue Mountain Lake, NY: Adirondack Museum; Syracuse, NY: Syracuse University Press.

Thomashow, Mitchell. 1999. "Toward a Cosmopolitan Bioregionalism." In *Bioregionalism,* ed. Michael V. McGinnis, 121–32. New York: Routledge.

Further Readings on Bioregionalism

Aberley, Doug, ed. 1993. *Boundaries of Home: Mapping for Local Empowerment*. Gabriola Island, Canada: New Society.

Alexander, Donald. "Bioregionalism: Science or Sensibility?" *Environmental Ethics* 12 (Summer): 161–73.

Berg, Peter. 2009. *Envisioning Sustainability*. USA: Subculture Books.

———, ed. 1978. *Reinhabiting a Separate Country: A Bioregional Anthology of Northern California*. San Francisco: Planet Drum.

Carr, Mike. 2004. *Bioregionalism and Civil Society: Democratic Challenges to Corporate Globalism*. Vancouver: University of British Columbia Press.

Evanoff, Richard. 2011. *Bioregionalism and Global Ethics*. London: Routledge.

Frenkel, Stephen. 1994. "Old Theories in New Places? Environmental Determinism and Bioregionalism." *The Professional Geographer* 46 (3): 289–95.

McTaggart, W. Donald. 1993. "Bioregionalism and Regional Geography: Place, People, and Networks." *The Canadian Geographer* 37 (Winter): 307–19.

Mills, Stephanie. 1996. *In Service of the Wild: Restoring and Reinhabiting Damaged Land*. Boston: Beacon Press.

Sale, Kirkpatrick. 2000. *Dwellers in the Land: The Bioregional Vision*. Athens: University of Georgia Press.

Snyder, Gary. 1990. *The Practice of the Wild*. New York: North Point Press.

———. 1995. *A Place in Space: Ethics, Aesthetics, and Watersheds*. Washington DC: Counterpoint.

Thayer, Robert L. 2003. *LifePlace: Bioregional Thought and Practice*. Berkeley: University of California Press.

II

Permaculture

Chapter Five

Environmental Anthropology Engaging Permaculture

Moving Theory and Practice Toward Sustainability

James R. Veteto and Joshua Lockyer

Permaculture in Practice: One Anthropologist's Introduction

It's a cool, blustery day at Earthaven, a young ecovillage settlement nestled into the eastern slopes of the southern Appalachians. Breaking through the rustle of wind in the trees are the sounds of human activity, of people building their common future together, of children at play. In the distance you can hear the Earthaven Forestry Cooperative's portable sawmill cutting lumber from trees felled on the land. This is the sound of liberation. The Co-op's sawmill is allowing villagers and neighbors to create shelter, freeing themselves from the clutches of banks and clear-cutting timber barons while keeping materials and money within the village economy. These are radical acts. Should these and other permaculture-based strategies take hold in the larger society, corporate control might someday yield to an empowered, responsible, ecologically literate citizenry. We can hope it will be in time to pull humanity back from the brink of disaster brought on by our own folly.

A major first-generation challenge for the Permaculture movement and one of the main reasons for the creation of Earthaven, is to get enough working systems on the ground that we can make informed choices based on actual experience and begin to model bioregionally appropriate culture for our time and place. Creating and integrating ecologically responsible forestry and agriculture while developing natural building systems that conserve forest health, create jobs and generate renewable energy through good design has proved to be quite an ambitious undertaking. That we are doing all these things while feeling our way toward just and sustaining social and economic relations and maintaining democratic self-governance within a new village context still seems nearly miraculous, the more so the longer we persist. (Marsh 2002: 44)

In the fall of 2004, Lockyer initiated field research in an intentional community in the Appalachian Mountains of western North Carolina called Earthaven Ecovillage. Earthaven was founded in 1994 by a dozen people who started with a basic but ambitious goal of "creating a holistic, sustainable culture." They bought 320 acres of land and decided to form a community where they could support each other in creating a different way of life, one that is more socially intimate and less dependent on and integrated with unsustainable systems of production and consumption. Today, Earthaven has grown to over sixty members, forty-five of whom live "on the land," gradually implementing social, cultural, political, economic, and technological experiments in sustainability. Compared with most Americans, Earthaven's members live more communally and much closer to the economic resources that sustain them. They own, steward, and govern their land collectively using unique forms of land tenure and consensus decision making. Although some of them live in individual residential dwellings, they come together to eat, socialize, and govern themselves in common buildings and spaces. Members share common waste processing and water distribution systems that they construct and maintain themselves in addition to producing as much of their own food, energy, and material goods as they can manage (Lockyer 2007).

By aligning itself with the global ecovillage movement, the founders of Earthaven made it clear that they were committing themselves to exploring an alternative paradigm of development, an approach that takes responsibility for the effects of people's lifestyles and livelihoods on ecosystem function and human health and well-being, both present and future. Yet, how is one to go about developing a full-featured settlement in which human activities are harmlessly integrated into the natural world? How is one to create communities that can support healthy human development and that can simultaneously be continued into the indefinite future? As is necessarily true of any movement toward sustainability, these are lofty goals; achieving them will require significant forethought, risk taking, and expertise. As many environmental anthropologists would likely agree, achieving a just sustainability will entail actions grounded in detailed knowledge of local ecological, political-economic, and sociocultural systems combined with a global awareness and scientific acumen. But how is one to bring all of these components together in a way that makes sense and can lead to practical action?

> Permaculture is a holistic system of DESIGN, based on direct observation of nature, learning from traditional knowledge and the findings of modern science. Embodying a philosophy of positive action and grassroots education, Permaculture aims to restructure society by returning control of resources for living: food, water, shelter and the means of livelihood, to ordinary peo-

> ple in their communities, as the only antidote to centralized power. (*Permaculture Activist* 2004: 3)

The above quotation is on the inside cover of every edition of *Permaculture Activist* magazine, a publication that was edited by one of Earthaven's members during the time of Lockyer's fieldwork. As initial participant observation at Earthaven Ecovillage progressed, it became apparent that the permaculture paradigm provided a practical foundation that the members of Earthaven used to initiate practical steps toward their goal of developing a holistic, sustainable culture. Indeed, permaculture's ethical philosophy and material design principles provided the tools for translating the ecovillage concept from idealism into practice. At Earthaven Ecovillage, permaculture has been employed as one of the main tools for building bridges between global social and environmental awareness and concern and the development of local, sustainable practices. According to Earthaven's website:

> One of our first tasks was to create a permaculture-based site plan for developing our mountain forest property. We identified sacred sites; land to remain forested; areas for gardening, farming, and orchards; locations for ponds and hydro-power stations; locations for roads, paths, and common community buildings; and locations for residential neighborhoods. We agreed to build homes only on slopes and save flat bottom land for agriculture; retain as much water on the land as possible through roof water catchments, swales, and ponds; regenerate our soil with layers of organic biomass; protect our sacred sites; and not build on ridge tops. We build passive-solar heated buildings of natural Earth-friendly materials and generate our own off-grid power. We practice sustainable forestry and preserve many of our wilderness areas. We are not yet growing and raising most of our own food; however, this is important to us and is one of our next steps. (Earthaven Ecovillage n.d.)

Although Earthaven is by no means a purist rendering of permacultural thought in action, time spent there does make it clear that the permaculture paradigm provides a holistic and commonsense approach that recognizes humans as an integrated part of ecosystems. Permaculture challenges humans to take responsibility for themselves and the economy that sustains them by designing and practicing permanent, sustainable cultural and agricultural systems created in accordance with environmental knowledge.

A Historical and Conceptual Overview of the Permaculture Paradigm

Permaculture is a global grassroots development[1] philosophy and sustainability movement that encompasses a set of ethical principles and design guidelines and techniques for creating sustainable, permanent culture and agriculture. Indeed, permaculture is an agglomeration of those three words: permanent, culture, and agriculture. Permaculture models its designs for agroecosystems, buildings, and communities on patterns observed in nature, but, perhaps more importantly, permaculture views humans and human creations and activities as part of the natural world. Rather than focusing on human creations—agroecosystems, buildings, and communities—permaculture emphasizes the interconnections among these creations, humans, and the natural world. Permaculturists believe that this focus on interconnections is the best way to create systems that function in a sustainable manner. Permaculture is an eclectic and adaptive approach that emphasizes local and bioregional perspective and practice. At the same time, it is informed by a global view, maintains a strong tradition of technology and knowledge transfer across diverse areas and cultural traditions, and is fundamentally based on empirical observation and experimentation.

These foundations came into being in the 1970s when it became increasingly clear that the prevailing model of development was not creating ecologically sound, economically prosperous communities and was, to the contrary, actively destroying such communities. The conceptual and practical rubric for permaculture was initially developed in Australia by Bill Mollison and David Holmgren beginning in 1974. In Mollison's words, they "jointly evolved a framework for a sustainable agricultural system based on a multi-crop of perennial trees, shrubs, herbs, ... fungi, and root systems, for which I coined the word 'permaculture.' We spent a lot of time working out the principles of permaculture and building a species-rich garden" (1991: preface). The result was the publication in 1978 of a detailed volume entitled *Permaculture One,* a work that still stands as a permaculturalist's bible (Mollison and Holmgren 1978).

The academic response to Mollison and Holmgren's work was mixed, but largely negative; the disciplinary specialization of the academy was not prepared for the holistic approach that they offered, even in the face of the emerging and increasingly acknowledged socioenvironmental crisis. The academic world would have to wait some twenty years before interdisciplinary work became a dominant research paradigm—permaculture was way ahead of its time. Mollison's words again: "The professional community was outraged, because we were combining architecture with biology, agriculture with forestry, and forestry with animal husbandry, so that almost everybody who considered themselves to be a specialist felt a bit offended" (Mollison 1991: preface). Similarly, Holmgren notes that "permaculture was conceived within academia. Many who are involved in large-scale agriculture and land use policy saw it as theoretical, utopian and impractical because it was difficult to apply within the prevailing social, market and policy environment" (Holmgren 2002: xxii). Although permaculture has been taken seriously by some academics, resulting in occasional sporadic publications over the years (e.g., Strange 1984a, 1984b; Jungt 1985; Kennedy 1991), it has been largely ignored. This has been the case particularly among anthropologists, as a literature search within anthropology provided us with no scholarly articles or monographs that we could locate.

However, the public reaction was quite different; small-scale agriculturalists especially gravitated toward Mollison and Holmgren's ideas, as they sought a more ecological approach to food production. In the late 1970s Mollison resigned from his university post and committed himself full-time to experimenting with, teaching, and promoting permaculture design. By 1981, Mollison had garnered a Right Livelihood Award (the "Alternative Nobel Prize") and had graduated an initial group of people from a standardized permaculture design course that he taught in Australia. These graduates moved on to teach others, initiating a pattern that continues to this day and that has resulted in at least one hundred thousand trained permaculture practitioners throughout the world (Holmgren 2002).

The permaculture movement today is represented by an eclectic network of local practitioners and demonstration centers and by a number of publications, such as *Permaculture Activist* magazine. Semi-structured permaculture design certification courses are offered throughout the world based on a curriculum that was codified in 1984 (Holmgren 2002). These courses are often hands-on events that take place at permaculture experimentation and demonstration sites, such as Earthaven Ecovillage, that have been created by people who can often trace their permaculture genealogy through their teachers back to Bill Mollison and David Holmgren. People who participate in these courses often find them "life-changing" and go on to establish their own permaculture experiments and demonstration centers. The semi-formalized structure of permaculture certification has created some concerns regarding lack of standardization; however, the flexibility inherent in this horizontal approach is valued because it allows the core of the permaculture rubric to be adapted to widely varying cultural and ecological contexts. According to Holmgren, permaculture is represented by "a worldwide network and movement of individuals and groups who are working in both rich and poor countries on all continents to demonstrate and spread permaculture design solutions. Largely unsupported by government or business, these people are contributing to a more sustainable future by reorganizing their lives and work around permaculture design principles" (Holmgren 2002: xx).

While Mollison, now in his eighties, has become less active in the movement, Holmgren continues to promote permaculture as a powerful, commonsense approach to sustainability and an antidote to "the prevailing industrial culture" (Holmgren 2002). In his book *Permaculture: Principles and Pathways Beyond Sustainability*, Holmgren defines permaculture as follows:

> Consciously designed landscapes which mimic the patterns and relationships found in nature, while yielding an abundance of food, fibre and energy for the provision of local needs. People, their buildings and the ways they organise themselves are central to permaculture ... It draws together the diverse ideas, skills and ways of living which need to be rediscovered and developed in order to empower us to move from being dependent consumers to becoming responsible and productive citizens. (Holmgren 2002: xix)

Holmgren's book emphasizes both the ethical philosophy and design principles that together comprise the permaculture rubric.

Permaculture begins with a set of ethical principles that are based on some fundamental assumptions. First, "[t]he environmental crisis is real and of a magnitude that will certainly transform modern global industrial society beyond recognition. In the process, the well-being and even survival of the world's expanding population is directly threatened" (Holmgren 2002: xv). In addition, "the inevitable depletion of fossil fuels within a few generations will see a return to the general patterns observable in nature and pre-industrial societies dependent on renewable energy and resources" (Holmgren 2002: xvi). With these assumptions in mind, permaculture seeks to enable people to become more self-reliant and, in the process, to relieve the social injustices and ecological degradation created by the global political economy. In this aim, permaculture's critique of the modern, Western, industrialized political economy and culture is clear:

> The fact is that our own comfort is based on the rape of planetary wealth, depriving other people (and future generations) of their own local resources. Our own "hard work" and the so-called "creativity" of our economy and "fairness" of our system of government are all secondary factors in creating our privilege. Once we understand the massive structural inequities between rich and poor nations, urban and rural communities and human resources and natural resources, the emphasis on providing for one's own needs is seen in a different light. *As we reduce our dependence on the global economy and replace it with household and local economies, we reduce the demand that drives current inequities. Thus "look after yourself first" is not an invitation to greed but a challenge to grow up through self-reliance and personal responsibility.* (Holmgren 2002: 7, emphasis in original)

At a fundamental level, permaculture holds that "the process of providing for people's needs within ecological limits requires a cultural revolution" (Holmgren 2002: xxv).

Based on this cultural critique and utopian vision, permaculture combines insights gleaned from traditional ecological knowledge and modern scientific knowledge into designs for sustainable human settlements and production systems. As mentioned before, the core of the permaculture paradigm consists of a basic ethical philosophy and a set of design principles or guidelines. Permaculture's three ethical principles are basic and fundamental: (1) care for the earth, (2) care for people, and (3) set limits to consumption and reproduction and redistribute surplus (Holmgren 2002). These ethical principles are grounded in the assumptions discussed above and provide a permacultural foundation for designing and enacting a more just, equitable, and sustainable world.

Permaculture's design principles, initially presented in Mollison (1991) and recapitulated in Holmgren (2002), are grounded in the science of ecology, and more particularly in systems ecology, landscape geography, and ethnobiology (Holmgren 2002). The overall aim of these design principles is to develop closed-loop, symbiotic, self-sustaining human habitats and production systems that do not result in ecological degradation or social injustice. Although the design of such systems is necessarily dependent upon the particular local context, the permaculture rubric provides general guidelines for considering environmental variables and patterns in designing buildings, home gardens, orchards, farms, livestock operations, aquaculture systems, and community and urban areas (Mollison 1991).

While we do not have space here for an extensive discussion of all twelve permaculture design principles (see Figure 0.2), we provide an example of each principle in action at Earthaven and refer the reader to publications such as *Permaculture Activist* and to the published work of Mollison and Holmgren (Holmgren 1996, 2002; Mollison and Holmgren 1978; Mollison 1988, 1991) for further elaboration. Permaculturalists believe that these principles provide a framework for situating humans in nature as we seek a sustainable development strategy. This framework is a foundation for experimentation in places like Earthaven, where an adaptive management approach is leading to the creation of an increasingly self-reliant ecovillage.

1. *Observe and Interact:* Earthaven's founders spent over a year observing their property—becoming familiar with the flows of energy (wind, solar, water) across the landscape—before they began developing the ecovillage. This process continues to this day as they recognize and learn from their mistakes and seek to more fully integrate their human community into the natural community of their property and bioregion.

2. *Catch and Store Energy:* Renewable energy systems are the most obvious example of this principle in practice at Earthaven. From photovoltaic solar arrays to their micro hydro generating station, Earthaven's members

capture and store readily available energy. The same could also be said of the water distribution system, which uses the force of gravity rather than fossil fuel–powered pumps to deliver water to households and other facilities throughout the ecovillage.

3. *Obtain a Yield:* Earthaven manifests this principle on a very local scale. They have a long-term, ecologically sensitive forest management plan for their property under which they harvest wood and use it in the construction of their own houses. A variety of agroecological production systems are also being developed so that Earthaven's members can begin to provide for their own food needs.

4. *Apply Self-Regulation and Accept Feedback:* Referring back to the first principle above, Earthaven's members are constantly involved in reevaluating what they have done in terms of the physical development of their land. Regular meetings of the strategic planning committee provide opportunities to change course or choose another development strategy that seems more appropriate based on recent experience. For instance, Earthaven has chosen to stop allowing the development of outlying neighborhoods until the center of their community has become more fully functional, recognizing that this pattern had led to the fragmentation of their social community and that they have subconsciously copied the unsustainable suburban model in which most of them were raised.

5. *Use and Value Renewable Resources and Services:* Again, the obvious manifestation of this principle is Earthaven's renewable energy systems, primarily photovoltaic solar and micro hydro. However, this principle is also apparent in Earthaven's emphasis on composting food scraps and human waste for use as future fertilizers, completing a more closed-loop nutrient cycle.

6. *Produce No Waste:* The emphasis on compost in the fifth principle above is an excellent illustration of this principle in action at Earthaven. However, Earthaven has taken this a step further in terms of putting society's waste to good use. For example, a large house at Earthaven that often serves as a bed and breakfast for visitors was constructed using parts from a dismantled bridge and frozen fruit juice concentrate shipping pallets that were destined for the local landfill.

7. *Design from Patterns to Details:* A pattern that is evident anywhere on earth is the sun's cycle throughout the year, and many cultures have oriented their architecture around this cycle. Earthaven requires all of its buildings to be built using a passive solar orientation; that is they are designed to absorb the sun's rays when it is low in the southern sky during the winter, providing natural renewable heat for the home, and to reflect sunlight during the hotter months. However, this has not led to an orthodoxy of building style; rather, each building, while being oriented for pas-

sive solar gain, is designed uniquely for its particular site in the landscape and its particular occupants.

8. *Integrate rather than Segregate:* Industrial agricultural systems are characterized by large-scale fields of monocrops. Earthaven's approach is to use a variety of inter- and multi-cropping methods to enhance pest control and soil regeneration. Beyond that, Earthaven has moved toward a reintegration of natural and agricultural systems through the creation of a "forest garden," where food crops are interspersed with existing, partially harvested forest.

9. *Use Small and Slow Solutions:* Earthaven itself is a small and slow solution. It has taken fifteen years to put in basic, minimal infrastructure, establish a system of communal self-governance, build a few dozen buildings, and begin small-scale food production. This stands in contrast to the rapidity of suburban construction, suggesting that small and slow approaches are inherently more sustainable and more fulfilling.

10. *Use and Value Diversity:* Many of Earthaven's members know their landscape intimately. During Lockyer's fieldwork at Earthaven, there was a group of young men who would regularly go out for "plant walks," during which they would identify as many different species as they could. On one particular occasion, they returned with specimens of over twenty types of edible mushrooms. This reflects a wider pattern at Earthaven whereby ecovillage members know how to identify and use the biological diversity that exists on their property.

11. *Use Edges and Value the Marginal:* Many of Earthaven's buildings are built on slopes that mainstream builders would consider marginally appropriate. However, Earthaveners have chosen to turn this problem into an opportunity, taking advantage of natural features such as south-facing slopes to build passive solar-oriented houses. With regards to edges, many of Earthaven's farmers use the edges of their fields (where there are defined fields) to plant flowers that are simultaneously aesthetically pleasing and act as a form of pest control or edible plants and trees such as wineberries *(Rubus phoenicolasius)* or hazelnuts *(Corylus avellana).*

12. *Creatively Use and Respond to Change:* One of the biggest changes that has taken place at Earthaven is an influx of younger members of little financial means. Earthaven's founders were mostly older and many of them had significant financial resources. Under the original membership process, buying into the community required a significant financial investment. When these younger, poorer people began arriving in higher numbers, Earthaven's members made a consensus decision to open up a "sweat equity track" to membership and landholding. This enabled people of lesser financial means to pay their membership and site lease fees by contributing labor to community agricultural projects, thus en-

abling a larger, more diverse membership and simultaneously moving Earthaven's much desired agroecosystems forward.

As a result of the growth of the permaculture network, permaculture principles are increasingly being employed by individuals, communities—intentional and otherwise—and even local and national governments (Cuba, Vietnam, Brazil, Senegal) in the development of more just, equitable, and sustainable human habitations, communities, and agricultural production systems. The permaculture paradigm represents one path among many that should be explored as society seeks to address impending socioenvironmental crises. As environmental anthropologists, we recognize that current models of development are on an unsustainable trajectory and we advocate for more socially just and ecologically sustainable forms of development. However, too often our critiques of current approaches to development are unaccompanied by viable solutions, especially solutions that recognize that we in the Global North must take responsibility for our contributions to contemporary socioenvironmental problems. One reason for this is that suggesting such solutions entails a political agenda that clashes with our role as supposedly dispassionate scientific researchers. A way around this conundrum is the strategic choice of research foci. As social scientists we can choose to focus our methods and theoretical frameworks on people who have taken the politically active step of saying "no" to current development hegemonies and experimenting with alternative development strategies.

We hold that the permaculture movement acts as a sort of natural laboratory wherein potentially sustainable solutions are experimented with. Furthermore, we believe that by engaging with this movement, we can create a powerful dialectic between anthropological theory and practice on the one hand and cultural critique in action for sustainability on the other. In engaging in this dialectic we seek to help construct an anthropology that can productively contribute to an understanding not only of how the world is and how it got that way, but also of how the world could be and how we can get there.

Environmental Anthropology Engaging Permaculture: Areas of Theoretical and Applied Compatibility

There are numerous promising theoretical and applied perspectives within environmental anthropology that seem to us to present potential cross-fertilization opportunities with permaculture. In this section we will identify those perspectives and give some preliminary suggestions for collaboration. In the concluding section we suggest that this sort of collaboration is one major direction in which environmental anthropology could move. Examples and discussion are also presented that make a case for narrowing the gap between sustainability practices that researchers idealize in their academic approaches and the examples that they present in their personal lives, thereby taking steps to minimize the great divide between the consumption patterns of those who conduct research and their typically resource-poor subjects of study. This is a practical step toward or beyond the current sustainability paradigm that is almost never addressed in environmental anthropology.

Several research programs in environmental anthropology offer excellent opportunities for permaculture-based scholarship and practice. Though certainly not limited to these approaches alone, this section will focus on cultural ecology, agricultural anthropology, historical ecology, ethnoecology, and political ecology as particularly fruitful avenues for engaging permaculture.

Cultural ecologists have focused their research on three fundamental ethnographic questions: (1) How do [a certain people] make a living? (2) How do they organize themselves to make that living? and (3) How do they rationalize the way they make that living? Though cultural ecology is no longer a dominant approach within anthropology (it is still major research strategy in geography), its focus on environmental adaptations of different groups of people in different places around the globe from the 1950s to the 1980s produced an impressive amount of empirical data (e.g., Netting 1968, 1981, 1993; Bennett 1969). This data, and particularly with respect to smallholder agriculture, is exactly the type of empirical information that permaculturalists can use in their applied approach to bioregionally sustainable adaptations. Whether it be Chinese smallholder agricultural strategies spanning thousands of years (Netting 1993), Andean, Alpine, and Himalayan adaptations to alpine mountainous areas of vertical zonation (Rhoades and Thompson 1975), or the complex adaptive strategies of four different social groups to the Canadian plains (Bennett 1969), cultural ecologists have outlined in substantial detail how people have managed to survive in ways that are (arguably) sustainable. A cultural ecology database that was made available for anthropologists engaged in permaculture research and application as well as to permaculture practitioners would be of practical value. This informational cross-linkage has the potential to ground permaculture projects in empirical data detailing successful environmental adaptations and can give cultural ecologists a productive new framework in which to apply and interpret their research.

Agricultural anthropology, a relevant subdiscipline that has used the methodology of cultural ecology prominently in its practice, has excellent potential for contributing to the understanding and improvement of permaculture and vice versa. It has been prominent in international agriculture and development circles and has contributed to the emergence of horizontal and participatory development approaches such as "farmer-back-to-farmer" (Rhoades and Booth 1982) and "farmer first" (Chambers, Pacey, and Thrupp 1989). Long-term experimentation in agricultural anthropology with more egalitarian research relationships provides methodologies that can be applied in permaculture settings. Sustainable and alternative agriculture is also a current major research focus for agricultural anthropologists. Permaculture, with its emphasis on designing sustainable agroecosystems, has been understudied, but has much to add to the knowledge and practice of agricultural anthropology, particularly in regard to creating a multilayered perennial polyculture agriculture.

The merging of historical ecology with permaculture can provide practitioners with long-term data on how human-environment interactions have taken place in specific places. A central concept used to organize historical ecology approaches to human behavior and agency in the environment is *landscape,* a term that has is its origins in historical geography. Landscape is also the multi-scale domain that permaculture takes as its field of operation (Mollison 1988). Therefore, historical ecology and permaculture are theoretically aligned on at least one basic level. Both permaculture and historical ecology also have a shared interest in the applied realm, as applied historical ecologists are cognizant of their role in supplying baseline data related to time depth and traditional knowledge that can be used to restore past landscapes (Balée 2006; Swetnam, Allen, and Betancourt 1999). Similarly, permaculturists seek to improve the sustainability of present landscapes through various design principles (see above). A major finding within historical ecology is that human cultures do not always reduce environmental landscapes into barren wastelands of low diversity (which sometimes, obviously, they do), but that, conversely, human communities often heighten species diversity in local environments through ongoing resource management strategies that increase landscape heterogeneity—particularly local and indigenous gardening and agroforestry practices (Balée 2006; Fairhead and Leach 1996). This theoretical realization and resulting empirical reports on how species diversity is increased through time in specific landscapes is consistent with permaculture design principles that seek to maximize species diversity and stability for providing basic human needs (Mollison 1988). Permaculturalists can take information gleaned from historical ecology to weigh their design options, particularly when deciding whether or not certain architectural plans, agroecological designs, or plant introductions are contextually appropriate. In short, historical ecology offers data that can help applied permaculturalists to "learn from the past," and permaculturalists provide historical ecologists with unique and diverse natural laboratory settings to see the findings of their research incorporated into dynamic and applied approaches to landscape design. In addition, historical ecologists who investigate permaculture sites will be providing baseline data for future studies of those particular landscapes.

Ethnoecology is another subfield that offers opportunity for collaboration with permaculture. In the last six decades of ethnoecological research, thousands of studies featuring particular or specific aspects of indigenous ecological knowledge systems have been produced and are available in anthropological and other literatures. This wide variety of ethnoecological studies of local knowledge can help permaculturalists to garner ideas about the application of their own and borrowed technologies and practices. Furthermore, the study of indigenous classification systems and classifying behaviors (Ellen 1993, 2005; Berlin 1992) can help permaculture practitioners challenge their own conceptualizations of the biological world from perspectives outside of the Western tradition. Anthropological challenges to and debates surrounding the appropriation of indigenous materials and intellectual property rights can also help to ensure that cultural borrowings are appropriately contextualized, acknowledged, left alone if needed, traded, or compensated for (Sillitoe 1998, 2006; Agrawal 2002; Cleveland and Murray 1997; Dewalt 1994). Ethnoecologists can also study permaculture sites as dynamic cultural arenas and natural laboratories where people in various bioregions across the world are incorporating, classifying, reclassifying, and hybridizing locally appropriate technologies and biological knowledges. This seems to us a necessary step for ethnoecology if it wants to contribute to on-the-ground solutions toward sustainability.

Political ecology has brought issues of political economy and power to the forefront of an ecological analysis that is assumed to have been oversimplified and apolitical in its more traditional approach (Robbins 2004). Approaches such as world systems theory (Wallerstein 1974) and poststructuralism (Escobar 1999) point out how limited access to and control over resources—combined with the essentializing tendencies of "otherness"—tend to disempower individuals, communities, and the environments in which they dwell. Analysis has centered largely on the relationship of governmental and corporate power/capital hegemonies in the Global North to nations and communities on the periphery of the capitalist world economy, particularly in the Global South. The political ecology approach articulates well with permaculture ethics and cultural critique, which encourage modern individuals to take responsibility for their own actions, reduce their consumption and waste, and live a more simple and ecological lifestyle, thereby enacting a more democratic and fair division of and access to the world's environmental resources (Holmgren 2002). Both permaculture and many prominent strains of political ecology are engaged in critique of current globalization trends emerging from a capitalism whose political power is centered largely in the Global North. Permaculture offers political ecology the opportunity to study how citizens, particularly in the Global North, are providing lifestyle and community changes to meet the sustainability challenge and inherent inequalities in the current global economic system.

Conclusion

Fictional Scenario One

An environmental anthropologist gets up in the morning, takes his customary twenty-minute hot shower, throws on his best five-hundred-dollar suit (one of over twenty-five suits he has accumulated over the years), walks out of his two-story suburban house, and jumps in his SUV, quickly navigating the thirty-minute drive through rush hour to take care of a few things in his university office. After packing his briefcase with the necessary papers, he jumps back in the SUV and makes the hour-long trek to the nearest regional airport. Breakfast, as so often these days, is eaten on the go as he runs through a McDonalds drive-thru and orders a bacon, egg, and cheese McMuffin, hashbrowns, and a cup of coffee to go. NPR plays on the radio on the way to the airport and gives him quick snippets of global happenings. This will be the last of eighteen roundtrip flights he has made this year (most of them international). Several hours later the plane touches down in Washington DC. Outside the terminal he catches the first taxi ride available and tells the cab driver from Nigeria to take him directly to the five-star hotel where the American Anthropology Association annual meeting will take place. By the time he and several thousand other anthropologists complete their weekend trips, they will have probably consumed more resources than many of the communities that they study will in a year.

Fictional Scenario Two

An environmental anthropologist gets up in the morning, takes her five-minute solar hot water shower, and puts on her just-casual-enough/just-business-enough hemp/organic cotton sweater that was made by the homespun seamstress in the ecovillage. She cooks a quick pot of oatmeal (purchased in a bulk order from the village co-op) and checks e-mail on her solar-powered laptop. The fair trade coffee is done just in time and she pours it into her trusty to-go mug and hops out the front door of her passive solar cob house. She walks past several other residences (one post-and-beam passive solar and the other cordwood construction, both built by the ecovillage forestry co-op) and then out through the extensive village gardens and orchards. She swipes a Limbertwig apple from a nearby tree and picks a few kale and mustard greens to chew on. She waves to two of her graduate students, who are collecting data for their applied research projects, as she gets in the community hybrid SUV that she has reserved for her drive to Washington DC. She picks up several of her colleagues at the department, and within thirty minutes they are on the road. It is a four-and-a-half-hour drive, but within the eight-hour radius of a pact they have made with each other for their one conference presentation a year. This may not be the best way to get ahead in their profession, but it sure does make their life less hectic and keep their ecological footprint down. A Global Ecovillages compilation CD sets the background as they head to the AAA meeting. They had heard that this year the anthropology and environment section of the AAA had made some real progress in reducing the waste produced by the annual meeting, and each of them was curious to see what had been done.

These two fictional scenarios depict two opposite extremes of a continuum and serve to illustrate a point that we are trying to make. We all probably know at least someone who (at least loosely) fits the description of first scenario. It is fairly unlikely that we know anyone who fits the second scenario (though not completely out of the realm of possibility), even if we may know several environmental anthropologists who would ideally live in such a way. Most of us probably fit in somewhere between these opposite extremes, navigating the constraints of our personal and professional lives to try and be as minimally wasteful as we can without driving ourselves crazy in the process. Perhaps a minority of environmental anthropologists do not care how much they consume and are explicit about their wasteful choices. We will not judge them here, and it certainly does not mean they cannot produce excellent research and theory. But our call for a dialogue between anthropology and permaculture will probably be of much more use to those who are interested in the greening of our profession and to some extent "practicing what they preach." Taking responsibility for our own personal consumption patterns and demonstrating to others in our consumption-oriented culture that an environmentally sustainable future is a very real alternative development option is a major promise of the engagement between permaculture and environmental anthropology. It has the potential to bring us down to earth and onto a more level playing field with the subjects of our research as well.

Permaculture, at present, is not a significant approach in the international agriculture centers (CGIAR) and other international development arenas, such as the World Bank. We propose that it should probably remain so. Agricultural and environmental anthropologists do excellent work in governmental hierarchal structures such as the CGIAR. However, permaculture provides an alternative, bioregionally organized, horizontal network of practitioners, ecovillages, and research sites that we feel would only suffer in the context of the current top-down (despite significant strides made toward more participatory bottom-up approaches) international development approach. Environmental anthropologists who want to work in sustainable development and agriculture outside of the CGIAR and other such mainstream development arenas may find permaculture to be a suitable venue. The significant theoretical insights, applied experience, and grant-writing skills of anthropologists would almost certainly be a welcomed addition to the international permaculture network. Decades of anthropological insights gained from the fields of political ecology and ethnoecology can help to caution permaculturists against potentially unethical cultural borrowings by bringing to light current debates concerning traditional environmental knowledge (TEK) (Sillitoe 1998; Cleveland and Murray 1997). Inversely, permaculture in practice potentially gives environmental anthropologists an on-the-ground forum for working out the often controversial theoretical and ethical implications of TEK in a more decentralized, grassroots fashion.

Applied projects led by anthropologists have already been instrumental in promoting sustainable agriculture on campus (Barlett and Chase 2004) and in local US communities (Andreatta 2005). Permaculture projects led or participated in by anthropologists hold a lot of promise for further research that goes beyond the current sustainability framework. In the future it may be possible for environmental anthropologists to walk out their front door and enter the (eco)village instead of having to fly halfway around the world to get there. When that happens we will have done much to solve the current environmental crisis that those of us in the Global North have played a major role in perpetuating through our current consumption habits. It may then be possible to speak of a true "global village" and reach out in more democratic ways with our work and our lives toward those that we conduct research with.

Notes

This chapter is reprinted with permission and slight modification from *Culture and Agriculture* 30 (1–2): 47–58.

1. Development is used here for lack of a better word. The general idea of development—the improvement of the human condition—retains its value. However, development has become synonymous with a certain kind of development, one based on distinctly Euro-American, sociocultural, and political-economic models and one driven by the dictates of global capital. Most permaculturalists would undoubtedly balk at the cultural baggage carried by the concept of development; however, we do not have space to debate the viability of the term here.

References

Agrawal, Arun. 2002. "Indigenous Knowledge and the Politics of Classification." *International Social Science Journal* 173: 287–97.

Andreatta, Susan. 2005. "Urban Connections to Locally Grown Produce." In *Urban Place: Reconnecting with the Natural World,* ed. Peggy F. Barlett, 117–40. Cambridge, MA: MIT Press.

Balée, William. 2006. "The Research Program of Historical Ecology." *Annual Reviews in Anthropology* 35: 75–98.

Barlett, Peggy F., and Geoffrey W. Chase. 2004. *Sustainability on Campus: Stories and Strategies for Change.* Cambridge, MA: MIT Press.

Bennett, John W. 1969. *Northern Plainsmen: Adaptive Strategy and Agrarian Life.* Chicago: Aldine.

Berlin, Brent. 1992. *Ethnobiological Classification: Principles of Categorization of Plants and Animals in Traditional Societies.* Princeton, NJ: Princeton University Press.

Chambers, Robert, Arnold Pacey, and Lori Ann Thrupp. 1989. *Farmer First: Farmer Innovation and Agricultural Research.* London: Intermediate Technology Publications.

Cleveland, David, and Stephen Murray. 1997. "The World's Crop Genetic Resources and the Rights of Indigenous Farmers." *Current Anthropology* 38 (4): 477–515.

Dewalt, Billie R. 1994. "Using Indigenous Knowledge to Improve Agriculture and Natural Resource Management." *Human Organization* 53 (2): 163–89.

Earthaven Ecovillage. n.d. "Ecological Living at Earthaven." http://www.earthaven.org/ecological_living.php (accessed on 5 May 2008).

Ellen, Roy. 1993. *The Cultural Relations of Classification: Analysis of Nualu Animal Categories from Central Seram.* Cambridge: Cambridge University Press.

———. 2005. *The Categorical Impulse: Essays in the Anthropology of Classifying Behavior.* New York: Berghahn Books.

Escobar, Arturo. 1999. "Beyond Nature: Steps to an Anti-essentialist Political Ecology." *Current Anthropology* 40 (1): 1–30.

Fairhead, James, and Melissa Leach. 1996. *Misreading the African Landscape: Society and Ecology in a Forest-savannah Mosaic.* Cambridge: Cambridge University Press.

Holmgren, David. 1996. *Melliodora (Hepburn Permaculture Gardens): Ten Years of Sustainable Living.* Hepburn, Australia: Holmgren Design Services.

———. 2002. *Permaculture: Principles & Pathways Beyond Sustainability.* Hepburn, Australia: Holmgren Design Services.

Jungt, J. R. 1985. "Perennial Polyculture, Permaculture, and Preservation—the Principle of Diversity." *American Biology Teacher* 47 (2): 72–75.

Kennedy, Declan. 1991. "Permaculture and the Sustainable City." *Ekistics—the Problems and Science of Human Settlements* 58 (348–49): 210–15.

Lockyer, Joshua. 2007. "Sustainability and Utopianism: An Ethnography of Cultural Critique in Contemporary Intentional Communities." (PhD diss., University of Georgia).

Marsh, Chuck. 2002. "Earthaven and the Promise of Permaculture." *Permaculture Activist* 49 (Winter): 44–47.

Mollison, Bill. 1988. *Permaculture: A Designer's Manual.* Sisters Creek, Australia: Tagari Publications.

———. 1991. *Introduction to Permaculture.* Sisters Creek, Australia: Tagari Publications.

Mollison, Bill, and David Holmgren. 1978. *Permaculture One.* Sisters Creek, Australia: Tagari Publications.

Netting, Robert McC. 1968. *Hill Farmers of Nigeria: Cultural Ecology of the Kofyar of the Jos Plateau.* Seattle: University of Washington Press.

———. 1981. *Balancing on an Alp: Ecological Change and Continuity in a Swiss Mountain Community.* Cambridge: Cambridge University Press.

———. 1993. *Smallholders, Householders: Farm Families and the Ecology of Intensive, Sustainable Agriculture.* Palo Alto, CA: Stanford University Press.

Permaculture Activist. 2004. "What is Permaculture?" *Permaculture Activist* 53: 3.

Rhoades, Robert E., and Robert Booth. 1982. "Farmer-Back-to-Farmer: A Model for Generating Acceptable Agricultural Technology." *Agricultural Administration* 11: 127–37.

Rhoades, Robert E., and Stephen I. Thompson. 1975. "Adaptive Strategies in Alpine Environments: Beyond Ecological Particularism." *American Ethnologist* 2 (3): 535–51.

Robbins, Paul. 2004. *Political Ecology.* Malden, MA: Blackwell Publishing.

Sillitoe, Paul. 1998. "The Development of Indigenous Knowledge." *Current Anthropology* 39 (2): 223–52.

———. 2006. "Ethnobiology and Applied Anthropology: Rapprochement of the Academic with the Practical." *Journal of the Royal Anthropological Institute* SI: S119–S142.

Strange, P. 1984a. "Permaculture—Practical Design for Town and Country in Permanent Agriculture." *Ecologist* 13 (2–3): 88–94.

———. 1984b. "Permaculture—Give it a Chance." *Ecologist* 14 (1): 47–48.

Swetnam, Thomas W., Craig D. Allen, and Julio L. Betancourt. 1999. "Applied Historical Ecology: Using the Past to Manage for the Future." *Ecological Applications* 9 (4): 1189–1206.

Wallerstein, Immanuel. 1974. *Modern World-system: Capitalist Agriculture and the Origins of the European World-economy in the Sixteenth Century.* New York: Academic Press.

Chapter Six

Weeds or Wisdom?

Permaculture in the Eye of the Beholder on Latvian Eco-Health Farms

Guntra A. Aistara

On a tour of organic farms in Austria in 2006, one farmer proudly showed off her raised garden beds brimming with a diversity of herbs, medicinal plants, and vegetables, explaining that these were permaculture beds, whereby plants reseeded themselves, grew where they "felt best," and worked in ecological systems with neighboring plants. Some of the Latvian organic farmers on the tour were shocked and amused, however, by this, their first encounter with permaculture, and what they described as "farming amidst weeds." "Well, in that case I have permaculture everywhere in my farm," muttered one farmer. Another commented that it all depends on how you present things to visitors: "When you come visit me, and I explain to you that this is *permakultūra* ... don't criticize it, because it comes from *Eiropa* [Europe]." Other farmers insisted that permaculture meant farming as wisely as nature does, and that we might learn from it.[1]

The Latvian farmers' identification of what they saw in Austria as "lazy farming" may have been accurate,[2] but the interpretation of whether this is a positive or negative characteristic is a matter of opinion. What the Austrian permaculture farmer saw as wisdom was to some Latvian observers just too many weeds. This chapter traces Latvian farmers' reactions to permaculture principles and the articulation of their own practices with those principles. It is based on a participatory research project with the *Vides un veselības saime* (Latvian Eco-Health Farm Network; henceforth EHF Network) in the summer of 2010.[3] Latvia's EHF Network is a group of approximately fifty certified organic farms that have been working since 2000 to integrate healthy agroecosystems with human health, rural tourism, and community environmental education. The founders of the EHF network describe their approach as "recuperating our ancestor's knowledge, wisdom, and traditions, and enhancing these with knowledge from contemporary doctors and scientists both in Latvia and abroad."[4] This has proven an effective strategy in the prolonged transition of Latvia from a republic in the former Soviet Union to a new European Union (EU) member state, where farmers have faced a string of political and economic changes and challenges over the past twenty years that have now culminated in the current global economic crisis. The eco-health farmers have embraced these changes through a process of constant learning and adapting new techniques to their conditions. As one farmer put it, this has allowed them to "choose to ignore the economic crisis."[5]

These organic farmers promote their way of life as a site for environmental education and community building, catering mostly to educational excursions for local schoolchildren; residents of the capital city, Riga, escaping city life for a weekend; and some foreign tourists. Every year the group invites guest lecturers to lead discussions about a variety of topics, such as nutrition, massage, or eco-tourism. In 2010 I helped organize a series of on-farm permaculture workshops.[6] As all of the participants had a wealth of experience in trying to construct systems of alternative living and farming in Latvia, our collective discussions were aimed at discovering the "edge" of where permaculture complements local efforts. Together we explored how Latvian eco-health farm practices contribute to socioecological resilience, and how these practices articulate with permaculture principles and practices.

Many Latvian EHF farmers actively engaged aspects of permaculture that relate to biodiversity conservation, yet some remained unconvinced of a few field crop management techniques characteristic of permaculture approaches. I argue that this is in part because farmers in post-socialist Latvia are facing multiple pressures negotiating the mingling of EU dictates regarding farm modernization with the revival of traditional practices, and permaculture represents a new hybrid which thus far fits neither scenario. I relate this to Latour's (1993) analysis of the processes of "purification" and the "proliferation of hybrids" underlying modernity, and reflect on how farmers might take advantage of this permaculture "edge" to form alternative modernities.

The first section of this chapter gives a brief overview of two key concepts in permaculture, edges and diversity, and shows how they articulate with anthropological theories of modernity and ecological theories of resilience. The second section shows how Latvian EHF farmers have been working toward diversity and resilience through a revival of traditional herbal sauna practices, and how these practices correlate with permaculture principles. The third section discusses the barriers of acceptance by Latvian EHF farmers of some permaculture practices. Finally, I reflect on what these barriers show about the relationship between permaculture's ideals and the realities of the Latvian countryside, as well as what we can learn from the Latvian example about how farmers integrate new ideas with traditional practices to create new hybrid forms.

Permaculture versus "Modern" Agriculture

Bill Mollison and David Holmgren originally defined permaculture as "an integrated, evolving system of perennial or self-perpetuating plant and animal species useful to man" (Mollison and Holmgren [1978] 1990: 1). Now the concept has been expanded to include not just agriculture, but also a sense of ethics for sustainability and a conscious mingling of social and ecological responsibility. Explaining the evolution of the term in the 1990s, Mollison and Slay (1990, quoted in Whitefield 2004: 5) emphasize that "the word itself is a contraction not only of permanent agriculture but also of permanent culture, as cultures cannot survive for long without a sustainable agricultural base and landuse ethic." Permaculture is operationalized using Holmgren's (2002) twelve permaculture principles (see Figure 0.2), which are designed to be adapted and implemented in diverse climates and cultures.

There are noteworthy parallels among permaculture principles, Latour's (1993) theories on modernity, and Ingold's (2000) analysis of diversity. Exploring two permaculture principles in particular, "use edges and value the marginal" and "use and value diversity" (Holmgren 2002), can help us understand the sometimes contradictory responses of the Latvian eco-health farmers to some permaculture practices, as well as evaluate the future potential for articulation between Latvian practices and permaculture principles.

Scholars of both permaculture and science technology studies are concerned with exploring intermingled "naturecultures" (Haraway 1997), rather than maintaining an artificial separation between the two realms (Puig de la Bellacasa 2010). Latour has argued that what we call modernity is built up of two parallel processes: striving for "purification," or the separation of nature and culture, on the one hand, and "translation," or the "proliferation of hybrids" of nature-cultures, on the other. He suggests that these two processes contradict yet reinforce each other, thus making modernity ultimately unattainable:

> The first set of practices, by "translation," creates mixtures between entirely new types of beings, hybrids of nature and culture. The second, by "purification," creates two entirely distinct ontological zones: that of human beings on the one hand; that of nonhumans on the other. Without the first set, the

> practices of purification would be fruitless or pointless. Without the second, the work of translation would be slowed down, limited, or even ruled out. (Latour 1993: 10–11)

Permaculture can be understood as a practice of consciously and explicitly creating nature-culture hybrids. The very idea of "cultivated ecology" (Mollison and Holmgren [1978] 1990: 3), essentially designing an ecosystem, is the quintessential hybrid of nature and culture. Permaculture is conceived as a conscious alternative to modern industrial agriculture, in which growing dependence on technology increasingly separates people from their environments. Mollison and Holmgren noticed that issues such as soil fertility and weeds are not problems in natural ecosystems, and thus resolved to create a system that works with nature rather than against it. Permaculture practitioners aim to design agroecosystems that integrate natural and cultural systems, rather than continue their segregation (Holmgren 2002).

One example of nature-culture hybrids in permaculture is the concept of "edges." Permaculture practitioners note that the margin between two ecosystems is often 30 percent more diverse than either ecosystem on its own, a phenomenon known as "the edge effect" (Whitefield 2004: 24). One goal is to design farms using patterns that maximize edges, in order to increase diversity on the farm, and edges in permaculture are seen as "the place where the most interesting events take place" (Holmgren 2002: 223). In a practical sense, much of the biodiversity in such edges is, from the point of view of farmers, labeled as weeds. And while permaculture practitioners often quote Ralph Waldo Emerson's statement that "a weed is a plant whose virtues have not yet been discovered," in conventional and organic agriculture alike, weeds are often the bane of farmers' existence, and organic farmers often expend much effort eliminating them mechanically.

The constant incursion of weeds into the cultivated field is the proliferation of hybrids between nature and culture, whereas the creation of neat, weed-free fields represents an act of purification. This act places the farmer unquestionably on the side of culture, having dominated over nature. As Michael Pollan has noted: "To weed is to apply culture to nature—which is why we say, when we are weeding, that we are cultivating the soil" (Pollan 1989). Having individual crops in separate fields or rows is also a way of maintaining order and neatness, or the "legibility" that is also associated with what Scott (1998) calls high modernism in agriculture.

Latour (1993) notes that a part of modernity is the active denial of such hybrids. He urges instead that scholars study them explicitly, by exploring the role that nonhuman actors have in determining social relations. Weeds are an ideal example of such nonhuman actors, or what Latour calls "actants" (2005).

> Plants act, and can be considered actors of a kind. This is perhaps most obviously the case with weeds, which grow fast, adapt quickly to changing conditions, cause problems and induce emotional reactions … they stir things up by trespassing across otherwise carefully tended edges and boundaries. They do not know their place, and they disregard human design. (Despard 2008: 91)

Tsing (2005: 174) notes that "weeds have been of little interest to conservationists; we think of them only as indicators of disturbance." Yet she notes that it is exactly such "weedy, mixed forest landscapes" that make up a large part of what we consider biodiversity. She argues that with a change in perspective such weedy, messy areas, or "gaps," that exist between two systems can also become spaces of creativity and potential. Other scholars have also extended the notion of edges to understanding cultural interactions and their effects on socioecological resilience (Henfrey in press; Turner, Davidson-Hunt, and O'Flaherty 2003), as well as cultural barriers.[7] Permaculture practitioners encourage edges and acknowledge the agency of weeds, but try to transform barriers into productive "gaps" by discovering the virtues of useful and edible perennial plants, leaving less room for "weeds" with as yet undiscovered virtues.

Thus, taking edges and the weeds that grow in them as an important part of the landscape also means taking a different view of diversity. In permaculture, specialists emphasize that diversity should not be understood just as having more "things" on the farm, but rather as increasing the number of relationships between elements on the farm, as well as in the wider community. "Some people see the emphasis on diversity in permaculture as meaning that a random mix of species makes a system stable. In response, Bill Mollison suggests that it is the number of functional connections between species, rather than the number of species, which makes for stability" (Holmgren 2002: 213). Therefore, choosing the relative location of each element becomes a key design feature in permaculture, because this enables relationships to form and function.

This view of diversity, based on connections rather than objects, resonates with Ingold's (2000: 138) observations of diversity in different cosmological systems. He asserts that in genealogical models "diversity is the measure of difference … that presumes a world already divided into discrete, unit-entities—'things-in-themselves'—which may then be grouped into classes of progressively higher order on the basis of perceived likeness." In contrast, a relational approach places diversity in a dynamic context, rather than a static one. What makes things the same or different is "the shared experience of inhabiting particular places and following particular paths in an environment … The relational model, in short, *renders difference not as diversity but as positionality*" (Ingold 2000: 148–49, emphasis in original). Ingold's approach, like permaculture, emphasizes both relationships and location, as well as the inclusion of both human and nonhuman actors. This is also part of Latour's project to "reassemble the social" by tracing associations and connections "between things that are not themselves social" (Latour 2005: 5). In this understanding, diversity is a social network of connections, rather than a mere species count, and edges are the spaces for connection.

The creative potential for change, as represented in edges, and the integration of social and ecological networks are also key elements in the concept of socioecological resilience. Folke (2006: 259) notes that while we typically think about resilience as the "capacity to absorb shocks and still maintain function," resilience "is not simply about resistance to change and conservation of existing structures … It is also about the opportunities that disturbance opens up in terms of recombination of evolved structures and processes, renewal of the system and emergence of new trajectories." Biodiversity is of central importance for resilience. Folke (2006: 258) notes that while some species may seem "redundant," they can actually be the most valuable for regenerating the system after disturbance and disruption. If we consider the definition of biodiversity as a network of social and ecological connections, not just the number of species, it may become even more important for responding to crisis.

Permaculture's innovative approach to edges and understanding diversity reveals some of the tensions between modern agriculture and conservation. First, modern agriculture tries to eliminate edges and interactions rather than promote them. It is through this separation, in fact, that modern agriculture is placed in opposition to conservation, while in permaculture they are integrated into one whole. The separation between nature and culture in modernity promotes a static view of diversity. Attention to biodiversity at the species or gene level as countable objects allows our biodiversity monitoring to fixate on a calculation of perpetual loss. A reevaluation of biodiversity as built upon relationships allows for the possibility to actively identify and promote new connections, among both human and nonhuman actors, thus potentially increasing diversity (Aistara 2011). This is in fact what permaculture is attempting to do, in the process increasing social, ecological, and economic resilience. I will now turn to how Latvian eco-health farmers have utilized edges and imagined connections and networks of diversity on their farms, and how this has contributed to their resilience.

Sweating for Sustainability

It is often commented that the philosophy and practices of permaculture are not new, but rather a recombination of traditional and ecological knowledge from various cultures presented in a systematic, holistic fashion (Whitefield 2004: 4). Indeed, Latvian EHF farmers found that much of the "wisdom" of permaculture resonated with traditional practices that they have already been connecting with modern practices into their own hybrid forms. Thus, many practices used by Latvian EHFs are already a good reflection of permaculture principles, although they were not necessarily formed by design. Farmers' initial reaction to the principles was often, "Ah, we already do that," or, "That's a good reminder." One woman even noted that it is not so far off from the basics of agricultural training: "We are taught all of this in classical agronomy as well. It's just that when people are taught about chemicals and fertilizers, they forget the rest."[8]

As we toured farmers' land, participants began to see their own and their neighbors' farms through different eyes, and identified ways in which Latvian farmers are already using practices in line with permaculture principles. On one farm we found a small greenhouse on the south-facing wall of the sauna building that looked almost exactly like an illustration of permaculture design seen in books where the sauna, greenhouse, compost pile, and chicken coop are all grouped together to create a warm microclimate. On this farm, the grape vine growing next to the sauna attested to the warm microclimate that was indeed created. Participants in the seminars sometimes pointed out elements that the farmers themselves took for granted, such as the "stacking effect" of having medicinal herbs growing in front of apple trees, or a line of tall trees bracing the far northern edge of the farm acting as a sun trap, even though the trees' size testified to the fact that they were planted generations before the term "permaculture design" came to Latvia.

Perhaps the most striking example of how Latvian EHF farmers are weaving webs of connections and diversity, both social and ecological, is through the revival of the Latvian traditional *zāļu pirts* (wood-fired herbal steam sauna, or bathhouse). The *pirts* was the traditional place for washing in a Latvian farmstead, as well as a place for relaxation after a week of hard work on the farm. The traditional Saturday evening bathing ritual was also connected with spiritual purification, and the *pirts* is even likened to a church in historic literature (Virza [1933] 1989). Although many farmers today have indoor plumbing, the *pirts* remains a central ritual to country life, and one of the main attractions for city residents who escape for a country weekend.

Below I elaborate on how the *pirts* functions as a node where several permaculture principles meet, in particular the concepts of edges and diversity. I will use the example of Anta's farm, where she grazes beef cattle and sheep and grows potatoes, a selection of vegetables, fruit trees, and herbs. In recent years her specialization has become medicinal herbs, although it was not her original plan. "It all started with the *pirts,*"[9] she told me. She decided to build the *pirts* after going to a seminar sponsored by the EHF network and attending *pirts* courses, and within a few years her *pirts* had become a popular spot for locals and tourists from Riga as well as an integral part of her farm.

The traditional *pirts* ritual includes various rounds of heating up in the sauna, cooling off in a pond, and a *pēriens*—a gentle beating with a brush of birch branches tied together into a soft *slota* (broom) that acts as an exfoliation technique. In recent years, however, herbal specialists have been reviving and reconfiguring traditional knowledge and folk beliefs about the medicinal properties of various other trees, herbs, and medicinal plants that can be used in a *pirts,* depending on the desired health effects. A full herbal *pirts* procedure at Anta's farm can take up to four hours, and includes various stages of gradually warming up; an exfoliating rub with baking soda and salt; an energizing and then a warming *pēriens* with different types of *pirts slota*s; a honey mask; and a final massage. Each round in the *pirts* is followed by dips in a cold-water pond or rolls in the snow or dew, and copious amounts of herbal teas that promote sweating, increase the metabolism beforehand, and help replenish liquids, vitamins, and minerals afterward. A light meal of homegrown organic food and overnight lodging on aromatic straw mattresses in a loft above the *pirts* are also available. In the way Anta's *pirts* connects with other elements on her farm, we can identify the interaction of several of Holmgren's permaculture principles, as I discuss below.

Use Edges and Value the Marginal

Anta's farm is unique in that the diversity on her farm is maintained partially by the grazing of wild horses and wild cattle that she introduced to recreate historical herbivore-grassland ecological relationships (Schwartz 2005). This practice has gained popularity in recent years to help prevent forestation of grassland areas. Reforestation results in the loss of the "edge effect," because one ecosystem outcompetes the other when a crucial component (herbivores) is missing. Anta explained, "It's a wall of alders now; these aren't the traditional forest edges of the Latvian landscape."[10] Thus, the wild horses help promote the diversity of grasses, as well as the intermingling edges of forest and meadow ecosystems through their uneven grazing. These edges are important for the *pirts,* because, as one seminar participant noted, forest edges are the place where the best birch trees grow to be cut for the *pirts slotas*. Indeed, Anta's natural grazing meadows have been recognized by a number of experts for their high levels of diversity and rare species.

Use and Value Diversity

Anta collects a great variety of wild herbs and flowers in her meadows and grows others for use in *pirts slotas* and herbal teas. Plants are combined for their aromatic and healing properties. For example, in one *pirts* procedure she used *slotas* from birch, currant, and mugwort leaves in the first round, yarrow, oregano, and celery in the second round, and maple, birch, chamomile, plum, clover, and ash leaves in the third. She says she wants to demonstrate that everything she uses in the *pirts* can be obtained from the farm, and that everything is natural (Tooma 2005). Thus, the diversity on her farm is maintained through connections between the wild horses, meadow grasses, and humans who collect the grasses for various uses.

Within permaculture, networks of diversity refer not only to ecological relationships on the farm, but also to a broader web of social relations. Indeed, the connections stemming out from Anta's *pirts* reach far beyond the farm and into the community as well. As her *pirts* became more popular, Anta began employing local assistants to collect wild plants, and began making herbal balms and rubs. She now sells some plants to a local organic cosmetic company that makes upscale lotions for local sale and export within Europe. The *pirts* also serves as a central node for environmental education activities on the farm. The *pirts* is often what attracts visitors to the farm, but in the process they learn more about the diversity of herbs and grasses and their uses, about sustainable local food production and rural living, and how to see the landscape with different eyes through observing wild horses in the meadows.

Anta's *pirts* has also served as a node for integration of a variety of local organizations outside the EHF Network. As we sat around her picnic table discussing permaculture principles, other participants were from at least three different active networks that intersect on Anta's farm. The wool yarn from her sheep attracts a circle of craftspeople who sell some of their final products to tourists through Anta's farm. She is also part of a Heifer International project on livestock management, and a local tourism development foundation that is cooperating with Estonian organizations to promote bioregional cultural exchanges. As we discussed these multiple connections at the seminar, the women gathered around the picnic

Figure 6.1. Diverse medicinal herbs and tree leaves drying for use in herbal teas and sauna procedures. Photo by Guntra A. Aistara.

table joked that they themselves were like "beneficial insects" attracted by Anta's *pirts* and innovative farming practices.[11]

Design from Patterns to Details

In analyzing Anta's farm, it is also noteworthy to mention another permaculture design feature, according to which the elements of farms are arranged in five zones imagined as concentric circles going out from the house—Zone One being the closest and most frequently accessed. Anta's natural grazing areas on the outskirts of the farm serve as an ideal example of Zone Five, which is meant to be the wildlife zone farthest from the house, with limited or no human interference. Anta also commented on the multifunctionality of the bushes in that zone, which serve as browsing fodder for the horses during the winter when the snow covers the grasses and as firewood after the snow melts.

Within permaculture design, plantings are often arranged in patterns that maximize edges, such as spirals and mandalas. As we were discussing her farm's arrangement, one participant suddenly observed, "We are talking here about mandala gardens, but really if we were to look from above, the whole farm is arranged like a mandala, with paths going out from the house in different directions to all parts of the farm."[12] This mandala represents how attention to diversity and productive edges in Anta's meadows has given rise to a range of other products and processes, serving to form hybrids of local and global, ecological and economic activities—in short, of nature and culture. At the end of the seminar Anta noted, "You see how a very permacultural spider's web has formed here, all on its own."[13]

Permaculture on the "Edges" of Modernity

Despite the examples above, where permaculture principles can be identified as already working in the realm of biodiversity conservation, other practices seem to remain on the borders of acceptability by EHF farmers. In field crops and soil management, permaculture involves some relatively unconventional practices, and this is where there was the most skepticism. In permaculture, soil fertility is not managed through yearly tilling and cultivating of the soil, because digging and turning the soil disturbs soil structure. And while turning the soil liberates nutrients, it does so more quickly than the plants can use, thus leading to soil degradation (Whitefield 2004). Thus, nutrients are added using techniques such as sheet mulching, rather than digging.[14] In larger areas, cash crops are integrated with hedges and trees, or planted directly into clover, to help maintain soil fertility (Whitefield 2004).

At one seminar, where the hosting farm was already using permanent beds prepared by sheet mulching, cultivated only with a flat hoe and the addition of compost and mulch in place of tilling, a long discussion emerged among participants about whether the garden paths and beds should be inverted the next year, or at least after a few years. Some farmers saw the clover-covered paths as good land left fallow, which when turned over would lead to healthy soil for cultivation. According to permaculture methods, however, the soil under the paths is compacted and thus should always remain a path, while in the garden beds the addition of organic matter and the growing of leguminous crops build soil and a healthy population of microorganisms. Disturbing it even every few years would destroy several years' worth of biological activity. As opinions clashed about whether or not the soil in the beds would get "tired" from constant cultivation or "disturbed" by digging, one older farmer said, "I would just work this land as one piece … dig it up, have several larger fields and rotate them … but I guess that's the old agronomy school."[15]

The integration of various crops also met with mixed reactions. Some traditional combinations, like oats and peas or onions and carrots, were taken for granted, but going beyond two or so crops was seen by some as going too far: "This is for you younger generations—it is psychologically not acceptable to us … having everything mixed up like that."[16]

Perhaps most universal was the dislike of weeds. Although it was often the object of good-natured joking, this seemed to constitute the real barrier where permaculture ceased to be an acceptable alternative. While it is untrue that permaculture necessarily implies weed-infested fields, the half-wild perennial combinations often have a "messier" look. Some farmers had recently visited some permaculture farms in Germany and commented that they, personally, would be ashamed to bring visitors to their farms if they were so unkempt. One farmer objected very emphatically, "On the issue of weeds I disagree!" She liked having her potato fields clean and clear so she didn't have to "search for her potatoes."[17]

This skepticism by some Latvian EHF farmers to permaculture field crop management practices is rooted in the fact that these practices seem to fall into a "gap," neither traditional nor modern, and this is exactly the "edge" that Latvian farmers are still negotiating in their prolonged post-Soviet transition to managing their regained family farmsteads in a new European modernity.

Traditional farming practices include crop rotation and tilling of soil after letting it lie fallow for some time, as suggested in the comment above by the older farmer. On the other hand, the most visible embodiment of the norms of modern agriculture in Latvia, the EU regulations, are constantly encouraging upgrades of farming technology and modernization of practices toward greater industrialization. Land consolidation is increasing, often in the hands of foreign companies and farmers. For example, many Danish farmers now manage farmland in Latvia and are expanding the use of herbicides and pesticides, large machinery, and modern infrastructure. Thus, if for the past twenty years Latvian organic farmers were constantly explaining how they differed from their conventional neighbors, who also didn't use pesticides for lack of income, they are now becoming a much more striking contrast to their neighbors. In one county I visited, 50 percent of the farmland is owned or managed by only a few Danish-Latvian joint ventures. There are only two organic farmers in the county, and an extension agent reported that they are now increasingly hassled by their neighbors about their "untidy" fields. Thus, they are being reminded that not becoming modern is still seen as a retreat backward: "Time's arrow is unambiguous: one can go forward, but then one must break with the past; one can choose to go backward, but then one has to break with the modernizing avant-gardes, which have broken radically with their own past" (Latour 1993: 69). These new permaculture methods were perplexing to some, because on the one hand, they brought more weeds, which were a sign of backwardness. On the other hand, the EHF had encountered these practices in western Europe, which is itself representative of modernity.

This also relates to a second issue—the cultural values of *tīrība, kārtība,* and *sakoptība* (cleanliness, order, and tidiness) in the Latvian countryside. Even the Latvian word for a cultivated field, *tīrums,* signifies a clean or tidy place. Thus, the perception of weeds in the countryside as contradictory to these values is not surprising. In fact, much of the post-decollectivization history has been one of returning the countryside to its romanticized, independence-era tidiness (Eglitis 2002; Schwartz 2006). There are even regular competitions for the most tidy farmsteads and counties (Berķis, Hānbergs, and Ziedonis 2001). Thus, these norms of tidiness and order also have a deeper cultural significance, and constitute what Latour (1993) calls "purification," quite literally.

Because permaculture's soil management practices do not really fit any existing categories of Latvian farmers, either traditional or modern, they also do not immediately fit as an option for "serious farming." Rather, permaculture practices sometimes get relegated to the margins of the main income-generating activities. They are seen as very appropriate for Zone One, by the house, such as an herb spiral by the door, or for Zone Five, such as Anta's grassland meadows, yet are not considered feasible—at least not without more information and experimenting—for large-scale production of cash crops. For the Latvian farmers, this is as much an economic issue as one of aesthetics or modernity. It is seen as cheaper and more efficient to work one field with a tractor (especially with fuel tax exemptions) than to work in smaller beds without technology and more manual labor. Labor is not only expensive, but also hard to find, given large-scale emigration from the countryside to Ireland and other EU countries. The current global financial crisis has also hit Latvia harder than many other countries, so a large-scale reorganization of farming might indeed be a risky endeavor.

Finally, the Latvian EHF farmers' reactions are related to current EU regulations. Even for EHF farmers who are disillusioned with the push to modern agriculture, there is one final, practical hurdle. What Latour (1993) calls the "modern constitution" has been transcribed onto paper and institutionalized in regulations. Purification is the norm, even in the EU agri-environmental support payment program. Those farmers most interested in integrating biodiversity conservation practices with food production are the ones having the most trouble with the regulations (Aistara 2009). For example, the regulations do not allow trees and shrubs in grazing areas or agricultural fields, and require a minimum size of 0.3 hectares of one type of crop. Such norms are contrary to the formation of edges and encouraging biodiversity. In the reality of the Latvian countryside, EU regulations impose "modernity," with all of its implied segregation.

Thus, it seems permaculture will for now remain on the edges of Latvian farms, which are themselves perceived to be on the far edges of modernity, given historic constructions of eastern Europe as the backward "other" to western Europe (Wolff 1994). As the EHF farmers attempt to turn that edge into one that is full of potential, diversity, and connections, they must continue to evaluate how permaculture and other new practices fit with their own productive new hybrids.

Conclusion

What can we learn from the Latvian EHF examples of how their practices articulate with permaculture principles? These examples raise interesting questions about what constitute both the productive "edges" and the divisive "frontiers" of permaculture practices and their acceptance by some Latvian EHF farmers. We can analyze what these margins signify about the acceptability of permaculture as an alternative way of organizing rural livelihoods in Latvia and elsewhere.

In my assessment, the jury is still out on how the farmers' initial skepticism about these practices will play out and affect the diversity, networks, and resilience of their farms. The pessimistic view would be that farmers' doubts reveal a separation between ideas of "living" and "farming," where the use of more conventional farming techniques for "serious production" serves to reinforce segregation between nature and culture as a form of purification. Traditional values of tidiness combined with EU regulations and pressures for modernization would thus translate into limiting diversity and innovative networks on these farms.

On the other hand, it is noteworthy that the types of connections that the permaculture principles are intended to promote have happened in Latvia, not by design, but rather as an almost accidental outgrowth of combining traditional cultural practices like the *pirts* with new knowledge and an ecological sensibility. This can serve as a reminder that networks based on existing cultural traditions—rather than completely new elements—may be the most appropriate, as what Holmgren calls "small and slow solutions" (Holmgren 2002). It shows how EHF farmers are turning their location on the margins of Europe into a productive "edge," and using their innovative integration of human and ecosystem health issues to enrich permaculture practices in new ways.

This brings us back to theories about resilience. Folke (2006: 259) discusses the productive tension between continuity and innovation in resilience: "Memory is the accumulated experience and history of the system, and it provides context and sources for renewal, recombination, innovation, novelty, and self-organization following disturbance." This suggests that perhaps farmers' initial skepticism is only the first step, to be followed by experimentation, analysis, and the slow intermingling of new practices with local, traditional ones. If so, then this approach may in fact be vital to promoting both cultural and ecological resilience in the future.

The Latvian case also exposes some noteworthy contradictions. First, it shows that in the European project of modernity, even regulations that are intended to support agri-environmental integration sometimes prevent the creation of hybrid systems that may actually lead to greater economic and ecological resilience. Second, the Latvian farmers' careful evaluation of the practicality of permaculture solutions for their circumstances also holds a lesson for promoters of permaculture. I expect that there are a great many farmers in the world who might accept permaculture as a wise solution for the borders of their home and the outskirts of their farms, but who might not be swayed for a large-scale redesign of their main productive activities—for economic as well as cultural reasons. Permaculture texts emphasize that more people should be involved in small-scale food production rather than society relying on large-scale farms producing monocrops, but this division leaves out a whole range of medium-sized, diverse farms that are struggling to make a living and protect the environment in the modernized world of food production. This should make those interested in advocating permaculture as a wide-scale model for sustainable living—and a step toward ecotopia—consider how better to engage not only growing numbers of urban environmentalists and suburban gardeners, but also the populations who *are* currently producing our food.

Notes

1 All comments in this paragraph made anonymously by farmers on a trip to Austria, 22 April 2006.
2. Permaculture is referred to as "lazy faming" to emphasize the fact that once ecological processes are established through proper design, they require less intervention.
3. This chapter builds on earlier ethnographic research conducted in Latvia from 2005 to 2009; all names are changed and all translations are my own. I wish to express my gratitude to Māra Bergmane for the invitation to run the seminars and to the members of the Latvian Eco-health Farm Network for welcoming me in their midst. I wish to thank Dace Dzenovska, Gundega Jēkabsone, Hadley Renkin, and the editors for helpful comments on earlier drafts. The writing of this article was sponsored by Central European University Foundation, Budapest (CEUBPF). The views expressed herein represent the ideas of the

author, and do not necessarily reflect the opinion of CEUBPF or other funding sources.

4. Founder of EHF Network, email to author, 1 March 2008.
5. Anonymous farmer comment at seminar, 16 March 2010.
6. I shared my knowledge about permaculture principles gained from permaculture design courses, while farmers shared their practical experience of local farming conditions and practices, and analysis of how permaculture principles align with their farm design.
7. Tom Henfrey has differentiated between "fringes" as zones of human enhancement of biodiversity, "cultural edges" as areas of social and cultural exchange of ideas and objects, and "cultural and ecological frontiers" as where intercultural interactions lead to a loss of diversity (in press).
8. Anonymous farmer comment at seminar, 16 June 2010.
9. Anta, comment at seminar, 24 July 2010.
10. Anta, comment at seminar, 24 July 2010.
11. Anonymous farmer comment at seminar, 24 July 2010.
12. Anonymous farmer comment at seminar, 24 July 2010.
13. Anta, comment at seminar, 24 July 2010.
14. In sheet mulching, layers of sheets of cardboard or newspaper are topped with manure, compost, or other organic matter and used for planting. These materials block out weeds and gradually break down to add nutrients to the soil. See, for example, Whitefield (2004: 195).
15. Anonymous farmer comment at seminar, 16 June 2010.
16. Anonymous farmer comment at seminar, 16 June 2010.
17. Anonymous farmer comment at seminar, 24 July 2010.

References

Aistara, Guntra. 2009. "Maps from Space: Latvian Organic Farmers Negotiate Their Place in the European Union." *Sociologia Ruralis* 49 (2): 132–50.

_____. 2011. "Seeds of Kin, Kin of Seeds: The Commodification of Organic Seeds and Social Relations in Costa Rica and Latvia." *Ethnography* 12 (4): 490–517.

Berķis, Aivars, Ēriks Hānbergs, and Imants Ziedonis. 2001. *Lauku Sēta Ir Gudra.* Rīga: Jumava.

Despard, Erin. 2008. "Creative Weeding and Other Everyday Experiments in the Garden." *The Brock Review* 10: 86–96.

Eglitis, Daina. 2002. *Imagining the Nation: History, Modernity and Revolution in Latvia.* University Park: Pennsylvania State University Press.

Folke, Carl. 2006. "Resilience: The Emergence of a Perspective for Social-Ecological Systems Analyses." *Global Environmental Change* 16: 253–67.

Haraway, Donna. 1997. *Modest_Witness@Second_Millennium. Femaleman©_Meets_Oncomouse™: Feminism and Technoscience.* New York: Routledge.

Henfrey, Thomas. In press. *Edges, Frontiers, and Fringes.* New York: Berghahn Books.

Holmgren, David. 2002. *Permaculture: Principles and Pathways Beyond Sustainability.* Hepburn, Australia: Holmgren Design Services.

Ingold, Tim. 2000. *The Perception of the Environment: Essays in Livelihood, Dwelling and Skill.* New York: Routledge.

Latour, Bruno. 1993. *We Have Never Been Modern.* Cambridge, MA: Harvard University Press.

———. 2005. *Reassembling the Social: An Introduction to Actor-Network-Theory.* Oxford: Oxford University Press.

Mollison, Bill, and David Holmgren. [1978] 1990. *Permaculture One: A Perennial Agriculture for Human Settlements.* Tyalgum, Australia: Tagari.

Pollan, Michael. 1989. "Weeds Are Us." *New York Times Magazine,* 5 November.

Puig de la Bellacasa, Maria. 2010. "Ethical Doings in Naturecultures." *Ethics, Place, and Environment* 13: 2.

Schwartz, Katrina Z. S. 2005. "Wild Horses in a 'European Wilderness': Imagining Sustainable Development in the Post-Communist Countryside." *Cultural Geographies* 12 (3): 292–320.

———. 2006. *Nature and National Identity after Communism: Globalizing the Ethnoscape.* Pittsburgh, PA: University of Pittsburgh Press.

Scott, James. 1998. *Seeing Like a State: How Certain Schemes to Improve the Human Condition Have Failed.* New Haven, CT: Yale University Press.

Tooma, Anitra. 2005. "Medains Pēriens Nekurzemē." *Vides vēstis* 78 (3): 42–45.

Tsing, Anna Lowenhaupt. 2005. *Friction: An Ethnography of Global Connection.* Princeton, NJ: Princeton University Press.

Turner, Nancy, Iain Davidson-Hunt, and Michael O'Flaherty. 2003. "Living on the Edge: Ecological and Cultural Edges as Sources of Diversity for Social-Ecological Resilience." *Human Ecology* 31 (3): 439–61.

Virza, Edvarts. [1933] 1989. *Straumēni: Vecā Zemgales Māja Gada Gaitās.* Rīga: Liesma.

Whitefield, Patrick. 2004. *The Earth Care Manual: A Permaculture Handbook for Britain and Other Temperate Climates.* Hampshire, UK: Permanent Publications.

Wolff, Larry. 1994. *Inventing Eastern Europe: The Map of Civilization on the Mind of the Enlightenment.* Palo Alto, CA: Stanford University Press.

Chapter Seven

Permaculture in the City

Ecological Habitus and the Distributed Ecovillage

Randolph Haluza-DeLay and Ron Berezan

The wild strawberries are close enough to reach as Randy writes. He feasts on a half dozen every sentence, attracted by their succulence. He watches another bus pass, as they do every twenty minutes, and picks another handful of the tiny berries. Butterflies flit from columbines to columbines and hollyhocks. The apple tree has finally established itself after a couple years of struggle and a couple dozen plump spheres, ripe in a couple of weeks, are reachable from the sidewalk. A potato patch towers next to the saskatoon bushes. Several pumpkin blooms show brilliant yellow against the red cedar wood chips that carpet winding paths among the vegetation. Bean vines entwine up the sunflowers that will be autumn food for chickadees. A wren chitters from the spruce tree near the birdhouse it occupies with its partner: a first resident after five years of no inhabitants. A year ago—except for the three-year-old apple tree—this was all grass lawn.

Later today, Randy will water some of it from the barrels that hold rainwater diverted from the city runoff system. Another eaves trough feeds a landscaped stream and pond. Eventually, so will the wash water and bath drains. The view from the front window looks like a wild tangle of greenery and subtle colors one finds in forests rather than the floridly hued landscaping more common in the city. The family now shares space with birds, butterflies, and large rabbits that populate the neighborhood. But the yardscape also yields food. And it provokes a sense of place different from that of the lawn; maybe it also grows a way of thinking more in line with sustainability.

Ron is known as "The Urban Farmer"; he is a gardener, social activist, and educator in the field known today as "permaculture"—the movement toward a "permanent culture" in which the human species is integrated within natural systems, even within urban spaces that have typically sought to manage out the "other-than-human." Ron describes his work as empowering urbanites to reclaim their connection to nature within the city and to restore and regenerate barren urban landscapes into places rich in biodiversity, beauty, and productivity. Randy is a permaculture acolyte. He is also a former wilderness guide, and now a social scientist with a professional focus on environmental sustainability.

The community network that the urban permaculture movement has created serves, we argue, as a *"distributed ecovillage"* and a social field productive of an *ecological habitus,* that is, an orientation that generates lifestyle practices and institutional forms that effectively fit the ecological conditions of place (Haluza-DeLay 2008). As Veteto and Lockyer (2008) identified, there is astonishingly little research on permaculture, and most of that is not in a Global North context. Our key concern is not whether permaculture can contribute to local urban sustainability, but how learning occurs in ways that connect residents to their place.

In this chapter we try to use the storytelling employed by permaculturalists when describing their *design systems*—that is, the transformation of their yards, gardens, community spaces, and public places. The dialogical model for the chapter will have each of us commenting on key themes and each other's comments from our vantages as reflective practitioner (Ron, in italics) and activist-scholar (Randy, non-italicized). As one principle of permaculture is *enhancing diversity,* we hope that our epistemological diversity can illumine the analysis of the development of a permaculture network in Edmonton, Alberta. If the modern world is one of disenchantment (Gibson 2009), in some senses permaculture is about re-enchanting the city (Haluza-DeLay 1997) and bringing the social and ecological together. Academic language can be equally distancing, so we bring it in conversation with the praxis of permaculture practitioners.

This chapter relies on techniques best called an autoethnographic approach. The root of the term—"ethnography"—evokes a common research method with a history in the social sciences. *Auto*ethnography places the researcher's experience as something to be studied. The approach here is consistent with the style Anderson (2006) called "analytic autoethnography," rather than "evocative autoethnography" as advocated by Ellis and Bochner (2000). Analytic autoethnography commits to deriving theoretical understanding of the phenomenon from close examination of researcher experience. As Ron has been a central node in the development of the permaculture network in Edmonton, his experience is an invaluable source of knowledge. Randy's sociotheoretical background helps to position this knowledge amidst broader scholarly questions and explanations of social movements toward a sustainable future. As Bullough and Pinneager

(2001: 15) explain in their assessment of "self-study" techniques: "Articulation of the personal trouble or issue never really becomes research until it is connected through evidence and analysis to the issues and troubles of a time and place." Autoethnography deemphasizes abstract and categorical knowledge, giving preference to the testimony of narrative (Polkinghorne 1988). Permaculture principles emphasize *starting where you are* and being attentive to the biological integrity of the locality. This principle can be and is extended toward social integrity as well. We start where we are and engage each other in dialogue—one of us a social scientist, and the other a permaculture practitioner and mentor.

Starting Where You Are

Both sets of my grandparents settled on the edge of this city nearly one hundred years ago. They were attracted by the similarity of the landscape to their eastern European homelands and chose to live a peri-urban life with small mixed farms but close proximity to the concentration of urban resources and opportunities. Within one generation, their smallholdings were annexed by the municipality and converted to suburban neighborhoods. I consider myself something of a dual citizen—thoroughly steeped in the urban reality from birth and attracted to the intensity and social possibilities of the city, but equally formed by my early childhood small farm experiences and my frequent forays into the wild edges both on the city's perimeter and in the river valley and ravines that meander through it. By the time I had children of my own, I became fascinated by the prospects for extending that "wild edge" into our own yard, both in terms of fostering biodiversity but also through creating an intensely productive urban microfarming environment. My quest eventually led me to the "permaculture narrative," which offered a systematic framework for the values and vision that we as a family were attempting to live out.

Permaculture is a broad synthesis of traditional and scientific knowledge aimed at the design of sustainable human habitat that suggests a trajectory toward the reintegration of the human species within local ecologies. While the primary emphasis in permaculture has been on sustainable food production, the movement increasingly concerns itself with the domains of alternative economy, natural building, energy systems, water systems, ecological restoration, community development, education, and spirituality. Permaculture understands that given the fact the human species has created tremendous disturbance on the planet, we have both the responsibility and the capacity to heal impoverished lands and to nurture biodiversity. Through the articulation of numerous ecological design principles, permaculturalists (who affectionately call themselves "permies") strive to work with nature in this restorative work. As a movement, permaculture has evolved a pedagogical framework of popularizing this vision through one-, two-, and fourteen-day permaculture workshops. All are encouraged to be teachers as well as learners in this process.

Slowly, I began to apply my permaculture knowledge to the transformation of our inner-city yard from concrete and lawn into a diverse, resilient, and productive landscape. This began in small steps—careful observations of the sun and water patterns on our site, converting lawn to vegetable beds through a sheet mulching technique, planting every edible or otherwise useful perennial I could find, and establishing fruit and berry trees in key locations. The deeper I progressed into this transformation, the more possibilities for new interrelationships between elements in the landscape were discovered. Soon there were synergies created between the house and the landscape, such as the development of a grey water wetland to recycle bath water and create a new biological habitat, the placement of cold frames on the south side of the house to extend the growing season, and the collection of rainwater from rooftops into large barrels with drip lines to deliver water to where it was most needed. At this time, I was largely unaware of any others in my city adopting the permaculture approach, and indeed I traveled great distances for additional permaculture training and networking.

Edmonton is a northern city of nearly one million people in the metropolitan area—at fifty-three degrees latitude it is the most northern city in North America of that size. The city itself sprawls over 264 square miles, partly owing to the generally flat to gently rolling terrain of the prairie upon which the city sits. The North Saskatchewan River valley bisects the city, with many ravines veining down to the deep river valley that flows from the Rocky Mountains several hundred kilometers away. The river valley and many of the ravines make up one of the largest urban parks in the world, and beaver and coyote and an occasional moose make their way along the river parks. Edmonton sits at the intersection of the prairie and aspen parkland ecoregions and has a fairly dry climate, warm summers, and cold winters. The growing season runs from mid-May to late September, with a long-term average of 140 frost-free days. The northern location means long sunny days, with over seventeen hours of daylight at summer solstice. Average January temperatures are approximately –11.7°C (10.9°F), ranging to a July average of 17.5°C (63.5°F). Extremes of –30°C are generally achieved approximately five times a winter, while summer days occasionally reach 30°C. The city is classified as USDA Plant Hardiness Zone 3a, important information for knowing which plants can survive in the city.

Such pieces of information are aspects of a sense of place essential to planting and growing. Environmental scholars and theorists often emphasize the important role of place knowledge in developing attention to and care for places (Gruenewald 2003; Haluza-DeLay 2010). More important to Edmonton permaculturalists is the intimate knowledge of their own yards and the communities where they work. The key locations Ron mentions in his own description include microclimates of sunny or wet spots, depressions where mushrooms might promulgate, spots of wind or wind shelter. Permaculturalists know their soils (or soon learn it) and how water flows around the property. They draw on many resources, including the sharing of books (Pearman and Pike 2000; Williams 1997) and personal knowledge. "Zone 3a" is only a beginning to coaxing productive growth out of a permaculture site.

There is a particularly interesting microclimate in the northeastern part of Edmonton that has been a site of community activism for several decades (Spaling and Wood 1998). Blessed by unique soils, slightly warmer average temperatures, and more frost-free days, this region hosts a number of market gardens. The land use plan approved in 2010 provides some protection for agricultural production in city limits (although the council has since backtracked and rezoned the land for housing and industrial development). An important focal organization in the urban agriculture campaign was the Greater Edmonton Alliance, which mobilized several hundred people to city hall on several occasions in 2009, and publicized a "great potato giveaway" by one of the market gardeners that shocked many Edmontonians into realizing how productive this microregion in the city truly was. Edmonton also has an extensive community garden program, with up to sixty-five community gardens listed by the Community Garden Network of Edmonton and Area. The network began in the early 1990s, although the nonprofit organization was only incorporated in 2003. In 1993 Ron was instrumental in organizing only the third community garden in the Edmonton area. Several other permaculturalists have had past or current connections to the community gardening in Edmonton, often under the perception that "any food growing is good growing."

Facilitating Interrelations

Another permaculture design principle is to "facilitate interrelations." My journey eventually led to the abandoning of my long-term employment in the nonprofit sector for the creation of a small business, The Urban Farmer, focused on offering permaculture design for the transformation and regeneration of urban spaces. As this vision and methodology were relatively unknown in the local region, our own yard became both laboratory and classroom for the emerging permaculture community within the city of Edmonton. The transformation of our inner-city yard from concrete and lawn into a wonderfully diverse (over 180 different plant species), resilient, and productive landscape showed what could be done. In the spring of 2005, I offered my first formal workshop from my home, Backyard Permaculture—Creating an Urban Oasis, which included twenty participants. This eight-hour event generated a great deal of enthusiasm and participants pledged to "keep in touch" at the conclusion of the day, though no formal means for doing this was established at that time. Additional workshops soon followed and public awareness of permaculture in our city began to grow. From grey water systems to edible forest gardens to building with cob, our space grew to function as a central node for permaculture learning and networking in the Edmonton area.

In the summer of 2006, I developed a partnership with another permaculture enthusiast who began to assist with my workshops. On her initiative, we organized our first permaculture potluck supper, which attracted twenty-five people. Attendees were primarily folks who had attended permaculture workshops with me in the past. At that gathering, informal conversations led to the shared conclusion that we should develop the means for ongoing networking to support each other's efforts in permaculture learning and in living more sustainable, ecologically integrated lives. Thus the Edmonton Permaculture Network (EPN) was born.

To facilitate ongoing information and resource sharing, an EPN listserv was established with an initial twenty-five members. At first, this listserv was seldom used and primarily functioned as a way for people to share information about events happening within the city. As additional workshop graduates signed onto the list and our numbers doubled within a few more months, the level of activity increased. Soon there were regular posts by people who had excess plants to give away, those who were looking for used windows to build cold frames, and others who were trying to find mulching materials for their yards, etc. Before long, the listserv also evolved into a series of what became known as "permie crawls," whereby members who had a project in mind for the transformation of their yard could post an invitation to a "work bee" to other members of the group. There were front yards that were transformed from lawn into edible forest gardens in an afternoon, herb spiral gardens built from discarded materials in an evening, ponds dug and brought to life on a Saturday afternoon, and visioning sessions where twelve sets of eyes would converge on a backyard with powerful collective observations and ideas for the homeowner in their efforts to create their space along permaculture lines. All of these group gatherings injected additional energy and motivation into the life of the EPN. By 2009, our numbers had grown to over one hundred people on the listserv.

Considerable research has shown how important social networks are to the diffusion of innovation (Hildreth and Kimble 2004; D. R. White 2007). More importantly, they are one of the key ways that humans interact. Networks are durable patterns of relationships that perform functions for members, and social movements have been studied extensively from this perspective (Diani and McAdam 2003). For humans in networks, the functions may be friendship, economic exchange, information, or production and utilization of social capital. As noted above, the EPN has served to distribute materials, time, and other resources, as well as the perhaps even more important social support, which we will discuss below.

Networks consist of nodes and ties. Nodes are the members, while ties are the connections between them. Ties can be assessed on the basis of their strength and type. Nodes can be assessed on the basis of such measures as centrality (meaning the strength of links attached) or density (number of ties relative to the total number of ties in the entire network). Network theory assumes that for the most part, individuals are less significant than the ways that they are embedded in networks.

As he has identified, Ron has been a key node in the EPN. His workshops have formed a key meeting place, and he has been a conduit for many forms of resources. But as we will show later, he has not been the only node, and the network has clustered in new patterns recently. Social network analysis, of the mathematical type at least, is often handicapped by lack of attention to the meaning of the relationships (Crossley 2008), just the sort of data that ethnographic methods are very capable of discerning. More important than the number and strength of ties Ron has is the meaning that Ron has had for Edmonton permaculturalists and others. In summer 2010 he was acknowledged with the first Edmonton Growing Green Leader award from a diverse range of social and environmental groups. Currently, most participants in the EPN have some reference to Ron. As the network evolves over time, it will be interesting to see how Ron's role and the meanings people attach to it will change.

Networks are key to diffusion of knowledge and innovation. For example, the permaculture network in Edmonton may become a stimulus for broader socioecological transformation. Kenworthy (2006: 68–69) lists several key dimensions for urban sustainability. The first two are clearly values and practices of permaculture:

> a. The city has a compact, mixed-use urban form that uses land efficiently and protects the natural environment, biodiversity and food-producing areas …
>
> b. The natural environment permeates the city's spaces and embraces the city, while the city and its hinterland provide a major proportion of its food needs.

A key question for consideration is the extent to which permaculture as a practice can assist cities like Edmonton toward institutionalization of such key dimensions. "Nature" is usually "out of sight, out of mind" in city planning and even academic literature on cities. For example, one of the premier Canadian texts in urban sociology completely ignores the environment (Hiller 2009). Clearly, this approach contrasts with one acknowledging the environment as the foundation for human living, especially in terms of supplying the material resources, waste absorption, and other ecosystem services that are part of urban metabolism. Permaculture specifically means one cannot ignore this "metabolic rift," that is, the gap between the taking of nutrients and energy from nature far in excess of what is returned to the environment (Foster 2002). Permaculturalists are zealous in an effort to maintain "metabolic value"—a "rift-healing contribution" to the imbalance (Salleh 2010)—and are even evangelistic about the need to reconfigure urban environments in this fashion.[1]

In time, additional spin-off groups have formed out of the EPN, making for new nodes. The Rivercity Chickens Collective has been working for over two years to have the municipal bylaws changed to allow for backyard chicken keeping. Operation Fruit Rescue Edmonton (OFRE) was created to glean fruit from local untended fruit trees, offering one-third of the harvest to the homeowner, another third to the food bank, and the final third to the volunteers who do the picking. A guerrilla gardening group has developed with the goal of naturalizing degraded public spaces. One-hundred-mile diet activism was featured on local radio for an entire year and has motivated faith communities and other groups. Edmonton also now has an active Transition Town group that grew out of members of the EPN. In April 2010, the EPN organized the Edmonton Permaculture Convergence, a full-day gathering of permaculture workshops and networking opportunities. This event was facilitated completely by volunteers and drew 126 people.

At the time of writing, the EPN listserv has 180 active members. In the past two years, there have been three complete twelve-day Permaculture Design Certificate courses in the province of Alberta, which have produced a host of new teachers and permaculture-related businesses, many of whom have been active in the EPN. Introduction to Permaculture workshops are now being facilitated by people other than myself, and there are permaculture landscaping businesses, permaculture consultants and designers, and other related businesses emerging. An EPN member has started a permaculture group within a local high school and several community gardens with a permaculture emphasis have been initiated. Now that there are many other private yards in the city implementing permaculture principles, I organize an annual Edible Garden Tour to offer the public the opportunity to see a range of examples of urban permaculture gardens. The sixth annual tour ran in August 2010. Another group organizes a bike tour of community gardens. My own yard continues to function as a central node for permaculture activities, and additional workshops have been developed, such as Building with Cob, No-Till Vegetable Gardens, Raising Fungi in the Garden, Backyard Bees, and many others.

Densifying

The expanding permaculture diversity fits another permaculture principle, that of *densifying*. This highlights a valuable component of the Edmonton permaculture network—applied to human communities, this means *densifying social capital*. The Urban Farmer still serves as a key node in the EPN, but over time, the movement diversified, meaning there are a number of nodes. Community gardens have been shown to have citizenship and social capital benefits (e.g., Glover, Parry, and Shinew 2005). The practice of permaculture also has such benefits. Furthermore, geographic and foci distribution is key to the proliferation of network impact. Corresponding to permaculture principles that seek to maximize biodiversity and interdependence, a multiplicity of nodes has more resiliency and diversity. Networks are "clumpy," that is, nodes cluster with a variety of similar types of links, meaning that subcultures form in any network. Such groupings are a key means of network differentiation, information transmission, and innovation. Lave and Wenger (1991) call these "communities of practice" and asserted that the most significant forms of learning are situated in such social relations. In his study of value innovation and cultural change, Rochon (1998) identifies the important role of "critical communities." New ideas start with key thinkers "whose experiences, reading, and interaction with each other help them to develop a set of cultural values that is out of step with the larger society" (Rochon 1998: 8). But innovations of ideas or practices require social support to maintain that out-of-stepness. This challenge is especially trenchant when one's ecological sensibilities do not correspond to the rather non-ecological orientation of contemporary society.

The development of the permaculture movement in Edmonton has unearthed the strong desire that many members of the EPN have for meaningful connections with others who share strong ecological values and who are attempting to live more consciously sustainable lives. Many of my permaculture workshop students have identified a sense of isolation, a dissatisfaction with the anonymity they experience in their neighborhoods, and a strong desire to live a more vibrant, engaged, and environmentally sensitive community life. Often this has been expressed in the desire to "start an ecovillage," either in a rural area or within the city itself. Indeed, the global ecovillage movement shares many similar origins and trajectories with permaculture. The success rate for such initiatives is not high, however, in part because of the many financial, social, and regulatory challenges they must overcome. In any case, this is not a feasible option for many city dwellers already embedded in the existing urban milieu. The alternative that has emerged, somewhat organically, from our Edmonton experience is the intentional affiliation of a growing body of citizens who share the interest and desire to live ac-

cording to permaculture principles and ethics. Thus we can consider this community of urbanites with shared passion and interest for permaculture as somewhat of a "distributed ecovillage." Not only are participants in the EPN supported in their efforts to internalize and "make normal" a lifestyle that is more connected to the landscape in which they live, but they become the social edge in their diverse communities, where their living out alternative strategies becomes a counterpoint to the non-ecological but well-entrenched milieus in which they live.

In this case, the network is distributed throughout the city. Other researchers have shown that one of the values of geographically concentrated lifeworlds as exemplified by ecovillages is that they "institute and reinforce an alternative paradigm" to the outmoded but still dominant Western worldview of human-nature independence (Kasper 2008: 12). However, the extensive built environments of cities already exist, with the path-dependency of their sunk costs. It is unlikely that many people will remove themselves from everyday and routine worlds for specifically developed ecovillages, even if they desired to do so. The intensity of living together maximizes the strong ties of a network, but research into such homophily also shows that it can weaken the diffusion of the innovations as members lose their bridges to nonmembers (Newman and Dale 2007). The permaculture network in Edmonton, although diffuse, performed a similar function, as identified by research on ecovillages. The EPN provides social conditions to serve as communities of practice in which alternative ecological practices and place/nature attentiveness could flourish.

Haluza-DeLay (2008) argued that a sustainable society needs the internalized dispositions such that we can "live environmentally without trying"; or, drawing on Bourdieu (1990), sustainability requires an "ecological habitus." An ecological habitus is "a practical logic of how to live well in this place, that is, in a socially and ecologically integrated manner" (Haluza-DeLay 2008: 44). Simply, Bourdieu described society as a set of interlocking *fields*. Each social field generates internalized dispositions in participants that participants draw on to act, which then reproduces the social fields in which their habitus is normalized. As embodied dispositions, habitus structures everyday choices—Bourdieu's "theory of practice":

> The theory of action that I propose (with the notion of habitus) amounts to saying that most human actions have as a basis something quite different from intention, that is, acquired dispositions which make it so that an action can and should be interpreted as oriented toward one objective or another without anyone being able to claim that that objective was a conscious design. (Bourdieu 1998: 97–98)

Most human action, therefore, is non-cognitive, a "practical sense" (the French term Bourdieu uses is *sens pratique,* translated into English as a "logic of practice"). Primarily, life is a "feel for the game" (one of Bourdieu's favorite metaphors), in which "individuals can exercise various strategies within the generative capacities of his or her habitus" (Reed-Danahay 25: 105). According to most commentators (and Bourdieu himself), habitus is conservative, being unlikely to diverge much from the normed routinization of the surrounding social field. Therefore, we might assume that habitus formed in one social field—such as that of a society that does not exhibit environmental sustainability—is unlikely to generate practices commensurate with other social conditions, such as genuine environmental sustainability.

So on one hand, "the practices generated by an ecological habitus are attentive to its place as a socioecological milieu" (Haluza-DeLay 2008: 214), but on the other hand, an ecological habitus is challenged by the very conditions that have generated unsustainable North American cities. One could say it is "mis-fit." Bourdieu emphasized the "fit" of a habitus to its social field as constitutive of the success of a person in navigating their social position. A conclusion we could draw is that ecological awareness is likely to be marginalized, or will reconfigure itself toward the mainstream, as it faces pressure from others to *not* subvert conventional social norms, unless there is a social field in which such an orientation does fit.

Involvement in permaculture helps participants begin to learn their bioregion—what plants grow, how to deal with climatic conditions, where their food comes from, the direction of the sun, source of water and by extension, their energy sources, housing construction products, etc., that are elements of a sustainable lifestyle. Most of all, involvement in the permaculture field legitimizes such place and nature attentiveness as practices that "fit" the permaculture field. Thus, diffusion in the field involves deliberate educational efforts, but the interrelations of the network may be even more influential in producing new norms of ecologically attentive practice. Still, permaculture remains a minor thread in Edmonton land management and yardscaping. Rochon (1998: 15) points out that "the end point of cultural change with respect to some value occurs when the value is diffused into the wider society to such a degree that it is no longer a matter of contention, or even necessarily of conscious awareness." Such an end point—where environmental behavior is not of conscious design—is exactly what the social fields of a sustainable society underpinned by ecological habitus would presumably manifest. As a distributed ecovillage, the EPN facilitated such an orientation in its affiliates, with social support and a context in which it "made sense." A key question is the degree to which permaculture can influence others toward its logic of place-based practice and substantially contribute to the trajectory toward this sustainable future.

Disturbance and Design Edges

Two other permaculture principles are relevant in considering from where ecologically sensitive lifestyle orientations can emerge. *Disturbance* provides for the possibility of new growth, wherein pioneer species with their nutrient densification initiate ecological transformation. For Bourdieu, change came only when some sort of disturbance *(hysteresis)* troubled the fit between habitus and the structure of the field (Mesny 2002). Design that *creates edges* allows diversity to flourish and different perspectives and practices to more readily encounter each other. Permaculture is edgework that disturbs the routinization of urban North America, providing invasive space for a habitus attentive to its place.

Within a couple of years, attention to proliferating naturalized yards and media about The Urban Farmer engaged city administration. Such engagement helped morph Master Gardner programs into Master Composter and Master Naturalist programs, and helped foster a movement toward a citywide municipal development master plan that embraces the possibilities of urban agriculture. This was not without controversy, as the unique microclimate of northeastern Edmonton was only protected after large-scale civil society mobilization. But participants have found that urban permaculture is disturbing in other ways. Ecoscaping yards has challenged neighborhood "nuisance" codes. One network member described trying to let the grass grow "naturally," especially as a rabbit family was being raised under a front yard bench, only to find a neighbor had mowed the yard for him. Front yard food production troubles local norms about lawns. Extending permaculture principles for growing food plants to growing animals has yielded effort to change bylaws to allow chickens in the city. Finally, permaculture principles are gleaned from observations of nature. Urban permaculture creates hybridities of nature, which are at variance with conventional assumptions about nature in terms of managed gardens or lawns, aesthetically powerful flowers, or "wild" nature from which humans are removed. Design edges—such as these hybrid "socionatures" (D. White 2006)—are among the most fertile spaces, for food production as well as for changing perspectives.

But perhaps in contrast, a rather unanticipated but integral thread that has woven its way through this permaculture tapestry has been the development of visible and invisible community structures. As the transformation of our physical space began to occur, it was simultaneously reinforced by increasing and stronger social connections. With every new development of our yard, additional neighbors stopped by to lend a hand, ask some questions, or have a look around. As the saskatoon (Amelanchier alnifolia) *hedge on the outer, public edge of our property began to produce, neighborhood children, their parents often in tow, came around for a feed. I have connected with many "old-timers" in the neighborhood who were gardening and raising chickens in the city decades before I was born. To them I can go for advice on grafting my fruit trees, digging a cold cellar, making wine, or pruning tomatoes. My immediate neighbor offered up approximately 3,500 square feet of unused backyard space where we have created an edible forest garden that offers a tremendous harvest of edible and medicinal species while attracting numerous birds, bees, butterflies, and other wildlife to our community. Out of these casual interactions have grown many strong connections within the neighborhood, with functional interrelationships ("I scratch your back, you scratch mine") set in place. The transformation of our yard has not only offered me an intimate partnership with the local ecology, it has woven the social connections back into the living system that is this place. We now harvest a significant portion of our annual diet of fresh produce (fruit, berries, vegetables, and herbs) from here; but the social, emotional, and spiritual yields are equally valuable to us.*

Discussion and Conclusion

Permaculture adds to the "culture of enchantment" lacking in the modern North American urban world. It also contributes a place awareness and interrelationship of social and ecological linkages that can be a foundation for increased orientation toward sustainability. In direct contest with modernity's attempted erasures of nature and dualisms of nature-society, permaculture weaves them together again. The urban dynamic is a messy hybrid of "socionatures"—interacting natural and social features that are combinations of what we casually segregate as either "social" or "natural." In permaculture the "natural" and "cultural" are indissoluble. While those engaging in permaculture are a community of interest, the practice also facilitates social networks and communities of geographical connections as well.

Participants in the Edmonton permaculture network derive a variety of self-described benefits from their involvement. The majority of participants in the introductory workshops had no previous involvement in permaculture but frequently remarked that they had been searching for something like this for a long time. Many participants resonate with the "solutions-focused" nature of permaculture practice. Permaculture training offers a tool kit of concrete, context-specific strategies for making positive changes right where a person is. Approximately one-third of workshop participants choose to become active in the EPN following their experience. Some participants are active in other sustainability initiatives. Others take their learning into their own lives and many seek out ongoing contact with the broader permaculture community.

The permaculture network is a learning community. First, participants learn that their *place* matters, from their microplace (as in a front yard) to larger places such as Edmonton. Place has been claimed as an important way of thinking about public policy (Bradford 2005). Second, participants continue to build a different awareness than the mainstream population, part of which includes the perhaps obvious but important notion that the ecology of place should be a source of attention. Their permaculture practices do, in some cases, blend into other place-relevant practices, such as alternative economies or public transit. Finally, permaculture network participants engage (in various ways) with relations in community. This community is important as a source of social support for the place-oriented, environmental awareness that has already been identified and that has been described as an "ecological habitus."

The notion of an ecological habitus is the final valuable outcome of this study. As an expertise developed from a sense of place, ecological habitus contributes to a practical logic of how to live well in this place; that is, in a socially and ecologically integrated manner. Bourdieu's social anthropology demonstrates that behavior is always a product of active relations between social institutions and networks and the variety of agents operating in them. Environmentally consistent behavior is similarly shaped by this interplay of agents and fields, undergirded by their understanding of "how to play the game" in contemporary society. The genius of permaculture is that it says a different game is afoot. Such a perspective is more likely to gain traction when supported by social relations in which these new rules of reintegrating human be-ing and local ecologies are encouraged, facilitated, supported, and made sensible.

Notes

1. Salleh's work reminds us of the need to attribute political economic analyses, along with gender, to the political ecologies of environmental degradation and restoration. In the EPN there are many more women than men. For space reasons, we do not interrogate this in this paper.

References

Anderson, Leon. 2006. "Analytic Autoethnography." *Journal of Contemporary Ethnography* 35 (4): 73–95.

Bourdieu, Pierre. 1990. *The Logic of Reason*. Stanford: Stanford University Press.

———. 1998. *Practical Reason*. Cambridge: Polity Press.

Bradford, Neil. 2005. *Place-Based Public Policy: Towards a New Urban and Community Agenda for Canada*. Ottawa: Canadian Policy Research Networks. Available at http://cprn.org/doc.cfm?doc=1186&l=en.

Bullough, R. V., and S. Pinneager. 2001. "Guidelines for Quality in Autobiographical Forms of Self-Study Research." *Educational Researcher* 30 (3): 13–21.

Crossley, Nick. 2008. "Small-World Networks, Complex Systems and Sociology." *Sociology* 42 (2): 261–77.

Diani, Mario, and Doug McAdam. 2003. *Social Movements and Networks: Relational Approaches to Collective Action.* Oxford: Oxford University Press.

Ellis, Carolyn, and Arthur P. Bochner. 2000. "Autoethnography, Personal Narrative, Reflexivity: Researcher As Subject." In *Handbook of Qualitative Research,* 2nd ed., ed. Norman K. Denzin and Yvonne S. Lincoln. Thousand Oaks, CA: Sage Publications.

Foster, John Bellamy. 2002. *Ecology Against Capitalism.* New York: Monthly Review Press.

Gibson, James William. 2009. *A Reenchanted World: The Quest for a New Kinship with Nature.* New York: Metropolitan Books.

Glover, Troy D., Diana C. Parry, and Kimberly J. Shinew. 2005. "Building Relationships, Accessing Resources: Mobilizing Social Capital in Community Garden Contexts." *Journal of Leisure Research* 37 (4): 450–74.

Gruenewald, David A. 2003. "Foundations of Place: A Multidisciplinary Framework for Place-Conscious Education." *American Educational Research Journal* 40 (3): 619–54.

Haluza-DeLay, Randolph B. 1997. "Remystifying the City." *Green Teacher* 52: 5–8.

———. 2008. "A Theory of Practice for Social Movements: Environmentalism and Ecological Habitus." *Mobilization* 13 (2): 205–18.

———. 2010. "Place." In *The Encyclopedia of Sustainability, Vol. 1: The Spirit of Sustainability,* ed. Willis Jenkins. Great Barrington, MA: Berkshire.

Hildreth, Paul M., and Chris Kimble. 2004. *Knowledge Networks: Innovation through Communities of Practice.* London: Idea Group.

Hiller, Harry. 2009. *Urban Canada.* 2nd ed. Toronto: Oxford University Press.

Kasper, Debbie V. S. 2008. "Redefining Community in the Ecovillage." *Human Ecology Review* 15 (1): 12–24.

Kenworthy, Jeffrey R. 2006. "The Eco-City: Ten Key Transport and Planning Dimensions for Sustainable City Development." *Environment and Urbanization* 18 (1): 67–85.

Lave, Jean, and Etienne Wenger. 1991. *Situated Learning: Legitimate Peripheral Participation.* Cambridge: Cambridge University Press.

Mesny, Anne. 2002. "A View on Bourdieu's Legacy: *Sens pratique* v. *Hysteresis.*" *Canadian Journal of Sociology* 27 (1): 59–67.

Newman, Lenore, and Ann Dale. 2007. "Homophily and Agency: Creating Effective Sustainable Development Networks." *Environment, Development and Sustainability* 9 (1): 79–90.

Pearman, Myrna, and Ted Pike. 2000. *NatureScape Alberta: Creating and Caring for Wildlife Habitat at Home.* Edmonton: Federation of Alberta Naturalists.

Polkinghorne, Donald. 1988. *Narrative Knowing and the Human Sciences.* Albany: State University of New York Press.

Reed-Danahay, Deborah. 2005. *Locating Bourdieu.* Bloomington, IN: Indiana University Press.

Rochon, Thomas. 1998. *Culture Moves: Ideas, Activism and Changing Values.* Princeton, NJ: Princeton University Press.

Salleh, Ariel. 2010. "From Metabolic Rift to 'Metabolic Value': Reflections on Environmental Sociology and the Alternative Globalization Movement." *Organization and Environment* 23 (2): 205–19.

Spaling, Harry, and John R. Wood. 1998. "Greed, Need or Creed? Farmland Ethics in the Rural-Urban Fringe." *Land Use Policy* 15 (2): 105–18.

Veteto, James R., and Joshua Lockyer. 2008. "Environmental Anthropology Engaging Permaculture: Moving Theory and Practice Toward Sustainability." *Culture & Agriculture* 30 (1–2): 47–58.

White, Damian. 2006. "A Political Sociology of Socionatures: Revisionist Manoeuvres in Environmental Sociology." *Environmental Politics* 15 (1): 59–77.

White, Douglas R. 2007. "Innovation in the Context of Networks, Hierarchies, and Cohesion." *A New Perspective on Innovation and Social Change,* ed. David Lane, Geoff West, Sander van der Leeuw, and Denise Pumain. Dordrecht, the Netherlands: Springer Methodos Series.

Williams, Sara. 1997. *Creating the Prairie Xeriscape.* Saskatoon: University of Saskatchewan Press.

Chapter Eight

Culture, Permaculture, and Experimental Anthropology in the Houston Foodshed

Bob Randall

For twenty-one years beginning in 1987, I directed Urban Harvest, Inc. (UHI), and its predecessor at the Interfaith Hunger Coalition. UHI is an effort to alter agricultural and horticultural land use in Houston, the United States' fourth largest city and sixth largest metropolitan area. Starting with no desk or telephone, an increasing number of us gradually built an organization that today has over a dozen staff, a one-million-dollar budget, a large network of volunteers, and interacts with thousands of people weekly (Urban Harvest n.d.). More importantly, it has had a significant impact on the horticultural land use and diet within the Houston metropolitan area, and through emulation of its programs has had impacts elsewhere. In a significant way, this development was made possible by combining permaculture design concepts with cognitive-linguistic–derived ethnographic theories of adaptation and culture change.

My work with UHI was not in the applied anthropology tradition of helping an existing agency achieve its goals. Rather, I used anthropological concepts and methods to start and lead an agency designed to affect a solution. As such, I played a primary role in formulating and implementing strategies, so my effort was thus consciously closer to the classic scientific tradition of using experiments to test theories. None of these experimental strategies were tried solely because of my decisions, however, and the reasons others in the group backed particular courses of action were only in part the same as mine. Inevitably, therefore, what follows is a better portrayal of my observations and analysis, and is a less accurate portrayal of the many others who contributed in major ways to our successes.

Using Permaculture to Reform the Foodshed

Permaculture is a branch of applied human ecology with three key global end goals: *care of people, care of earth,* and *share the surplus fairly.* Its power to achieve these goals for individuals and bioregions derives from a remarkable synthesis of design-build principles developed worldwide over many years by Australians Bill Mollison and David Holmgren, their students, and students of their students (Mollison and Holmgren 1978). These principles derive in part from rigorous attention to:

- The stabilizing connections and processes in forest ecology
- Ancient and modern ideas from anywhere on the planet that promote the key end goals
- Energy both in the form of daily human labor and as it flows through a system
- Energy as it is embodied in the production, transportation, use, and decomposition of tools, supplies, equipment, and structures

Permaculture posits that earth care is an urgent global problem that requires sharing among populations; restricting all forms of energy consumption; and working locally in small-scale projects. Typically, permaculturally designed landscapes, homes, and villages reduce waste and effort while increasing benefits. Permaculture's main ideas are found in several texts, in particular Mollison's *Permaculture: A Designers' Manual* (1988); in the core design and ethical principles (SEED International n.d.a, n.d.b); and in the curriculum of the Permaculture Design Certificate course (Permaculture Institute 2010). There is also a rich implementation history in all of the world's biomes and regions.[1]

Mollison has sometimes described permaculture as the effort to design engineered ecosystems, and more bluntly as the art of not defecating in your own bed (1991b). Broadly, permaculture is an intelligent critique of the destructive design of civilization and the less than consistent attention all large organizations have historically paid to sustainability issues. As Mollison described it in his early works, modern life is based on ever-depleting fossil fuels, ecosystem collapse, and climate-destroying emissions, so all people on the planet need to urgently redesign their food, housing, transportation, and other systems before life becomes impossible. Mollison says, "People are the most difficult factor in any design," because they thoughtlessly commit "Type One Errors" (1988: 58, 32). Rather than cooperate with nature, people unnecessarily battle ecosystems and physics. Our task, then, is to help people organize bioregions permaculturally before they and other species perish.

Permaculture, Culture, and Subsistence Cognition

In permacultural discourse, the definition of *culture* has always been tacit and not considered problematic. Permaculture derives from the common etymological roots of *agriculture* and *culture* in everyday English (Mollison 1991a). As Mollison put it decades ago (1981), societies without a permanent (sustainable) agriculture cannot have a sustainable culture either, and very likely will not last.

Culture, in Mollison's usage, is what is in jeopardy. Its relation to the problems and their solutions is therefore not the main part of his inquiry. Few permaculturists, accordingly, have paid attention to anthropological debates about the meaning of culture or believe it makes much of a difference to the fate of the planet. But in social and other sciences, concepts do matter and definitions point out what needs attention, so a good definition of culture could help permaculturists be effective.

In the long run, our concept of culture must not be at odds with what we know about culture change, subsistence, economics, or human knowledge and its mental and neural manifestation in memory. If permacultural end goals are to be achieved, our concept of culture must make the task of instigating sustainable changes easier. We need to understand how people conceptualize their basic life support activities and how they engage in problem-solving strategies concerning them. A different way of life needs to be substituted, so cultural investigation needs to uncover underlying principles of subsistence knowledge and thinking that will make the substitution easier to achieve.

At Urban Harvest, I used an understanding of cultural knowledge about subsistence change derived from research I did among Philippine Samal fishermen-farmers (Randall 1977, 1987). I used a cognitive understanding of subsistence culture to determine if the food system could be changed easily; concepts of metaphorical and analogical framing to enlist and empower organizational supporters; and permacultural design to create a highly functional organization that has effects over a large area. In order to explain how this happened, I need to briefly review my research on Samal subsistence change.

Adaptive Subsistence Plan Making

The Samal I studied practiced over seventy long and arduous types of fishing and farming for both cash and subsistence (Randall 1977). One type of night fishing *(aglaway,* "multihooking the purse-eyed scad") involved about fourteen hours of activity derived from a plan that sequenced hundreds of subplans. The exact sequence was routinely altered based on "current conditions," "moon brightness," "how well the fish were biting," "how healthy the fisherman was," whether there were "pirates in the area" or "high seas," and much more. If one studies many such routine plans, it becomes obvious that plans for achieving major life goals consist of hundreds of subplans having the same basic abstract goal structure. These giant plans are not rote-memorized, but, as in sentences in language, are strung together correctly in context as needed.

To make a "desired change" one must have a subplan to acquire all kinds of necessary means. They therefore must be possessed, located where they can be used, and in usable condition. One must also prevent anything or anyone who will prevent the desired change. Then after one uses an activity to implement the change to the desired state, one must then prevent change to an undesired state. Since getting each means and "preventing preventers" are themselves "desired changes" needing means, it is easy to see how human subsistence plans can be very large while having a relatively simple, highly repetitive, generative goal structure (Randall 1987).

More importantly, my analysis made it fairly obvious how and why Samal technology sometimes changed and sometimes did not (Randall 1977). Change happened quickly if:

- An alternative preferred subsistence plan was known to fishermen-farmers
- The means were easily available to implement the plan
- No one or thing was expected to prevent it

Change did not happen when villagers thought one or more of these preconditions were absent. In Houston, as we will see, this checklist for assessing change possibilities proved very helpful in selecting strategies that worked.

Early Efforts to Reform the Foodshed

Many of the programs and services UHI has today drew from beginning efforts in community gardens, hunger relief, and organic food and gardening prior to 1987 (Cutler 2006). With Mollison's visits to Texas and Houston from 1987 to 1994, these fledgling efforts were all conceptually connected by those few of us who knew about his work.

In the 1980s, food insecurity, hunger, and malnutrition rose dramatically across the United States (Physician Task Force on Hunger in America 1985), and by 1986 there were a million requests for emergency food in the Houston area. In this context, the Interfaith Hunger Coalition decided to start a food gardening program. An advisory group of mainly anti-hunger activists from impoverished neighborhoods recruited me as a volunteer advisor.

During the course of my volunteer year, I wondered why there was so much hunger and malnutrition in an area that had bountiful supplies of available land and nearly perfect year-round conditions for growing the widest selection of crops. I analyzed the situation using my subsistence planning theories and found no obvious impediments to change:

- The goal of providing adequate high quality food should be a high-level goal shared by everyone in the area.
- The means for growing cheap food could be made cheaply available to those that wanted to garden.
- Several well-connected Houstonians confirmed no one wanted to prevent this change.

So our project to reduce hunger substantially through community gardening projects seemed like it had a very high potential for success.

However, in 1988, when they hired me to manage the community gardening project, I discovered it would not be easy. We lost three of our first four gardens because antihunger activists designed them poorly and were short on labor, money, and knowledge. For the next six years, we gradually learned what worked and what did not. We learned to work with groups rather than individuals; required garden starters to take classes first; and learned from experience how to design gardens appropriate to communities, goals, and means.

What started as an antihunger project expanded in scope as we discovered that the food problems of the poor were related to the problems of all residents. By 1990, we believed that the Houston area food system was doing a mediocre job providing food to the 85 percent who were food secure, and a bad job providing it to the 15 percent who were not (Randall [1986] 2006; Randall and Taylor 1991). Moreover, we believed the system to be unsustainable over the longer run. We found that:

- The food system is based on a fossil fuel– and import-intensive world market that is potentially vulnerable to disruption in fuel costs, exchange rates, or climate-induced food shortages (Randall 1995a).
- The long-distance trade in food favors energy-dense meats and starches (as well as pesticide-laden produce selected for transportability and long shelf lives) over fresh, local produce selected for taste and nutrition (Hardy 1990; Randall 1995b).
- Taste is "improved" by salt, fat, sugar, and additives, rather than natural flavors. The result is a disease-causing diet and major health, economic, and educational problems for cities and their rural surroundings (Randall 1995a).

In general, the high-level goal everyone has for good food is not achieved by the long-distance food system, so this analysis suggested the system could be replaced with a better one if enough people became aware of an affordable alternative. How to make them aware became our main strategic question, and for that we turned to cognitive frames.

Metaphor, Analogy, and Organizational Strategy

There is an impressive body of research in linguistics, cognitive psychology, psychiatry, and anthropology that roots much of human reasoning and behavior in conceptualizing one thing as being "like" another. Young children learn to distinguish birds from bees and airplanes (Piaget [1926] 1999). Language speakers master fairly arbitrary grammatical categories, and use narrative *frames* about typical actors, scenes, and activities to understand what people are talking about (Fillmore 1985). More abstract comparisons between similar things like analogies, metaphors, and similes are constantly used to understand, reason, explain, convince, complain, manipulate, organize, and even invent (Goffman 1974; Schön 1983; Gavetti and Rivkin 2005; Feldman 2006; Lakoff 2008).

The general point is that people endlessly classify their experiences and draw analogical and metaphorical parallels based on them. They do this mostly unconsciously while communicating, interacting, and problem solving. For permaculture to be an effective sustainability strategy for remaking the planet, it must make use of analogical and metaphorical frames people already have to help them develop ecological practices and frames they currently do not employ. Permaculturists observe "patterns," and in humans, frames of many types are important patterns guiding behavior.

Much of what we did to make Houstonians aware of gardening required persuasive communication. In 1987, most area residents had a concept of "food," "farming," and "gardening" that was quite different from what we wanted them to have. Their frames involved supermarkets and restaurants for "getting food;" out-of-state agribusiness for "farms"; and lawns or azaleas for "gardening." We wanted to change these frames toward local, small-scale, organic food that would benefit the poor.

The Positive Contagion Frame

In 1988, we did not have the means to communicate the ease, productivity, and quality of the local gardening alternative directly to the poor. Because of this lack of resources, our first strategy was to use a *contagion* spreading analogy. Nature is full of contagious diseases and many other phenomena (pioneer species, fire spread, gas diffusion, cloud formation, insect infestation) that mimic the pattern of one isolated or concentrated incidence spreading outward in ever-increasing scope. Ideas too are said to be "contagious" or even "viral." A good idea supposedly spreads with little effort.

Permaculture exploits nature's patterns in its designs, but in 1988, our strategy was dominated less by permaculture than by pedagogical and community-organizing ideas related to demonstration projects. Broadly, our strategy was to put an example of good public food gardening where residents would see it and learn from it. This fit our means, borrowed from Agricultural Extension's time-tested approach, and needed very few participants or resources to create what amounted to a billboard for better food.

In those years, our few exemplary community gardens were sometimes copied when both the exemplary garden and the copy operated in similar situations. So part of our strategy was to show potential community gardeners sites similar to those they contemplated. Later, we taught classes that matched the design needs of a potential community gardener to their situation.

There were some spectacular successes. Inner-city, food-pantry gardens at churches in low-income African American communities produced and distributed tons of food and were emulated many times. We developed ways to design specific types of community gardens: where families rent allotments, at community action agencies, at homeless shelters, in parks, at schools, and at church food pantries. We also figured out how to teach adult gardening classes and used these skills to design more successful classes. In 2001, UHI began an annual fruit tree sale, providing the best fruit plants in one place, and the idea of fruit tree sales spread. The school district helped us develop outdoor classrooms at schools and UHI's farmers' markets ideas spread. Accounts of UHI gardens and ideas also spread nationally—San Antonio, Waco, Atlanta, and other cities studied UHI programs and copied them.

Our contagion strategy also produced many failures. Most of the poor knew almost nothing about how to grow food efficiently, nor did they know its potential advantages. They frequently had disabilities that interfered with gardening, they moved frequently, and addiction and incarceration rates were high. In addition, in low-income communities, paying work was valued over volunteer work, and physical labor jobs made volunteer physical labor like gardening unattractive. Additionally, many residents or their relatives had fled a hard life of agricultural labor, so they and those they influenced hated food growing. In contagion terms, many people were "immune" to infection even by virulent strains of "great gardening."

As well, community garden builders often had little money and had a steep learning curve in gardening and organizing, so their gardens often were not exemplary or emulated. Media and potential financial supporters too did not know or value food gardening, so they often ignored our efforts. Also, our small staff and board had little life experience trying to "infect" anything, so even a wonderful inner-city project failed to spread.

Put in the permaculture terms just beginning to spread through Texas at the time, infections spread in nature only to some individuals. We should have realized from the start that people might have many reasons for not growing food. "Good gardening" ideas stubbornly refused to spread themselves, as a real *contagion* should, so we needed an alternative strategy.

In subsistence planning terms, we did not have the means easily available to spread the gardening ideas ourselves. For that we needed an agency with a broader mission able to acquire more resources. We needed help from government, media, religious congregations, and the well off. However, they did not themselves understand the possibilities. Moreover, most of them, we gradually concluded, did not have "Feeding the Hungry" among their higher goals. So in 1995, we converted this goal into "Healthy Quality Food for Everyone." By converting the first goal into the second, we helped create a program where every resident stood to benefit, so everyone had a reason to support us. What seven years of the contagion approach got us was about a dozen dedicated and skilled supporters who in 1994 formed Urban Harvest.

Strategic Planning Frames for Businesses and Nonprofits

When UHI incorporated to receive charitable donations in the mid-1990s, it took on many similarities to for-profit organizations: vision, mission, board, officers, tax accounting, attorneys, timesheets, and much else. It also took on an increasing number of supporters with business development experience. Inevitably, these supporters drew analogies with business planning ideas. "Urban Harvest is a business" was a common metaphoric frame used in their strategic arguments.

Accordingly, UHI adopted a corporate-modeled strategic plan. The idea was to have a short and clear vision, a mission, and a strategic plan. Each volunteer committee became "a department" that had a small number of quantitative goals, a timeline, and reporting requirements. By focusing on a small number of goals, resources were supposed to be concentrated, thus increasing the likelihood of success. However, by dropping from prominence goals that some supporters held dear, we lost effort and enthusiasm. There were fewer resources, not more.

Nonprofits like ours needed to attract "supporters." These are donors, staff working at below-market wages, and skilled volunteers who donate labor and resources. Supporters want to work successfully on what they think is important. If they are successful, they will work even harder and recruit more supporters. We therefore learned to take seriously any supporter-driven, feasible, strategic goal related to foodshed improvement, and our subsequent strategic plans focused on attracting, using, and keeping supporters (cf. Kretzmann and McKnight 1993).

Accordingly, our more successful strategic plans for 2001 and 2006 were lengthy, multiple-goaled, and incorporated preferences and plans of all supporter groups. One result was a rapid increase in funding, staff, and capacity to spread food reform ideas. Put in permacultural terms, our programs were increasingly designed to achieve many purposes, to have backups for key functions such as fundraising, and to use low-cost supporter labor highly effectively.

The Schooling Frame

We needed an easy way to explain to supporters what we were trying to do. However, the area's educated and affluent had no idea how to grow food, nor had they eaten the many tasty and nutritious fruits and vegetables only available from local production. So enlisting their labor or monetary support was difficult. We needed a better way to do this.

Anyone who speaks publicly about the benefits of gardening often hears "I just don't have a green thumb" given as a reason for not gardening. Because I had worked with book illiterates, I was familiar with a similar excuse: "I never seemed to get the hang of reading and writing." In reality, of course, illiterates probably had no opportunity to learn, so they think they were "born stupid." One day, I noticed the green thumb resemblance to the literacy frame and realized we could describe the problem we were fighting as "overcoming horticultural and ecological illiteracy." This helped us attract funders, frame our outreach and teaching effort, and motivate volunteers.

By 2001, we started talking about "hortliteracy" and "our school system to teach gardening horticulture." In this frame, the neighborhood "horticulture elementary schools" were community and school gardens; the "high schools" taught adults in multisession gardening classes; and our "higher education" taught permaculture and offered workshops for farmers, teachers, and organic landscapers. In that strategic plan, our long-term goal became "extending hortliteracy to everyone." We defined "everyone" as: the urban, rural, and suburban; the affluent, poor, and middle class; the educated and uneducated; and all ages, abilities, and languages.

This strategy helped UHI grow dramatically because people knew the literacy frame. Once they understood that most people were "gardening illiterate," they increasingly supported horticultural illiteracy's eradication. More importantly, the frame helped our supporters participate effectively and enthusiastically in our efforts. In frame analysis terms, we substituted a common cultural narrative about schools, teachers, and literacy for residents' previous frames regarding food, farms, supermarkets, and gardening. In permacultural terms, we used a commonly observed pattern in the culture to design an effective campaign to change the foodshed toward permaculture end goals.

By itself, the gardening school frame could not create mass hortliteracy, or achieve deeper bioregional sustainability goals. This "schooling" only attracted those already curious about gardening. So we asked, how could we reach horticulturally illiterate adults uninterested in community gardens and classes? Since all residents eat or make landscaping decisions, we launched programs for non-gardeners. We launched Houston's first certified farmers' market in seventy years and started an organic education alliance of horticultural businesses. Both efforts have since multiplied many times in size and scope.

The farmers' markets provided weekly education for people who liked to eat well. By demonstrating the quality of local food, additional support for local farming was created. Because of rural farmer participation, urban farmers' markets also exported ideas about sustainable horticulture to rural areas. Similarly, the organic horticultural business alliance provided education about organic landscaping to businesses that manage multiple parcels of land for large organizations and wealthy individuals. Their new knowledge inevitably exported to their upper-income clients.

Permaculturally Designed Ecosystem Frames

UHI creates designs for gardens, outdoor classrooms, farmers' markets, classes, fruit tree sales, and its own organization. Although the term *permaculture* is only rarely part of UHI's public face, it has nevertheless been a major part of its designs since 1996. Probably two dozen staff and board members have been permaculturists, naturalists, organic gardeners, or all of these, so the principles and analogies of ecology, organic gardening, and permaculture have greatly influenced UHI's designs.

By 1997, Urban Harvest was running many food-related programs: classes for adults, a demonstration garden, community and school gardens, market gardening, and more. As discussed above, all this activity led the corporate planning frame advocates to support narrowing goals. The permaculturists saw it differently. They wanted to use *ecological growth* analogies to guide UHI's advance.

By background, our 1998 board president was a published naturalist and organic advocate. During one debate, he argued successfully that UHI "needed to grow organically." He believed we should grow capacity by evolving slowly like ecosystems do. The development of one process, he said, will make another one possible; and the resiliency, functionality, and stability of a mature ecosystem will eventually be obtained. We permaculturists argued that a polycultural farm is less risky than a monocropped one, and a mature, highly diverse, interconnected natural ecosystem out-produces a lawn or a wheat farm. We said analogously that promoting many diverse programs designed to reform the foodshed would be more productive and less risky than specializing in schools only, hunger prevention only, or farmers' markets only. The permacultural frame prevailed and played a crucial role in Urban Harvest's subsequent rapid rise.

As a result, my gardening book became a local best seller (Randall 2006) and our board president's habitat gardening books became influential in landscaping (cf. Bowen 1998); numbers of classes and attendance doubled and doubled again; the permaculture designers' curriculum was offered cheaply and constantly; the annual fruit tree sale grew from $14,000 to $140,000; community gardens grew to over 150; outdoor classrooms at schools grew to 70; and the number of farmers' markets grew to two dozen.

Zoning Frames

Mollison points out that farms, kitchens, and all aspects of design should be organized by permaculturists to minimize labor (Mollison 1988: 48–57). A farm should be *zoned* to have daily activities nearby with less frequent activity functions more distant. UHI used the zone analogy to organize its staffing.

Today, for example, UHI has three main programs: community gardens, farmers' markets, and education. Each of these three core programs has subprograms designed to promote the higher-level goal of each program. There is an effort to fund, staff, and guide all of these with staff oversight or volunteer committees assigned to run them. As such, they have a resemblance to the hierarchical branching organizational structures common in large organizations.

However, at UHI the permaculture zone frame overlays the branch pattern. The programs and subprograms are all zoned for resource efficiency according to how much paid and volunteer labor is required. Core administrative functions—including staff support, relations with other agencies, fund-raising, some outreach, and finance—use a lot of paid staff resources. Similarly, adult classes, the farmers' markets, contract community garden, and school garden services all use daily paid labor resources. By comparison, programs like organic landscaping are run almost entirely by volunteers.

Sector Frames

A core principle of permaculture is to use free resources rather than waste them. Designers should pay attention to exogenous *sector* energies and resources (like sunlight, rain, dust, birds, or even windblown trash) that enter and exit system boundaries unaided (Mollison 1988: 48–57). Supporters and community-donated assets are the main nonprofit free resource. So UHI designed outreach activities at the farmers' markets and at gardening classes to funnel potential supporters into other programs. These designs attracted and retained volunteers and donors because they incorporated supporters' passions successfully. The permaculture frame focused our attention on the necessity of looking for free resources and using them.

Symbiotic Frames

For additional functionality, UHI also densely connected these programs. In nature, food-webs are everywhere, but not all connections are of the predator-prey type. Guilds of symbiotic species gain benefits from connections that neither could obtain by themselves. For example, mycorrhizal fungi provide minerals and nitrogen to plant roots and get sugars in return. Permaculturists use this idea in design to connect both living and nonliving design elements beneficially (Mollison 1988: 58).

UHI began to connect different programs together. For example, in the farmers' markets, thousands of people per week have been educated about what grows in season, so the market is used to recruit students for gardening and permaculture classes. Classes are used to recruit school and community gardeners and customers for the farmers' market. The organic business alliance uses local farm produce for their meetings, thus introducing organic landscapers (and maybe their clients) to both sustainable food and farmers' markets.

The power of this permacultural organizing frame, however, is greater than mere symbiosis. In permaculture, the emergent benefits of connection and edge are designed and used. By connecting the outdoor classrooms to the farmers' markets, we conceived "Kids' Market Day." School children sell produce they grow, display garden art they make, and also learn both art and arithmetic. Parents visit the market and become customers, so both programs benefit by the connection. Wealthy customers at the market also interact with low-income school children and their art. Thus, everyone learns something new to appreciate about their community and its schools.

Function Stacking Frames

Mollison also argues that wise resource use runs counter to single-purpose design elements. In forests, trees perform many functions. Analogously, permaculturists should design to achieve multiple goals from all energy investments. Space should be *stacked with functions* vertically, horizontally, and over time.

We assessed how well each part of the Urban Harvest effort achieved multiple goals, listed the multiple goals UHI subprograms were intended to achieve, and assessed the degree to which they achieved them (Table 8.1). We then used this result to plan how to do a better job of achieving those goals, and made plans to increase the number of goals each subprogram achieved. Over time, UHI has increased function stacking in its programs. For example, the fruit tree sale was originally patronized only by the more affluent, but over time we have increased the food security and science education functions of the sale by involving schools and gardens from low-income neighborhoods.

Organizations with many programs densely woven together contribute to an overall perception of the organization's abilities, worth, and frugal use of donated funds. Supporters make comments like, "I am amazed how much Urban Harvest does with what it has." This sort of perception attracts more volunteers and donors, and as in ecosystems, high functionality and interconnectedness promote growth. More importantly, there is evidence that Urban Harvest is increasingly able to help area residents achieve permacultural end goals.

Substantive Results

It is not possible to trace the effect of our early food system critiques on the national movement for organic and local foods (Randall and Taylor 1991; Dromgoole 1992; Randall 1995a, 1995b), nor is it easy to understand that movement's effects on Houston. So our effect locally is uncertain. By

Table 8.1. Urban Harvest function stacking and labor allocation by program. Table by Bob Randall.

KEY: V= very; H= high; M= medium; L= low; Neg: Negative	Com. Gardens	Schools	Market Farming	Adult Classes	Fundraising	Oversight	Outreach	Landscaping	Permaculture	Fruit Sale
Function										
Community Development	H	H	H	M	VL	VL	M	L	H	L
Food Security	VH	VH	VH	H	VL	VL	H	VL	M	VH
Quality of Life	H	H	VH	VH	VL	VL	M	M	H	VH
Health Nutrition	VH	VH	H	H	VL	VL	H	M	M	VH
Hort. Literacy	H	VH	L	VH	L	VL	VH	VH	M	VH
Science Ed	L	VH	VL	M	VL	VL	L	VH	H	M
Value of Nature	VL	H	VL	M	VL	VL	M	H	VH	L
Envir. Stability & Sustainability	M	H	M	H	VL	VL	H	VH	VH	VH
Sust. Economic Development	L	L	H	H	VL	VL	H	VH	M	VH
Economic Empowerment	M	M	VH	VH	VL	VL	M	H	L	M
Net Income	Neg	M	VL	M	VH	Neg	M	L	L	VH
Labor Zone 1	1	2	3							
Staff & $ Cost	VH	VH	VH	H	VH	VH	M	—	—	—
Vol. Labor	VH	VL	M	H	VH	VH	H	—	—	—
Labor Zone 2	4	5	6							
Staff & $ Cost	M	L	VL	—	—	—	—	—	—	—
Vol. Labor	VH	L	L	—	—	—	—	—	—	—
Labor Zone 3	7	8	9							
Staff & $ Cost	L	VL	VL	—	—	—	—	VL	L	L

[1] Contract projects in low-income neighborhoods.
[2] After-school programs
[3] Urban Harvest Farmers' Markets
[4] "High Leverage" community garden projects.
[5] Other youth projects in low-income neighborhoods.
[6] Efforts to promote market farming by low-income
[7] Other promising community garden projects
[8] Other youth projects.
[9] Other farmer education and support.

almost any easily researched criterion, however, the UHI experiment has been a substantial success.

When we started, few people knew food could be grown locally (Hardy 1990). An independent 2009 scientific survey says 42 percent of Houston's Harris County residents now consider the *ability to buy local food very important,* and 83 percent consider it at least *somewhat important* (Klineberg 2010: 18).

Less direct successes include:

- UHI started with $500 in 1994 and now budgets $1,000,000.
- The city of Houston is promoting UHI's programs. It built more community gardens in 2010 than in its previous history, and the mayor has opened both a farmers' market and a community garden at city hall (Galvez 2010; Cook 2010).
- Weekly farmers' markets grew from zero to twenty-four; annual fruit tree sales from zero to nine; adult organic gardening classes from one to ninety-six; community and school gardens from three to one hundred and fifty; organic horticultural business alliance members from five to one hundred and twenty.
- Four hundred and seventy volunteers have been given awards for five years or more of service.
- Locally owned garden supply stores have mostly shifted to organic products and many more gardeners are trying to attract birds and butterflies.
- UHI's rise was listed in the 1 January 2000 Millennial Edition of Texas's largest newspaper as one of top ten most influential area gardening developments ever (Huber 2000). I was given several major public awards for hunger alleviation, environmental sustainability, peace, and justice, including one for $50,000 in public health leadership.

Broadly, permaculture ethical goals, together with the use of ethnographically discovered frames and permacultural design frames—as well as lengthy effort—have resulted in substantial transformation of the metropolitan foodshed.

Theoretical Results and Implications

This effort provides some experimental evidence that both permacultural and ethnographically salient frames can be used effectively to achieve permaculture end goals, because they are also widely sought-after life goals. If this approach can be replicated elsewhere, permaculturists will have a powerful theory for creating adaptive change. To carry out such changes, however, one needs an agency that is managed or strongly influenced by ethnographically and permaculture-trained personnel. More than likely, to be effective in implementing the permaculture end goals such personnel need to experiment with frames like the ones proposed above.

The Urban Harvest approach appears to work especially when the proposed change fits the subsistence planning rule cognition theory I have proposed elsewhere (Randall 1987). Specifically, this change happens if a better alternative is known and people agree it is better; the proposed change accomplishes a very high-level goal for nearly everyone and is not easily prevented; and the means to implement the change are easily and cheaply available. Advocates of change need to look for opportunities with these characteristics, because they are easier changes to make—and success may help acquire the resources necessary to tackle more challenging problems involving opposition or scarce means.

Notes

1. See The Permaculture Activist website at www.permacultureactivist.net or video search "permaculture" for examples.

References

Bowen, Mark. 1998. *Habitat Gardening for Houston and Southeast Texas.* Houston: River Bend.

Cook, Alison. 2010. "Wednesday City Hall Farmers Market Could Be a Turning Point." *Houston Chronicle,* 16 October, Star sec. Available at http://blogs.chron.com/cookstour/archives/2010/10/wednesday_city.html.

Cutler, Leigh H. 2006. "On Common Ground: A History Of The Community Gardening Movement in Twentieth-Century Houston" (MA thesis, University of Houston).

Dromgoole, John. 1992. "Community Gardens." *The New Garden.* No. 213. San Antonio, TX: PBS Television.

Feldman, Jerome. 2006. *From Molecule to Metaphor.* Cambridge, MA: MIT Press.

Fillmore, Charles. 1985. "Frames and the Semantics of Understanding." *Quaderni di Semantica* 6: 222–53.

Galvez, Melissa. 2010. "Vegetable Gardens At City Hall." Public Television Channel 8, Houston, 7 June. http://app1.kuhf.org/houston_public_radio-news-display.php?articles_id=1275884496 (accessed 2 September 2010).

Gavetti, Giovanni, and Jan Rivkin. 2005. "How Strategists Really Think: The Power of Analogy." *Harvard Business Review* (April): 1–11.

Goffman, Erving. 1974. *Frame Analysis: An Essay in the Organization of Experience.* New York: Harper & Row.

Hardy, Jean. 1990. "Alternatives to Chemicals: Organic Gardening in Houston." *Houston Metropolitan Magazine* (August): 33–40.

Huber, Kathy. 2000. "Time to Look Back at Gardening Roots." *Houston Chronicle,* 1 January, Star sec. timeline insert.

Klineberg, Stephen. 2010. *The Changing Face Of Houston: Tracking the Economic and Demographic Transformations Through 29 Years of Houston Surveys.* Houston: Rice University Institute for Urban Research. Available at http://houstonareasurvey.org/uploadedFiles/2009_Findings/HAS-2010_(Complete).pdf.

Kretzmann, John, and John McKnight. 1993. *Building Communities from the Inside Out: A Path Toward Finding and Mobilizing a Community's Assets.* Evanston, IL: Institute for Policy Research.

Lakoff, George, 2008. *The Political Mind.* New York: Viking Press.

Mollison, Bill. 1981. "This Terrible Time of Day." In *Transcript of the Permaculture Design Course.* Wilton, NH: Yankee Permaculture.

———. 1988. *Permaculture: A Designers' Manual.* Tyalgum, Australia: Tagari Publications.

———. 1991a. *The Global Gardener.* Oley, Pennsylvania: 220 Productions. Reissued at www.youtube.com/watch?v=lyJLENVyNQQ.

———. 1991b. "Permaculture: Design for Living." *In Context* 28. Reissued at http://www.context.org/ICLIB/IC28/Mollison.htm.

Mollison, Bill, and David Holmgren. 1978. *Permaculture One.* Stanley, Australia: Transworld.

Permaculture Institute. 2010. *Permaculture Design Certificate Course.* Santa Fe, NM: Permaculture Institute. Available at www.permaculture.org/nm/images/uploads/PDC_cert_book_.pdf.

Physician Task Force on Hunger in America. 1985. *Hunger in America: The Growing Epidemic.* Middletown, CT: Wesleyan University Press.

Piaget, Jean. [1926] 1999. *The Child's Conception of the World.* Reprint ed. London: Routledge.

Randall, Robert A. 1977. "Change and Variation in Samal Fishing: Making Plans to Make a Living in the Southern Philippines" (PhD diss., University of California, Berkeley).

———. [1986] 2006. *Year Round Vegetables, Fruits, and Flowers for Metro-Houston: A Natural Organic Approach Using Ecology.* 12th ed. Houston: Year Round Gardening Press.

———. 1987. "Planning in Cross-cultural Settings." In *Blueprints for Thinking: The Role of Planning in Cognitive Development,* ed. Sarah L. Friedman, Ellin Kofsky Scholnick, and Rodney R. Cocking. Cambridge: Cambridge University Press.

———. 1995a. "Rediscovering Our Horticultural Heritage." *American Horticulturist* (December): 40–41.

———. 1995b. "Food Supply Quality." In *Houston Environment 1995: A Report of the 8-county Houston Environmental Foresight Multi-year Task Force.* The Woodlands, TX: Houston Advanced Research Center.

Randall, Bob, and Clarence Taylor. 1991. "A Garden." In *50 More Things You Can Do to Save the Planet*, ed. Earth Works Group. Kansas City: Andrews and McMeel.

Schön, Donald A. 1983. *The Reflective Practitioner: How Professionals Think in Action.* London: Temple Smith.

SEED International. n.d.a. *Permaculture Principles.* www.seedinternational.com.au/pc_principles.html (accessed 21 September 2010).

———. n.d.b. *Permaculture Ethics.* www.seedinternational.com.au/pc_ethics.html (accessed 21 September 2010).

Urban Harvest. n.d. "Homepage." www.urbanharvest.org (accessed 5 August 2010).

Chapter Nine

Putting Permaculture Ethics to Work

Commons Thinking, Progress, and Hope

Katy Fox

> Sustainability is interpreted by many politicians as sustaining the way we live at the moment rather than living sustainably. There's quite a big difference because at the moment we're not living sustainably. We're polluting, we're using up all the resources, we're taking more than our fair share, there's repression of people everywhere.
>
> —Sarah, permaculture teacher[1]

This chapter builds on both my doctoral ethnographic research (2006–2008) with inhabitants of rural Romania who practice subsistence agriculture as well as research (ongoing since 2009) with people who practice permaculture in the UK. I stumbled upon permaculture after witnessing the highly destructive, structurally violent effects of modern agriculture and the European Union's (EU) Common Agricultural Policy (CAP) on locally embedded, subsistence-based ways of living in rural Romania during my doctoral fieldwork. During this time, I lived in several villages in the Romanian Carpathian Mountains and was particularly interested in people's life stories, work, and livelihoods before and after Romania's accession to the EU. This political change devalued subsistence farmers' livelihoods even more than had been the case during previous historical periods. EU membership produced a great deal of suffering among villagers, as well as new strategies for resilience, creativity, and hope. Permaculture ways of living presented a lot of resonance with the devalued ways of life of rural Romanians, but were based on different premises of what was desirable in one's life. I started to reflect on commons thinking, progress, and hope and on how people in different contexts envisage the possibilities of their lives unfolding because of the words of one participant in a permaculture design course (PDC): "[I]n many ways, people have always been doing permaculture, even if they did not call it that."[2] This person explained to me that, usually, when faced with life's challenges, people seek and find solutions by paying close practical attention to context, conditions, and possibilities.

In this chapter, I will look at how two different groups (Romanian peasants and UK permaculturists) engage with change in the context of crisis, focusing particularly on how progress and hope were differently imagined and practiced. The differences between the two groups in imagining progress and hope are not just a function of their relative marginalization vis-à-vis mainstream society, but are born also from the differing extent to which they want to imagine and live in ways other than the dominant models of progress. At the heart of this chapter—and of anthropological inquiries into social change in general—is the question of whether collective action is to be shaped to bring about desirable social change. I argue that desirable change works with Romanian peasants rather than being imposed on them by EU law alien to their socioeconomic context. Change works with—rather than against—nature in permaculture land-based design. Permaculturists try to make dynamics between collaborators explicit through group building, so as to work with these dynamics and have them disrupt the creative process as little as possible. In Romania, people did not agree with the way in which the EU's agrarian policy influenced them from the outset, but rather preferred to remain practical, vague if necessary, engaged throughout the work process, and to retain a degree of flexibility to adapt their practices throughout. I will argue that the logic of growth inherent in the economic practices of capitalism is sidelined in both the Romanian peasant and the permaculture contexts in favor of a logic of careful balance and prioritizing. In both groups, desirable change is directed, but not controlling.

Epistemologies of Dominance and Commons Thinking

I use the contrast between dominance thinking and commons thinking as an epistemological tool to inform my ethnographic findings about how implicit and explicit visioning of the future relates to action in the present life of human beings in divergent contexts. The contrast is taken from anthropologist Justin Kenrick (2005, 2009), who has worked with Mbuti people in central Africa and sex workers in Scotland, and who, more recently, has become involved in the Transition movement in Scotland. Kenrick (2009) poses the question of directed social change in the following way: how do we make the transition from a system in which problems are made worse by the way solutions are imposed to a system that no longer divides the world into superior and inferior realms? One of his examples concerns development aid, and the need to recognize "that ending poverty in Africa does not require the supposedly 'superior' wealthy and educated West to intervene with charity, but requires the 'West' to stop building its wealth on forces of extraction and domination that impoverish Africa" (2009: 55). Kenrick's argument is inspired by the way in which common property regimes (CPRs) have persisted in a world where colonization, enclosure, and commodification of the environment have long prevailed. In this chapter, I use Kenrick's epistemological insights to ground my argument on progress and hope, and do not draw on the vast literature on CPRs (e.g., Ostrom 1990; Dolsak and Ostrom 2003).

According to Kenrick (2009), dominance thinking, which has been the main epistemological mode of Western modernity, assumes that one's well-being ultimately depends on controlling the devalued other (whether other life forms, other humans, or other aspects of oneself). Problems are about the lack of such control and involve the dominant realm (e.g., the mind, civilization, the development expert, the adult) imposing their solution on the inferior realm (e.g., the peasant, the woman, the child) to stop it from being a problem. Moving toward a society based on commons thinking requires relinquishing the dominance approach, the dualistic problem-solving approach underpinning non-egalitarian and unsustainable social systems, and collectively relearning the political and personal skills of envisaging and enabling a viable common future.

Commons thinking, then, is one important skill for rebuilding political, community, and personal resilience. Unlike the separation into separate realms required by dominance thinking, the epistemology of commons thinking assumes that we live in a common lifeworld, not necessarily synonymous with the ecosystem or the biosphere, but recognizing the relationality of human life on earth upon which we all depend. Problems within socioenvironmental relations stem from not considering existing relationships between elements of ecosystems, and, in order for people to thrive within socioenvironmental relations, these relationships need to be restored, nurtured, and cared for. Thus, people practicing permaculture in their garden, for instance, were highly aware and explicit about the fact that ecosystems present complex interdependent relationships and that certain elements within the system may have emergent properties relating to and stemming from this interdependence. Similarly, peasants in Romania explained to me the interconnectedness of upriver (where they lived) and downriver (the cities of the Romanian plain), and argued that if the peasants are not doing well, neither are the urbanites. Kenrick holds that the assumptions of abundance, trust, and mutuality distinguish commons thinking from dominance thinking:

> Commons thinking recognizes the rich resources available to us by starting from ensuring the well-being of locality, and the well-being of others in their localities, rather than from a system of competition over resources made scarce by that very competition. Resources are assumed to be abundant, and are made abundant by ensuring that all people and other species (all ecosystems) have sufficient resources to meet their needs and to ensure their flourishing. This is predicated on the notion that my well-being depends on your well-being, and on the assumption that solving problems involves working to restore relationships of trust rather than to impose solutions on others. (2009: 55)

Commons thinking endorses the management of socioenvironmental relations in a way that attends to the *finite* nature of human and natural systems (which paradoxically ensures their *infinite* abundance) and grounds responsibility in every person.[3] I will maneuver back and forth between the two ethnographic contexts under scrutiny, illuminating my argument as I go along.

The Unity of Permaculture Principles, Ethics, and Practice

One of my permaculture teachers, whom I will call Sarah, once gave the following definition of permaculture: "[I]t is about finding ways to live in harmony with ourselves and with the planet; it's about creating abundance in our lives, finding solutions through looking to how nature solves problems."[4] She then memorably explained that permaculture was different from other environmentalist visions, as it endorses, within its community of practitioners, the connection between permaculture principles, ethics, and design, and thus, in a significant way, between the framework for action (normative) and action itself (actual). The twelve "permaculture principles" (see Figure 0.2) and the threefold division of permaculture ethics (earth care, people care, fair shares) popularized by David Holmgren (2002) are a pragmatic and dynamic framework for concrete, situated action toward sustainable living.

Permaculture is not a static framework; it is alive and growing with the people who use it. It does not stand apart from its instantiations in practice. To my question of how permaculture connects to peasant, worker, and various other anti-capitalist struggles, Sarah replied that "[permaculture is] about who's doing it, and who sees, and who acts. Rather than permaculture reaching into those areas [of struggle], it's rather the people reaching out to permaculture."[5] This shows how permaculture principles work against reification by their constant dynamic looping back to concrete situations within which they can be put into practice, or "put to work," as one permaculturist friend put it.[6]

"Struggle" was not Sarah's choice of term but mine: it had been on my mind when I spoke to her because of my previous research in Romania. Sarah attached much more importance to integrating how she lived her family life in South Wales in accordance with permaculture ethics and practice than leading some kind of struggle or being part of a formal movement for change that would function within a political program of sorts. This is perhaps unsurprising given her relatively more privileged position in comparison to Romanian peasants. Yet, she felt quite strongly about the connections between hierarchy and orthodoxy, which made her weary of organized or institutionally led change. She took seriously walking the walk and reducing the gap between what she practiced in her life and what she taught in the permaculture design courses she helped facilitate.

In line with Holmgren's (2002) principle of "maximizing edges," she had made the conscious decision at one point for herself that margins and edges could be very productive places to do things, both in the meaning of ecosystem edges that are most diverse, and in the sense of worrying little about "mainstreaming" permaculture. Sarah wanted to work with people who had some affinity with permaculture already, rather than attempt to compel those who had never heard of it. I had encountered this valuing of diversity and edges before when I was living and working with people who called themselves peasants—to differentiate the way in which they made a living from that of entrepreneurs or commercial farmers—in rural Romania. They were, however, encumbered by the way in which dominant practices of farming endorsed by the new EU agricultural policies were devaluing their own agricultural and production practices and techniques. Rather than envisioning their marginality as a liberating kind of space, they found the edge was encroached on by dominant practices. Their responses to this state of affairs were, on the whole, rather different from those of people engaged with permaculture in the UK, although they presented some surprising similarities in practice.

Progress: Modernity, Growth, and "Making Do"

In Romania's rural areas, people were living their lives very much *in spite of* the legal, political, and economic frameworks that sought to change their ways of being as well as their peasant ways of doing and making things (see Fox 2009a, 2009b, 2010a). People's livelihoods were considered "black" market practices, and judged as inadequate by the state apparatus implementing the EU's agrarian policy. This policy did not, however, give peasants a space, capital, or encouragement to change their livelihoods, as it was geared toward larger-scale commercial farmers. Any complaint in peasants' narratives was frequently concluded by rhetorically asking, "What can we do? We have to keep on working." In narratives of what was wrong in Romania, elites point to the inadequacies of peasants and peasants to the inadequacies of the state or elites. The claim by peasants to define the problem as belonging to the "top of the pyramid" was a direct consequence of a very polarized, unequal society, and needs to be understood in this context. Sometimes, when they were not blaming the "top" or the "bottom," people admitted that there was a more generalized problem. This was often explained through a story that—after the revolution in 1989—Romanians had misunderstood the notions freedom and democracy, and it was felt that any idea of social obligation had been lost, that people were stealing, and the country had been sold out.

However, complaint narratives did not necessarily go hand in hand with an explicit call to action for desirable change that would go against the grain of the self-diagnosed "increasing individualization," "separation of people from one another," and "loss or failure of [social] growth," even though, within their communities, people did work together, and extend active reciprocity and mutuality to one another. People persistently used the native category of "transition" to express the feeling about human and social progress in their local or national context. However, it was one thing to complain about the lack of progress and quite another to get through life resourcefully. In practice, the response entailed that people implicitly used permaculture principles such as using resources efficiently, producing no waste, and making do with what they had. The older generations in particular saw the benefits of self-imposed frugality, and managed to retain the valuing of the old ways, although this was disputed by younger generations. Young people who chose not to emigrate often worked along the same principles.

Peasants acutely felt the powerlessness that accompanied EU membership as the culmination of a long history of devaluation of their way of being. However, in their narratives, it became evident that people in Romania still hoped that the future would be brighter and current shortcomings would be remedied. People's ideas about the future and a better quality of life were influenced by a long history of modern political projects of improvement (Li 2007, 2008) and stories of economic growth. The working practices of states (and of the capitalist economy, with which states are so entwined) are highly powerful tools with which to parcel the world. However, they also have unintended epistemological consequences, of which dominance thinking is one example. The logic of growth in living systems is organic and can be captured analytically with the concept of peasant personhood, where people adapt their ways of being to the situation at hand, making do with what they have, and seize opportunities as they come along. Growth in relation to modern projects is premised on notions of profit, multiplication, and incorporation. This kind of growth is not particularly well suited to incorporate dynamic, historically evolving phenomena. I will now examine the relationship people had to their future through the notion of "transition."

"Transition" in the Postsocialist and Permaculture Contexts

Two very different ideas of "transition" were mobilized in the two contexts I worked in. "Transition" in postsocialist settings is deeply enmeshed with the transformation of former socialist economies into so-called viable capitalist economies through processes of restructuring and imposing trade policies. Despite ongoing critique of the concept in anthropology (see Burawoy and Verdery 1999; Buyandelgeriyn 2008; Hann 2002; Humphrey and Mandel 2002; Verdery 1993) because of its implied teleology, "transition" as a native term was very alive in Romania and in the UK. In the context of UK permaculturists, "transition" denoted the deliberative steps toward adapting to a post–peak oil, postcarbon economy as inspired by Rob Hopkins and the Transition (Town) movement. This movement emphasizes the need for cooperation, resilience, and local self-organization to face up to the twin challenges of peak oil and climate change. People involved in the movement are explicit about the fact that they do not know where "transition" is headed. They want to provide alternative stories about peak oil to create "desire lines" (Bachelard [1958] 1969) for people to act upon in the present.

After Romania attained EU membership, rural people's lives went on as they had before, with the exception of punctuated activity around policies that affected them. Along with the discourse on transition—appropriated mainly by village elites—appeared another, paradoxical discourse of "things not moving *at all.*" This discourse projected defeatist connotations, "that nothing was ever going to change in Romania," expressed sometimes through "maybe we will get richer, but we will never get civilized." For those excluded from the benefits of EU membership and integration, it felt as though transformations were happening elsewhere; while the discourse of transition seemed to soothe and ascertain that, with patience, things were going to change even here. The normative pull to "Westernize" and "civilize," or, in other words, dominance thinking, was quite strong and it was hard to make a living as a peasant household. The fundamental practical question for people in Romania became: what kinds of movements and change are appropriate in our lives, in the here and now? These are moments of reflection and evaluation of the past against the present, begging the questions, "Where are we going?" and "What are our sources of hope?" However, Romanian peasants arguably did not muster enough power, leadership, and commons thinking to envision the future on their own terms, separate from the enticing "desire lines" of Western modernity and economic growth.

In the permaculture context, the narratives around "civilization" or "wealth" are not compelling in and of themselves. Instead, my interlocutors who practiced permaculture often focused on experiential moments to explain what compelled and inspired them to make the choice of practicing "transition." Sarah explained that it was not so much what her tutor had been *telling* her that convinced her of permaculture as a worthwhile way of achieving change, but what she had seen when visiting his garden. "What really convinced me was seeing his garden. It was a tiny patio, absolutely crammed full of plants and containers ... [we were] eating his fresh salads ... it was the experiential that made me think more than what he said to me earlier. It was the experience of the garden that made me want to know more."[7] The idea of emancipation through action came through very strongly in her narrative, as she recounted how she felt inspired by people who were very practical and active, and who were taking control of their own lives. While the Romanian peasants did not express this idea as explicitly, there was the idea that "beautiful talk" (i.e., eloquent, wordy, or clever talk, often associated with village elites) was ambiguous: it could be sincere, but it could turn into deceit and manipulation quickly, into "ugly talk." "Beautiful action" was more tangible and less dangerous, as it left more traces than "empty talk."

Amy, whom I met during a permaculture course, is working toward being "a light-hearted permaculturist."[8] She was, in her own words, "aspiring to find rest in motion," and contrasted the way in which progress was imagined in permaculture with "mainstream progress" in the following way: "Progress in permaculture could be said to achieve a state of balance, as opposed to mainstream progress as repeated linear movement like lemmings off cliffs; or the rise and fall of successive civilizations, each containing its own destruction within its culture."[9] In summary, then, Romanian peasants and permaculturists had similar ideas of relational connection between distinct places and the importance of measure, balance, and reciprocity between humans and their environment. However, in the Romanian case, the notion of "transition" is not divorced entirely from Western ideals of progress and economic growth, which is related to the way in which dominance thinking is not explicitly countered by an alternative discourse, as is happening in the permaculture and Transition movements. In both contexts, however, people used a certain degree of forward thinking as part of how they lived and did things and how they evaluated their current place in comparison with the past and the future. It is in terms of this consonance that I would like to argue that hope was part of people's everyday practices, be they Romanian peasants or UK permaculturists.

Hope: Uncertainty, Trust, and Common Sense

My work with both Romanian peasants and UK permaculturists shows that their livelihood practices contained elements of hope, but that these found very different expressions. My research (Fox 2009a) has not framed hope as a mere attitude or a matter of faith, but as a fundamentally human capacity. I suggest thinking about hope as a human faculty or a sense of openness to the world. Any sense of hope is built on the trust that there is a life worth living in uncertain times (Zournazi 2002: 16). The sense of hope with which people live their lives goes against those political and economic grids that shape their lives and endorses a different personhood ideal. In dominant capitalist discourse, couched in neoliberal theories of economics—the epitome of dominance thinking—the prevalent notion of the person prescribes an individual separate from its environment and absolutely free to act in accordance with the rational, self-maximizing principles underlying most of modern economic theory. Through the lens of the concept of hope, this normative, aspirational notion of personhood becomes attenuated, and space is held for alternative, relational ways of being a person in practice.

Even though free agent personhood was dominant in both groups, it had different consequences because of historical conditions that people found themselves in and the corollary epistemological constructions of their own life projects. In the Romanian context, the dominant ideal of personhood endorsed and furthered inequality. Because of an insecure environment that traced back to socialism and intensified during post-socialism, people were suspicious of each other and, due to the illegality of their economic practices, often were not open with their activities. As a consequence, the idea proliferated that people were untrustworthy or tricky, and intensified the feeling that nothing could be done against economic inequality and exploitation.

In contrast, in permaculture circles, the dominant notion of personhood was made less convincing and desirable through explicit critique and an embracing of commons thinking. The resulting relationality puts human-environment and human-human relationships on an equal footing in what I have called here "socioenvironmental relations." Embracing relationality along with commons thinking, permaculturists felt strongly that there were resonances between the ways in which humans treated each other and the ways they treated their environments. They expressed this visually in their teaching through relating the notions of "earth care" and "people care" and balancing them with "fair shares." They advocated that in order to bring about transition, one needed new stories that could envision a different future. They felt strongly that the postcarbon society is not one of deprivation; rather, they proliferated visions of other kinds of abundance lacking in today's society. At one permaculture course I attended, a motto that became a running joke was that "if it is not fun, it is not sustainable."[10] People in the permaculture and Transition movements ask questions such as: What is real wealth? How do we want to live more happily (and—as a side effect—more sustainably)? How can we bring about a future that is desirable and healthy? In order to bring about a positive transformation and a viable future, they use visioning techniques such as "dreaming" the future and group-building activities, and offer alternatives to the strong experience of grief, fragmentation, and denial arising from daily media representations of cataclysm, violence, and destruction.

In Romania, this visioning did not take place in the same way—even though narratives indicated, symptomatically, what people felt was amiss in their social environment. For peasants, the environment of insecurity along with dominance thinking made people draw strong boundaries between people they trusted and people they did not. They complained, in narrative, that there had been a loss of "common sense," because people were just looking after themselves. In the Romanian villages where I conducted research, this was expressed in stories by allusions to fragmented social worlds peopled by two-legged wolves. From these stories, the idea emerged that "common sense" had been reduced to the meaning of "generally known sense" through the felt fragmentation of social worlds, and that the other meaning of "shared and connected sense"—a sense of community that went beyond the immediate neighborhood—had been somewhat eclipsed, and needed to be revived. In the permaculture context, commons thinking is a cluster of practices that helped bring about a genuine awareness of the interdependence of people, and of people and their environments, through games and visioning exercises that people felt were carried over to their everyday lives. In the Romanian context, interdependence was considered very important within one's own local community, but it was often not extended to people in other places—especially within urban areas, as these places were considered different and unequal in terms of hierarchical ideas of Western progress.

As I moved from my Romanian research context, which was premised on inequality and dominance thinking, to working with permaculturists, it took me awhile to understand to what extent permaculture practitioners work not just *against* hierarchies present in mainstream society but also *for* creating different kinds of relationships and practices. In their tightly interwoven ethics and practice, they took commons thinking, with its sincerely egalitarian and collective thrust, seriously. The ethics embedded in permaculture principles and action, as indicated above, are based on people care, earth care, and fair shares. They do not foreground one of these, but assume a strong interdependence between humans, their environment, and concerns of justice or egalitarianism. As Sarah explained to me, these "principles are to be balanced in any design for sustainable change, whether this be on a personal level, on a community scale, or even on a global scale."[11] She went on to say that permaculture is common sense, at least to some degree. However, she felt strongly that this "common sense" was not so common today, and that it needed to be recovered by a certain mindfulness about how things connect, echoing the Romanian claims.

Carefully Connecting Social and Environmental Relations

Reflecting on her own practice, Sarah also suggested that perhaps there was "no point to teach any more earth care skills, if people cannot work out the people care skills."[12] It was in the area of people care skills that she perceived the most serious challenges with regard to the courses she had been teaching. People did not see how they had to change the ways in which they behaved toward one another. This made it very difficult to appreciate any kind of base-level social interconnectedness. She said that because permaculture was usually perceived, from the perspective of relative outsiders, as being about how to cultivate one's land in the paradigm of permanent agriculture and not about changing one's being in any way, people sometimes reacted badly to the idea that person-to-person relationships were regarded as crucial in the restoring and reconfiguring of socioenvironmental relations. Permaculture ethics and principles put to work in everyday practice pointed to the co-arising and coevolution of person and environment, informing the minutest everyday act often implicitly—but also made explicit sometimes, especially in the context of permaculture design courses.

One of the most striking things about permaculture practitioners is their rejection of hierarchy and the embrace of working on the edges of hierarchy. Amy put it thus: "Permaculture is certainly a common sense and practical way to design change but it's also ingenious, elegant, feasible and approachable. And you don't have to worship Bill Mollison—there is genuinely no hierarchy. That's unusual."[13] Sarah, who homeschooled her own daughter, noted that getting an education did not necessarily entail being encouraged to think for oneself:

> In mainstream education, there is a real hierarchy. You have to go through the hoops, do your GCSEs, your A-levels, your degree—the more you go through the hoops, the more you are listened to. However, this discredits our innate intelligence, and almost blocks that off … And actually, who wants to hear *don't do* all the time. We all heard that enough as children. Don'ts and shoulds and musts are all just big turnoffs for people. What people want to hear is: it's fun. *You personally* are going to benefit from this very quickly. Look I'm having fun, I am free in my life. However it manifests in us brings people in, rather than to scare them away.[14]

I suggest that Sarah indirectly reveals several central points about why in Romania, hierarchy was, at least explicitly in narrative, seen as unavoidable. Making one's future was about yielding to the dominant idea of progress and seeing hope in the threads that dominance thinking indicated, or, if the state were to continuously fail to provide social and economic welfare, seeing hope in kinship and community relationships. *Designing* desirable change was never the issue.

This is the main crux of the difference between how the two groups envision their future: what they imagine as feasible and desirable is very different, and, for the permaculturists, this vision runs explicitly counter to dominant ideas of "wealth" and "prestige" that were common in Romanian visions of the future. Peasants in Romania may know they may not achieve this kind of "wealth," but they still tend to believe in the story of Western progress and civilization. In other words, their disappointment is possible only because they believe in the golden age of modernity and improvement originating from the state that they had partially witnessed in 1950s and 1960s socialism. In the Romanian context, then, a dissonance between normativity (expressed in narratives) and actuality (actions) existed. In other words, the belief in progress was still alive, even though people's everyday lives had to go on with or without it. This explains why there was a certain amount of complaint in people's narratives, but that, at the same time, people resourcefully made do with what they had. One Romanian put it thus: "The mafia is controlling this country. There are two different sets of laws, and there is a problem with the money. The state doesn't really get to our villages, and so there is nothing happening. Have you seen the state of the roads? Earlier on, this was all a vibrant area of wood industry … Now everything is broken."[15] People felt deep belonging to their place, but they were angry at how it had ended up—destitute—and, according to them, without many opportunities or future prospects. Still, they needed to make a living, and they just kept working with their animals and their patches of land, trading the fruits of their labor on the black market, and making some money on the side with homemade clothing, brandy, and other local produce.

In a way, permaculturists chose a different livelihood, even though they could have participated in the UK economy. They had turned away from Western ideals of progress and modernity, because of their detrimental environmental and social impacts, and they were specifically advocating alternatives. One of the alternatives they practiced was to liberate people from the fear that they found to be at the heart of the capitalist economy. Sarah was at her most energetic and vibrant when it came to playing games in groups. She finds them very enjoyable, because she likes

> the way the inner child just comes up with the games. And the laughter. You can tell some people haven't laughed like that for years, not without stimulants anyways. To actually just genuinely let that laughter out. I really enjoy seeing people get really silly, which kind of may sound quite superficial or trivial, but actually I think it goes quite deep with people who may not have laughed like that for a few decades. And I think that's quite significant to actually enable that to happen. Partly what happens on [permaculture] design courses is that whole breaking down of barriers. It's what happened to me too. This box of who you are, this person, to actually breaking it down and becoming who you want to be and actually laughing hysterically if you want to be and speaking your mind and asking deep and meaningful questions of each other. Expanding each other. I find the courses very expansive for each other and I really enjoy watching that and being part of that … People really shine on courses … I think that's what I enjoy most. Seeing that empowerment of people and often seeing that anything is possible. That doorway that opens and some people really embrace it and just go right through it.[16]

Sarah describes the high emotions and empowering and motivating effects emerging from the playful space afforded by the permaculture design courses, in which people can reimagine their possible futures paradoxically by not focusing their attention on them directly, and in which people can take their first conscious steps toward a different kind of future.

Conclusion

From Environmentalist to Environmental Thinking and Action

Even though there was a strong notion of the existence of various kinds of crises (e.g., economic, environmental, and community) with both UK permaculturists and Romanian peasants, the two groups appropriated the spaces on the edge of this crisis very differently. I have argued that this was so because different epistemological principles underpinned people's life projects and their evaluations of the past and the future. In the Romanian case, a normative ideal of personhood was influenced by dominance thinking and the principle of "scarcity," which both originate from the economic paradigm of capitalism, and which cause fragmentation and reification in epistemological terms and socioenvironmental relations. However, Romanian peasants often adopted practices resembling those of permaculturists for reasons of necessity, even though their belief in progress differed quite radically from that of permaculturists. For permaculture practitioners, on the other hand, the underlying assumption was that an abundant relationality was at the core of all aspects of life, and, much in line with commons thinking, restoring appropriate relationships helped solve entrenched problems.

Comparing two groups from such widely divergent social and historical contexts in a chapter of this length cannot adequately address all the larger issues at stake in such a comparison. Structural sociopolitical relationships disempowered Romanian peasants in how they felt they could make change, and one could argue that peasants are not environmentalists. Indeed, orthodox environmentalist tenets have been embraced largely by a middle-class audience, who for the most part do not work *in* nature, unlike peasants or farmers. The biases and persistent myths of this orthodox environmentalist thinking include primitive ecological wisdom, conservation and separation of nature, and practices that strategically segregate one "cause" from another (e.g., climate change versus peak oil). Richard White is one of the few commentators who has drawn attention to the way in which work in nature has not been addressed as a central issue within the environmental movement, and has convincingly shown that the choice between "condemning all work in nature and sentimentalizing vanishing forms of work is simply not an adequate choice" (1995: 174).

While I do acknowledge the critique that repressive conditions of life are not particularly conducive to orthodox environmentalist thinking, my research bears witness to burgeoning socioenvironmental thought and praxis across the board. Atypical environmental thinkers and activists such as peasants and permaculturists, that is, people from very different walks of life, are deeply concerned about the way in which their social, economic, and ecological environments have been evolving. They are actively implementing ways of being and living that are different from the mainstream, often starting from the edges: local currencies, community building, resilient food systems, eco-building, reduced energy needs and consumption, and social enterprise. Romanian peasants may not label their practices as "new" at all, but they provide a proactive stance of community action, if looked at in the context of a postsocialist state that is not intervening in their favor. Both permaculturists and peasants start with what is at hand and with an imperative for connecting principle and practice on a local scale. Neither attempts to exclude human intervention from an exterior, reified nature—instead endorsing a balanced, careful approach to working with the natural world.

Notes

1. Sarah is a fictional name. Interview with author, 24 March 2010.
2. Tom (fictional name). Conversation with author, 23 January 2010.
3. The idea of personalizing responsibility is a problematic claim for underprivileged and highly unequal contexts, such as Romania, even if one were to reject partially the idea of poverty as produced by postsocialist inequality and the market economy, and this chapter only goes some way to solve this issue. Indeed, neoliberal forces have helped to shift self-responsibility from elites to disadvantaged communities as decentralization and privatization have increased. In this sense, I remain deeply uncomfortable with the resonance of horizontal "personal responsibility" evoked by permaculturist groups, as it unwittingly, and rather unfortunately, echoes that of neoliberal discourse. It appears as though responsibility itself is understood in two different, incommensurable ways: in neoliberal discourse, shifting the blame away from the state or any social institution onto the private person; and in permaculture discourse, taking full responsibility for one's own actions in an interconnected world, that is, being able to respond empathically to their environment and other persons. The difference can be captured by the contrast of dominance and commons thinking in this chapter.
4. Sarah. Interview with author, 24 March 2010.
5. Sarah. Phone conversation with author, 27 March 2010.
6. Chris (fictional name). Email to author, 15 February 2010.
7. Sarah. Phone conversation with author, 27 March 2010.
8. Amy (fictional name). Email to author, 24 April 2010.
9. Amy. Email to author, 24 April 2010.
10. Joke initiated by Chris and Sarah, January 2010.
11. Sarah. Interview with author, 24 March 2010.
12. Sarah. Interview with author, 24 March 2010.
13. Amy. Email to author, 24 April 2010.
14. Sarah. Interview with author, 24 March 2010.
15. Gaby (fictional name). Conversation with author, 15 September 2007.
16. Sarah. Interview with author, 24 March 2010.

References

Bachelard, Gaston. [1958] 1969. *The Poetics of Space.* Boston: Beacon Press.

Burawoy, Michael, and Katherine Verdery, eds. 1999. *Uncertain Transition: Ethnographies of Change in the Postsocialist World.* Oxford: Rowman and Littlefield.

Buyandelgeriyn, Manduhai. 2008. "Post-Post-Transition Theories: Walking on Multiple Paths." *Annual Review of Anthropology* 37: 235–50.

Dolsak, Nives, and Elinor Ostrom, eds. 2003. *The Commons in the New Millennium: Challenges and Adaptation.* Cambridge, MA: MIT Press.

Fox, Katy. 2009a. "The Principle of Hope: Relating to the European Union in Rural Romania." In *The Resilience of Hope,* ed. Janette McDonald and Andrea Stephenson. Amsterdam: Rodopi.

———. 2009b. "Confusion, Secrecy and Power: Direct Payments and European Integration in Romania." In "Private Property: Postsocialist Promises and Experiences," special issue ed. Stefan Dorondel and Thomas Sikor, *Annuaire Roumain d'Anthropologie* 46: 63–75.

———. 2010a. "Despre autopoiesis si angrenajul structural." In *Teme in Antropologia Sociala din Europa de Sud Est. Volum dedicat memoriei Profesorului Paul Stahl,* ed. Stelu Serban, 21–44. Bucharest: Paideia.

Hann, Chris M., ed. 2002. *Postsocialism: Ideals, Ideologies and Practices in Eurasia.* London: Routledge.

Holmgren, David. 2002. *Permaculture: Principles and Pathways beyond Sustainability.* Hepburn, Australia: Holmgren Design Services.

Humphrey, Caroline, and Ruth Mandel, eds. 2002. *Markets and Moralities: Ethnographies of Postsocialism.* Oxford: Berg.

Kenrick, Justin. 2005. "Equalising Processes, Processes of Discrimination and the Forest People of Central Africa." In *Property and Equality: Vol. 2, Encapsulation, Commercialization, Discrimination,* ed. Thomas Widlock and Wolde Dossa Tadesse. Oxford: Berghahn.

———. 2009. "Commons Thinking: The Ability to Envisage and Enable A Viable Future Through Connected Action." In *The Handbook of Sustainability Literacy: Skills for A Changing World,* ed. Arran Stibbe. Foxhole, UK: Green Books.

Li, Tanya Murray. 2007. *The Will to Improve: Governmentality, Development, and the Practice of Politics.* Durham, NC: Duke University Press.

———. 2008. "Social Reproduction, Situated Politics and *The Will to Improve.*" *Focaal* 52: 111–18.

Ostrom, Elinor. 1990. *Governing the Commons: The Evolution of Institutions for Collective Action.* Cambridge: Cambridge University Press.

Verdery, Katherine. 1993. "Nationalism and National Sentiment in Post-Socialist Romania." *Slavic Review* 52 (2): 179–203.

White, Richard. 1995. "'Are you an Environmentalist or Do You Work for a Living?': Work and Nature." In *Uncommon Ground: Rethinking the Human Place in Nature,* ed. Richard Cronon. London: W.W. Norton.

Zournazi, Mary. 2002. *Hope: New Philosophies for Change.* Annandale, Australia: Pluto Press Australia.

Chapter Ten

Permaculture in Practice

Low Impact Development in Britain

Jenny Pickerill

Introduction

The principles of permaculture offer practical guidance on how to live more sustainably. Permaculture is designed to be a holistic, integrated practice that can build functioning sustainable alternatives that balance the needs of nature with the needs of humans. In Britain permaculture has been predominantly practiced as an approach to food production and gardening, eschewing many of its wider implications for the built environment, land tenure, planning, and economics. However, an emerging movement of Low Impact Developments[1] (LIDs) are broadening the way in which permaculture is practiced by applying it to all aspects of collective eco-living on a village scale.

As permaculture is essentially a design system, not a rigid set of rules, it is important to understand how its principles are actually practiced in order to critically explore its value in different contexts, and its possibilities as a guide for sustainability. As Holmgren notes, "permaculture remains an environmentally friendly method of growing food, rather than the design and philosophical basis of the community itself" (2002: 175). Examining permaculture practice in several LIDs in Britain, this chapter details the shift beyond food production to a more holistic implementation of permaculture principles. However, it also identifies how the lack of a shared interpretation of what permaculture means in practice, the lack of experience of residents in working collectively using permaculture, the tensions of implementing it in practice, and the lack of large-scale collective working examples of permaculture in Britain (unlike, for example, Tamera in Portugal or Crystal Waters in Australia [Barton 1998]), has hindered the possibilities of permaculture in fully shaping sustainable ecological living. Of particular interest is the collective implementation of permaculture in all aspects of living, including building, land tenure, personal relationships, and resilience to climate change.

Low Impact Development is a radical approach to housing, livelihoods, and everyday living that began in Britain in the 1990s as a grassroots response to the overlapping crises of sustainability. LID employs approaches that dramatically reduce humans' impact upon the environment, demonstrating that human settlements and livelihoods, when done appropriately, can enhance rather than diminish ecological diversity (Fairlie 1996; Halfacree 2007). LID is also a direct response to the need for low-cost housing, an anti-capitalist strategy forging alternative economic possibilities, and a holistic approach to living that pays attention to the personal as well as the political. As such, LID is "engaged in social transformation through everyday-lived practice" (Woods 2008: 132). This is a subset of the broader ecovillage movement. Although it shares many concerns with ecovillages, LID places a particular emphasis upon being low impact by being visually unobtrusive (integrating nature into its designs), using natural and local building materials (such as straw and wood), being of an appropriate scale (according to what the land can support), being autonomous in terms of water, waste, and energy, and providing the majority of their food needs from their land, and is often linked to sustainable land-based livelihoods (such as fruit growing, bee keeping, and vegetable box schemes) (Maxey 2009; Jacob 2006).

LID is in essence about localizing all aspects of living to reduce the need for consumption and travel. However, this does not involve residents segregating themselves from society. Rather, many LIDs invest considerable time and energy in building links with local communities, establishing educational projects, and research (Pickerill and Maxey 2009a). It is estimated that ten thousand people live in LIDs in Britain; however, the size of settlements tend to be small in scale, with few having more than twenty residents (Chapter 7 2003). Examples include Hockerton Housing Project (Nottinghamshire, England), Lammas (Pembrokeshire, Wales), Landmatters (Devon, England), Green Hill (Scotland), and roundhouses at Brithdir Mawr (Pembrokeshire, Wales) (Map 10.1).

The empirical material on which this chapter is based is drawn from an engagement with several LIDs since 2006. The level of participation and involvement has varied according to the needs and desires of each community. The author has been extensively involved with the Lammas Low Impact Initiative (Pembrokeshire), which was granted planning permission for nine LID smallholdings and dwellings in August 2009. This included repeated site visits, researching and preparing reports for the planning application, interviews, participation in meetings and events, and, most

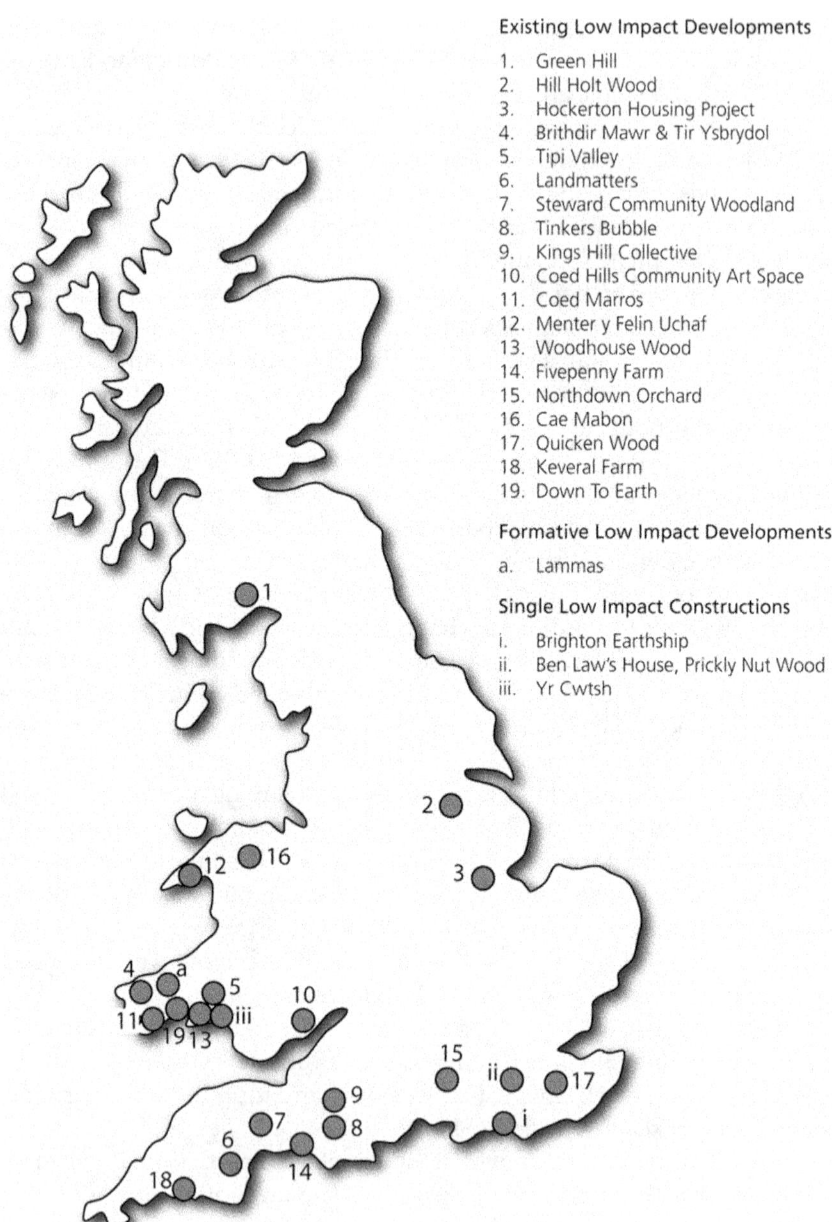

Map 10.1. Map of low-impact developments in Britain. Map by Jenny Pickerill.

recently (April 2010), volunteering in the construction of new dwellings. Similarly, repeated visits were made to Green Hill (Scotland) to volunteer, participate in the vegetable box scheme, and conduct interviews. Research was also done through volunteering at Tinkers Bubble (Somerset), while day visits incorporating an informal site tour and interviews with participants were conducted at Steward Community Woodland (Devon) and Landmatters (Devon). At more established LIDs such as Hockerton Housing Project (Nottinghamshire) and Hill Holt Wood (Lincolnshire), official tours were attended and interviews were conducted, and both places have since become regular sites for teaching field trips run by the author. For more details about each site, see Pickerill and Maxey (2009a, 2009b).

Minimizing Impact through Integration

There is a synergy between LIDs and permaculture in that they are both design systems that at their heart seek to interconnect processes of life and create more sustainable systems. They are both based upon understanding and creating systems of cooperation that encompass ecology, people, and equality.

The British Permaculture Association defines permaculture as "about living lightly on the planet and making sure that we can sustain human activities for many generations to come, in harmony with nature" (n.d.). Permaculture is about designing systems whereby the needs of people *and* the environment are met in a way that creates balance and harmony and is inspired by close observation of nature's own systems of stability, resilience, and productivity (Kennedy 1991). Thus, "practitioners should learn from, mimic, and work with—rather than against—nature. This implies that we should design complex, integrated, even multi-stored, systems within which all organisms … perform not single and competitive, but multiple and mutualistic functions" (Mulligan and Hill 2001: 205).

These interconnections can be explored by understanding the three ethics that underpin permaculture (earth care, people care, fair share), and how attention to each of these ethics is required to create a holistic, harmonious, and balanced way of life. Earth care reduces our impact upon the natural environment and works in harmony with natural systems. The aim of such an ethic is to enable existing natural systems to flourish and replicate with ease and is focused on valuing ecological systems and preventing their destruction and pollution. Such an ethic informs how we manage land and design systems that supply our needs in a low-impact way.

People care concerns the needs and well-being of people and communities. This involves defining the resources we need and ensuring that we have access to them. This includes access to good food, water, and shelter. There is an emphasis within this ethic that people care involves collective approaches to better managing resources for our needs, such as collectively organizing better public transport systems or organic food provision. Good design is used to maximize use of resources for collective benefit. It is about developing environmentally friendly lifestyles that sustain ourselves and the environment simultaneously. There is another important element to people care, however, and that is care for self and an understanding that "to be able to contribute to a wider good, one must be healthy and secure" (Holmgren 2002: 7). Indeed, as Whitefield notes, "we largely know how we need to change our agriculture and industry in order to make them sustainable. How to deal with human emotions, such as fear and greed, is less simple however, and these are what really prevent us from making progress" (1997: 6). Thus, we need to pay attention to personal emotions and human needs, and develop skills such as communication and listening. This involves valuing nonmaterial well-being as well.

Finally, an ethic of fair share determines that the limited resources we have available to us are shared equally between all beings. These "beings" include all people, animals, plants, and, perhaps most importantly, future generations. According to some interpretations this involves setting limits to population growth to create a "stable" population (Holmgren 2002). While this idea remains controversial, the ethic certainly requires a limit to consumption and a check upon what we perceive as essential for our needs. We thus need to better "match our consumption to need" (Whitefield 1997: 7).

Permaculture has had a big influence on green ideas in Britain in recent years, but in the main this has been expressed through changing practices of gardening and food production. Many of the key advocates and designers of LIDs are trained in permaculture design (for example, Ben Law, who built an LID in Prickly Nut Wood, East Sussex, has a diploma in applied permaculture design), though others describe themselves as "accidental" permaculturists (a point we will return to). As such, LID has been described by Tony Wrench, of Brithdir Mawr, "as being a catalyst for letting permaculture happen in the countryside and letting people with no money or very little money, live a balanced lifestyle that will survive economic crises, and will survive peak oil"[2] (see also Wrench 2001).

LID reflects the ethics of permaculture in two keys ways: in its holistic approach and in its emphasis upon the importance of people and the personal. LID takes holism—the idea that we need to understand the whole of a system (physical, social, economic, and psychological) and that the properties of a system cannot be understood by its component parts alone—as its approach to understanding how humans should interact with the environment (Pickerill and Maxey 2009a). For Will of Green Hill, this holism is central to permaculture: "One of the things that defines permaculture is to try and—for an individual or a group—do the whole process, be both implementer and designer and observer, and evaluator as well, to learn lessons ... because it's incorporating people and the earth and trying to get that fair share ... that defines it as being holistic."[3]

Thus, LID and permaculture advocate that in addition to physical changes, we must attend to the personal and emotional too (Brown and Pickerill 2009). This very much reflects a permaculture ethic of seeking to work in harmony with nature's systems and of people care, and an acknowledgement that the personal politics of change are as important as protecting the natural environment.

Principles in Practice

Given the breadth of this ethical framework, it is important to explore what this has meant in practice in LIDs. This can be assessed by how the twelve permaculture guidelines developed by Holmgren (2002—see Figure 0.2) have been put into practice. These guidelines are a set of principles to ensure energy-efficient design (Laughton 2008). In other words, permaculture "can only be achieved by means of careful design. Useful connections can only be made between things if they are put in the right place relative to each other" (Whitefield 1997: 3). This is part of permaculture's appeal for LIDs: "What I particularly like about permaculture is that it offers a set of design principles, but does not necessarily tell you how to do something ... This gives you flexibility in responding to location and situation."[4]

Permaculture is a deliberate and assertive approach to sustainability, and its practice in British LIDs will be explored through the examination of the interpretation and implementation of four principles: catch and store energy (number 2); integrate rather than segregate (8); design from patterns to details (7); and creatively use and respond to change (12).

Catch and Store Energy

The principle of *catch and store energy* is often applied to arranging plant growth to best store energy in the landscape, such as creating areas of biomass like trees or through the protection and nurturing of healthy soils. However, it can equally be applied to constructing highly energy-efficient buildings that naturally store solar energy. If orientated to the south, buildings can benefit from passive solar gain, which both heats and lights a space for free. Often this solar gain can be stored in walls with high thermal mass to heat the space overnight or during cloudy days. Moreover, photovoltaic panels and solar thermal water heating catch solar energy and store it for use in the home. The use of natural materials often facilitates the process of storing energy too; for example, straw bales or adobe create thick walls that help to store solar energy.

An example of the use of this principle is the design of the dwellings at Hockerton Housing Project, Nottinghamshire. Built in the mid-1990s, the five-house terrace has thick concrete walls and is earth-sheltered to the north. All the windows face south, with a large conservatory designed to capture the sun's energy but also to prevent overheating and thus stabilize the internal temperature of homes. The homes rarely need heating (using wood stoves), and electricity is generated by photovoltaic panels and two wind turbines.

There is a tension in the application of this principle, however. In order to create such a dense thermal mass, a large amount of concrete was used in construction. This potentially works against some of the other principles such as *use and value renewable resources and services* (number 5) and *produce no waste* (6). Thus, permaculture in practice often has to be pragmatic. At LIDs such as Tinkers Bubble (Somerset) and Landmatters (Devon), their ecobuildings are made predominantly from more natural materials (largely wood), often not perfectly positioned for solar gain—which consequently do not catch and store energy with the same efficiency as those at Hockerton. They also lack airtightness and thermal mass. LIDs in Britain have not yet resolved the tension as to whether it is better to use non-natural materials to increase energy efficiency in building, or to compromise efficiency and avoid the use of polluting building materials. This example illustrates that although permaculture design principles are being incorporated into house building in LIDs, compromise is often needed to make such principles work in British contexts.

Integrate rather than Segregate

Permaculture principle number 8, *integrate rather than segregate,* identifies that the relationships between things are vital to the successful operation of a system as a whole. Moreover, by working together synergies are created, which means that "the whole is greater than the sum of its parts" (Macnamara 2009: 10). Thus, it is important to generate connections and intersections. This principle overlaps with another—*produce no waste*—as ideally a system is created whereby the needs of one are supplied by another.

Although often applied to food production, for example, by ensuring that food is supplied by a broad variety of sources (main crops, wild food, orchards, and exchange with others), integrate rather than segregate can also be conceived as a principle to be applied to designing how we live together and with others. In theory this suggests, for example, that we locate chickens near parts of the garden that require pest control, and then use chickens for meat, feathers, and eggs (Whitefield 1997). If we apply this more broadly to ecoliving, it requires us to structure our dwellings, infrastructure, and livelihoods in ways that maximize sharing and communal use. Thus, we locate according to needs that could also increase the ability to share and to generate multiple uses from one resource. This principle then speaks to the need for collective approaches to sustainability.

Lammas[5] is a new LID, with construction of nine smallholdings and a community hub on seventy-six acres of mixed pasture and woodland near Glandwr, Pembrokeshire, Wales, begun in the autumn of 2009. Lammas deliberately structured its design around principle number 8, employing permaculture design specialist Looby Macnamara to aid plot plans. She argued that "the sharing of infrastructure, resources such as tools, labour and transport greatly reduces costs and ecological footprints compared with having nine separate smallholdings" (Macnamara 2009: 10). Lammas is not an intentional community, however, and they wished to create a supportive village environment whereby residents shared resources but also maintained maximum personal freedom. Thus, they used permaculture to design a way to work collectively when necessary but ultimately each have their own space, freedom, and choices in how they use their plot and make their livelihood, experimenting with permaculture to create new ways to live together. The result is a village with a strong sense of mutual solidarity, sharing, and kindness. People care becomes as important as earth care, as there is recognition of the importance of personal autonomy and space for individual emotions. This personal need for some separation, however, naturally limits the amount of integration possible, and although tools and labor are often shared at Lammas, most residents have their own vehicle and are building their own homes predominantly by themselves. Holmgren, as an advocate of intentional communities, argues that ideally we should cooperate even more than this; "the belief that human nature demands that we live segregated and uncooperative lives is arguably a greater impediment to a sustainable future than the belief that technology and human brilliance can solve environmental problems" (2002: 176).

At other LIDs the attempt to integrate rather than segregate has been hampered by a lack of shared interpretation of what permaculture means in practice. Laughton notes that many "projects had naturally arrived at permaculture-style solutions without labeling them as such" (2008: 81). Landmatters (Devon) struggled with agreeing on a collective definition of permaculture despite many residents having attended permaculture training. As a result,

> we soon realized that everybody had a different interpretation of it … most people might consider their own design as permaculture, but we have not really done it on the scale of the whole site. Several decisions which we have made would have been different if we were taking a whole-site permaculture approach … which means that some odd decisions have been made, such as the location of the communal building, which I have always thought should have been more central and on the village green.[6]

Thus, while individually residents in LIDs may be practicing permaculture—or some permaculture principles—and certainly applying it to more than simply food production, there remains a lack of experience of residents in working collectively using permaculture as an encompassing design approach.

Design from Patterns to Details

Permaculture seeks to use patterns evident in nature to aid efficient design (number 7). Thinking about patterns aids the development of large-scale permaculture plans for a project. Pattern design can include zoning (dividing a site according to which sections need more attention), sector analysis (considering how sun and wind flows through a site), and elevation planning (ensuring appropriate use of slopes and altitude). This approach facilitates planning use of a site before thinking about the detail.

At Green Hill LID (Scotland), principle number 7 has been used to design the entire site, including location of homes, and zoning was used to consider human energy use for daily tasks. Since 2001 this community has been living without planning permission in a woodland. They have recently completed a timber-framed straw bale house. Rainwater is used for everything except drinking, power is generated by wind and solar, and houses are heated by wood-fired stoves. Income is generated through a vegetable box scheme from their extensive gardens and by hosting training courses. The pattern design process is also used when changes are required:

> The movement of the hen house recently … we observed the two main places we thought it feasible to take it to … and thought about the pros and cons of each of those sites and how that would work and opted for putting it next to the sheep enclosure because of that design process we went through—how that would be easy in terms of the day to day flow of our pattern, going to feed the hens, check on the sheep—they're both in the same place … we can

> feed at the same time, and the collectivisation of our resources, so the water can come off the roofs of both of the buildings, that can be collected together and that then becomes a shared resource for hens and sheep.[7]

At each stage of design the OBREDIM (observation, boundaries, resources, evaluation, design, implement, and maintain) approach was used. For Green Hill this enabled a broad variety of influences—aspects from the three ethics and all principles—to be incorporated and considered at each stage. Thus, the role of climatic conditions was considered alongside human energy levels and security from possible thieves. When considering the expansion of their food production area, "we didn't know whether we wanted to go east or west ... So one side in terms of observations is quite exposed, quite windy, but more secure, less interaction with the public. On the other side, more sheltered, got a good windbreak around it, but potentially less secure, next to a public footpath, so potential nicking of vegetables."[8] The main disadvantage with this process is the time that it takes to do it thoroughly, which Will argued would take at least a year. This was problematic because of the heavy demands on the residents' time (looking after young children and generating their income from land-based livelihoods) and because some members of the community preferred to make decisions more quickly than such a process enabled.

Creatively Use and Respond to Change

Permaculture encourages a creative and positive response to change, both in planning to encourage ecological succession (for example, from bare land to mature forest) and in reacting to larger-scale shifts such as climate change. Thus, while known changes can be planned for (such as changing seasons), there is also a need to be able to respond to changes that might have less well understood consequences. For Holmgren, "one of the great challenges in energy descent is to replace mass solutions and systems with a great diversity of systems and solutions to suit the particular needs of sites, situations and cultural contexts" (2002: 242). This response to change is as much about social change and knowing how to work together and collectively as it is about ecological response. As the Permaculture Association notes, "working with people is just as important in permaculture as working with plants (which are much easier!)" (n.d.).

The emphasis on diversity as a form of ecological and social resilience is evident in several LIDs in Britain. Landmatters is a forty-two acre eco-community in Devon (England) that currently only has temporary planning permission and is restricted to temporary dwellings. There are currently twelve adults on-site and seven houses, and all land is collectively owned. Permaculture was core to the creation of the community: "[W]e had all done a permaculture course, so had that philosophy as a common commitment" (Rodker 2009: 64), even if in practice they struggled to agree on its finer details. Diversity was evident in their food growing to an extent: "[W]e can create resilience via diversity. We are not sure yet whether it is going to become wetter or drier and we could start growing for both knowing that we might waste some, but also that some will survive. Really it is about diversity, which we do anyway, and growing a huge range of crops, such as the variety of salads that I have."[9] However, in other ways Landmatters is not very diverse, and this has led to both personal tensions and a narrow skill base, because "although shared beliefs and co-operative behavior are fundamental to the success of intentional communities, too much similarity in skills, ages and needs and personalities encourages competitive rather than co-operative relationships" (Holmgren 2002: 176). This similarity of types of people attracted to LIDs is something most residents are very aware of and continue to seek to rectify.

LIDs actually have quite a flexible approach to change rather than simply being resilient; in other words, they have incorporated permaculture less in planning resilience and more in their spontaneous flexibility to change as it happens. LID is an ongoing experiment, and Landmatters residents continue to invent and create as they evolve. Their design provides flexibility in response to change in part because their dwellings are temporary, self-built, and modular (and thus can be easily modified), their needs change and are adapted to (for example, many couples now have young children and have had to change their lifestyles), and their land management evolves (with the intention of generating more land-based income but with an approach that is open to new opportunities).

Transitions to a Sustainable Future

The greater incorporation of permaculture into LIDs in Britain has occurred alongside the emergence of the Transition Town movement. Transition Towns, also known as the Transition movement, are a social movement where communities collectively decide to prepare for the consequences of peak oil and to mitigate the impact of climate change. This tends to involve groups of campaigners raising awareness of environmental issues within their local town, practical efforts to reduce energy use, and attempts to build resilience to climate change by, for example, establishing communal allotments and designing an energy descent plan (North 2011). The aim is to engage the whole community in planning for a more resilient way of life in a hopeful and productive way, with the slogan "Peak oil makes it inevitable. Transition initiatives make it feasible, viable and attractive" (Transition Towns n.d.). Transition Towns have been greatly inspired by permaculture; the movement's founder, Rob Hopkins, is an active permaculture teacher, and much of its approach mirrors a permaculture understanding of natural systems and resilience. Transition Towns are in effect a re-imagination of permaculture:

> Transition Towns are a remarketing of permaculture. It's a reflection that permaculture has grown to such an extent that it's able to think about stuff at a town/city level, rather than in the 80s or the 90s at a garden level or allotment level. One of the reasons why the transition town movement exists is because it's stopped saying permaculture is just about gardening … Permaculture has always wanted to be a whole society thing … we've got to join everything up, we've got to find some way of involving the community a lot more … The resilience that the transition town movement talks about is the same resilience that is talked about in early permaculture teachings … it's like nature's really resilient, how do we match that?[10]

This re-imagination illustrates, in much the same way as LIDs, that permaculture is a flexible and useful tool for outlining the possibilities of sustainable living. In both Transition Towns and LIDs, there is a strong acknowledgment of the need to survive increasing climate change and that to do this requires a process of experimentation and closer observation of nature's systems. Both try to put into practice the original intention of Mollison and Holmgren (1978): of a new way of living that involves radical changes far beyond simply producing our food differently.

Conclusions

> Low Impact Developments seek to operate with the least energy input and the least negative impact. This is very similar to the permaculture principle of minimum input for maximum output. Overall the aim is to make a positive contribution to the natural world, locally and globally. In other words, have a positive relationship with nature which is beneficial for all.[11]

LIDs in Britain have used permaculture as a way to structure their communities, food production, house building, and livelihoods. Increasingly, they have been able to shift beyond food production to a more holistic implementation of permaculture principles, just as it was originally intended, and as a result be part of "the permaculture movement [which] acts as a sort of a natural laboratory wherein potentially sustainable solutions are experimented with" (Veteto and Lockyer 2008: 53).

In examining LIDs, we are able to critically examine the successes and tensions of permaculture in practice in the particular national context of Britain. Permaculture has been used to shape site plan decisions, to make best use of resources and energy, to support the processes of integration rather than segregation, and to assert the importance of being flexible in the face of change. However, the partial implementation of permaculture principles and ethics highlights the struggle many LIDs have had with implementing permaculture collectively and in building integrated and communal ways of living. Whether this is an assertive rejection of the full implications of collectivity and thus a critique of permaculture, or more a reflection of the stage at which LIDs find themselves is unclear. Few LIDs have been able to put permaculture fully into practice because of a difficulty of collectively agreeing on the finer details of what permaculture is, and for the lack of large-scale collective working examples of permaculture in Britain.

Moreover, there are many "accidental" permaculturalists who have come upon it and practice what they call "commonsense" approaches to ecoliving, which could be conceived by others as permaculture practice. Permaculture has openly and deliberately built upon a myriad of understandings of nature's systems, both indigenous and Western-scientific, and as a result is conceived by many as being about "looking at some of those traditional ways of farming and working the land and traditional communities and saying what works and what doesn't work?"[12] Other permaculture advocates have argued that in practice it is "only by reconnecting ourselves with our local resources can we move towards a sustainable society" (Whitefield 1997: 8). This, however, confuses the wider lessons of permaculture in that it is a hybrid of principles, some about localism, but others about connection, integration, and the balancing of needs of the earth and people. There are also tensions about the time needed to closely observe a site before any plans are made (advised to take twelve months) amid the acknowledgment of the need to evolve systems quickly to cope with climate change.

My analysis of only partial success in the implementation of permaculture in LIDs is not meant as an assertion of its failure, but rather as a celebration of its successes thus far. Britain is in a transitional period of making permaculture work on a large scale in collective spaces. However, it is the broader lessons that permaculture teaches that have been embraced by LIDs where hope really lies. In balancing the needs of the earth with those of people, of asserting the importance of equality, and, crucially, in tying these together with a focus on holism, sustainable ecological living has begun to become a reality.

Notes

1. I use the term Low Impact Development after Fairlie (1996) to refer to a radical approach to living, as opposed to use of the term in the United States for

a storm water management system that seeks to disperse storm water using biologically inspired design. Such an approach in Britain is referred to as a sustainable urban design system, and is very different from what is explored in this article. However, recent work in North Carolina has used permaculture design in improving these storm water management systems; see Ormond et al. 2010.

2. Interview with Tony Wrench, Brithdir Mawr, 15 August 2006.
3. Interview with Will, Green Hill, 15 May 2006.
4. Interview with Josh, Landmatters, 18 May 2010. These are the personal views of Josh and are not necessarily shared by all residents at Landmatters.
5. An intentional community seeks to operate according to an agreed set of principles to which all residents comply—hence, they act with intention, be it around spiritual beliefs, dietary constraints, or minimizing environmental impact. Lammas decided to have as few rules as possible and seeks to encourage individual freedom in decisions about spirituality, eating meat, and the ownership of individual motorized vehicles.
6. Interview with Josh, Landmatters, 18 May 2010.
7. Interview with Will, Green Hill, 15 May 2006.
8. Interview with Will, Green Hill, 15 May 2006.
9. Interview with Josh, Landmatters, 18 May 2010.
10. Interview with Will, Green Hill, 15 May 2006.
11. Interview with Will, Green Hill, 15 May 2006.
12. Interview with Will, Green Hill, 15 May 2006.

References

Barton, Hugh. 1998. "Eco-neighbourhoods: A Review of Projects." *Local Environment* 3 (2): 159–77.

Brown, Gavin, and Jenny Pickerill. 2009. "Space for Emotion in the Spaces of Activism." *Emotion, Space and Society* 2 (1): 24–35.

Chapter 7. 2003. *Sustainable Homes and Livelihoods in the Countryside.* South Petherton, UK: Chapter 7.

Fairlie, Simon. 1996. *Low Impact Development: Planning and People in a Sustainable Countryside.* Oxford, UK: Jon Carpenter.

Halfacree, Keith. 2007. "Back-to-the-Land in the Twenty-First Century—Making Connections with Rurality." *Tijdschrift voor Economische en Sociale Geografie* 98 (1): 3–8.

Holmgren, David. 2002. *Permaculture: Principles and Pathways Beyond Sustainability.* Hepburn, Australia: Holmgren Design Services.

Jacob, Jeffrey. 2006. *New Pioneers: The Back-to-the-Land Movement and the Search for a Sustainable Future.* University Park: Pennsylvania State University Press.

Kennedy, Declan. 1991. "Permaculture and the Sustainable City." *Ekistics—The Problems and Science of Human Settlements* 58 (348–349): 210–15.

Laughton, Rebecca. 2008. *Surviving and Thriving on the Land: How to Use Your Time and Energy to Run a Successful Smallholding.* Devon, UK: Green Books.

Macnamara, Looby. 2009. *Permaculture Report for Lammas Low Impact Initiatives Ltd.* Designed Visions (Permaculture Design Consultancy). Available at http://www.lammas.org.uk/ecovillage/documents/Permaculturereport.pdf.

Maxey, Larch. 2009. "What is Low Impact Development?" In *Low Impact Development: The Future in Our Hands,* ed. Jenny Pickerill and Larch Maxey. Available at http://lowimpactdevelopment.wordpress.com.

Mollison, Bill, and David Holmgren. 1978. *Permaculture One.* Sisters Creek, Australia: Tagari Publications.

Mulligan, Martin, and Stuart Hill. 2001. *Ecological Pioneers: A Social History of Australian Ecological Thought and Action.* Cambridge: Cambridge University Press.

North, Peter J. 2011. "The Politics of Climate Activism in the UK: A Social Movement Analysis." *Environment and Planning A* 43 (7): 1581–98.

Ormond, Timothy, Bailey Mundy, Mary Weber, and Zev Friedman. 2010. "LID Meets Permaculture: Sustainable Stormwater Management in the Mountains of Western North Carolina." Proceedings of the 2010 International Low Impact Development Conference. San Francisco, CA, 11–14 April 2010.

Permaculture Association. n.d. "The Basics." http://www.permaculture.org.uk/knowledge-base/basics (accessed 24 May 2010).

Pickerill, Jenny, and Larch Maxey. 2009a. "Geographies of Sustainability: Low Impact Developments and Radical Spaces of Innovation." *Geography Compass* 3 (4): 1515–39.

———, eds. 2009b. *Low Impact Development: The Future in Our Hands.* Available at http://lowimpactdevelopment.wordpress.com.

Rodker, Oli. 2009. "Living the Dream … the Low Impact Way. In *Low Impact Development: The Future in Our Hands,* ed. Jenny Pickerill and Larch Maxey. Available at http://lowimpactdevelopment.wordpress.com.

Transition Towns. n.d. "What is a Transition Town (or Village/City/Forest/Island)?" http://www.transitiontowns.org/TransitionNetwork/TransitionInitiative (accessed 22 June 2010).

Veteto, James R., and Joshua Lockyer. 2008. "Environmental Anthropology Engaging Permaculture: Moving Theory and Practice Toward Sustainability." *Culture & Agriculture* 30 (1–2): 47–58.

Whitefield, Patrick. 1997. *Permaculture in a Nutshell.* Hampshire, UK: Permanent Publications.

Woods, Michael. 2008. "Social Movements and Rural Politics." *Journal of Rural Studies* 24: 129–37.

Wrench, Tony. 2001. *Building a Low-impact Roundhouse.* Hampshire, UK: Permanent Publications.

CHAPTER ELEVEN

In Search of Global Sustainability and Justice

How Permaculture Can Contribute to Development Policy

Aili Pyhälä

Introduction

In the past few decades, there has been a tendency among academics, politicians, and lay people to think of development and the preservation of the environment in antagonistic terms.[1] This human-nature dualism and alienation from nature has evolved to a point where, by "domesticating ourselves," we are ever more disassociated from our local ecosystems and thus becoming rootless economic entities geared toward limitless growth (Livingston 1994; Shepard 1998).

However, recent research shows that indefinite global economic growth is unsustainable (Jackson 2009; Simms and Johnson 2010). Each year we are consuming the earth's living resources faster than our planet can regenerate them, and producing more waste than it can assimilate—currently, we are exceeding the planet's regenerative capacity by about 30 percent (Wackernagel and Rees 1996; WWF 2008). Meanwhile, supposed "solutions" and strategies, such as the introduction of genetically modified organisms (GMOs) and the intensification of monoculture industrialized farming, both of which are often sold in the name of "development," have proven to be based on methods that seriously threaten the stability and diversity of ecosystems, while marginalizing and impoverishing small-scale farmers and undermining food sovereignty.

A recent report from the International Assessment of Agricultural Science and Technology for Development (IAASTD), drafted by over four hundred scientists and practitioners from around the globe, has stated that "business as usual" is no longer an option for tackling food insecurity;

and that a fundamental change in farming practice is needed to counteract soaring food prices, hunger, social inequities, and environmental disasters. They also state that small-scale farmers and nongenetically modified agroecological methods are the way forward, with indigenous and local knowledge playing as important a role as formal science (IAASTD 2008).

There is therefore much reason to start considering "development" in far more broad terms, not only as increases in income and material goods, but foundationally as the expansion of human freedoms, which are thoroughly dependent on the integrity of the environment (Apffel-Marglin and Marglin 1996; Sachs 1992; Escobar 1993; Deb 2009). This argument is complemented by a growing number of studies revealing that, beyond a certain point, economic growth no longer improves health, happiness, or measures of well-being (Solnick and Hemenway 1998; Easterlin 2003; Graham 2008; Easterlin and Angelescu 2009; Holmes 2010). On the contrary, as affluent societies have grown richer, rates of anxiety, depression, and numerous other social problems have increased (Kasser 2002; Wilkinson and Pickett 2010). In other words, despite their affluence, modern societies are, in many ways, social failures.

The development model currently advocated by the politically dominant mass-consumer culture is not only environmentally and socially unsustainable; it is also increasingly unjust. It is estimated that approximately 80 percent of the world's resources are being consumed by 20 percent of the world's people (Wilkinson and Pickett 2010), and the gap between the rich and the poor continues to grow. This injustice is exacerbated by the fact that the effects of climate change, peak oil, and other crises (such as those related to water, soil, and food insecurity) are falling disproportionately on the world's poorest countries, particularly in Africa, Asia, and South America (Patt et al. 2009). Hundreds of thousands of communities in these parts of the globe are more vulnerable than ever and facing an increasingly uncertain future.

Yet, despite all the evidence, the majority of affluent industrialized countries continue to advocate a model of development based on economic growth, holding poor countries locked in a system that keeps them dependent on serving the more rich and powerful, in the name of "development" (Escobar 1993). Ironically, the current trend will inevitably limit the possibilities of development, not only in poor countries, but also in richer nations, as they strive to maintain their prosperity. It is no surprise, then, that in the field of international development policy makers and practitioners are not only struggling to find solutions to the multiple problems facing many of the poorest communities in the world; they are also having to rethink their very own arguments and strategies regarding how to convincingly guide poorer populations down a development path that seems doomed to fail.

This chapter takes a look at development policy from a perspective of global environmental sustainability and social justice. I start by examining the shortcomings, contradictions, and failures of development aid, and question the reasoning for continued aid in its current form. I then address the question of whose sustainability we are really talking about in the discourse of "sustainable development."

Too often, critiques of current approaches to development are unaccompanied by viable solutions. This chapter attempts to counter this by exploring what one particular design system, *permaculture,* can offer in terms of solutions and approaches to current challenges in development aid. Presenting recent case studies from around the world, and drawing on both theory and personally collected data,[2] I argue that permaculture can synergistically resolve multiple problems and challenges facing both donors and recipients, while playing a central role in promoting self-determination and equity in development. I also suggest that new and different roles for development cooperation grounded in the permaculture paradigm be explored under a strategy that combines both bottom-up and top-down approaches.

Development Aid: A Moral Obligation or a Fundamentally Flawed Paradigm?

Development aid (also termed development cooperation or development assistance) is foreign aid that is concerned with overcoming world poverty wherein trajectories of foreign aid[3] flow from richer countries to poorer countries, and ostensibly to poor people. This aid aims to help address acute human suffering, contribute to human welfare, and reduce poverty (Riddell 2007). The reasoning for continued aid provision is largely a moral one: estimates suggest that in 2010–2012, 870 million people were chronically undernourished and 98 percent of the world's hungry lived in developing countries (FAO 2012).

Despite these figures, less than half of all official development aid (ODA) is channeled to the sixty-five poorest countries, and well over 10 percent of official aid goes to countries too rich to even qualify as recipients of ODA (Riddell 2007). Overall, current levels of ODA fall well short of what is needed to effectively address the problem of poverty in poor countries, and according to some analysts, even doubling current levels would prove insufficient (Collier 2007). Some observers claim that the gap between what is needed and what is currently provided is expected to grow even wider if problems caused by emergencies, disasters, climate change, and other factors rise in coming years, as has been predicted (UN Millennium Project 2005).

There is thus a grave mismatch between donors acknowledging their responsibility to respond to acute human suffering and the amounts of aid they currently give, suggesting that there are other criteria that matter just as much (if not more) in development aid than the humanitarian motives for providing aid. Perhaps even more paradoxical is that (1) more people live in extreme poverty today than they did twenty years ago—and certainly more than ever in the past (Sachs and Santarius 2007); (2) in some parts of the world, such as in sub-Saharan Africa, the percentage living in poverty has actually increased in the past three decades (World Bank 2007); and (3) the enormous contrast between the extreme poverty and suffering on the one hand and the rich minority on the other continues to grow (Milanovic 2005).

Studies on the distribution of wealth show that currently 80 percent of global wealth accrues to the fifty-two richest (high-income) countries, which contain 17 percent of the world's population. Meanwhile, only 3 percent of global wealth is produced in the sixty-two poorest (low-income) countries, which contain 37 percent of the world's population (World Bank 2006).[4] What is becoming increasingly clear is that rather than world economic integration, as promised by the current economic development model, a process of global *fragmentation* is taking place: the world is developing, but in two opposite directions.

There are further reasons to question the efficacy, effectiveness, and intentions of development aid. In terms of monitoring progress in poor countries, few aid-funded projects or programs have been successful in achieving or contributing to broader goals and outcomes in a lasting way, and some aid has even had adverse systemic effects (Riddell 2007). More deep-rooted, fundamental flaws of development aid—and development thinking in general—lie in the fact that aid effectiveness continues to be assessed mainly on its ability to make immediate and concrete differences to poverty levels in aid-recipient countries, and these poverty levels are assessed almost entirely based on *income.* However, single definitions and classifications of poverty can simply not be limited to indicators based on income (Bell and Morse 2008); the fact that one in five (over one billion) people in the world live on less than one US dollar per day says nothing about the *conditions* in which those people are living. Imposing a view that a single yardstick can be applied to all cultures is not only ethnocentric; it would also be naïve to think that the conventional economic mode of classification in any way discerns the *quality* of life in any particular society (Woodward 2010).

Another facet demonstrating this concern is that economic development statistics often fail to capture the losses and disadvantages that may accompany monetary gain. For instance, there is no standard practice for accounting for the effects that earning an income may have on social security and culture, when external labor often requires that workers migrate to the city, thereby no longer relying on family networks or local land bases. Entire forms of livelihood can disappear, and knowledge-rich traditions and customs along with them. Similarly, the tendency of monetary incomes to favor men goes unseen in quantitative accounting methods. Furthermore, all too often financial project aid ends up in the pockets of elites, encouraging corruption and failing to reach those who really need it, or for whom the resources were intended (Collier 2007). Indeed, vast amounts of aid have increased economic disparities; thus, simply increasing amounts of aid will not solve the issue.

The problem with current discourses of development is that they are firmly entrenched in Western modernity and economy. As a result, the process of needs interpretation and satisfaction is inextricably linked to the development apparatus, based on a liberal human rights discourse and on the "rational, scientific assessment and measurement of 'needs,' lacking a significant link to people's everyday experience" (Escobar 1993: 46).

For decades, scholars have provided critiques of the discourse and practice of development, many of them arguing for new ways of thinking about the meaning of development and the complexion of our economy (Frank [1969] 2000; Apffel-Marglin and Marglin 1996; Keare 2001; Chambers 2005; Cooper and Packard 2005), some even calling for alternatives *to* development, rejecting the entire paradigm (Escobar 1993, 1995; Deb 2009). Many of the critiques have tended to focus on one or more of the following: a critical stance with respect to established scientific knowledge; an interest in local autonomy, culture, and knowledge; and the defense of localized, pluralistic grassroots movements (Esteva 1987; Shiva 1989; Sachs 1992).

In sum, the idea that richer, developed societies do better than others is misleading, and there is as much reason to question the belief that those who live on less than one dollar a day can be classified as "poor" as there is need to start redefining "development" based on notions of equality (Agyeman, Bullard, and Evans 2003; Deneulin and Shahani 2009). This leads us to the notion of global justice and responsibility, and the following question: whose sustainability are we really talking about when we talk about *sustainable development?*

Whose Sustainability?

One of the first definitions of "sustainable development" is that published in the Brundtland Commission's 1987 report *Our Common Future,* where it is explained as "development that meets the needs of the present without compromising the ability of future generations to meet their own needs" (Brundtland 1987: 43). The same report goes on to argue that "sustainable development requires meeting the basic needs *of all* and extending *to all* the opportunity to fulfill their aspirations for a better life" (Brundtland 1987: 43, emphasis added). The "of all" and "to all" illustrate that the issue of not only intergenerational but also *intra*generational equity was laid out as fundamental to the concept of sustainable development when the concept was first being defined.

In 1992, when the international community agreed at the United Nations (UN) Conference on Environment and Development to devise national sustainable development strategies, the goal was set to "ensure socially responsible economic development while protecting the resource base and the environment for the benefits of future generations" (UN Department of Economic and Social Affairs 2010: chap. 8). What remained unclear was the question of *whose* future generations, and *where?*[5] Similarly, how and to what extent nation states should consider sustainability at the *global* scale was left open to interpretation.

There is mounting evidence suggesting that the issue of global responsibility and justice needs to be addressed. In their study, Srinivasan et al. (2008) found that the economic value of environmental damage to poor nations by high-income nations is greater than the total foreign debt of the poor countries affected. Similarly, there are many areas in the policy positions of industrialized countries that are currently at odds with global sustainability. Alongside development aid, large-scale programs driven today by governments and corporations are proving to be far more destructive both to the environment *and* to local populations than small-scale development could ever be—as modern industrial fisheries, intensive forestry, and mining are mostly geared to meet global demand for overconsumption, rather than to meet local basic needs (Arce and Long 2000).

As a result, many rural populations in developing countries remain stuck in a vicious cycle of poverty, disease, malnutrition, and environmental destruction—a cycle that has more to do with estrangement from culture, traditional practices, knowledge systems, livelihoods, and identity than it has to do with lack of income. With growing external pressure to gain higher economic incomes, poor families have been (and continue to be) driven to adopt unsustainable extractive activities. What were once nearby forests have often been hunted out and logged, cleared for agriculture for a few cycles until the nutrients are washed away, turned over to cattle pasture, or abandoned. The result is decreasing soil fertility, loss of biodiversity, increased resource scarcity and hardship, and mutually reinforcing cycles of poverty and environmental degradation (Stonich and DeWalt 1996).

What this boils down to is the need for *policy coherence*[6] to be an underlying and fundamental precondition for any policy integration, in keeping with the original idea of promoting sustainable development (OECD 1996). However, not much will change on the policy front while economic ground rules remain as they currently are: benefiting the rich at the expense of the poor. These are the same rules upon which the regulation of property, international trade, and commerce are based, as well as negotiation in current climate change talks (Klimaforum Declaration 2009).[7] The Greenhouse Development Rights report's analysis of how requirements for mitigation of climate change could be distributed in a "just" way concludes that much of the mitigation that takes place within the Global South must be enabled and supported by the Global North (Baer, Athanasiou, and Kartha 2007). Interestingly, however, although all the governments in the North are currently under pressure to sign up to an agreement to significantly lower their CO^2 emissions, the most promising actions being taken to meet these targets are coming not from governments, but from the grassroots.

The above critique of development is one covering many sectors and disciplines, thus calling for an equally broad-ranging approach that can simultaneously address the multiple facets and challenges of development. Permaculture is one such framework, which provides principles and tools for working with the social, economic, ecological, and cultural pillars of development in an integrated, holistic, and synergistic way.

What Permaculture Design Can Offer

Permaculture is a holistic and interdisciplinary system of design based on a set of design principles and techniques for developing closed-loop, symbiotic, self-sustaining human habitats and production systems that do not result in ecological degradation or social injustice (Mollison 1988). David Holmgren, the cofounder of permaculture (with Bill Mollison), writes that permaculture "draws together the diverse ideas, skills and ways of living which need to be rediscovered and developed in order to empower us to move from being dependent consumers to becoming responsible and productive citizens" (2002: xix). He goes on to stress the importance of providing for one's own needs through self-reliance and personal responsibility: "As we reduce our dependence on the global economy and replace it with household and local economies, we reduce the demand that drives current inequities" (Holmgren 2002: 7). Permaculture thus seeks to enable people to become more self-reliant and, in the process, to relieve the social injustices and ecological degradation created by the global political economy (Veteto and Lockyer 2008: 50).

One of the factors that differentiates permaculture from many other "sustainability sciences" is that permaculture aims not only for sustainability, but also for rapid regeneration and significant *improvements* in the natural resource base and yields. The philosophy behind permaculture is that it is no longer enough to simply conserve what is left of the natural world; we must also heal the damage we have done. Contrary to common belief, human cultures can, and often do, increase species diversity in local environments through natural resource management practices that incorporate local and indigenous knowledge, methods, and practices (Balée 2006). In other words, "sustainable" is not good enough, and what permaculture strives for is *abundance,* while enriching both cultural and biological diversity.[8]

Another unique characteristic of permaculture is that it encompasses a set of fundamental ethical principles, namely (1) care for the earth; (2) care for people; and (3) set limits to consumption and reproduction and redistribute surplus (Holmgren 2002). As such, permaculture provides a strong foundation for designing and enacting a more just, equitable, and sustainable world, in a holistic framework that bridges the grassroots and valuable traditional knowledge with modern science, innovation, and policy making. As an integrative systems science guided by logical principles, permaculture addresses root causes of current problems—rather than just symptoms—thereby avoiding falling into the trap of many of the controversies of current development "aid" mentioned above. The following case studies, compiled from around the world, present some examples of how permaculture design is already helping to address global sustainable development challenges at the local level.

Jordan

The Jordan Valley Permaculture (JVP) project, undertaken by the Permaculture Research Institute of Australia (PRI) in the Dead Sea Valley, Jordan, started as a pilot project to rehabilitate ten acres (four hectares) of otherwise nonproductive farmland in the southern Jordan Valley, which exists in conditions of extreme salinity and drought. The main environmental concerns that led to the project were the increasing shortage of freshwater resources for human uses and the decreasing quality of freshwater resources due to high salinity of water and other pollution—thereby also decreasing the quality of farm system production. Before the project, these systems were entirely dependent on chemical inputs—hence an economic burden on farmers—with significant impacts on the environment.

The aim of JVP was to establish a model project of sustainable arid land development, demonstrating that with the use of permaculture design, all basic needs can be met—even in harsh conditions—with low-cost, low-tech methods. Some of the specific techniques and permaculture principles applied were the following: (1) building rainwater harvesting contour swales (manifesting permaculture principles of "designing from patterns to details" and "catching and storing energy"); (2) planting a multitude of both nitrogen-fixing and fruit-bearing plants and trees along the swales (manifesting principles of "obtaining a yield" and "valuing diversity") and using all plant residue to cover swales so as to conserve water and improve soil properties (manifesting the principle of "producing no waste"); and (3) introducing animals to achieve plant-animal integration, generate income, and provide manure for different crops (manifesting principles of "integration" and "using and valuing renewable resources and services") (PRI 2008).

Both video and photographic documentation are proof of the dramatic positive impacts and results of the project (see Lawton 2007). Once an arid desert landscape, the project site now boasts abundant green cover and well-established permaculture ecosystems. The site is organically cultivated with different productive crops that serve both for subsistence and market purposes, thus helping to generate income for the local community. Over its course, the JVP project has involved over one hundred local people directly, with an additional estimated thirty thousand indirect beneficiaries, and the site is now being used as a training center for a regional water management program for all the agricultural communities within the Jordan Valley.

Peru

Another noteworthy development-focused permaculture project is the Redpal-Shipibo Permaculture Project near Pucallpa, in Peruvian Amazonia (Mellett 2004). The project started in the early 1990s, when a group of indigenous Shipibo settlements were relocated to an area that had previously been deforested and overgrazed. With few livelihood options and meager resources, the Shipibo decided to connect with the Latin American Permaculture Network (PAL), and together they formed RedPAL (the organization currently running the project) and began to design appropriate agroforestry systems to regenerate soil fertility and to meet some of the most basic immediate needs of the communities.

In direct response to local engagement and preferences (with the priority being food security), RedPAL set out to work primarily with sustainable aquaculture based on permaculture principles. The aquaculture ponds were designed so as to "maximize edge" (to enhance microclimates and biodiversity), and for "maximum interconnectedness and multiple functions" (surrounding trees and shrubs drop leaves and fruit into the water to directly feed fish and stimulate algal, plant, and insect growth that fish and other animals feed on). Using permaculture design has significantly reduced the need for inputs of supplementary feed and labor, rendering the system self-maintaining. Production is raised through increasing diversity and efficiency rather than increasing inputs, and the economic potential is estimated to be the equivalent of a fifteen-fold profit in income, thus making the project, from an economic standpoint, quite successful. It also has the effect of regenerating an area that not long ago was degraded, deforested, and impoverished land into a thriving ecosystem.

The wealth of traditional ecological knowledge (TEK) held by the Shipibo communities (particularly about the seasonal food chain interactions between different species of fish and plants) played a major part in the design process of the project. The combination of permaculture design principles and local TEK enabled the Shipibo to learn new innovative approaches to sustainable development while simultaneously tapping into their own knowledge systems and skills for ecosystem regeneration and management, giving new value to traditional knowledge. A committee of Shipibo families continues to manage the project, and plans are underway to set up an educational center for permaculture and ecovillage design near Pucallpa, with the aim being to spread knowledge, skills, and examples throughout Amazonia.

Nepal

The Himalayan Permaculture Centre (HPC) is a grassroots nongovernmental organization (NGO) set up by Chris Evans (a UK permaculture expert) and local permaculture-trained farmers from numerous villages in the Surkhet district (midwestern Nepal) to overcome the shortfalls of international development and implement sustainable rural development programs in Nepal (Permaculture Association n.d.). HPC has prioritized its work with affected communities that are marginalized by not only lack of access to key resources such as education, health care, food security, and credit; but that also live in marginalized environments characterized by high altitude, remoteness, and steepness, and with little supporting infrastructure. According to HPC, these are the people and places "where small inputs of appropriate technology and appropriate education can make huge differences" (HPC n.d.).

In a country where over 90 percent of the working population are dependent on agriculture for their livelihood, traditional subsistence agricultural practices have developed over time to be finely in tune with the local climate, the landscape, and people's needs, providing food, fuel, fodder, timber, and medicines. Recently, however, the nationalization of forests, in combination with a rising population and ineffective aid programs, has undermined the sustainability of traditional agriculture (HPC n.d.).

HPC's strategy revolves around three main activities: demonstration, training and education, and resources. The latter includes the distribution of seeds, seedlings, and published material (books, booklets, posters) translated into the local language (based on Vedic script—in Hindi or Sanskrit) for farmers and development workers to design and implement sustainable food, energy, and entire permaculture systems on their own land and in their communities. In addition, HPC carries out research to identify useful new species and cropping patterns (or combinations of those existing traditionally) that can be appropriated by local farmers (applying the principle of "observing and interacting").

HPC's "toolbox" contains methods and technologies developed with participatory methods such as participatory rural appraisal (PRA) and appreciative inquiry (AI)—where stakeholders themselves "pass" the technology on its merits, and frequently improve and adapt them to their local situation and needs (principle of "adapting to change"). These are then relearned by HPC for broader distribution, and are often taught directly from farmer to farmer (Chambers 2007), even in areas where HPC has not been active (principle of "self-regulation and feedback").

HPC is a strong proponent of "rolling permaculture" (Burnett 2009), the implementation of permaculture systems that do not displace traditional agricultural and social practices, but instead enhance them and allow them to flourish. For example, the use of green manures as an intercrop increases soil fertility by growing biomass—an agricultural resource—in between rotations of traditional grain crops. Such practices can thus be increased on-farm without displacing traditional yields. This is also achieved by planting suitable tree species on bare and unproductive land, improved seed selection and storage, and the planting of live fences that also produce fodder, wood for fuel, bee forage, and serve as barriers (principles of "multiple functions" and "integration"). Such systems increase the biomass needed to support agriculture (fodder and leaf litter for compost production close to the farm) without decreasing land under staple food production and without the need to increase land under agriculture, thus taking pressure off the forest, which farmers would otherwise exploit to create new farmland. These and other technologies are described in the Farmers' Handbook (Evans and Jespersen 2007), which—in addition to being a technical support document—is also designed to be used in literacy education.

Conclusions

It is increasingly questionable whether the overall paradigm of "development" is compatible with the long-term health of the planet. What we currently perceive as a model of successful development is far from what can be considered *sustainable* development. In the process of individual nations striving to improve the well-being of (parts of) their populations, many are losing track of the aim of sustainability, and falling into what we can call "excess"—the use of more resources than what the planet can provide and sustain.

Meanwhile, the ongoing and growing inequality within and between societies in the Global North and the Global South is shifting our attention from ever more pressing environmental and social problems, as efforts are predominantly focused on keeping the economic wheel turning. To enable global equal rights to a healthy environment, all scientific scenarios point to a need for the rich, high-consumer cultures to severely curb their ecological (and carbon) footprints. The South, in turn, is currently faced with the most immediate challenges and greatest burdens in dealing with and adapting to the multiple crises related to climate change, food and energy security, and loss of biocultural diversity. Permaculture can help address these challenges by reviving and strengthening traditional practices and knowledge systems in the Global South, allowing the diversity of cultures to flourish, and thereby addressing an essential component of truly sustainable development.

One of the great attractions of permaculture design is that it addresses justice and sustainability holistically—not only in the ecological, but also in the economic, social, and cultural dimensions. In addition, permaculture addresses the *root causes* of problems, exposing the illusion of progress promoted by conventional development aid that in reality does little other than enable further exploitation. It proposes a new framework that demonstrates, through research and development, that sustainability and justice *are* possible.

The permaculture project case studies presented above demonstrate that it is within human capacity and knowledge to enhance, improve, repair, and regenerate the environment and societies in which we live. From re-localization to regeneration and rehabilitation, new projects can draw upon a wide range of permaculture principles and techniques to reduce energy demand while incorporating local food and energy resilience, and strengthening local economies and cultures.

Applying permaculture in development cooperation projects can provide on-the-ground practitioners with a comprehensive toolbox for solving the often controversial ethical implications of development "aid" discussed above—as well as for the extension, planning, building, and managing of sustainable systems. Rather than going out to transform the traditions, values, and belief systems of other cultures, permaculture design—recognizing the value in TEK—offers opportunities for the *revitalization* of local traditional and indigenous culture, knowledge systems, and traditions, while simultaneously encouraging integration with modern science and technology. The approach is one that allows people and communities to define and design a path of sustainable living appropriate to their own environments, contexts, and worldviews.

Permaculture design also serves as a bridge between the grassroots and governments, between disciplines and knowledge systems, and between illiterate and literate. With an array of "living laboratories" and decades of experimentation around the world, permaculture networks and associations are already providing for the creative exchange and dissemination of information, skills, and expertise across and between levels and sectors—including farmers, planners, communities, governments, NGOs, businesses, and educational institutions (Veteto and Lockyer 2008).

The main challenge continues to be insufficient and irregular funding of such projects, which makes it difficult to plan for the longer term and to extend, scale up, and multiply projects. Yet, support for South-South exchange in permaculture and ecovillage design—complemented with more research, advocacy, and funding—has the potential of greatly strengthening local capacities and empowering grassroots initiatives in identifying a multitude of synergistic solutions to tackle future challenges. Furthermore—in order for the fundamental ethical principles laid out by permaculture to become legally influential—more pressure is needed to back the development of international law that is more ethical and just.

Achieving global social justice and environmental sustainability remains one of the greatest challenges facing us today. One of the most important obstacles to overcome is Western ethnocentrism and conventional epistemologies in the development arena. This demands a consequent shift toward supporting the right of each society to self-determination and cultural identity. Permaculture has the potential to integrate traditional and modern knowledge systems and technologies and, in offering sustainable and ethical solutions, can bring about revolutionary changes in the way humans relate to the earth and to each other. We might even wake up one day to find that instead of economic disparity being the dividing force of our world (which it has, for centuries), the knowledge and skills necessary to live in harmony with the earth and ourselves are the true guiding forces that lead us into a prosperous future.

Notes

I would like to express my deep gratitude to my dear friend and colleague Paulo Mellett, who introduced me to permaculture back in 2001 and who read and gave valuable comments on an early draft of this chapter.

1. The environment-development dualism is largely based on the centuries-long belief that humans are somehow separate from nature, dating back to Plato and Descartes, who, among other philosophers, strongly influenced Western thought with their theories on mind-body dualism (Encyclopaedia Britannica 2010).
2. During two years of working as a freelance researcher and consultant in the field of sustainable livelihoods (2008–2010), I have collected written material, made observations during project visits, and interviewed permaculture, ecovillage, and grassroots leaders from Africa, Australia, Europe, Asia, and North and South America.
3. Foreign aid consists of three very different but increasingly interlinked strands: (1) that of official development aid (ODA) (provided by governments and intergovernmental agencies); (2) that of development aid provided by NGOs and civil society organizations (CSOs); and (3) that of humanitarian and emergency aid, provided by official donors, UN agencies, the Red Cross, and NGOs. In this chapter, all three forms of aid are considered.
4. The income equality gap can also be analyzed in terms of the incomes of people, rather than countries. Analyses suggest that the income ratio of the richest 5 percent to the poorest 5 percent of people in the world is 165:1, the richest group earning in forty-eight hours what the poorest earn in a year. Meanwhile, the top 10 percent earn half the total world income, and the bottom 10 percent a mere 0.7 percent of world income (Milanovic 2005).
5. Similar questions, from the perspective of distributing the benefits of biodiversity, have been raised by Arturo Escobar (1998).
6. Policy coherence implies that the objectives, strategies, mechanisms, intentions, motives, and outcome pursued within a given policy framework are consistent with each other, and are not conflicting with objectives, strategies, mechanisms, motives, and outcome of other policy frameworks of the system (OECD 1996).
7. Many of the policy "solutions" in the climate change negotiations—mechanisms such as carbon capture and storage, Clean Development Mechanisms, genetically modified crops, geoengineering, and reducing emissions from deforestation and forest degradation (REDD)—are being opposed at the grassroots level, for they are perceived as only deepening social and environmental conflicts and inequalities (Klimaforum Declaration 2009).
8. Growing evidence shows that protecting and restoring biodiversity and maintaining and revitalizing cultural diversity are intimately interrelated, and that any hope for saving one is predicated on a concomitant effort to appreciate and protect the other (Maffi and Woodley 2010; Pilgrim and Pretty 2010; Verschuuren et al. 2010). Likewise, scholarly discussions have characterized

indigenous knowledge as a significant resource for development (Agarwal 1995, 2002).

References

Agarwal, Arun. 1995. "Dismantling the Divide Between Indigenous and Scientific Knowledge." *Development and Change* 26 (3): 413–39.

———. 2002. "Indigenous Knowledge and the Politics of Classification." *International Social Science Journal* 54 (173): 287–97.

Agyeman, Julian, Robert Doyle Bullard, and Bob Evans. 2003. *Just Sustainabilities: Development in an Unequal World.* London: Earthscan.

Apffel-Marglin, Frédérique, and Stephan Alan Marglin, eds. 1996. *Decolonizing Knowledge: From Development to Dialogue.* Oxford: Clarendon Press.

Arce, Alberto, and Norman Long. 2000. "Reconfiguring Modernity and Development from an Anthropological Perspective." In *Anthropology, Development and Modernities,* ed. Alberto Arce and Norman Long. London: Routledge.

Baer, Paul, Tom Athanasiou, and Sivan Kartha. 2007. *The Right to Development in a Climate Constrained World: The Greenhouse Development Rights Framework.* Berlin: Heinrich Böll Foundation.

Balée, William. 2006. "The Research Program of Historical Ecology." *Annual Reviews in Anthropology* 35: 75–98.

Bell, Simon, and Morse, Stephen. 2008. *Sustainability Indicators: Measuring the Immeasurable?* London: Earthscan.

Brundtland, Gro Harlem. 1987. *Our Common Future: The World Commission on Environment and Development.* Oxford: Oxford University Press.

Burnett, Graham. 2009. *Permaculture: A Beginners Guide.* Essex: Spiralseed.

Chambers, Robert. 2005. *Ideas for Development.* London: Earthscan.

———. 2007. "From PRA to PLA to Pluralism: Practice and Theory." IDS Working Paper 286. Brighton, UK: Institute of Development Studies.

Collier, Paul. 2007. *The Bottom Billion: Why the Poorest Countries are Failing and What Can Be Done About It.* Oxford: Oxford University Press.

Cooper, Frederick, and Randall Packard. 2005. "The History and Politics of Development Knowledge." In *The Anthropology of Development and Globalization: From Classical Political Economy to Contemporary Neoliberalism,* ed. Marc Edelman and Angelique Haugerud. Malden, MA: Blackwell.

Deb, Debal. 2009. *Beyond Developmentality: Constructing Inclusive Freedom and Sustainability.* London: Earthscan.

Deneulin, Séverine, and Lila Shahani, eds. 2009. *An Introduction to the Human Development and Capability Approach: Freedom and Agency.* London: Earthscan.

Easterlin, Richard A. 2003. "Explaining Happiness." *Proceedings of the National Academy of Sciences* 100 (19): 11176–83.

Easterlin, Richard A., and Laura Angelescu. 2009. "Happiness and Growth the World Over: Time Series Evidence on the Happiness-Income Paradox." IZA Discussion Paper No. 4060. Bonn, Germany: Institute for the Study of Labor.

Encyclopaedia Britannica. 2010. "Mind-Body Dualism." London: Encyclopaedia Britannica, International.
Escobar, Arturo. 1993. "Imagining a Post-Development Era? Critical Thought, Development and Social Movements." *Social Text* 31–32: 20–56.
———. 1995. *Encountering Development: The Making and Unmaking of the Third World.* Princeton, NJ: Princeton University Press.
———. 1998. "Whose Knowledge? Whose Nature? Biodiversity Conservation, and the Political Ecology of Social Movements." *Journal of Political Ecology* 5: 53–81.
Esteva, Gustavo. 1987. "Regenerating Peoples' Space." *Alternatives* 12 (1): 125–52.
Evans, Chris, and Jakob Jespersen. 2007. *Farmer's Handbook.* http://permaculture.org.au/2010/01/06/farmers-handbook/ (accessed 3 July 2010).
FAO. 2012. *The State of Food Insecurity in the World.* Rome: Food and Agriculture Organization of the United Nations.
Frank, Andre Gunder. [1969] 2000. "The Development of Underdevelopment." In *From Modernization to Globalization: Perspectives on Development and Social Change,* ed. J. Timmons Roberts and Amy Hite. Malden, MA: Blackwell.
Graham, Carol. 2008. "The Economics of Happiness." In *The New Palgrave Dictionary of Economics,* ed. Steven Durlaug and Lawrence Blume. 2nd ed. New York: Palgrave Macmillan. Available at http://www.dictionaryofeconomics.com/article?id=pde2008_H000015.
Himalayan Permaculture Centre (HPC). n.d. "Himalayan Permaculture Centre." http://himalayanpermaculture.com (accessed 14 May 2010).
Holmes, Bob. 2010. "Money Can Buy You Happiness—Up to a Point." *New Scientist,* 7 September.
Holmgren, David. 2002. *Permaculture: Principles and Pathways Beyond Sustainability.* Hepburn, Australia: Holmgren Design Services.
International Assessment on Agricultural Knowledge, Science and Technology for Development (IAASTD). 2008. "Global Summary for Decision Makers." Synthesis Report. Washington DC: Island Press.
Jackson, Tim. 2009. *Prosperity Without Growth?—The Transition to a Sustainable Economy.* London: Sustainable Development Commission.
Kasser, Tim. 2002. *The High Price of Materialism.* Cambridge, MA: MIT Press.
Keare, Douglas H. 2001. "Learning to Clap: Reflections on Top-Down Versus Bottom-Up Development." *Human Organization* 60 (2): 159–65.
Klimaforum Declaration. 2009. *System Change—Not Climate Change: A People's Declaration from Klimaforum09.* Copenhagen: Klimaforum.
Lawton, Geoff. 2007. *Greening the Desert.* Video of Jordan project converted into short Quicktime movie. Australia: Permaculture Research Institute. Available at http://www.youtube.com/watch?v=sohl6vnWZmk.
Livingston, John A. 1994. *Rogue Primate: An Exploration of Human Domestication.* Toronto: Key Porter Books.
Maffi, Luisa, and Ellen Woodley. 2010. *Biocultural Diversity Conservation: A Global Sourcebook.* London: Earthscan.
Mellett, Paul. 2004. "Silvo-aquaculture: Including Indigenous Resources in Amazonia's Blue Revolution" (BSc diss., University of East Anglia).

Milanovic, Branko. 2005. *Global Income Inequality: What It Is and Why It Matters.* Washington DC: World Bank.

Mollison, Bill. 1988. *Permaculture: A Designer's Manual.* Sisters Creek, Australia: Tagari Publications.

OECD. 1996. "Building Policy Coherence." In *Public Management Occasional Papers.* Paris: OECD.

Patt, Anthony, Dagmar Schröter, Richard J. Klein, and A. Cristina de la Vega-Leinart, eds. 2009. *Assessing Vulnerability to Global Environmental Change: Making Research Useful for Adaptation Decision Making and Policy.* London: Earthscan.

Permaculture Association. n.d. Profile of Chris Evans in "People Projects Places." http://www.permaculture.org.uk/user/chris-evans (accessed 15 May 2010).

Permaculture Research Institute of Australia (PRI). 2008. "Case Study: Jordan Valley Permaculture Project, Jordan." In *ProAct Network, The Role of Environmental Management and Eco-Engineering in Disaster Risk Reduction and Climate Change Adaptation.* Available at www.proactnetwork.org.

Pilgrim, Sarah, and Jules N. Pretty. 2010. *Nature and Culture: Rebuilding Lost Connections.* London: Earthscan.

Riddell, Roger C. 2007. *Does Foreign Aid Really Work?* Oxford: Oxford University Press.

Sachs, Wolfgang, ed. 1992. *The Development Dictionary: A Guide to Knowledge as Power.* London: Zed Books.

Sachs, Wolfgang, and Tilman Santarius. 2007. *Fair Future: Resource Conflicts, Security and Global Justice.* London: Zed Books; New York: Fernwood Publishing.

Shepard, Paul. 1998. *Nature and Madness.* Athens: University of Georgia Press.

Shiva, Vandana. 1989. *Staying Alive: Women, Ecology, and Development.* London: Zed Books.

Simms, Andrew, and Victoria Johnson. 2010. *Growth Isn't Possible: Why Rich Countries Need a New Economic Direction.* London: New Economics Foundation.

Solnick, Sara J., and David Hemenway. 1998. "Is More Always Better? A Survey on Positional Concerns." *Journal of Economic Behavior and Organization* 37: 373–83.

Srinivasan, U. Thara, Susan P. Carey, Eric Hallsteind, Paul A. T. Higgins, Amber C. Kerr, Laura E. Koteen, Adam B. Smith, Reg Watson, John Harte, and Richard B. Norgaard. 2008. "The Debt of Nations and the Distribution of Ecological Impacts from Human Activities." *Proceedings of the National Academy of Sciences of the USA* 105 (5): 1768–73.

Stonich, Susan C., and Billie R. DeWalt. 1996. "The Political Ecology of Deforestation in Honduras." In *Tropical Deforestation: The Human Dimension,* ed. Leslie E. Sponsel, Thomas N. Headland, and Robert C. Bailey. New York: Columbia University Press.

UN Department of Economic and Social Affairs. 2010. *Agenda 21.* http://www.un.org/esa/dsd/agenda21/res_agenda21_00.shtml (accessed 10 July 2010).

UN Millennium Project. 2005. *Investing in Development: A Practical Plan to Achieve the Millennium Development Goals.* London: Earthscan.

Verschuuren, Bas, Robert Wild, Jeffrey McNeely, and Gonzalo Oviedo. 2010. *Sacred Natural Sites: Conserving Nature and Culture.* London: Earthscan.

Veteto, James R., and Joshua Lockyer. 2008. "Environmental Anthropology Engaging Permaculture: Moving Theory and Practice Toward Sustainability." *Culture & Agriculture* 30 (1–2): 47–58.

Wackernagel, Mathis, and William Rees. 1996. *Our Ecological Footprint: Reducing Human Impact on the Earth.* Gabriola Island, Canada: New Society.

Wilkinson, Richard, and Kate Pickett. 2010. *The Spirit Level: Why Equality is Better for Everyone.* London: Penguin Books.

Woodward, David. 2010. *How Poor is "Poor"?* London: New Economics Foundation.

World Bank. 2006. *World Development Indicators (WDI).* Economic and Social Data Service International. Manchester: Mimas.

———. 2007. *The Atlas of World Development.* Washington DC: Harper Collins.

World Wide Fund for Nature (WWF). 2008. *Living Planet Report 2008.* Gland, Switzerland: WWF International.

Further Readings on Permaculture

Bane, Peter. 2012. *The Permaculture Handbook: Gardening for Town and Country.* Gabriola Island, Canada: New Society.

Dawborn, Kerry, and Caroline Smith, eds. *Permaculture Pioneers: Stories from the New Frontier.* Hepburn, Australia: Holmgren Design Services.

Hemenway, Toby. 2000. *Gaia's Garden: A Guide to Home-Scale Permaculture.* White River Junction, VT: Chelsea Green.

Holmgren, David. 2002. *Permaculture: Principles and Pathways Beyond Sustainability.* Hepburn, Australia: Holmgren Design Services.

———. 2007. *Essence of Permaculture.* Victoria, Australia: Holmgren Design Services. Available at http://permacultureprinciples.com/freedownloads_essence.php.

Mollison, Bill. 1988. *Permaculture: A Designer's Manual.* Tylagum, Australia: Tagari Publications.

———. 1990. *Permaculture: A Practical Guide for a Sustainable Future.* Washington DC: Island Press.

———. 1991. *Introduction to Permaculture.* Sisters Creek, Australia: Tagari Publications.

Mollison, Bill, and David Holmgren. 1978. *Permaculture One.* Sisters Creek, Australia: Tagari Publications.

Whitefield, Patrick. 1997. *Permaculture in a Nutshell.* Hampshire, UK: Permanent Publications.

III

Ecovillages

CHAPTER TWELVE

From Islands to Networks

The History and Future of the Ecovillage Movement

Jonathan Dawson

Introduction

Significant shifts have been visible within the ecovillage movement worldwide over the last decade that have fundamentally transformed the identity, role, and potential impact of ecovillages moving forward. In broad terms, the journey that ecovillages have undertaken is from being relatively isolated countercultural experiments offering a profoundly alternative vision and lifestyle to the cultural mainstream to increasingly working in formal and informal alliance with the more progressive elements in today's society. In short, ecovillages can no longer be described as standing outside of and in opposition to the mainstream.[1] The ecovillage vision, heterogeneous and disparate as it may be, is no longer alien or threatening to the wider society, and the relationships enjoyed by most ecovillages with their surrounding communities have improved, often beyond recognition, over the last decade or so.

As this has happened, the many social, economic, and ecological experiments that ecovillages have undertaken have spilled out of the confines of ecovillages themselves to flavor and transform their surrounding bioregions. Dense concentrations—or "islands"—of sustainability-related activities are giving way to networks of engagement in a wide array of social, economic, and ecological initiatives, with ecovillages serving as nodes in emerging bioregional networks. What happened to effect such a transformation? Interestingly, it seems to have had relatively little to do with conscious choices or increased outreach efforts made by ecovillages themselves—at least at the outset. From my perspective as a long-term ecovillage resident and former president of the Global Ecovillage Network (GEN), far more important have been changes in the wider society—in terms of both cultural orientation and policy formulation and implementation, changes that have made the activities of ecovillages appear more relevant.

This chapter looks at this issue from a broad historical perspective. Following an opening section on definitions, I explore the roots of today's ecovillage movement, identifying the various threads that are woven into the ecovillage tapestry. The second section explores recent trends within mainstream society that have made ecovillages more visible and relevant to its concerns. This section also describes some of the more prominent alliances that have developed in recent years between ecovillages and other actors in the public and private sectors. The third section describes some recent notable trends in ecovillages, and the final section explores how ecovillages might have the greatest impact in facilitating the transition to a low-energy future in which the human family has implemented ways of living well within its means.

Defining Ecovillages

The term "ecovillage" has proved famously difficult to define with any precision. The pioneers and leaders of the ecovillage movement have wrestled periodically with the thorny question of providing a clear and succinct definition. However, at each turn, the sheer diversity within the network has been so great that the definitions offered have been either incomplete, more aspirational than descriptive of the current reality, or both.

The first attempt at a definition, and still the one most commonly used, is Robert Gilman's: "A human-scale, full-featured settlement, in which human activities are harmlessly integrated into the natural world in a way that is supportive of healthy human development, and can be successfully continued into the indefinite future" (1991: 10). He added a later qualification in 1999 that ecovillages should also have "multiple centers of initiative," including governance structures, autonomous enterprises, associations, and projects of its residents—which together comprise the physical, economic, and social fabric of village life.

This is clearly aspirational in nature: few communities, with the exception of some traditional or indigenous groups, have consumption levels that are close to being sustainable into the indefinite future. Moreover, only relatively few intentional communities that call themselves ecovillages can truly be described as villages with multiple centers of initiative; most remain small in nature and limited in scope. The usefulness of Gilman's definition is further limited by the fact that in describing an end state rather than a strategy for its realization, it fails to adequately distinguish ecovillages from the growing number of sustainability-related community initiatives in more conventional towns and villages, as exemplified, for example, by the Transition movement.[2]

Subsequently, I offered the following five defining characteristics of ecovillages: "[p]rivate citizens' initiatives; in which the communitarian impulse is of central importance; that are seeking to win back some measure of control over community resources; that have a strong shared values base, often referred to as 'spirituality'; and that act as centers of research, demonstration and in most cases training" (Dawson 2006). This definition has the merit of greater precision, but at the cost of limiting itself to intentional communities located primarily in the Global North. Few existing indigenous communities could truly be described as being built around strong shared spiritual values and acting as research, demonstration, and training centers, even if there are groups and activities within Global South ecovillages to which these defining characteristics could apply.

Indeed, the most obvious distinction among ecovillage types is that between intentional community experiments, primarily but not exclusively located in the industrialized world; and existing communities—or more commonly, networks of existing communities—in the Global South. The former are small initiatives (only a handful have over one hundred members and many have significantly fewer) that are created around shared values and projects that relate to the journey toward a more sustainable society. The latter comprise communities in which local leaders understand the threat that economic globalization poses to the health of their communities and are seeking to wrest back some measure of control over their cultural, ecological, and economic resources. In fact, the largest members of the GEN are networks of Southern communities created by indigenous nongovernmental organizations (NGOs). Examples include Sarvodaya, a group that works with almost two thousand primarily rural communities across Sri Lanka; COLUFIFA (a French acronym meaning Committee for the Struggle to End Hunger), a network of two hundred and fifty communities spanning Guinea, Guinea-Bissau, Senegal, and Gambia; and GEN Senegal, an organization that networks over thirty communities in the west African state.

Common cause has been made between these two constituencies (Northern-based intentional communities and Southern networks of existing villages) around which alliances have been built focusing on economic relocalization, poverty alleviation and global justice, respect for cultural and spiritual diversity, and the evolution of a post-consumerist culture. However, it has proved difficult to provide a definition that satisfactorily encompasses the attributes of these two very different types of ecovillage. Since the themes addressed in this paper have impacted them somewhat differently, they are generally discussed separately.

Historical Development of the Ecovillage Movement

Various threads have been woven into the fabric of today's ecovillage movement, North and South, with multiple countercultural currents of the 1960s and 1970s playing a central role. While it is true that a small number of GEN members predate the 1960s—including the Icelandic ecovillage of Solheimar, which was created in 1931—these are very few in number, and even in such cases, themes strongly identified with the 1960s and 1970s are clearly present.

By the early 1960s, the Western world was emerging from a prolonged period of postwar austerity and had embarked on what was to be a sustained period of technological development and economic growth. It was a period of great optimism in the power of science and technology to create a better and wealthier world. The space race was on. Scientific advances created strong expectations for a high-technology, leisure-rich society. The "development" of the Third World was to be engineered, with the Green Revolution at its heart. In Britain, the Labour leader, Harold Wilson, won the 1966 general election on the back of the slogan "The White Heat of Technology."

By the beginning of the 1960s, Gandhi was dead, replaced at the helm of the Indian state by the modernizing Nehru, and there were few voices questioning the wisdom of the development path focused on science and industrial-scale technology. Today, we trace lineages of dissent back to such radical pioneers as Fritz Schumacher, Rachel Carson, and the authors of the *Limits to Growth* report (Meadows et al. 1972), but it is important to recognize that in the era in which they lived, these were lonely pioneers swimming against a mighty tide.

However, under the surface—and increasingly visible and audible as the 1960s progressed—were currents of collective dissent toward the dominant societal narrative of the time. One of the more durable manifestations of these diverse and interlinked counternarratives was the emergence of a range of communitarian experiments that were to flower into the intentional communities movement, primarily located in the industrialized world. The back-to-the-land and hippie movements were enormously important threads, representing a rejection by youth of mainstream, materialist values—and a yearning for reconnection with the land and vibrant, human-scale community. The cohousing movement, launched in Denmark and spreading outward internationally, represented a less radical but no less important attempt to create human settlements that tread more lightly on the earth while offering their residents a real sense of community and belonging.

Peace activism, given momentum by the anti–Vietnam War demonstrations, was a key element for resurgent intentional communities. In fact, one of the first usages of the term ecovillage—or rather, its German equivalent, *ökodorf*—was the name given by German peaceniks to the camps they created next to the nuclear power plants against which they were protesting. In an attempt to move beyond rejection of nuclear weapons, these temporary communities sought to model in microcosm the new society they were advocating in the design of their physical structures and systems as well as their decision-making procedures (Dawson 2006).

Many who were active in both the environmental and feminist movements began to see the links between the patriarchal oppression of women and the domination and destruction of the earth, which, like women, was seen by the industrial growth economy as a passive resource that would produce on demand and could be exploited for profit. The emerging small-scale, egalitarian communities were seen as ideal laboratories for the birthing of a new society based on ecological principles in which men and women might coexist as true equals.

Under the tutelage of intellectual giants such as Ivan Illich, radicalized groups came to look on state provision of services such as education and health as tools for the creation of artificial needs to be satisfied by emerging giant corporations and the general disempowerment of the populace (Illich 1971, 1977). Within the emerging intentional communities, radical experiments in holistic health and education proliferated. The Farm in Tennessee went so far as to set up its own primary health care system with laboratories, dispensary, infirmaries, outpatient care, ambulance service, neonatal ICU, holistic midwifery center, and training clinics for "barefoot doctors."

In contrast to the growing materialist and rationalist rhetoric of mainstream industrial society, there emerged on the margins, including within many intentional communities, a renewed interest in meditation, spiritual enquiry, and the merits of voluntary simplicity. The ancient teachings of indigenous and tribal traditions exerted an especial fascination, as exemplified by the cult popularity of the teachings of Paramahansa Yogananda and Black Elk, or the imaginative works of J. R. R. Tolkien and Carlos Castaneda.

Meanwhile, the Global South was seeing its own form of growing dissent and resistance to the grand scientific project of development that was being spread out across the Third World. The spirit of Gandhi was resurrected in the writings of E. F. Schumacher, who proposed intermediate technologies as key to the evolution of more human-scale and community-based societies (Schumacher 1973).

Critics of the dominant development model pointed to growing disparities in wealth, the degradation of ecological systems, the progressive displacement from the commons of communities who had managed them for centuries, and their simultaneous usurpation by multinational corporations. One of the responses, in all corners of the Global South, was the creation of networks of communities working in solidarity to resist these damaging trends and to regain greater control over their own social, economic, and cultural resources. Such networks included Wangari Maathai's Green Belt Movement, the Sarvodaya movement created by Ari Ariayaratne in Sri Lanka, the Ladakh project founded by Helena Norberg-Hodge, Vandana Shiva's Bija Satyagraha Movement, and COLUFIFA, the transnational network of rural communities created by Demba Mansare in west Africa. All of these networks are currently involved with the Global Ecovillage Network—as founders, members, friends, or allies.[3]

In summary, by the early 1970s, in opposition to the dominant scientific, materialist worldview (with its belief in technology and economic growth as the twin motors of progress), a radical fringe had emerged with a multiplicity of alternative narratives of the good society and how it was to be achieved. There were minimal connections between these two alternative paradigms. They operated in parallel realities, the former extremely well-funded and resourced, the latter largely homegrown.

For the Northern communards, meaningful contact with the wider society was generally very limited. They built their own houses, treated their own waste (in biological reed-bed systems and composting toilets), created enterprises to meet their own needs, built alternative schools for their own children (and those of like-minded people in the surrounding areas), worshipped or meditated in their own sanctuaries, and in some cases birthed their own children and healed their own sick. They neither asked for financial support from the state nor had any realistic chance of receiving any. Sustainability at the community level was implicitly equated with self-reliance and complete independence from a surrounding society that was assumed, with generally good reason, as being indifferent or even hostile.

In the Global South, meanwhile, ecovillage networks and the NGOs at their helm remained at the margins of the governmental development debate, which was dominated by the one-size-fits-all structural adjustment policies imposed by the World Bank and International Monetary Fund. Ecovillage movements did, however, begin to be recognized as valuable partners by some agencies within more progressive elements of the development community. Sarvodaya in Sri Lanka and the Permaculture Institute villages in Brazil, for example, have had little difficulty in attracting funding from both official donor agencies and Northern-based NGOs for the past several decades. As holistic, integrated rural development agencies in their own right, their activities are broadly recognized within the Northern aid community—particularly more grassroots-focused organizations like Oxfam and Save the Children. Nonetheless, most ecovillages continued to operate on the margins of the mainstream development debate.

From Islands to Networks

Today we are seeing a significant transformation in the relationship between ecovillages and mainstream society. This is more visible among the intentional community ecovillages of the industrialized world, where the trend is more recent. Here, alliances (a number of which are described below) are developing between ecovillages and central and local governments, as well as with other organizations in their own backyards that share similar values and visions. Increasingly, ecovillage-based consultants are taking the technologies and expertise developed in ecovillage settings out into conventional organizations and communities, while trainers in leadership skills and conflict facilitation have clients among corporations and statutory bodies.

Ecovillage educational programs, meanwhile, are attracting participants from across the social spectrum, and university students are gaining credits from conventional universities for semesters spent in ecovillages (see Greenberg, Chapter 15, this volume) and degrees from ecovillage-based institutes through the recently organized Gaia University. Furthermore, a growing number of academic research projects are focused on various aspects of the ecovillage experience. Even at the highest level, international bodies—including the United Nations (UN)—are entering into partnerships with ecovillages.

The following examples provide a small sample that illustrates the type of specific initiatives that are emerging between Northern ecovillages and their new partners. The Farm, near Nashville, Tennessee, in the southeastern United States, works with a variety of government and NGO partners on an array of initiatives. More than thirty years ago, its Save Our Water Now campaign organized local groups to stop deep-well injection into a regional aquifer by pesticide and herbicide companies. Today, The Farm is building social networks of youth to oppose a toxic waste landfill near the same location. Its Big Swan Headwaters Preserve drew together local conservation organizations, state and local governments, and international charities like Nature Conservancy to protect more than three thousand contiguous acres from logging, subdivision, and development.[4] The Farm has also organized an antiwar network—Peace Roots—that aligns veterans, farmers, students, and the general public in campaigns to oppose continued war spending.[5] An international charity based at the Farm—Plenty—works in emergency relief arenas like post-hurricane New Orleans, post-earthquake Haiti, and the Gulf Coast in the aftermath of the BP Deepwater Horizon disaster. Plenty performs long-term follow-ups in areas where they work, incubating community-based enterprises and essential services, and bringing together local stakeholder groups to insure long-term survival of the displaced and the populations most at risk.[6] With The Farm's leadership, the nearby seat of the county the community is located in became the twenty-fifth Transition Town in the United States and is progressing toward net carbon neutrality.

The German ecovillage ZEGG (*Zentrum für experimentelle Gesellschaftsgestaltung*, or Center for Experimental Cultural Design), located just outside Berlin, has in recent years developed an active program to disseminate appropriate technologies throughout its bioregion—including a biological wastewater treatment system, organic food production, and a CO^2-neutral community heating system fired by local wood chips. Their efforts include seminars, workshops, visitor days, and articles in regional newspapers. In addition, ZEGG has been an active partner in local initiatives to create a free school in the neighboring town of Belzig, an info-café that acts as a center for tolerance in the face of extremism and violence, projects with refugees and asylum seekers, a community currency system, a nature-based kindergarten, campaigns to promote fair-trade products, community supported agriculture, and many types of cultural activities, including music nights, art exhibitions, and theater productions. In 2004, ZEGG won the "Local Agenda 21" award set up by the regional administration of Potsdam-Mittelmark in the state of Brandenburg for the ensemble of its ecological work in the region.[7]

In Scotland, the Findhorn Foundation's growing alliances with local organizations began with two studies. The first found that Findhorn's initiatives contributed four hundred jobs and £5 million to the economy of the north of Scotland (Brian Burns Associates 2002). The second found that community residents have a per capita ecological footprint that is one-half of the UK national average (Dawson 2009). These studies won the community a level of credibility that opened doors previously closed to it. Today, the ecovillage hosts a UN CIFAL training center (one of eleven such centers worldwide), which provides sustainability-related training for local governments and other local actors.[8] This is made possible by political and financial support from the Scottish government and local government authorities. Findhorn teaches courses jointly with Scottish universities, is a training and demonstration center for the Highlands and Islands Food Network's community-supported agriculture (CSA) program, and has members who provide consultancy services for local organizations as diverse as the Cairngorm National Park and the Development Trusts Association of Scotland—local organizations whose mission is to promote economic, ecological, and community development.

The Centre for Alternative Technology, a founding member of the GEN, is a leading player in the Ecodyfi initiative in Wales, an effort that brings together local authorities, the Welsh Assembly, various community groups, and specialist organizations with the mission "to foster sustainable community regeneration in the Dyfi valley" in ways that are sustainable and build on local distinctiveness. The program includes community-level renewable energy generation, promotion of locally based farming systems, composting and recycling initiatives, sustainable tourism, and the involvement of young people in planning, design, and fund-raising for a sports facility.[9]

In the Global South, a similar trend can be discerned, although as explained above, it is a longer-term and more incremental process, as there is an element within the development community that has long recognized ecovillage networks as valuable partners. The most striking recent breakthrough has been the decision by the government of Senegal to create a National Agency for Ecovillages.[10] The declared aim of the agency is to transform all of Senegal's fourteen thousand villages into ecovillages. There are indications that the government of Senegal sees this as more or less a grand public works program, with interventions planned to improve water supply, build renewable energy facilities, increase organic agroforestry activities, and so on. However, senior figures from GEN Senegal are involved in exploratory discussions and are likely to emphasize the community empowerment aspects of the ecovillage model.

Other Southern ecovillage initiatives that have succeeded in winning greater official credibility and profile in recent years include La Caravana Arcoiris por la Paz (the Rainbow Caravan of Peace), a community of artists and ecological activists that have toured Latin America for the last ten years in a caravan of buses teaching sustainability through the arts. Between 2005 and 2008, La Caravana was commissioned by the Brazilian government to help develop fifty community-based cultural centers in Brazilian towns and villages. The legendary Brazilian singer Gilberto Gill, who as Brazil's Minister of Culture inspired this alliance, described La Caravana as "the most original socio-cultural experiment in Latin America" (Barnett n.d.). Today, La Caravana is doing similar work in cooperation with the Secretariat of Culture in the Coyoacán district of Mexico City.

Three ecovillages—Auroville in India, Sarvodaya in Sri Lanka, and The Farm in Tennessee—were active players alongside government and local community-based organizations in the clean-up and reconstruction activities following the south Asian tsunami and the 2009 earthquake in Port-au-Prince, Haiti.[11] In 2009, Sarvodaya was awarded the United Nations' prestigious UN Habitat Scroll of Honor in special recognition of its achievements in helping communities recover from the effects of the tsunami. For its work in protecting indigenous cultures of the Americas through Plenty, The Farm received the first Right Livelihood Award, presented in the Swedish parliament in Stockholm.

Finally, linking ecovillage initiatives North and South, Gaia Education has developed an educational curriculum drawn from best practice within ecovillages globally. This is built around the four dimensions of sustainability—social, economic, ecological, and worldviews/values. The curriculum, developed by educators based in ecovillages around the world, has been endorsed by the United Nations Institute for Training and Research (UNITAR) and welcomed by the United Nations Educational, Scientific and Cultural Organisation (UNESCO) as a valuable contribution to its UN Decade of Education for Sustainable Development. The course is now being taught in ecovillages, universities, and community centers on every continent and has been taught virtually for several years through the Open University of Catalunya in Spain, where it is now offered as a master's program.

What happened to trigger such a transformation—rapid and recent in the North, more incremental and long-term in the South? For the most part, the answer lies in changes in mainstream society rather than (initially at least) increased outreach efforts on the part of ecovillages. On the one hand, there have been subtle changes in society at large, even among those who are largely unaware of converging social, ecological, and financial crises. Concerns that not so long ago were limited to the margins of society—including healthy organic food, child-centered education, complementary medicine, meditation, and lifestyles based around lower levels of consumption—today attract interest in many sectors of society.

It has also become increasingly clear to policy makers and practitioners in a wide range of fields that the very issues ecovillagers have been working on in relative isolation over recent decades are precisely those that are of increasing relevance as we encounter more and more ecological limits. Work on renewable energy systems, energy-efficient housing, biological waste treatment systems, and organic agriculture—which had appeared quirky and irrelevant in a world of perceived energy abundance—are today attracting far more attention as the nature and scale of the energy descent that lies before us becomes more widely recognized. There is also a growing, if less widespread, recognition of the need to develop post-consumerist values and lifestyles that will make it possible to maintain a high quality of life with significantly reduced resource use. One study found that intentional communities in the United States were succeeding in maintaining a high quality of life despite significantly lower than average incomes by substituting social and natural capital for financial capital (Mulder, Costanza, and Erickson 2006).[12] In short, experiments at all levels that ecovillages have been undertaking—technological, organizational, values-based, and relating to governance—are increasingly recognized as being of relevance far beyond the confines of ecovillages themselves.

Recent Trends in Ecovillages

Paradoxically, at this moment when ecovillages are enjoying unprecedented influence and exposure, it has never been more difficult to create new ecovillage initiatives in the industrialized North. The primary factors contributing to this situation are land prices and planning regulations. In both areas, the barriers to entry for those seeking to create new ecovillages have risen steeply. Most intentional communities created in the 1960s and 1970s developed organically and without a master plan; settlements evolved in response to the emerging impulses and passions of their members. Today, would-be communards have to file applications with planning authorities detailing not only the technical specifications of the completed settlement, but also details of a financing package that has been worked out in advance. Navigating these obstacles is a world away from the spirit of spontaneous innovation in which most of today's established ecovillages were created. So great, in fact, are barriers to entry that in most parts of the industrialized world the formation of new ecovillages has slowed to a trickle. Those that are being created are tending to adopt cohousing or other similar models in which the design is established in advance and the models are more familiar to planning professionals.

A legitimate question arises concerning the need for and value of new ecovillages in the industrialized world. The golden age for the formation of most such communities was in the 1960s and 1970s when conditions were ideal—cheap land, lax regulations, and profound disaffection among a radical minority toward the values and aspiration of mainstream society. Today, it could be argued that none of these conditions exist. Not only has land become more expensive as regulations have tightened, but awareness of sustainability issues and the need to build community resilience have also spread dramatically in mainstream society. In short, most of the concerns that set ecovillages apart from mainstream society in the industrialized world of the 1960s and 1970s have today been absorbed by significant groups within it. The Transition Movement, in which existing communities are mobilizing their resources with the aim of building resilience and reducing their dependence on fossil fuels, is but one of a number of similar movements across the industrialized world. In short, it could be argued that concerned and committed citizens no longer need to abandon their towns and villages to create new communities in order to engage with like-minded people in sustainability-related activities.

Seen in this light, the difficulties inherent in creating new ecovillages in the industrialized North may be seen as being not so serious after all. In an era in which ecovillages stood apart from and in opposition to mainstream society, the push to create new intentional communities and to encourage as many people as possible to live in them was an appropriate strategy. However, when—as today—large sections of mainstream society are looking toward ecovillages and seeking to learn from their experience, and given the urgency of the need for building resilience into our existing communities, it is legitimate to ask whether the creation of new ecovillages (an enormously time-consuming exercise, even when conditions were more favorable) is the priority.

An emerging trend is for existing ecovillages in the industrialized world to become regional hubs for networks of sustainability-related initiatives. This path is best exemplified by the EcoDyfi initiative in Wales described above, but is to greater or lesser degrees evident in most Northern ecovillages, as the experiments and initiatives developed on ecovillage "islands" spill out into their progressively more receptive hinterlands. An interesting recent episode encapsulates this trend. Several years ago, the German ecovillage ZEGG was faced with a decision on how to meet increased demands for food from the community and the people who came to participate in educational courses they offer. Until relatively recently, enhancing self-reliance by increasing their own food production would have been the obvious choice. However, the community chose to buy more from local organic suppliers outside the ecovillage, at least in part to strengthen the web of interconnected sustainability initiatives in their bioregion.

The situation in the Global South is analogous. Here, the line between ecovillages and other rural community development initiatives has become blurred by the adoption of more holistic and integrated community-driven strategies by rural development agencies over recent decades. For example, many of the models pioneered in Sri Lanka by Sarvodaya—including mutual savings and loans clubs, microfinance, village-level banking, and linking microenterprise to local and national markets—have been adopted by more conventional rural development agencies. To some degree, Southern ecovillages can take the credit for playing a pioneering role. One consequence of their success is that they can sometimes look less distinctive and radical than previously.

Southern ecovillages do nonetheless retain a distinctive, pioneering flavor in some cases, and continue to develop and demonstrate models for sustainable community development. Vandana Shiva's Bija Satyagraha Movement, for example, is on the forefront of the battle between small-scale Indian farmers and multinational corporations over control of the production and use of seeds in the country. It is helping farmers to develop and manage seed banks and is successfully pursuing legal actions in the courts of both India and Europe to revoke patents taken out by Western multinationals.[13] The Green Belt Movement (GBM) in Kenya, meanwhile, sees its mission as mobilizing communities for self-determination, justice, equity, poverty reduction, and environmental conservation—not infrequently in the face of an aggressively hostile state—using trees as the entry point. The GBM currently has over six hundred community networks across Kenya that manages six thousand tree nurseries. Over the years these networks, along with individuals, have participated in planting more than thirty million trees on private and public land, protected reserves, sites with cultural significance, and in urban centers.[14] The work of the GBM was recognized by the awarding of the Nobel Peace Prize to its founder, Wangari Maathai, in 2004.[15]

These are grand, visionary crusading initiatives in the best traditions of the ecovillage movement. It is here, at the leading edges of the struggle for sustainability and justice, that ecovillages are likely to continue to play a distinctive, leading role.

The Role for Ecovillages in Today's World

So what is the likely role of ecovillages in helping facilitate the transition into a future defined by the disruption of climate patterns and depletion of natural resources, most notably fossil fuel reserves? To a significant extent, this depends on the trajectory that societies follow. David Holmgren's *Future Scenarios* provides some insights into how the near- to medium-term future may unfold and the likely relevance of initiatives that are based on ecological design principles, such as ecovillages (Holmgren 2009). He describes four possible future scenarios, depending on the speed and scale at which what he sees as the two key determinants of the shape of future society—peak oil and climate change—unfold.[16] Perhaps the key determinant in terms of the potential role of ecovillages is the speed with which peak oil proceeds. In both of Holmgren's scenarios in which energy descent occurs relatively slowly (one with slow and manageable climate change, the other where it is faster and destabilizing), the state continues to command enough energy to be able to play a central role in driving and implementing policy. Conversely, in those scenarios in which fossil fuels rapidly become much scarcer and more expensive, the state quickly shrinks, leaving communities and other local structures to play a lead role.

Clearly, in both these meta-scenarios—in which the lead role is played by the state or by local bodies—ecovillages have an important role to play. Alliances that have developed over the past several decades allow various experiments engaged in by ecovillages to be widely shared through institutional presence in the United Nations, university courses, research projects, and consultancy services aimed at official and nongovernmental agencies. Consequently, even in scenarios where sufficient cheap energy exists to enable the organs of the state to continue to play a lead role, the ecovillage experience is likely to remain both relevant and accessible.

That said, a more rapid onset of energy descent will create a greater role for ecovillages as the energy-starved state shrinks. Holmgren describes the more benign rapid energy descent scenario, "Earth Stewards," in the following terms:

> Global warming is slowed dramatically and reversed by the collapse of the global consumer economy and absence of large-scale investment in new energy infrastructure … [and, in some places at least, there occurs] a cultural and spiritual revolution as people are released from the rat race of addictive behaviours and begin to experience the gift of resurgent community and the simple abundance of nature to provide for basic needs … Organic and small farmers, close to markets and able to make use of labour and animal power thrive (to the extent security allows) in a context of relatively benign climate change. An explosion of home businesses based on building and equipment retrofit, maintenance and salvage starts to build a diversified economy. (Holmgren 2009: 79–80)

The building of bioregional networks of sustainability initiatives, in which ecovillages are increasingly engaged, is ideal foundation building for such a future. The work of ecovillages is clear: to consciously develop and implement strategies to further strengthen networks of resilience-building initiatives that will sustain society as government services falter and fail. These initiatives include community currencies, local investment and cooperative ownership of enterprise and other community facilities, economic diversification, community-based food production systems, building using locally available materials, and models for local governance, among many others. Whereas ecovillages have previously developed expertise in these fields, the challenge now is to disseminate models through research, education, and consultancy.

Under Holmgren's dystopian rapid energy descent scenario, "Lifeboats" (in which climate change is also rapid and disruptive), a starkly relevant role for ecovillages is also sketched out:

> In some localities, especially in favourable regions with accessible energy and agricultural resources, communities analogous to the monasteries of the early medieval period provide basic knowledge and skills to their surrounding communities and are thus protected by the locals from the ravages of local warlords and pirates. These communities, mostly in rural and suburban areas, and based on pre-collapse efforts of intentional communities or rich benefactors, pursue the task of saving and condensing knowledge and cultural values for the long dark ages ahead. (Holmgren 2009: 83–84)

This harks back to the decisive role played by Celtic monasteries in early Middle Ages Europe in safeguarding key elements of Greco-Roman culture and traditions in the wake of the collapse of the Roman Empire (Cahill 1996).

In short, we are in a highly dynamic situation. The direction in which our societies are headed is uncertain, even if many of the key trends that will shape them are more or less evident. What is clear, however, is that as the capacity of the state to provide the many services that it does today declines—in both the industrialized world and, if to a lesser extent, also in the global South—the greater will be the need for community mobilization and solidarity and the capacity to provide for needs on a local level with reduced availability of fossil fuels. This is, in myriad ways, precisely the grand project that ecovillages, North and South, have been working on for decades.

At present, prevailing conditions in the North—specifically, high land prices and tight planning regulations—make it more or less impossible for new ecovillages to emerge organically in response to the emergent needs and passions of their members. In this context, ecovillages represent less the model to be replicated than research, training, and demonstration centers for the wider sustainable communities movement and hubs that are able to act as catalysts for bioregional transformation. As the power of the state to regulate how settlements develop wanes, however, this may change.

In the South, the state is already much weaker, as a general rule, than in the North. As energy and food prices rise, it is likely to become weaker still. In this context, many possible scenarios—both benign and malign—could be envisaged. All, however, are improved by strong, mobilized, and networked communities of the type that ecovillages are developing.

In all of the attempts to create a definition of ecovillages referred to above, there is one common theme—namely, the primacy of community. This foundation stone of the ecovillage vision—that well-being, security, and resilience are ultimately built on a bedrock of strong, inclusive communities—is the gift the ecovillage movement bestows to societies seeking to navigate a sustainable path into a low-energy and uncertain future.

Notes

1. I am adopting a broad, commonsense definition of "mainstream society" as referring to that portion of the population subscribing to the dominant cultural narrative revolving around the merits of sophisticated technology, largeness of scale and economic growth—in opposition to which the ecovillage movement has been developing an alternative and contrary vision. This is not to imply homogeneity within "the mainstream," but rather to identify a sharp ideological line dividing it from the ecovillage movement.
2. The Transition movement is perhaps the most visible and well-known example of initiatives whose aim is to build the resilience and increase the sustainability of existing cities, towns, and villages. The Transition movement started in Ireland and the UK, but now has members across the world. For more details, see http://www.transitionnetwork.org.
3. A word of caution is in order here, once more relating to the thorny issue of definitions and terminology. Networks of community-based initiatives such as those mentioned above can in no way be seen as being synonymous with ecovillages or the GEN. That is, the great majority of such networks across the Global South have never had any contact with the GEN and, in most cases, likely have never heard of it. What is distinctive about the organizations mentioned here is that they all had prior personal contacts with the founding figures within the GEN and have since chosen to establish some form of affiliation with it. In short, while there is commonality of interest and, in some cases, of membership within the GEN, it would be inappropriate to refer to Southern-based networks of the type described here collectively as ecovillages, since this is not a term that most use to refer to themselves. The GEN is just one of the networks with which they have chosen to affiliate.
4. For further details, see http://www.swantrust.org.
5. For further details, see http://www.peaceroots.org.
6. For further details, see http://www.plenty.org.
7. For further details, see http://www.zegg.net.
8. CIFAL is an acronym for the Centre International pour la Formation d'Acteurs Locales (International Training Centre for Local Actors). The CIFAL network comes under the auspices of UNITAR (United Nations Institute for Training and Research). For further details, see http://www.cifalfindhorn.org.
9. For further details, see http://www.ecodyfi.org.uk.
10. Senegal is the African country in which the GEN has invested the most resources and in which, consequently, the ecovillage network is most developed. The decision was taken to focus on one country in Africa to develop an ecovillage model relevant to the continent's distinctive characteristics that

could be transferred and scaled up to other African countries. Senegal was chosen because of the contacts developed between the GEN and the network of eco-community activists that had cooperated in the creation of the Third Ecocities conference in Dakar in 1996. For further details, see http://www.afriqueavenir.org/en/2010/08/19/senegal-launch-eco-village-project-to-reduce-greenhouse-gases.

11. For further details, see http://www.sarvodaya.org/activities/tsunami and www.scribd.com/doc/.../Global-Eco-Village-Network-News-Issue-48.
12. Perhaps the most notable official recognition of the value of these various experiments in low-impact living (in ecovillages and elsewhere in society) comes in the recent publication *Prosperity Without Growth*, by UK Sustainable Development Commissioner (SDC) Tim Jackson (2009). The SDC was created with the mandate of advising the UK government on issues related to sustainable development. Jackson calls for a greater level of awareness of ecological limits in economic thought and planning and identifies the need to transition into a post-consumerist culture. He praises the Scottish ecovillage, Findhorn Foundation, as a model of a community that is seeking to delink levels of consumption from the achievement of well-being.
13. For further details, see http://www.rediff.com/news/2000/may/11neem.htm.
14. For further details, see http://greenbeltmovement.org/w.php?id=33.
15. Once again, the question of the definition of ecovillage arises, not least since neither of these examples are members of the GEN. It is, nonetheless, legitimate to include them here, since the models they represent—built around solidarity within networks of communities seeking to wrest greater control over their cultural, ecological, and economic resources—exactly matches that of ecovillages in the Global South given above.
16. Interestingly, and most usefully, he presents these scenarios not as competing but rather as potentially sequential, some following others; and also as possibly all existing simultaneously, nested within one another in organizations and territories of different scales and with different functions.

References

Barnett, Tracy L. n.d. "Coffee with the Subcoyote." http://theesperanzaproject.org/tag/rainbow-peace-caravan/ (accessed 4 May 2010).

Brian Burns Associates. 2002. Unpublished report. Findhorn Foundation, Scotland.

Cahill, Thomas. 1996. *How the Irish Saved Civilizatian.* New York: Anchor Books.

Dawson, Jonathan. 2006. *Ecovillages: New Frontiers for Sustainability.* Schumacher Briefing No. 12. Totnes, UK: Green Books.

———. 2009. "Findhorn's Incredible Shrinking Footprint." *Communities Magazine* 143: 26–27, 71.

Gilman, Robert. 1991. "The Eco-village Challenge." *In Context* 29. Available at http://www.context.org/ICLIB/IC29/Gilman1.thm.

Holmgren, David. 2009. *Future Scenarios: How Communities Can Adapt to Peak Oil and Climate Change.* White River Junction, VT: Chelsea Green.
Illich, Ivan. 1971. *Deschooling Society.* New York: Harper & Row.
———. 1977. *Limits to Medicine: Medical Nemesis, the Exploration of Health.* New York: Penguin.
Jackson, Tim. 2009. *Prosperity Without Growth: Economics for a Finite Planet.* London: Earthscan.
Meadows, Donella, Dennis L. Meadows, Jorgan Randers, and William W. Behrens III. 1972. *Limits to Growth.* New York: Universe Books.
Mulder, Kenneth, Robert Costanza, and Jon Erickson. 2006. "The Contribution of Built, Human, Social and Natural Capital to Quality of Life in Intentional and Unintentional Communities." *Ecological Economics* 59: 13–23.
Schumacher, E. F. 1973. *Small Is Beautiful: Economics as If People Mattered.* New York: Harper & Rowe.

CHAPTER THIRTEEN

Creating Alternative Political Ecologies through the Construction of Ecovillages and Ecovillagers in Colombia

Brian J. Burke and Beatriz Arjona

Ecovillages as Alternative Political Ecologies

Ecovillages are spaces and collectivities that are reinventing sustainability in its ecological, economic, communitarian, and worldview dimensions. They are experiences of life in community and in search of a more respectful relationship with the earth, others, the Other, and ourselves. Real and concrete paths for right livelihood and living well, now and in the future, they are pockets of hope. In this sense, ecovillages are laboratories for alternative political ecologies and their cultural and subjective underpinnings. They are experiments in alternative systems of relationships with the natural environment, human communities, productive processes, broader economic dynamics, and state structures. Global ecovillage movement supporters hope they will become lifestyle options "possible for everybody on the planet" (R. Jackson 2004: 2), and a broad range of actors have adapted the highly flexible ecovillage model to their local conditions.

In this chapter, we focus on two cases that highlight the wide range of ecovillage experiences in Colombia and, we hope, help advance the effort to make ecovillages a more widely accessible and realizable political ecological possibility. Beatriz Arjona's story exemplifies the most common ecovillage dynamic in Colombia—that of a disaffected middle- or upper-class urbanite seeking a more fulfilling life through new connections with nature and community. We especially examine the challenges she has faced in becoming an ecovillager, inspired by J. K. Gibson-Graham's assertion that "we must be ready with strategies for confronting what forcefully pushes back against the discursive imaginings and practical enactments [of] building a different economy" or political ecology (2006: xxii). We then turn to the exceptional case of Nashira, an ecovillage of low-income single mothers (many of whom are victims of violence and displacement) to consider possibilities for developing ecovillages among structurally disadvantaged populations. We hope that these two examples will help combat facile stereotypes of Global North and South that impede a clearer analysis of the actual social conditions that give rise to and constrain ecovillage projects throughout the world.

The longing for more sustainable human settlements has grown in response to the amply documented crises of recent decades, such as: peak oil and human-exacerbated climate change; the exhaustion of natural resources and declines in species, top soils, forest cover, fisheries, and accessible clean water; desertification and deforestation; an ecological footprint that outstrips global carrying capacity; devastating inequality, with more than a billion people living without adequate food and clean water; wars, violence, and massive displacement; the extermination of peoples, cultures, and languages; and the disintegration of families and communities. These crises derive largely from the dynamics of capitalist (and in some cases communist) development, but they do not simply exist in a world "out there." Those of us who participate in these development projects also produce these crises—just as we produce capitalism—through our own actions based on learned and deeply engrained values, desires, and expectations about the material and social conditions in which we "should" live and the social and ecological consequences of "progress" that are visible and acceptable.

As responses to these crises, ecovillages become places for recreating both society and ourselves. Experiences from Colombia show that ecovillages partially deviate from the reproduction of capitalist development by permitting alternative systems of production, consumption, and distribution based on different economic and social logics. This is the source of their radicalism, but also their greatest challenge. The Global Ecovillage Network's Ecovillage Design Education program recognizes the connections between social and subjective transformations: "Amidst these intense challenges, and largely catalyzed by them, lies the prospect for tremendous growth in human potential and consciousness. People and communities all over the globe are coming together to reclaim responsibility for creating their own living situations.... In the process, they are overcoming prior limitations and developing new talents, skills, knowledge and approaches" (Gaia Education 2006: 2). In the stories of Beatriz and Nashira, with additional context from other Colombian ecovillages, we hope to describe some of the new knowledge that has arisen from experi-

Figure 13.1. Ceremonial planting of organic rice, beans, sunflowers, and other seeds at the fourth "Llamado de la Montaña," the annual gathering of Colombian ecovillages and alternative communities, in 2010. Photo courtesy of the Colombian Ecovillage and Alternative Communities Network.

ments with alternative political ecologies, communities, and the subjects necessary to give them life.

Beatriz's Ecovillage Journey

Beatriz began her journey into ecovillages from a highly privileged economic position but with a profound and growing sense of discontentment. As she says:

> It started when I was young, and although I didn't know what was happening within me, it became clear that life should be more interesting, profound, holistic, and transcendent than what I saw in my social, family, and professional circles. Little by little, I felt an existential void growing within me, something I needed to find, something that affirmed my reason for being. By the time I was 38, this void, this imbalance between reason and heart, the growth of my bank account but not my stocks of happiness and fulfillment, provided the basis for my personal change.

> Several experiences illuminated my path: living in the Israeli Kibbutz and Moshav and with indigenous communities in the Colombian Amazon, and meeting the Rainbow Caravan of Peace, a nomadic ecovillage that traveled for 13 years around Latin America. Through them, I learned of ecovillages, permaculture, barter, consensus-based collectives, nomadism, pilgrimages, and the return to the simple and natural, spiritual ecology, deep ecology. I learned that it is possible to take a deeper and more holistic approach to life, where everything can be more interrelated, less fragmented and compartmentalized, where my approach to being could be deeper and not only based on reason. I learned that I wanted to walk in peace, with more consistency among thoughts, words, feelings, and action, being more conscious of my ecological footprint, my energy footprint. I learned that part of my mission was to light a beacon in the darkness of the generalized despair of a country with more than 50 years of civil war, with 18,000 violent deaths a year, with 30 children dying each day from malnutrition, with high rates of corruption and impunity, with extreme deterioration of natural resources, deforestation, waters and soils. I wanted to live a way of life centered on good-being (*bien-ser*), good-feeling (*bien-sentir*), and good-living (*bien-vivir*) more than on well-being (*bien-estar*) and well-having (*bien-tener*).[1]

Beatriz was struggling with a cultural or psychosocial contradiction of capitalism: achieving the economic advantages of a good job and a growing bank account pressured her to sacrifice fuller self-realization. Her economic self progressively colonized the intimate, spiritual, and social selves integral to holistic development. Achieving a more balanced life and new consciousness therefore required both internal and external changes. It is not surprising, then, that Beatriz found inspiration not only in spiritual possibilities, but also in political-ecological transformations (ecovillages, permaculture, alternative economies, consensus processes) and alternative ethical frameworks like deep ecology. The new self to whom she aspired was simply inconsistent with participation in the conventional capitalist political economy.

Beatriz was overcome by excitement when she discovered the liberatory possibilities of these alternatives, but her first attempt at change met with resistance:

> In 1997, when I shared my ecovillage dream, I found neither understanding nor interest. For everybody in my social world it was just another expression of utopian idealism, of altruism impossible to imagine and bring into being, especially in Colombia. Later, when I tried to buy a small farm where I could begin to live in the countryside, I came across a contradiction: the financial obligations of buying a farm would tie me even more to the work that was hampering my full self-realization. To free myself from the system, I would have to involve myself even more in it.

This is an important lesson about "the things that push back" against change. First, Beatriz encountered resistance even to creatively imagining other possible worlds. Her utopian thinking was cynically dismissed as an exercise in futility rather than celebrated as a valuable activity with revolutionary potential. This attitude shores up the status quo by stopping change before it starts; it creates an intellectual inertia that reinforces the idea that There Is No Alternative (as Margaret Thatcher famously put it), especially not here, not for us. Brushing aside the lack of support and continuing with her vision, Beatriz encountered a second problem: while she had overcome the intellectual barriers to imagining change, she still had to confront the economic barriers to materializing it. As an intermediate step, she bought an apartment at the edge of the city where she could enjoy the country while working and waiting for the seed of her ecovillage dream to germinate.

Two years later, inspiration struck again when she shared experiences with the Rainbow Caravan of Peace as co-organizer of the Bioregional Peace Gathering. As soon as this event ended, Beatriz threw the European ecovillage directory into her backpack and headed to the beach, full of hope. Unbeknownst to her, this trip was a rite of passage. She had to retreat from her daily life, her usual activities and relationships, and travel page after page into alternative worlds, in order to be reborn:

> There, supported by the immense force of the sea and the full moon, even though I didn't yet know the power of ceremonies, I did a little ritual to consecrate my life to ecovillages and commit myself to realizing my dream. And that's how I sealed my transformation into an ecovillager. And I asked the Great Spirit and the Universe to give me the tools and the wisdom necessary for my work.

She returned a new person with a different role in society, free to begin transforming her world. A couple of months later, her dream clearer and more insistent, Beatriz quit her job and began assembling the group with whom she would start her first ecovillage. Her colleagues and friends responded differently this time. Most admired her decision to put her dreams and happiness ahead of her work and lamented that they could not do the same. Their response reveals another barrier to change. In addition to constrained imaginations and material concerns like salaries, pensions, and health care, many people's identities and social lives are constructed through their activities within the conventional political ecology. To leave one's job in pursuit of something radically different unfixes and threatens this identity.

Beatriz's ecovillage journey has consisted of four experiences that have taught her important lessons about building a utopian dream in our complex reality. Each one can be seen as an experiment with the community structures and human-nature relationships that move her toward the overarching goal of spiritual development and sustainable living. Her first ecovillage experience lasted two years, during which she and her partner and accomplice Silvio lived with a group of four to seventeen people in Montaña Mágica, near the city of Medellín. They developed collective, egalitarian structures and activities—a shared house and kitchen; a common fund for expenses such as food, utilities, farm maintenance, and new projects; and the operation of a preexisting eco-hotel and small farm—in order to develop a shared commitment to a redesigned community. This was her first time farming and doing construction, but the biggest challenge by far was learning to live in community. The group found that they lacked tools, experiences, and wisdom to coexist in harmony, resolve conflicts, and make consensus an instrument of genuinely egalitarian, collaborative decision making.

When the collective decided to end the experiment, Beatriz and Silvio focused on developing a permaculture project on an adjoining property they had bought to expand Montaña Mágica. Amandaris ("Refuge of Peace" in Sanskrit) was their four-year project, a place to practice permaculture principles and ecovillage technologies. They built a home with traditional technologies, local and recycled materials, composting toilets, and rainwater harvesting; planted medicinal gardens; made wine and preserves from wild and organic fruits; participated in a barter/alternative currency group and the regional ecotourism network; and offered workshops on sustainability, ecovillages, permaculture, and nutrition. At Amandaris, they focused on ecological sustainability and personal growth, and their quick progress shows the relative ease of working in conventional family structures compared to larger groups. But there was something missing. They longed for the support and accompaniment of others and the growth that comes with sharing a life. Community was not just a strategy, a means to an end; it was also a central goal. So when they were ready and a new opportunity for communal living emerged, they left Amandaris and became founding members of Aldeafeliz.

Aldeafeliz began in 2006 through a visioning process led by Carlos Rojas. Out of the two hundred and thirty participants who shared their diverse dreams, twelve people, mostly urban professionals and academics, decided to test communal living on a rented farm an hour from Bogotá. Almost immediately they began developing strategies for the collective purchase of land, agreements for living together, and a membership structure that permitted different levels of involvement. They dedicated existing buildings to the community, forming a collective kitchen, dining room, laundry area, meeting pavilion, office, library, movie theater, and dressing room. Private spaces consisted of tents for the first two years, until some members began constructing their own houses. The community also began consolidating its economic base by planting gardens, improving coffee and fruit orchards, developing its own products (wine, granola, preserves, coffee, and soaps, among others), receiving visitors, conducting workshops on group dynamics and sustainability, and, recently, developing an eco-spa and offering eco-construction services.

During Aldeafeliz's subsequent productive but sometimes tumultuous years, its members have used a range of tools to develop a spirit of community and consensus processes, including discussion strategies (speaking circles, forums learned from the ZEGG ecovillage in Germany, and an indigenous technique called *mambeo*) and fun and spiritually rich group-building activities like sacred dances, dances of universal peace, yoga, and meditation. Like any collective, Aldeafeliz is growing and changing due to natural turnover of members, but also because residents themselves have developed new interests and capacities, new lifestyles and passions, and new tools for living together. The ecovillage now consists of twenty-nine members, eighteen of whom are residents. Beatriz's two years there were an opportunity for her to learn more about ecovillage living and work on her shadows and ego. In the end, however, she felt a growing distance from the community and realized that this was not the group that would best support her growth and personal journey.

Since 2008, Beatriz and Silvio have lived a fourth experience: a sustainability pilgrimage as volunteers for ecovillages, agroecology projects, and spiritual and alternative communities across Colombia. They are networking, teaching, living, and learning while representing Change the World Colombia and the Colombian Ecovillage Network. They have acquired new knowledge and experiences, woven community and strengthened their network, pollinated projects, and been pollinated in return by new places, people, experiences, and energies. Along the way, they have helped coordinate the Llamados de la Montaña, the annual gatherings of the Colombian Ecovillage Network. Their pilgrimage will continue until their path shows where and with whom they will live the next phase of their journey.

Beatriz's experiences show how personally fulfilling the ecovillage experience can be, but also how difficult it is to step onto this path and find one's home in an alternative political ecology rooted in community. One of the greatest challenges—and one of the biggest concerns of prospective ecovillagers—is to unlearn the sense of privacy and autonomy that seems so "natural" and adopt a new attitude that allows collectives to flourish while accommodating autonomy and individual needs. Challenges arise not only in big decisions such as ecovillage design, but also in the everyday realms of what to cook for dinner, how to wash the dishes, what color the communal house should be, and what music to listen to. Colombian ecovillages have found diverse ways of balancing the personal and the collective—ranging from the collectivization of almost all spaces, times, and decisions to near-total autonomy in a network of mutually supportive, privately owned, neighboring ecological projects. Some have also found the need to renegotiate this balance as communities mature, families grow, and members' desires change. There is no doubt that, in addition to formal structures and strategies, making ecovillages work depends on bonds of affection, solidarity, and a sense of common purpose.

The Nashira Ecological Community

While Beatriz began her ecovillage journey from a privileged economic position, many people in the North and South struggle to meet their basic needs. If ecovillages are to be a possibility for humanity, we need to examine the experiences and dilemmas faced in the most difficult conditions as well. What might motivate structurally disadvantaged people to adopt ecovillages, and how can these alternative political ecologies benefit them? How can vulnerable populations manage the economics of the ecovillage transition and ecovillage living, themes that have been challenging even among more privileged people? By examining the significant social, economic, and ecological successes of Nashira, we hope to show the importance and the potential of ecovillages in this context and examine how to make an ecovillage transition viable for people with few economic resources.

The women of Nashira began from extreme underprivilege created by violence, displacement, and urban poverty. Unfortunately, their experience is not rare. Colombia has between 3.9 and 5.5 million internally displaced people (the largest number of any country in the world) who have fled rural areas made increasingly uninhabitable by physical and psychological violence, forced recruitment, land expropriation, and livelihood unsustainability due to illicit crop eradication and effects on nearby licit crops (Reyes Posadas 2009; Ross 2003, 2007).[2] The national consequences of such high levels of displacement include rural depopulation and the restructuring of land tenancy, urban expansion and related problems of service provision and public order, changes in the electoral map, and problems with free expression and political organization (Conferencia Episcopal de Colombia 1995). Displaced families face numerous disadvantages. Almost half of displaced households are headed by single women. Dealing with trauma, lack of social supports, and high rates of illiteracy, they suffer from higher rates of poverty, inadequate housing, and poor health and nutrition than other subgroups among the urban poor. Studies show that 96 percent of displaced families in small- and medium-sized cities are vulnerable to food insecurity, and 76 percent are extremely vulnerable (Pérez

Marcia 2006); these families spend 50 percent of their income on food, often cheap and low-quality items, and 85 percent reduce the number of meals they consume for lack of money (World Food Program 2005).

Governments and nongovernmental organizations have responded with programs to return people safely to their home communities and conventional social supports for their lives in the city. Nashira offers a different kind of response to the physical, psychological, and structural violence experienced by displaced people and the urban poor more generally. Established in 2003 in Palmira, a town located thirty minutes from the city of Cali, the ecological development of Nashira grew out of the Association of Women Heads of Household (ASOMUCAF), an organization led by Angela Cuevas, a feminist, lawyer, and member of the women's peace network. ASOMUCAF formed in 1993 to support women heads of household with low incomes and no access to capital. The group ran a collective paper-recycling project, turning kitchens into workshops for producing paper cups, picture frames, and other decorative objects to sell in a collaborating store in Cali.

By 2003, with the paper project safely under their belt, the women of ASOMUCAF began examining other ways to improve their lives. They were especially concerned with supplementing their incomes, addressing housing needs, and improving their families' health and nutrition. None of the women imagined creating an ecovillage, but as they discussed these three issues in tandem, the general contours of an alternative political ecology emerged. The experiment became possible when Cuevas donated three hectares (seven and a half acres) of her family's land, as well as an extraordinary amount of time and energy to help raise funds and design the project. With the land, their far-fetched idea became a real possibility, and the women of ASOMUCAF developed a clearer vision: Nashira would provide a space for eighty-eight member families to live and work together, improve their food security, and earn a minimum-wage income to complement earnings from other livelihood activities.

Today, they have fully designed the site and finished building the first forty-one eco-houses; they continue to raise funds for the remaining forty-seven. Each family works in one of Nashira's eleven agroecology production groups focused on raising small animals (hens, guinea pigs, ducks, rabbits, or quail), tending fruit orchards and making fruit products (especially derived from bananas, plantains, and noni), worm composting, agritourism, and a green market. These groups improve nutrition and increase self-sufficiency and sustainability while providing earnings that are reinvested and divided evenly among member families. With the help of Change the World, Nashira is also creating the first Colombian solar restaurant.

To a large extent, Nashira's members' principal interest is economic—not social, spiritual, or ecological—and the ecovillage structure provides a very different set of possibilities in this regard. Rather than depending entirely on competition in the wage labor market, they have re-appropriated the means of production and collectivized the work process. The women and their extended families helped build their own homes, providing "sweat equity" that reduced monetary costs. By ameliorating major sources of vulnerability like housing, nutrition, and income problems, these women have shown that ecovillages could be important elements of social policy for marginalized populations. As a fundamental reorganization of political-ecological dynamics, ecovillages address root causes of vulnerability and poverty while providing holistic solutions that incorporate economic, ecological, and sociocultural issues. In this sense, they offer a valuable counterproposal to conventional developmentalist "solutions" like economic integration, job creation, microfinance, and safety nets.

While the economy might have been their primary interest, some of the most important benefits for the women of Nashira have been psychosocial. Elcy, a mother of seven and former president of ASOMUCAF, explains that she joined the Nashira project because her housing situation was insecure and made it difficult for her to work and her children to study. But like many of the members, when she describes Nashira, she emphasizes how it taught her that she can face people and talk to them without fear, without a sense of inferiority, and that she does not need to depend on a man in order to live. As a woman she is able to improve herself, take control of her life, pay the bills, and even pick up a shovel to grow food or a hammer to build her own house. Although they are not collectivizing their daily lives to the extent of Beatriz and other ecovillages, they too have developed new skills for group work and solidarity. As Elcy states, "one can accomplish anything that one proposes" and "as a group we can do things even better and quicker." This new sense of capability and agency is a major triumph, as important perhaps as the economic security of a home and sustenance, because it interrupts the psychosocial effects of structural violence that tend to reproduce poverty across generations. Nashira achieved this by actively involving women in group work, dialogues, design processes, home construction, agricultural production, and a broad range of training courses. The material, psychological, and social benefits of Nashira's experimentation have combined to permit Elcy's greatest pride: all her children have completed university.

The ecological element has also not been ignored at Nashira, and goes far beyond gardening. The community designed and built prefabricated eco-homes made of recycled materials, including reclaimed concrete, industrial ash, and refurbished electrical installations. Also—with help from

Change the World, the employees' fund of Electricité de France, and a water resources research institute at the Universidad del Valle (CINARA)—they developed community-level sustainable infrastructure, including artificial wetland wastewater treatment systems, a solar restaurant, and dry composting toilets made of local bamboo and plastic bottles filled with reclaimed materials. The community also offers agritourism options to educate visitors about sustainability.

One of the most important questions we need to address to make ecovillages a possibility for all people is how to make them economically viable, particularly for people who lack start-up capital and economic cushions to sustain them during transition periods. Nashira represents a new current of ecovillages that do not aspire to autonomous self-reliance. In fact, with only three hectares of land for eighty-eight families, there is no chance of becoming food self-sufficient. Instead, ecovillage economies are increasingly designed as complementary economies, with links to government and the private sector as appropriate (Dawson 2006, Chapter 12, this volume). The women of Nashira have managed these alliances in very effective and creative ways, taking advantage of special resources available to marginalized communities. With the help of Angela Cuevas, they have leveraged finances from USAID and both municipal and state governments. Nongovernmental organizations like Change the World have provided training and advisory services. And the most innovative approach was a connection forged with the Fundación Pagesos Solidaris, an organization that linked Spanish agricultural businesses with migrant workers committed to social work in their home communities. Through this program, thirty-nine men and women traveled to Spain under an agreement that they would donate a portion of their earnings not to their own families but to the entire Nashira collective to help construct the first forty-one houses. Communities like the urban poor and displaced people certainly face economic disadvantages, but they can also make claims to state resources that are not available to other social groups. Nashira has shown that well-organized communities can take advantage of state resources and capitalist integration and collectivize the appropriation and distribution of surplus in a way that supports the development of alternative—and hopefully more ecologically and socioeconomically sustainable—communities.

Discussion

One of the most important tasks before us today is to create more ecologically sustainable, socially just, and personally fulfilling communities.

Ecovillages stand at the forefront of this movement, providing valuable experiments in what alternative political ecologies might look like, what strategies might bring them into being and sustain them, and what types of personal changes we need to adopt to become subjects capable of enacting these alternatives. Although much of the ecovillage literature has focused on examples from the Global North, prominent authors have begun to recognize Southern ecovillage projects as well (Dawson 2006, Chapter 12, this volume). This is encouraging. To make ecovillages a possibility for all people, we need to analyze experiments from around the globe, considering how lessons from one context might be applied in another.

However, effective analysis requires that we describe non-Northern experiences without falling into common stereotypes of Southerners as either fully comprehensible via the lens of poverty or as idyllic villagers with a natural, intuitive, almost magical "traditional" knowledge of ecovillage living. Such essentialized preconceptions impede critical reflection on the actual lived experiences that give rise to and result from alternative political ecologies in the Global South. The same might be said for stereotypes of the North as a land of economic privilege, social alienation, and lifestyle-based ecological devastation. The truth is far more interesting and useful.

For example, Ross Jackson's argument that "people in the South grasp the revolutionary potential of ecovillages much quicker than Northerners" because "they still have their social fabric more or less intact and see the ecovillage model as fully compatible with their village-based culture" leads us to misunderstand the context for and challenges of creating ecovillages in the South (2004: 8). While some places match his description, many people in the South live in cities, having never known village life or having abandoned it long ago, and their social fabrics and cultural dynamics reflect this. Most importantly, many of these urban dwellers actively reject "village-based cultures" and ecovillage ideals of material simplicity, traditional/appropriate technologies, and food, water, and energy self-reliance in favor of hegemonic notions of wealth, development, and progress. Finally, the highly unequal (and worsening) distribution of land and the willingness of the elite to employ violence to resist redistribution pose serious obstacles to broad-scale ecovillage development. Far more than romantic stereotypes, we need honest discussion of the real challenges to imagining, promoting, creating, and maintaining alternative political ecologies such as ecovillages in the South.

In this chapter, we have offered a glimpse of the diverse ecovillage experiences in Colombia. Colombia has been a particularly fertile ground for ecovillage experiments. As of 2010, the Colombian Network of Ecovillages and Alternative Communities includes fifteen active communities and several in various stages of development.[3] Together, they house fewer than two hundred people living on less than two hundred and fifty hectares. This group is small, no doubt, but hopeful that their experiments will generate a snowball effect of inspired thought and action.

Each community has devised its own approach to ecological, economic, social, and worldview transformations, and they have shared lessons through annual encounters and the wanderings of ecovillage pilgrims. Ecologically, they have advanced in eco-construction, food security and sovereignty, appropriate technologies and alternative energies, and biodiversity and watershed conservation. Economically, they have sought to support themselves by living simply and self-provisioning to the greatest extent possible, generating incomes through individual, communal, and mixed enterprises, developing commercial and barter relationships among ecovillages, and tapping into external resources (as illustrated by Nashira). Developing the social dimension of ecovillages has benefited from diverse communication tools and tremendous intention and energy dedicated to creating "community glue" through women's circles, group prayer and meditation, techniques for "emotional discharge," collective work, the assumption of big responsibilities like hosting the annual ecovillage gathering, and a very healthy dose of fun. This is certainly a revolution with dancing! Ecovillagers often begin with an unconventional worldview and seek to deepen their commitment to sustainability and justice through economic, ecological, and social life changes; many also pursue worldview changes directly through spiritual work, drawing on indigenous, alternative Judeo-Christian and Eastern traditions (Arjona 2010).

The two experiences we have highlighted here are instructive for ecovillages in the North and South. Beatriz's story reveals the material and conceptual challenges to becoming an ecovillager, as well as several viable strategies for exploiting fissures in the hegemony of the conventional political ecology in order to liberate imaginations for the construction of alternatives. Resignation and fear can be overcome—and discontent made productive—through inspiring encounters with actually existing alternatives. Also, the threat of losing a (conventional) identity can be minimized by assuming a new and celebrated ecovillager identity. Ecovillage networks provide a community of dreamers to support this new identity.

The women of Nashira demonstrate how people around the world might overcome the economic limitations to ecovillage living. They took advantage of particular resources that are not universally accessible, but they also used bonds of trust and solidarity to effectively combine noncapitalist labor (such as production groups and sweat equity) with capitalist (migrant) labor within a framework that collectivizes resources and surplus for common goals. Other ecovillages can also put the conventional economy to their service by participating in ways that meet community needs, generate and collectivize surplus, and enrich the commons (see Gibson-Graham 2006).

Finally, it is important to recognize that the challenges that ecovillagers face do not end once the village is up and running. As Beatriz explained, turning a utopian dream into a complex reality takes ongoing work that is both external—in the realm of community relations and ecological or productive projects—and internal and very intimate. Becoming an ecovillager is a commitment to working on one's ego and self-limitations, supported by the sometimes unflattering reflections shared by other community members and in light of the grand responsibility of living differently. It is a commitment to transcend jealousies, conflicts, and self-centeredness in order to develop a community that supports spiritual, social, environmental, and economic change and more profound self-realization.

In his "critical introduction" to political ecology, Paul Robbins mentions the need for more "political ecologies of success" (2004: 213). It is premature to treat ecovillages as successes; even loyal ecovillage promoters repeatedly emphasize that the ideal ecovillage does not yet exist (R. Jackson 2004; Gaia Trust n.d.; H. Jackson 1998). As Beatriz says:

> The road rolls on ahead of us, even after ten years of walking the ecovillage path, of learning and unlearning, of transforming difficulties into challenges, limitations into learning opportunities, relationships with others into growth in the deepest parts of my soul, and of searching for partners in a collective life that enhances our personal and spiritual growth, our service to Mother Earth and other humans.

Ecovillages may not be (finished) successes, but we like to think of them as experiments in alternative political ecologies, works in progress inspired by imagined possibilities. This very idealism may mean that "success" is never achieved—always lying ahead in a future that we will create through continued hard work and self-critique—but this constant ethical striving might just be the movement's true success. Ecovillagers in Colombia are walking toward a dream, toward diverse dreams, and learning to integrate economic, ecological, social, and cultural change as part of a greater transformation of both society and themselves. In the process they are demonstrating that "*sí se puede*!" It is possible to live more sustainably, reduce our ecological footprints, unlearn competitive and individualistic attitudes, and live in community. And through these communities they are trying to create a future of greater harmony, peace, and sustainability in a country—and world—in need.

Notes

1. All extended quotations from Beatriz Arjona are from a series of conversations between the two authors during the initial writing of this chapter, 7–10 May 2010, near Pereira, Colombia.
2. Counting the displaced people in Colombia provokes heated debate, but the population is likely between the 3.9 million people officially registered with the government since 2000 and the 5.5 million counted by the reputable non-governmental organization Consultoría para los Derechos Humanos y Desplazamiento (CODHES) since 1985 (CODHES 2012; IDMC 2012). Displaced people comprise approximately 8–11 percent of the national population, the equivalent of twenty-six to thirty-six million internal refugees in the United States.
3. This is not meant to belittle other ecovillage and sustainability projects in Colombia, but rather to highlight those that self-identify as ecovillages and work to strengthen the Colombian Ecovillage Network. Other experiences include a number of ecovillages that have not joined the network and at least thirty possible ecovillages in formation.

References

Arjona, Beatriz. 2010. Las ecoaldeas: Una alternativa para soñar y disoñar el buen-vivir en el presente y el futuro. Soñar y Disoñar Múltiples Caminos Conference. La Cocha, Nariño, Colombia.

Conferencia Episcopal de Colombia. 1995. *Desplazados por la Violencia.* Bogotá: Kimpres.

Consultoría para los Derechos Humanos y el Desplazamiento (CODHES). 2012. *Desplazamiento Creciente y Crisis Humanitaria Invisibilizada.* Boletín Número 79. Bogotá: Consultoría para los Derechos Humanos y el Desplazamiento.

Dawson, Jonathan. 2006. *Ecovillages: New Frontiers for Sustainability.* Schumacher Briefing No. 12. White River Junction, VT: Chelsea Green.

Gaia Education. 2006. *Ecovillage Design Education.* Version 4.0. Developed by the Global Ecovillage Educators for a Sustainable Earth and endorsed by the United Nations Institute for Training and Research. Findhorn, Scotland: Global Ecovillage Network.

Gaia Trust. n.d. *EcoVillages: Introduction.* Foreningen Gaia Trust. Available at http://www.gaia.org/gaia/ecovillage/ (accessed 24 May 2010).

Gibson-Graham, J. K. 2006. *A Postcapitalist Politics.* Minneapolis: University of Minnesota Press.

Internal Displacement Monitoring Centre. 2012. *Global Overview 2011: People Internally Displaced by Conflict and Violence.* Geneva: Norwegian Refugee Council.

Jackson, Hildur. 1998. "What is an Ecovillage?" Gaia Trust Education Seminar. Thy, Denmark.

Jackson, Ross. 2004. "The Ecovillage Movement." *Permaculture Magazine* (Summer).

Perez Marcia, Luis Eduardo. 2006. *La Vulnerabilidad Alimentaria de Hogares Desplazados y no Desplazados: Un Estudio de Caso en Ocho Departamentos de Colombia.* Bogotá: World Food Program.

Reyes Posadas, Alejandro. 2009. *Guerreros y Campesinos. El Despojo de la Tierra en Colombia.* Bogotá: Editorial Norma.

Robbins, Paul. 2004. *Political Ecology: A Critical Introduction.* London: Blackwell.

Ross, Eric B. 2003. "Modernisation, Clearance and the Continuum of Violence in Colombia." Institute for Social Studies Working Papers 383. The Hague: Institute for Social Studies.

———. 2007. "Clearance as Development Strategy in Rural Colombia." *Peace Review: A Journal of Social Justice* 19 (1): 59–65.

World Food Program. 2005. *Estado Nutricional, de Alimentación, y Condiciones de Salud de la Población Desplazada por la Violencia en Seis Subregiones del País. Informe Final.* Bogotá: World Food Program.

CHAPTER FOURTEEN

Globalizing the Ecovillage Ideal

Networks of Empowerment, Seeds of Hope

Todd LeVasseur

Figure 14.1. Participants in the Findhorn ecovillage training program, February 2000. Photo by Todd LeVasseur.

From 5 February to 4 March 2000, approximately thirty-five full-time participants in residence and twenty-five part-time participants attended an ecovillage training program at the Findhorn Foundation community in Findhorn, Scotland. This five-week training program included attendees from all over the world: Japan, Australia, various European countries, Brazil, Sri Lanka, Israel, Turkey, Canada, the United States, Russia, El Salvador, Taiwan, Bangladesh, Ghana, the Philippines, and Egypt. For many people there, the training was not only a chance to learn about ecovillages, but also to make lasting international friendships.

The Findhorn Foundation is an intentional community located in northern Scotland.[1] Their main campus is called The Park and it is located a short walk from the town of Findhorn, located on Findhorn Bay. The husband and wife team of Peter and Eileen Caddy, along with their friend Dorothy Maclean, founded the community in 1962. All three were spiritual visionaries, and the community became a popular destination on the New Age circuit of the late 1960s, 1970s, and 1980s. The community subsequently became famous for Dorothy's communication with nature spirits and nature divas; Eileen's spiritual insights; and Peter's hard work in transforming what was a run-down caravan park into a thriving eco-garden and living center. Findhorn is still famous both for its sustainable farming and spiritual vision and receives thousands of visitors from around the world each year. In 1985 the community began to transition itself into an ecovillage, which is still an ongoing process, with new "green" structures being added annually.[2] As one of the leading ecovillages in Europe, Findhorn was instrumental in helping set up the Global Ecovillage Network (GEN) and is accredited by GEN to offer ecovillage training programs.

The ecovillage training program I attended in 2000 was organized and conducted by Findhorn community residents May East and Craig Gibsone, who were in charge of logistics, scheduling, and organizing the guest trainers, who led individual modules. These modules were designed to introduce participants to major themes and issues that they thought participants needed to know about ecovillages, and included training in:

1. *Ecovillages and the Emerging Paradigm*—this served as an introductory module to what ecovillages are and the worldviews that underpin their creation.
2. *Permaculture: Design for Sustainability*—many ecovillages are structured upon the principles of permaculture design. This three-day module introduced participants to some of the basics of permaculture (this aspect of ecovillages and the training program had a profound influence on many participants.)
3. *Building for the Next Millennium*—this module included tours of many of The Park's sustainable buildings and offered participants an opportunity to learn how Findhorn is continually transitioning their infrastructure to be more sustainable.
4. *Sustainable Economics*—this module investigated local exchange trading systems (LETS), and participants learned strategies to construct alternative, localized economies.
5. *Earth Share: Food, Farming, and Community*—this module investigated community supported agriculture (CSA) schemes and included visits to Findhorn's various agricultural fields.

6. *Building Effective Groups: Democracy, Empowerment, and Creativity*—this module addressed community dynamics and how to interface with local governmental bodies and other citizen groups in order to start the process of beginning an ecovillage.
7. *The Healing Power of Community*—this module explored the "pitfalls" of living in community, as well as the challenges and joys that come with sharing lives in an intentional community setting.
8. *Global Communication, Technology, and Networking*—this module introduced participants to social networking strategies around ecovillage ideals at regional, national, and international levels.
9. *Fundraising and Networking*—this module addressed some of the challenges of generating sufficient capital funds for beginning an ecovillage project.
10. *Wilderness, Conservation, and Eco-restoration*—the final module included a visit to Trees For Life's efforts to reforest the region with indigenous Scottish pine trees. Participants also learned how ecovillages can help with bioremediation and environmental restoration on their own property and within local bioregions.

The above training provided by Findhorn reflects a worldview that can be said to be common to an "ecovillage milieu." In the following passage, Hildur Jackson and Karen Svensson (2002: 5) give the impetus behind ecovillages and their milieu: "Over the past decades, people around the world have experimented with alternatives to a society, which they consider destructive. The ecovillage vision was born out of these experiments, providing solutions both urban and rural; both in the northern and in the southern hemisphere; and on every scale, from the family nucleus to local communities and global organizations. They embody a mindful lifestyle, which can be continued indefinitely in the future. As such, they are shaping nothing less than a new culture, designed to restore the Earth and her people."

Ecovillages: Ideals, Attributes, and Rationales

The above vision hints that ecovillages aim to be alternative experiments that bring together individuals, families, and/or communities who tend to be dissatisfied with the patterns of community interaction and consumption that their respective cultures practice. One of the underlying rationales behind ecovillages is a critique of the ubiquitous individualism and rampant consumption of modern lifestyles. Ecovillage idealists criticize this lifestyle, as they claim it leads to social and economic actions that degrade various communities. In regards to the earth, these communities are ecological, biological, and geochemical; for humans, these communities are familial, spiritual, mental, and physical. Furthermore, many in the GEN are sympathetic to and agree with the various criticisms of post–Bretton Woods global capitalism—as exemplified in Washington Consensus policies—wherein the ongoing neoliberalization of the global commons is seen to be harmful to human and nonhuman communities (Mander and Goldsmith 1996). Many buttress these criticisms by claiming that the modern consumer lifestyle championed by neoliberalization is imperialistic and leads to a destructive and rampant individualism, such that our communities are breaking down, leading to spiritual and ecological anomie. To borrow a phrase from Félix Guattari (2000: 30), ecovillages can be said to be a protest of the "mass-media serialism (the same ideal standards of living, the same fashions and types of rock music, etc.)" that has come to define the reality of many humans living in the twenty-first century. Ecovillages are, in part, a protest against the externalized ecological and social footprints that attend to this serialism.

Furthermore, the ecovillage movement—along with permaculture, bioregionalism, and other environmental justice and horizontal development-from-below movements—are living examples of a growing "blessed unrest" that Paul Hawken theorizes is changing the world (2007).[3] For Hawken (2007: 18), "a broad nonideological movement has come into being that does not invoke the masses' fantasized will but rather engages citizens' localized needs." Ecovillages are emblematic of these new social movements and are creations of local citizens concerned about local needs. Yet, these citizens are also concerned about global environmental issues. These concerns and the urge to build a more sustainable future leads ecovillagers to attempt to build sustainable communities and to join national and international ecovillage networks.[4]

Moreover, a strong ecocentric spirituality of interconnectedness permeates ecovillage subcultures.[5] This affective interconnectedness views humans as both biological and spiritual kin of nonhuman creation and is often ritualized in song, dance, poetry, and art (as participants experienced in many such rituals during the five-week training at Findhorn). Such a spirituality of interconnectedness views not only all humans as brothers and sisters of equal relations regardless of race, class, or nation-state; it also views nonhumans as being worthy of our reverence and as being equal members of a larger sacred earth-community. Ecovillages are places where this type of spirituality can possibly and even explicitly be lived out.

Although ecovillages are a pan-global phenomenon, they are theoretically designed to suit local needs and thus reflect local culture. My own experience as an attendee of an ecovillage training program in a Global North country is that the ecovillage ideal and movement reflects a Global North understanding of community and environmental problems. This friction was evident in our time at Findhorn, with those participants from the Global South having different needs, starting points, and concerns than those from a post-materialistic North (Guha 2006). For a truly pan-human and pan-global ecovillage network to emerge and have a chance of flourishing, these different cultural and historical pasts and different present needs and concerns need to be addressed.

Along these lines, a common starting point is that ecovillagers, North and South, recognize that Global North countries, as well as elites in the Global South, consume more than their share of the earth's resources. Ecovillages are thus, in one respect, a concerted attempt to create an antidote to the extreme power differentials on various scales made possible by modern capitalist markets and politics. They become living communities where members can attempt to enact values and patterns of consumption geared toward sustainability that are at odds with the dominant culture, especially in the North.

Starting an ecovillage is no easy task. It requires capital, a willing community, land, and patience. Unfortunately, many potential ecovillagers have not been given the skills that living in community requires. As the Scottish land campaigner Alastair McIntosh states (2008: 27), "the principles of community are neither obvious nor desirable to everyone." Therefore, ecovillages must have a community decision-making process in place so that our human need to gossip, deliberate, express differences of opinion, and then move toward reconciliation can be met (Baker and Lee 1996). Ecovillages are also susceptible to self-selective homogeneity, dogmatic purity, and assuming away cultural differences. Sadly, there is an all too real history of failure when people try to create a safe, healthy community—some ecovillages become habitats for demagogues while others have disbanded after just a few years. Thus, attrition and failure are real scenarios for each ecovillage—especially in a highly mobile, individualistic society.

Where there are mechanisms in place (for example, countries that are signatories of the Rio Earth Summit and have Agenda 21 funds) or in countries with more intact regional identities and cultures, chances for success at creating and maintaining an ecovillage are higher. However, it is naïve fantasy to think that it is easy to just begin an ecovillage from scratch and expect the whole culture (both within and without the ecovillage) to change. Rather, ecovillages are often "seeds," and the more successful, famous, and long-lasting ones become learning centers where the seeds born of practice are disseminated through training programs and workshops.[6]

Ecovillages are founded upon a reading of the anthropological record, in that for the majority of human history, humans have lived in face-to-face, small settlements and villages of twenty to a few hundred people. Ecovillagers believe that this scale of human settlement leads to healthy relations among humans and between humans and the nonhuman world. As it is neither feasible nor practical to expect that all humans are willing or able to downscale and deurbanize, many in the ecovillage movement instead hope that megacities develop interconnected, ecovillage-styled neighborhoods that utilize appropriate technologies. The city of Curitiba, Brazil is often held up as an example of a metropolis that is incorporating ecovillage ideals and appropriate-scale technologies into its planning.[7]

Lastly, ecovillages resemble what Edward Casey (1998) argues is an ongoing reemergence of concern for "place"; they reflect the growing ecological consciousness that is permeating the global commons (Worster 1996); and they are constituted by unique regional and cultural identities, concerns, and responses to neoliberalization (Escobar and Alvarez 1992; Veltmeyer and Petras 2000). Ecovillages therefore are "settled" at the vanguard of human attempts to reinhabit local place-based regions by incorporating insights of ecology and concerns for sustainability. The ecovillage effort to sustainably settle into place is molded and shaped by both local and regional identities and modes of thought and communication, and is tempered by a respect for local biological limits.

Five Global Perspectives on Ecovillages

This chapter is, in part, a ten-year retrospective that looks back at a utopian moment in the lives of sixty people who learned about ecovillages at Findhorn. Many of the participants in the training program have remained in touch via the Internet, developing networks and friendships. Given that the ecovillage phenomenon has emerged only in the last few decades, this chapter presents an opportunity for an international perspective on ecovillages that covers a ten-year period of action and reflection.

In April 2010, I selected peers from the Findhorn ecovillage training program, using them to develop a case study approach to understanding ecovillages. Given their situated perspective as participants in the 2000 training, coupled with their subsequent active pursuit of putting this training into practice, their insights help generate a multivocal perspective of the ecovillage milieu. To carry out this research, I adopted a semi-structured interview format that allowed for open-ended responses from the participants. All five participants were emailed a set of questions and were asked to submit responses no longer than six hundred words. The questions asked the respondents to briefly share their experience at the Findhorn ecovillage training in 2000, including how this training shaped and influenced their understanding of ecovillages; to provide a current understanding of ecovillages; and to share what they have done in the past ten years to try to create an ecovillage—including obstacles and barriers to success they might have faced. In what follows I will reflect on the differences and commonalities and the greater value of the collective experiences of this diverse group of people. Special attention will be paid to analyzing indicative phrases and experiences that help shed light on contemporary insights about ecovillages.[8]

Bert Peters, Full-Time Participant from the Philippines[9]

Bert Peters moved from Belgium to the Philippines in 1990. He subsequently married a Filipino, and they are raising a family and attempting to create their own permaculture and ecovillage-inspired learning center.[10] After moving to the Philippines, Bert helped with sustainable development initiatives. However, his experience was that "[p]eople just felt that we were experts with little real life experience, but instead loads of theoretical perception. So I [began] an active search for a system or model that could answer" local needs and questions. Bert shares that "I clearly understood that a comprehensive framework was needed. Attending a course on eco-village development in Findhorn was the first eye-opener for me … Permaculture became the key word and foundation" that emerged from the ecovillage training for Bert. Because Bert felt the holistic framework needed to create an ecovillage rests on principles of permaculture, "it lead to attending a series of permaculture courses in Australia and Hawaii. And ultimately, it lead to the birth of Cabiokid foundation, a permaculture development site on Luzon Island in the Philippines."

Bert feels that ecovillages must be designed to resemble natural systems. He also claims that "[w]hile a design is geared towards improving its surroundings and the users, it also entails a great level of responsibility from its birth onwards … The creation of eco-villages would be one [part of a] greater challenge [that] lies in undoing the damage in existing communities [with a goal of creating] little paradises or eco-villages within such existing or thriving communities."

Bert shares that "from the years 2000–2010, I carefully used the word eco-village since it carried a connotation that would not always match very well with the context of developing nations. The social fabric within communities [in developing nations] is still very strong, while [at the same time they see] all the wrongs of un-sustainable development brought to them by developed nations." For Bert, this means that "[e]co-village development in the first place is a mind-set. It is a way of life that one should practice wherever. An eco-village is a learning area where people can experiment with and experience … nature in its most beautiful form." To this end, Bert and his family and some close friends "have set up Cabiokid [a permaculture garden and training center] as a development and experimental site. People live there and form a community bonding with the surrounding community. Our experiments are open for residents of the nearby community to see and explore." This training center was inspired by seeing how Findhorn hosts permaculture and ecovillage training programs. Therefore, for Bert, "[m]y insight became that the real fabric is all about permaculture. Permaculture holds the key of any eco-village development and provides the essential understanding on how to tap in [to] nature's wealth and eventually to enable someone to benefit from it." Since founding Cabiokid, Bert shares that "[w]e continue to immerse with people whose realities are very grounded but who are often denied equal access to resources. Eco-village design is in the first place about creating equal opportunities for residents in a certain bioregion." For Bert, ecovillages have become a place where building community by offering workshops based on the regenerative models of natural systems and permaculture design can empower disenfranchised farmers and poor rural residents of Global South regions.

Juan Rojas, Full-Time Participant from El Salvador[11]

Juan Rojas entered into the ecovillage milieu from a permaculture perspective. Juan heard about Findhorn's training module while attending permaculture training programs at the ecovillage Crystal Waters in Australia. Thus, "in 2000 I joined an international band of ecological minded people at Findhorn Ecological Village. I was sponsored to attend by May East and Craig Gibsone … This [training] helped me to understand an English or European model of ecovillages [and] help[ed] broaden my understanding of [ecovillages]." Juan explains that by living at Findhorn during the training, he was able to see firsthand appropriate technologies that ecovillages can design and build to help lessen their footprints. For example, he was impressed by Findhorn's wind turbine; the on-site black and grey water "living machine" designed by John Todd; the amount of locally grown organic produce used in the cafeteria; and various "green" building practices. Juan also pointed out that "[f]reedom based on the spiritual journey of the pioneers can be sensed all over the place," and this to him was an important component of Findhorn's ecovillage. Overall, Juan "got the sense that [Findhorn] was one of the best models to reproduce at the European region because it is achievable and affordable by most people."

However, Juan shares that he is from a poor, rural farming region in El Salvador that was decimated by his country's civil war. Furthermore, "[i]n January and February 2001 there were a couple of earthquakes which devastated El Salvador. I was in those days building my house on two acres of property I owned in La Florida Farming Cooperative located in Santa Tecla, La Libertad Department of El Salvador." Juan and his colleagues in El Salvador's permaculture network developed a "permaculture strategy for rebuilding [their] rural community with the aim to set the bases for a future ecovillage with a Salvadoran style."[12] Juan's community of La Florida "benefited with an award from the Mennonite and Christian Churches in US and Canada of around $75,000 USD," and in two years they achieved a variety of regional infrastructure improvement. As Juan explains, he and his permaculture network employed ecovillage design concepts (e.g., creating sustainable physical and communal structures within the farming region of La Florida) to implement and generate a variety of successful community-level enterprises and strategies. These include building twenty-six permanent anti-earthquake and hurricane dwellings; introducing agroecology to counteract the negative effects of conventional farming practices that were used prior in the region; and the creation of a certified organic coffee cash crop over a three year period. Other successes include providing water sanitation and rainwater catchment tanks to various households in the community; building dry compost latrines for every household; and building wood saver stoves for every kitchen. Juan shared that these projects were successful because mutual aid work was offered and supported with a food-for-work scheme which was fundamental for helping the community support the reconstruction process. This included periodical indoor and outdoor community activities (such as shared meals, work parties, religious gatherings, and dances), which Juan claims were a must in the process as they helped overcome the collective psychological trauma of the earthquakes.

Juan's experience over the ten years was between two worlds. In one, he had been at leading permaculture and ecovillage communities in the Global North: Crystal Waters in Australia and Findhorn in Scotland. The other world was his home country of El Salvador, where he returned after the training, and which suffered a devastating earthquake. Juan's experience was that the ecovillage training was informative, and is a valid Global North model. Given the needs and realities (political, financial, and historical) of his home country, Juan feels that a European/Global North model is not necessarily transferable. Juan's experience with ecovillages led him to observe that the capital-intensive and spiritually based ecovillage model of Findhorn is a Global North phenomenon not readily replicated in poor rural farming areas of the Global South, which have suffered under colonialism and the demands of international commodity markets. Juan writes that "[a]fter a period of four years La Florida farming community was on track again, looking forward for new ways, alternative ways, innovative ways of knowing how to deal with its own destiny. Out of that symbiosis, the Permaculture Institute of El Salvador was born and started a promotion of permaculture through a network of the Farmer-to-Farmer movement based on community development nationwide." Juan writes that this network has transformed his rural community, which has since "become the experimental ground for hundreds of trainees in Permaculture Design. I have lived with that community for the last ten years in a wonderful relationship and continue working on permaculture issues from there." In essence, Juan has left behind the ecovillage concept as it was presented at Findhorn, and has instead tailored permaculture to meet the regional social, environmental, and political needs of his community. For Juan, ecovillages represent a Global North phenomenon; they are viable alternatives in Global North contexts, but he does not use the same vocabulary and goals in his native context.

Karen Inwood, Full-Time Participant from England[13]

Karen Inwood, a native of England, was a resident of Findhorn at the time of the training program. She had first visited Findhorn as a participant in their 1999 permaculture training course, which she claims was a life-changing event, prompting her to move "to Findhorn to study permaculture and experience community living."

Karen feels that "the highlight of EVT 2000 was meeting people from so many different cultures and realities and creating a network of international friendship." For her, the "[ecovillage] model is one of a group of people acquiring land, designing an ecological co-housing community and developing harmonious ways of living together."

Despite having lived in an ecovillage, an experience she "personally enjoyed," Karen nonetheless felt that "as a community worker my interest was, and still is, how to support existing communities to transition to an ecologically sustainable way of living. If our vision is to transform society, then we need to work with what we have and find solutions for positive, participative change." She feels that "[d]espite the participation of many people from the global south, the model and specific technologies presented [at the training] were high tech, expensive and based on western needs and western thinking—a lost opportunity to share ideas, experience and technologies between our very internationally varied group." Because of this tension and missed opportunity, Karen explains that "[b]y the end of the course my passion was still to find out how to apply permaculture within existing communities as a tool for the transformation of society. So a few weeks later, I left Findhorn for good and joined Juan Rojas in El Salvador to learn from his Farmer-to-Farmer permaculture project and help build a permaculture teaching institute there."

Like Juan, Karen felt the Global North perspective of an ecovillage that was presented at Findhorn was not readily transferable to the existing realities of the Global South. Indeed, "[t]en years later, I'm still in El Salvador working as Director of the Permaculture Institute which we set up with a group of peasant farmers in 2002. Together, we've built a movement of thousands of farming families working to transform their lives, their villages and their municipalities—using permaculture thinking to transition to a more ecological way of life." For Karen, "[t]he beauty of permaculture is that it allows you to create your own models—rooted in place, in local culture, spirituality, history and reality ... It teaches us to ... find small, simple and slow solutions to change our reality."

Karen explains that "[o]urs is long-term strategic work to build the capacity of individuals, of communities and of social institutions to find ecologically sustainable solutions to the overwhelming complexity of problems we face." This sentiment fits into those expressed by many within the ecovillage milieu, in that it recognizes the complex problems we face and the long-term, bottom-up solutions that are required, and of which ecovillages are but one part. Karen shares how "[t]he municipal ecological community networks are influencing local strategies, encouraging institutional cooperation, educating local organizations and demonstrating a very different vision for local development ... We can hardly keep up with the interest being generated—from local universities, overseas visitors, local government and development agencies."

The above success gave Karen pause for reflection. She writes that "looking back at the EVT course and how it has contributed to our work here, I have to say that it is not a relevant model for our reality, but rather our task has been and still is, to equip Salvadorans to find their own solutions and develop their own models." She explains how "[t]he poor of El Salvador have suffered for centuries from the imposition of western models, both those designed to exploit as well as those designed to help. Despite the millions of dollars poured in after the civil war, the conditions of the poor have changed little because the solutions didn't arise from their own culture, history, conditions and capacity." Karen still cares and is passionate about the same issues that brought her to Findhorn. However, her reality is now that of living in El Salvador. While the goals of ecovillagers might be held in common with the farmers she works with in El Salvador, the material needs and political strategies differ: "After all, the resilience of nature and therefore of humans, depends on diversity, on creativity and on adaptation."

Luiz Midea, Full-Time Participant from Brazil[14]

Luiz Midea was one of two participants from Brazil. He came as the representative and current resident of a Brazilian ecovillage, Matutu.[15] Matutu sent Luiz to learn concepts and skills that he could bring back to his ecovillage, located in southeastern Brazil. As Luiz explains, "[prior to beginning community life], I had lived for six years in the field, practicing [sustainable] agriculture and producing natural foods. What led me to seek [living in an intentional community] was precisely the search for alternatives to [the] urban model in which I lived for the first twenty years of my life." Living in crowded cities made Luiz realize that "the lack of meaning [that came with] disorderly development generated pollution and violence. [I saw] the need to build new ways of living close to nature and [the need to develop] friendly relations with the [peasant farmers]." As with many others in the ecovillage milieu who have had a similar realization, Luiz was prompted to move to the countryside to practice sustainable farming techniques. This precipitated his subsequent move to Matutu, "an intentional community with approximately one hundred and twenty people located in a beautiful valley at 1500 meters in altitude and where the group's experience with nature [is incredibly deep]." For Luiz, "my main [experience living in an] ecovillage was a discovery of possibilities to live together and [to] share life in nature." He found that "more than application of eco-technologies, an ecovillage offered the opportunity to create a collective culture, a rational basis for subsistence and a new sense of social [reality]."

Luiz shares that his current "understanding of an ecovillage is the realization that we must be open to learning and free of any model [of domination or coercion]." He continues, stating that "[e]covillages [should] support a local infrastructure [of residency, agriculture, and employment]" and "should pay [close] attention to their development process and [how they are] managed." Furthermore, ecovillages should develop a healthy, sustainable village structure so that "[t]he 'eco' is expressed in [healthy] relationships within the group and [between] the group and its environment."

Luiz's experience is that "[t]hese [human-human] relationships are the greatest resource available in the ecovillage and can also be its greatest obstacle. After my return from Findhorn, I could see how this feature of the [ecovillage], or lack thereof, can alter and change established systems, making them obsolete and of little significance to reinvigorating the group or its aims." Luiz finds that community relationships are strengthened with the following practices:

- Living together on a daily basis
- Holding collective celebrations
- Having transparent and participatory decision-making processes
- Maintaining solidarity and common purpose
- Having effective communication and information dissemination
- Encouraging cooperation for income generation and production
- Sharing ceremonies and spiritual practices

Luiz's experience living at Matutu is that "when one of these practices [is] not given due attention, the group open[s] a space for conflict and [this demands] precious energy to solve." Nonetheless, "when [those in Matutu exhibit] balanced and cooperative relations, based on a circle of sincere friendship and [shared living], the conditions to build sustainable systems (including around infrastructure, education, production and organizational management) become favorable and there is an expression of these natural values in group activities."

Luiz has moved to land next to Matutu, where, "along with my wife, [we grow] agroecological crops [and] have had visitors as our house guests." He shares that "while the forms of organization have changed a lot around here, I realize that these changes are just cycles of higher learning and not a hindrance. There is only one way to walk as an [ecovillage] pioneer: where there is [space] to recognize [both] the individual and the collective, in every challenge and every situation."

Martin Kirchner, Full-Time Participant from Austria[16]

Martin Kirchner traveled to Findhorn from his native Austria. A guitarist and computer programmer, he was one of the leaders of those in the group who were in their twenties, and spent a considerable amount of time tape recording interviews with a variety of participants to gain further insights into ecovillages and intentional living. Martin writes that "[t]o me, the Ecovillage training in 2000 was a turning point in my life at the age of twenty-five. Many of my interests and passions came together in the Ecovillage Training Curriculum. I saw it clearly as the most sensible thing to do: to spend my life's energy on creating positive examples for a culturally creative environment for sustainable lifestyles." He explains how "[m]y time in Findhorn touched me deeply, being together with changemakers from all around the world for almost five extremely intense weeks, learning from each other, celebrating the richness of diversity in the group, feeling human connection beyond cultural differences … It all left a deep impression on me and a ground tone, a reference vibration for the many years which were to come."

Upon returning to Austria, Martin "wrote up articles and a concept paper about how an Ecovillage in Austria could look. Starting with this document an Ecovillage initiative formed with many dozens of people involved, lasting for one year without [our group] being able to decide for a piece of land." Martin also "traveled to visit Ecovillage projects in more than twelve countries, to learn and understand more about them and to prepare for co-creating one. I got in touch with the Global Ecovillage Network and [have] joined many of the yearly General Assemblies since then." Furthermore, in Austria, Martin co-organized summer gatherings for people wanting to live in community and co-initiated the Austrotopia Network for Living in Community, linking up a couple of Austrian initiatives.

Martin relates that during the past ten years, "my understanding of the Ecovillage concept shifted from a largely autonomous village to a more open picture, integrated well within a region. Since Austria is quite a densely populated country it also always felt a bit awkward to build new villages." He relates how "[i]n 2004 I [was introduced to] the Co-housing concept and to me it was a much more appropriate approach to start an intentional community as a hub and culturally creative center within an existing village or small town." With family and friends, Martin "set up an association and put a lot of effort in looking for a good piece of land and attracting people." However, "[a]fter years of major setbacks with landowners and core groups which eventually dissolved, I got tired and ritually let go of the whole thing. And (this seems to be a universal pattern) not long after the right piece of land and the right people appeared and together we had enough critical mass to get a project going, [with] me being more determined than ever." Martin shares that "[n]ow in summer 2010 we are almost fifty beautiful people who have bought the land [and completed] the design for almost thirty units and communal facilities. Building will start next spring. To me it feels like the beginning of a journey, a great adventure together with 'soul family' people, where Cohousing will certainly not be an end in itself but a stepping stone to something more radical."

Martin shares that his "personal vision is connecting Ecovillages in the Global South with communities in Austria and to live in a very cosmopolitan, vibrant and spiritual place—like Findhorn is, but much warmer!" Looking back, Martin feels that "the Ecovillage Training was also extremely inspiring in terms of learning design. In 2010 I initiated and am leading a year-long training course for young changemakers called 'Pioneers of

Change,' which draws a lot from the setting and spirit of the Ecovillage Training which was so powerful to me.[17] I feel so much gratitude that I was able to have such an experience in my younger years."

Summary and Conclusion

What insights about ecovillages in the twenty-first century can be gleaned from these responses from dedicated ecovillage activists? One is the importance of permaculture, as both a gateway into the larger ecovillage milieu, and also as a foundational building block upon which ecovillage design can be built. Another is the different needs, expectations, and cultural paradigms of Global North and Global South citizens in today's world. Although an extremely small sample size, it is telling that three of the five respondents have lived in Europe and traveled widely, but are now in Global South countries attempting to create permaculture/ecovillage communities—all three point out the political, cultural, and economic disjunctures between North and South realities regarding ecovillages.

All five responses also engage in a dialectic with scale, negotiating whether they are working toward creating autonomous ecovillages, or incorporating their vision into a larger network across a geographical region. Most point out that their project is an educational center and/or a place to visit and that they are part of a larger process that involves educating local peoples about ecovillages and permaculture.

Lastly, all five describe the dedication and small victories that come with creating ecovillages. It was no small feat to take five weeks to travel to Findhorn to learn about ecovillages—such a trip requires great commitment, resources, and passion. Indeed, the attendees are at the forefront of the emerging ecovillage movement. Despite these passions, it has taken hard work and perseverance to put ecovillage concepts into action, and even then, only Luiz currently lives in an "ecovillage" proper. Yet, all maintain that the energy and effort they have put into building alternatives have been worth the journey. Furthermore, all still hold to the initial concerns and passions that brought them to learn about ecovillages in the first place—commitments to environmental justice, sustainability, and creating healthy human communities. It seems that one of the driving forces behind those involved in ecovillage subcultures is that ecovillages represent a utopia. As Peter Stillman explains, "for many utopians the central concern is the process of raising and reflecting on alternatives, thinking about the present in light of them, and acting where warranted … one central characterization of utopias is that they involve the stating and thinking through of norms, principles, or patterns that are alternatives to the values of contemporary society" (2001: 11). What ecovillages offer is the ability to plan, present, and put into practice such alternatives. For many, ecovillages become a place to embody and articulate utopian norms, patterns, and principles that explore sustainability and holistic living. These are seen by ecovillagers to be alternatives to the larger hegemonic society in which they live. By creating and residing in ecovillages, people are able to help shift their utopian imaginaries into a lived reality; they are able to bridge the gap of putting holistic values related to community, sustainability, and justice into lived practice. Although in relative infancy, the ecovillage milieu has the potential to help reshape human societies in this and coming centuries. Indeed, the practices developed and put forth over the last ten years by the participants in the Findhorn workshop are helping to lay the groundwork for an alternative vision to the serialism of late capitalism.

Notes

1. See http://www.findhorn.org/index.php. On its famous gardens, see the community's self-authored 1976 book, *The Findhorn Garden.*
2. See http://www.findhorn.org/whatwedo/ecovillage/ecovillage.php.
3. For an exploration of the type of skills such movements require and/or attempt to develop, see Stibbe (2009).
4. The author admits that the term "sustainable" is fraught with politics and inconsistencies. However, the concept is commonly used within ecovillage subcultures and in ecovillage literature—sustainability is one of the key goals of ecovillages.
5. For a look at this type of nature-related spirituality and how it manifests and thus influences radical environmental subcultures and, increasingly, mainstream culture, see Taylor (2010). It must be noted that many in the larger communities movement, especially in Western countries, are called to live in community because of specific religious beliefs and identities (Fellowship for Intentional Community 1996; see also *Communities* magazine at http://communities.ic.org/). These people have affinities with ecovillagers, and many are even creating faith-based ecovillages. Others in the intentional community and ecovillage milieu are motivated by deep ecology to build "ecosteries" (Drengson 1993; see also http://www.ecostery.org/default.htm). Religious belief and spiritual faith also motivate community and ecovillage movements in the Global South; see, for example, the Sarvodaya movement in Sri Lanka and Auroville ecovillage in India (Jackson and Svensson 2002).
6. Ecovillage training programs are now held at The Farm in Tennessee, USA; Crystal Waters in Australia; and Auroville in India, to name a few. For an in-depth exploration of how people succeed and do not succeed in putting values into practice, see Peterson (2009).

7. For an in-depth exploration of another Global South exemplar of a city built upon appropriate technologies and ecovillage ideals, see Weisman (2008).
8. It should be noted that English is the second language for four of the five respondents. I also asked for clarification on each response, so that respondents revisited their answer at least once.
9. All quotations in this subsection are taken from Bert Peters, emails to author on 15 March 2010 and 25 March 2010.
10. For more information see http://cabiokid.org.
11. All quotations in this subsection are taken from Juan Rojas, emails to author on 7 April 2010 and 24 April 2010.
12. For more information see http://www.permacultura.org.
13. All quotations in this subsection are taken from Karen Inwood, emails to author on 10 April 2010 and 2 May 2010.
14. All quotations in this subsection are taken from Luiz Midea, emails to author on 24 March 2010, 5 April 2010, and 19 April 2010.
15. For more information see www.patrimoniodomatutu.com.br.
16. All quotations in this subsection are taken from Martin Kirchner, emails to author on 14 April 2010 and 28 April 2010.
17. For more information see http://www.pioneersofchange.at.

References

Baker, Harvey, and Barbara Lee. 1996. "Community Building for the Long Term." In *Communities Directory: A Guide to Cooperative Living*, ed. Fellowship of Intentional Community. Rutledge, MO: Fellowship for Intentional Community.

Casey, Edward. 1998. *The Fate of Place: A Philosophical History*. Berkeley: University of California Press.

Drengson, Alan. 2003. *Doc Forest and Blue Mountain Ecostery: A Narrative on Creating Ecological Harmony in Daily Life*. Victoria, Australia: Ecostery House.

Escobar, Arturo, and Sonia E. Alvarez. 1992. *The Making of Social Movements in Latin America: Identity, Strategy, and Democracy*. Boulder, CO: Westview Press.

Fellowship for Intentional Community. 2007. *Communities Directory: A Guide to Cooperative Living*. Rutledge, MO: Fellowship of Intentional Community.

Findhorn. 1976. *The Findhorn Garden: Pioneering a New Vision of Man and Nature in Cooperation*. New York: HarperCollins.

Guha, Ramachandra. 2006. *How Much Should a Person Consume? Thinking Through the Environment*. Ranikhet, India: Permanent Black.

Guattari, Félix. 2000. *The Three Ecologies*. London: Athlone Press.

Hawken, Paul. 2007. *Blessed Unrest: How the Largest Social Movement in History is Restoring Grace, Justice, and Beauty to the World*. New York: Penguin Books.

Jackson, Hildur, and Karen Svensson, eds. 2002. *Ecovillage Living: Restoring the Earth and Her People*. Totnes, UK: Green Books.

Mander, Jerry, and Edward Goldsmith. 1996. *The Case Against the Global Economy and For a Turn Toward the Local*. San Francisco: Sierra Club Books.

McIntosh, Alastair. 2008. *Rekindling Community: Connecting People, Environment and Spirituality.* Schumacher Briefings 15. Totnes, UK: Green Books.

Peterson, Anna. 2009. *Everyday Ethics and Social Change: The Education of Desire.* New York: Columbia University Press.

Stibbe, Arran, ed. 2009. *The Handbook of Sustainability Literacy: Skills for a Changing World.* Totnes, UK: Green Books.

Stillman, Peter. 2001. "'Nothing Is But What Is Not': Utopias as Practical Political Philosophy." In *The Philosophy of Utopia,* ed. Barbara Goodwin. London: Frank Cass.

Taylor, Bron. 2010. *Dark Green Religion: Nature Spirituality and the Planetary Future.* Berkeley: University of California Press.

Veltmeyer, Henry, and James Petras. 2000. *The Dynamics of Social Change in Latin America.* London: Macmillan.

Weisman, Alan. 2008. *Gaviotas: A Village to Reinvent the World.* 10th anniversary ed. White River Junction, VT: Chelsea Green.

Worster, Donald. 1996. *Nature's Economy: A History of Ecological Ideas.* New York: Cambridge University Press.

Chapter Fifteen

Academia's Hidden Curriculum and Ecovillages as Campuses for Sustainability Education

Daniel Greenberg

We are living in a unique time, not just in human history, but also in *planetary* history. From the recent war in Iraq to the war on rainforests, from global markets to global warming—it is clear we *must* learn to live in ways that honor all life.

Yet we continue to dig deeper and faster into the earth's resources. Best estimates are that humans exceeded the earth's biocapacity sometime in the late 1970s and our global ecological footprint is now over one and a half planets (WWF 2010: 7). How is this even possible, given we only have one planet? We are living off the stored capital, or "ghost acreage," of fossil fuels that have accumulated over millions of years.

Unfortunately, our cupboard is getting barer every day. Many experts agree we are close to global peak oil and the difficulty and cost of extraction will continue to rise in coming years (e.g., Heinberg 2004). In addition, a century of burning oil, coal, and natural gas has dramatically increased atmospheric concentrations of carbon dioxide and is ushering in a period of rapid climate destabilization. Given our current (and increasing!) dependence on oil, these twin issues will likely have dramatic impacts on all sectors of society.

Donella Meadows, systems analyst and Dartmouth professor, once wrote that "[t]here is nothing so powerful as an exponential whose time has come" (1991: 53). Whether we are talking about species extinction, population growth, social inequity, deforestation, or acidification of the oceans, we are now witnessing unsustainable exponential growth (or decline) in a whole host of domains. Yet, as a species, humans seem evolutionarily unequipped to understand exponentials and unprepared to address the global issues facing us. For the most part, business is going on as usual: governments—at best—are thinking ahead only to the next election, and, as Oberlin professor David Orr has said, "[w]e are still educating the young as if there were no planetary emergency" (1994: 27).

We need to pause, take a step back, and consider how we can educate for a post-carrying capacity world—for a post-peak oil world. We need to move beyond the industrial era and train leaders who know how to *heal* the earth and build durable economies and sustainable communities. But how? Einstein once said that "[w]e can't solve problems by using the same kind of thinking we used when we created them." So we also need to move beyond the ivory towers of traditional academia and create campuses and pedagogies that are better able to educate for a sustainable future. This is where ecovillages come in.

What is an ecovillage? The classic definition was offered by Robert Gilman in 1991 when he wrote "an ecovillage is a human-scale, full-featured settlement in which human activities are harmlessly integrated into the natural world in a way that is supportive of healthy human development and can be successfully continued into the indefinite future" (1991: 10). Unfortunately, using a strict interpretation of this definition, one could argue there are *zero* ecovillages on the planet. So, practically, the term is better thought of as a *process* than as a product. Ecovillages are communities striving to achieve this ideal, rather than completed utopias.

Ecovillages are living laboratories—"beta test centers"—for a more sustainable future. In order to survive, humans need to both reduce the eco-

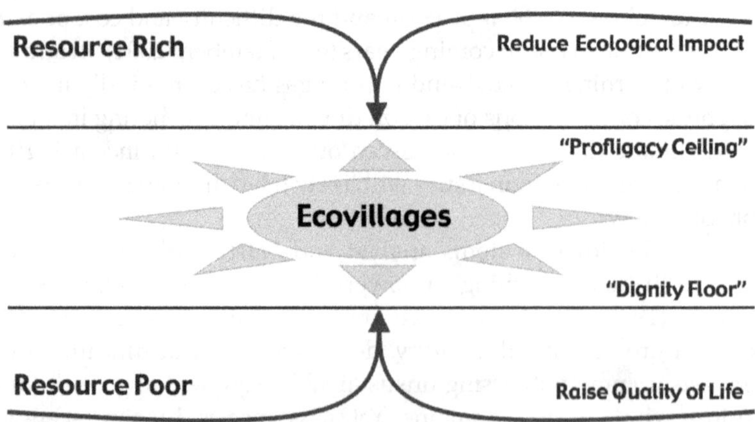

Figure 15.1. Living laboratories for a sustainable future. Design by Daniel Greenberg.

logical impacts of the resource rich and raise the quality of life among the resource poor. Julian Agyeman refers to these thresholds as humanity's "profligacy ceiling" (aka "carrying capacity") and "dignity floor" (Monani 2009: 60).

Ecovillages have essentially staked out a middle ground between the resource rich and resource poor and are experimenting with how we can live high quality lifestyles with low ecological impacts. How can we live well and lightly—together? This is likely the most important question of the twenty-first century.

Seen in this way, it becomes clear there are actually two directions toward the ecovillage model. Top-down ecovillages are typically intentionally created communities within developed, resource-rich countries in which members are exploring how they can reduce their footprints while maintaining high-quality lifestyles. Bottom-up ecovillages are more often indigenous, traditional communities attempting to develop in ways that preserve their local culture and resources. Both directions are valid and necessary and both are creating models of sustainable, human-scale communities.

According to the Global Ecovillage Network (GEN), an international network of sustainable communities and initiatives, over five hundred ecovillages are currently developing and refining ecological and social tools, such as community-scale renewable energy systems, ecological design, organic farming, holistic health and nutrition, consensus decision making, local economies, and mindfulness practices (GEN n.d.). It is important to note, however, that ecovillages are generally not on the cutting edge of sustainable development. There are few initiatives being attempted in ecovillages that are not—*on their own*—being done better elsewhere. One can easily find more successful organic farms, renewable energy facilities, green buildings, and even decision-making processes outside of ecovillages. What makes ecovillages unique and relevant is how they are putting these pieces together into wholes that are greater than the sum of their parts. They are, in effect, creating new cultures, new "stories" about what it means to live interdependently with each other and our planet.

Recognizing this core work, ecovillages are increasingly being viewed as "campuses" where students can learn about sustainability while actually living it. Many ecovillages have already had considerable successes creating educational centers and ongoing partnerships with government agencies, research centers, and schools of higher learning.

Living Routes is one such organization helping to build bridges between ecovillages and academia by creating college-level programs based in ecovillages around the world (Living Routes n.d.). Founded in 1999,

Living Routes is an educational nonprofit that partners with the University of Massachusetts–Amherst to offer fall and spring semester programs in India (Auroville), Scotland (Findhorn), Costa Rica (Monteverde) and Israel (Kibbutz Lotan); three week winter term programs in Mexico (Huehuecoyotl) and India (Auroville); and summer programs in Peru (Sachamama), Brazil (Ecocentro IPEC), Australia (Crystal Waters), and the United States (Sirius Community, Massachusetts). To date, over fifteen hundred students from over four hundred colleges and universities have completed a Living Routes program. These alumni have become more inspired and knowledgeable about topics such as permaculture, group dynamics, ecological design, worldview development, peace and social justice, and sustainable community development.

Living Routes works closely with another nongovernmental organization (NGO) called Gaia Education, which was created by a group of approximately twenty international ecovillage educators and GEN advocates known as the Global Ecovillage Educators for a Sustainable Earth (GEESE; Gaia Education n.d.). This group convened five times from 1998 to 2008 for the purpose of developing an ecovillage design curriculum, which attempts to offer an exhaustive and mutually exclusive outline of twenty design modules held within four dimensions of social, economic, ecological, and spiritual development. The curriculum is now available online in seven languages and has been deemed an official contribution to the UN Decade of Education for Sustainable Development (UNDESD) 2005–2014. Gaia Education was formally launched by the GEESE in 2005 and has since supported the delivery of over sixty intensive training programs on five continents, providing a core understanding of ecovillage design. While not specifically focused on academia, Gaia Education has partnered with a number of universities, and most of Living Routes' semester programs have been certified as ecovillage design education courses.

Why Academia Needs Ecovillages

To understand why ecovillages offer ideal campuses for sustainability education, it is helpful to unpack the "hidden curriculum" embedded within higher education as compared to ecovillages. Anyone who has been in school understands that students learn not only through their school's official curricula, but also implicitly through their day-to-day participation in that institution. For example, regardless of the topic being taught, students at most schools are expected to listen attentively to the instructor, be organized, and follow instructions. These unspoken yet powerful expectations are often referred to as an organization's "hidden curriculum."

While higher education is changing, its tacit structure, "story," or metanarrative is still more aligned with producing industrial-age specialists rather than the neorenaissance generalists and practitioners that are required if we are to slow down and reverse this juggernaut of destruction we have become. As David Orr so eloquently put it, "The plain fact is that the planet does not need more successful people. But it does desperately need more peacemakers, healers, restorers, storytellers, and lovers of every kind. It needs people who live well in their places. It needs people of moral courage willing to join the fight to make the world more habitable and humane. And these qualities have little to do with success as our culture defined it" (1994: 12).

How do we educate for this? And where? The following are ten examples of how academia and ecovillages offer contrasting hidden curricula that either hinder or support the development of the new type of leader that Orr describes. While these examples may seem provocative, and notable exceptions exist within each, it is hoped that the gestalt will ring true.

1. Conventional versus Experimental

Universities tend to be burdened by cumbersome bureaucracies that resist change. In fact, the basic structure of universities has not significantly evolved since the Middle Ages. This structure was effective during an industrial economy when a college degree conveyed a scarce premium and a bureaucratic "command and control" mindset was a market advantage, but less so in more networked and service-oriented societies that need real-world leaders and problem solvers who are not wedded to convention. When even the simple task of creating departmental letterhead can take months of meetings, review sessions, and calls for bids, one begins to understand why a deep structural reorientation toward sustainability is often a painfully slow process in many colleges and universities.

Ecovillages are physical and social "laboratories," experimenting with new technologies, social structures, and worldviews. They tend to have a trial and error mentality and are quick to adjust to changing conditions, challenges, and opportunities. At Sirius Community, a small ecovillage in western Massachusetts, a 1,000-square-foot greenhouse was built onto the community center using timber frame construction. This may seem odd as the thick timbers block sunlight, but these were the resources and skills available at that time, and after a few experiments and calculations, it was discovered they could build an effective (and beautiful!) greenhouse using this method. In addition, they used (literally) tons of stones held together by chicken wire as thermal mass and a low-watt fan that continually circulates air through the stones, thus heating them in the day and drawing heat out at night. This greenhouse provides about one-third of the heating needs for the community center. The best part is that above the stones is a dining space, which is particularly appreciated in the colder months of New England. Living Routes now runs a green building course at Sirius, and students benefit from these experiments by learning how to design and construct a greenhouse using timber frame, cob, and strawbale. The future is not fixed, and nimble minds will be required to effectively respond to coming challenges and opportunities.

2. *Hierarchical versus Heterarchical*

The power structure of universities is very top-down, with power emanating from the president down to the provosts, deans, faculty—and, at the bottom rung, students. While students often call for change, administrators know they can often wait out the activists, as they generally graduate in a year or two. This hierarchical system also supports the idea of a fixed curriculum that must be determined, filtered, and disseminated by the academic elite. The hidden agenda is one of "power over" and submission to authority, which is consistent with the conventional attitude that humans are meant to dominate and subdue nature.

In ecovillages, there is a wide diversity of relationships, and members tend to interact on a more or less equal footing. Living Routes programs try to model the ancient Indian *gurukula* model of education, where the teachers live and learn alongside students. In addition to leading seminars, research projects, and field visits, faculty, students, and community members might find themselves cooking a meal, playing sports, music, or a game, or planting trees or harvesting vegetables together. Living Routes also works with authentic and peer-based assessments, where students are given training and opportunities to reflect on and critique their own and each other's portfolios of work. These interdependent sets of relationships are more bottom-up than top-down; they help members get to know each other on many levels and better understand the complexity of living systems.

3. *Competitive versus Cooperative*

Universities are competitive on all levels—among students for the best grades; among faculty for grants, tenure, and recognition; and among schools for prestige and endowments. Rather than encouraging individuals to follow their inner guidance, this system reinforces extrinsic motivations and a scarcity mentality that often leads to a tragedy of the commons, as individuals race to "get theirs" first. Ironically, this can even be seen within the field of sustainability, as departments occasionally compete for the right to claim the term as their own and be seen as the "green" department on campus.

While competition certainly exists within ecovillages, the norm tends toward cooperation, with members assuming as much responsibility as they are willing to handle. The success of individuals is typically viewed as inherently tied to the success of the community as a whole. Students in Living Routes programs often collaborate on group projects and rotate responsibilities such as health monitor, meal prep/cleanup, and community meeting facilitator. This support of each other naturally leads to a sense of competency, confidence, and agency in the world.

In a well-functioning ecovillage, or any other form of community, for that matter, one almost gets a sense of being an ant in an anthill, going about one's business, but also serving a greater whole. A question that begs to be asked is, does a single ant—*can* a single ant—have any awareness of the intelligence that exists on the level of the anthill? Similarly, is it possible there is a collective consciousness present within communities—and indeed the planet—that we, as individuals, are only dimly aware of? If so, then perhaps our highest goal is to become the best "ants" we can by finding that place where, as Frederick Buechner said, "our deep gladness and the world's deep hunger meet" (1973: 95). Communities of purpose, such as ecovillages, aim to support this level of cooperation with each other and the planet.

4. Fragmented Knowledge versus Transdisciplinary Knowledge

Universities have responded to the exponentially increasing rate of knowledge generation with ever more subspecializations within disciplines. Knowledge is continually stockpiled within discreet containers that are functionally isolated from each other. This is no small problem when, for example, atmospheric chemists, oceanographers, biologists, and ecologists are not sharing information about climate change. Turf wars and lack of incentives for faculty to collaborate across departments further reinforce this segregation.

This "silo" mentality is the core reason why "sustainability" is often such a challenging issue within academia. It's not a question of importance. The question is, "Where do we put *that*?" A common response is to add content within existing majors, to help students learn about sustainability through their own disciplinary lens. While valuable, in some ways this strategy is reminiscent of Ptolemy adding epicycles onto planetary orbits in an effort to maintain his geocentric model of the heavens. We now need a Copernican, heliocentric revolution within academia that recognizes that these are not fringe issues. Cornell president David Skorton nailed it when he said that "[s]ustainability is no longer an elective" (Underwood 2007: 60). Unfortunately, as Robert Costanza, director of the Center for Sustainable Processes and Practices at Portland State University, has observed, "universities in the U.S. have not yet risen to this challenge and many sustainability initiatives have dissolved into fragmented, tinkering reforms that fail to address the underlying workings of our complex socio-ecological systems" (n.d.: 1).

Ecovillages recognize that real-life issues rarely exist within the boundaries of disciplines. For example, the decision to put up a windmill requires knowledge within the fields of appropriate technology, engineering, regional and community planning, governance, and even sociology and anthropology. Creating an organic farm crosses disciplines of agriculture, nutrition, philosophy and ethics, business, education, and communications, among others. Living Routes courses such as sustainable community development, applied sustainability, ecological design, leadership for social change, and worldview development can often be cross-listed in multiple departments, because they do not fit neatly within academia's disciplinary structure. While able to train specialists, ecovillages are uniquely positioned and equipped to train much-needed *generalists* who possess a "lateral" rigor across disciplines to complement a more traditional "vertical" rigor within disciplines.

5. Academic Community versus Living Community

Many students claim that gaining a sense of community is a primary motivation to attend college. While this is certainly available and valuable, it is also true that most relationships in academia are compartmentalized within age groups and mediated by specific, rather narrow roles, such as student/teacher, fellow researcher, classmate, etc. It is amazing that for between twelve and twenty years of our lives, we are grouped among peers typically not more than six months older or younger than we are, but this is seldom true outside of school.

If a sense of community is a goal, ecovillages may be even more fulfilling, as they offer a "living" community where members have a wide range of relationships, hold a common vision, and are committed to each other's long-term growth and development. Growing up in "mainstream" settings, youth rarely have relationships with adults who aren't their parents, friends' parents, or teachers. In communities and ecovillages, however, such relationships are the norm. And while children and young adults may occasionally long for the anonymity available in a large school or city, they also benefit from having early, frequent, and enduring relationships with other children and adults that are often quite diverse in age and personality.

A sense of being in community with all life is fundamental to sustainable lifestyles. And it is not a new invention. Many anthropologists have pointed out that most of human history has taken place in small social groups. Robin Dunbar, a British evolutionary biologist, claimed that humans have a built-in cognitive limit of being able to maintain stable relationships with only approximately 150 individuals (Gladwell 2002: 179). It seems humans are hard-wired to "belong" within human-scale communities in which they can both know and be known by others. Tragically, many people in modern, "developed" countries have lost this sense of community so thoroughly that their closest acquaintances are characters on TV shows. This lack of connection is likely at the source of our unsustainable and often violent cultures.

Immersing students within ecovillages allows them to rekindle this sense of community and interdependence. Furthermore, small class sizes, the use of authentic assessment methods, and the creation of "learning communities" within these "living communities" in which students have opportunities to deeply reflect on and share about their experiences further support their learning and development. The sense of belonging that Living Routes students experience within ecovillages both awakens and fulfills a need that many did not even know they had. And once nourished, this sense of belonging tends to expand to include ever-broader communities—both human and nonhuman.

6. Theoretical versus Applied

University professors are often critiqued as "armchair theoreticians" who like to be in their heads and maintain a detached, abstract perspective of the world. From this point of view, knowledge appears decontextualized and passive and best transmitted through didactic lectures, dry textbooks, and multiple-choice exams. As a consequence, academia often creates knowledge, but rarely wisdom.

There is a belief within academia that it is possible to keep one's own values, opinions, and feelings separate from the object of study, but this is itself more fiction than fact. No research is value-free. The problems we choose to explore, how we observe, extract, and order information in the natural world, and how we present what we find are all reflections of who we are. As Rollo May put it, "We don't study nature, we investigate the investigator's relationship to nature" (May 1975). This is not meant to imply that science is a futile endeavor—only that the researcher is an integral part of the scientific equation.

This is true on at least two counts. First, the hard sciences have led the way in proving that whatever is observed is affected simply through the act of being observed. Second, whatever is observed is then filtered through the particular lens of the observer. Such filters are likely even more pervasive and profound in the social sciences, where our "objective" measures are so easily colored by our cultural contexts and personal experiences. As Gregory Bateson once wrote, "The probe we stick into human material always has another end which sticks into us" (cited in Haley 1972: 26).

While fundamental science and research is invaluable, it is very easy within academia to get lost down a rabbit hole, pursuing topics that are so esoteric and abstract that it becomes hard to imagine ever making a difference in the "real" world. Today's emerging young leaders face a changing and challenging world in which technological advances are outpacing our collective wisdom and maturity. Of course we need to train scientists. But also, and perhaps more importantly, we need to train community builders—applied scientists—with the knowledge, skills, and commitment to create sustainable models of living and working together in peaceful and productive ways.

Ecovillages, in order to survive and prosper, must focus on practical knowledge and wisdom that can be applied in real-world settings. Theory is in the service of "what works," rather than the other way around. Ecovillages are inherently participatory, discovery-based, and experiential, and ecovillage educators tend to value multiple intelligences and individualized learning. Living Routes students have helped regenerate the tropical dry evergreen forest in Tamil Nadu, India, and the Caledonian Forest of northern Scotland; they assisted in creating the first written fair-trade contract in Peru; they have built recycling centers in Mexico and the United States using local natural materials; and they have designed permaculture gardens for schools in Brazil. And it is clear that they learned more real-world knowledge and skills through these internships and service learning opportunities than in even the best seminars.

7. Secular versus Spiritual

Not only are most universities rather hands-off, most also separate our heads from our hearts—and typically only care about our heads. Consequently, they tend to support a Newtonian/Cartesian view of the universe as a soulless machine to be manipulated and controlled by humans. From physics to chemistry, from biology to psychology, if there is anything the past century has taught us, it's that John Muir was right: "When we try to pick anything out by itself, we find it hitched to everything else in the universe" (1911: 110). It is time we recognize that humanity is inextricably embedded within and dependent upon a web of relationships that we are not "in control" of. This paradigm of the world as "other" inherently discounts ecological relations and provided the basic rationale behind the industrial revolution. It is unlikely we could do what we do to the planet or other humans if we recognized our fundamental interdependence with each other and our environment.

While some are explicitly religious, most ecovillages embrace a larger, more eclectic spiritual container in which members are supported to be "in process" and engaged with large life questions such as: What do I believe? How did I come to believe it? And, perhaps most importantly, what are my options? At the very center of Auroville ecovillage's fourteen-square-kilometer expanse in India sits the Matrimandir, a large meditation sanctuary. This is not a place for religion or dogma. It is not even a place for groups. It is a place for individuals to go and be silent and seek inner peace and wisdom. Various types of yoga, meditation, and silent practices are common features of many ecovillages that Living Routes students participate in.

Where might this all lead? Thich Nhat Hanh, the Buddhist monk, teacher, and author, once proposed that the next enlightened being might not come in the form of an individual, but come rather in the form of a community (2008). What would an enlightened community look like? Could it be an ecovillage?

8. Large Footprint versus Small Footprint

Universities are beginning to recognize, measure, and reduce their footprints. For example, the Sustainability Tracking Assessment and Rating System (STARS) developed by the Association for the Advancement of Sustainability in Higher Education (AASHE) is helping colleges and universities gauge their progress toward sustainability (AASHE n.d.). For the most part, however, universities are still incredibly resource-intensive institutions and not very attuned to their impact on their region or the world. Recycling and compact fluorescents are recent phenomena on many campuses, and few campuses even attempt to buy local and organic food.

As previously noted (and hopefully implied by the word itself), ecovillages strive to live well, yet lightly. Through sharing resources, conscious consumption, local food production, and renewable energy systems, ecovillages offer worthy models of low-impact lifestyles. For example, a study conducted in 2006 by the Sustainable Development Research Centre reported that the Findhorn Foundation, perhaps the world's premier ecovillage, with around 450 residents on the north coast of Scotland, has an average ecological footprint of 2.71 hectares per person (Tinsley and George 2006). According to a Findhorn press release, this is "the lowest ecological footprint recorded for any permanent community ever measured in the industrialized world … The average resident in the community consumes just one half of the resources and generates one half of the waste of the average citizen of the UK" (Dawson 2007: 1). While certainly a noble achievement, it should also be noted that the 2.71 hectares appropriated per Findhorn resident is just about the average global per capita footprint of 2.70 hectares, and quite a bit above the 1.8 hectares per capita of available world biocapacity (WWF 2010: 34). While ecovillages are advancing toward Gilman's definition of "integrating harmlessly into the natural world," they still have a long way to go.

Many assume ecovillages aspire to self-sufficiency; however, this is rarely accurate. Most look to their bioregion or watershed as the unit of land and culture that should strive to become more self-reliant. Ecovillages often serve as regional catalysts for reducing ecological impacts by supporting local initiatives such as organic agriculture and local distribution networks so resources do not have to be shipped great distances.

If, as many experts predict, we are on the downslope of global oil—and energy—production, we can also reasonably predict this will lead to widespread re-localization efforts due to rising transportation costs. Communities will increasingly need to concentrate more on local production of food, energy, and goods, as well as the development of local governance, currencies, and cooperative cultures. Sound familiar? There is already a quickly growing global movement of Transition Towns, which are "community-led response[s] to the pressures of climate change, fossil fuel depletion and … economic contraction" (Transition Network n.d.). Essentially, Transition Initiatives are striving to create ecovillages in existing communities!

9. Cross-Cultural versus Cultural Immersion

Most campuses enroll students from a variety of cultural backgrounds. Yet typically these lifestyles and traditions are subsumed under the melting pot of the academic culture, with few opportunities for cultural expression or exchange. How many students have taken *years* of language courses, but can barely negotiate buying fruit in a local marketplace using that native tongue? How many universities have cultural literacy requirements but few opportunities to experience other lifestyles firsthand? How many campus-based cultural festivals are superficial or, worse, caricatures of the customs they are meant to promote?

Perhaps because ecovillages are "living" rather than "academic" communities, there tend to be fuller expressions of ecovillage members' cultural backgrounds through festivals, rituals, language, and food. Even further, in traditional, indigenous ecovillages in the Global South, students have the opportunity to truly immerse themselves in vivid and full-featured cultures that both honor the past and are consciously reaching toward the future. For example, during Living Routes' programs in Senegal, US and Senegalese students joined together to explore sustainable community development within indigenous ecovillages. Through cross-cultural exchange and understanding, students can experiment with and adopt wholly new ways of being and thinking.

10. Problem Oriented versus Solution Focused

Last, but far from least, universities tend to primarily focus on dissecting and understanding "problems." Introductory courses on environmental studies, conservation, and natural resources are often litanies of negative human impacts on species, communities, and ecosystems. It is of course essential that we continue to study and better understand the serious local and global issues facing us, but there comes a point when students "get it" and then need to either *do* something about it or risk becoming overwhelmed with negativity and despair. Worse, some students may even go numb emotionally in an unconscious effort to defend their hearts against the seemingly insurmountable social and environmental problems facing humanity and the earth.

Ecovillages give students powerful opportunities to be a part of the solution and learn how they can make a positive difference in the world. Using energy generated from local windmills or photovoltaics, eating organic vegetables harvested from the land, living in homes built from local, natural materials, participating in communal celebrations, economies, and decision-making processes; these are all chapters within larger stories that ecovillages are writing about how we can live well and lightly together. They are far from complete utopias, but after spending time living and learning in an ecovillage, students can never again say, "It can't be done," because they see people wholly devoted to right livelihood and creating a sustainable future. It then comes back to students to ask themselves, "What am *I* going to do? How can *I* make a difference in my own life and in my own community?"

Why Ecovillages Need Academia

The above comparisons may seem like an argument to *run,* not walk, away from traditional academia, but that is not the point. Yes, ecovillages offer integrated campuses in which to teach about sustainable community development, but we also *absolutely* need to be teaching about sustainability within all college and university settings. The point is that while doing so, we need to recognize and make explicit to our students that what academia "says" and what it "does" are often quite different matters. Otherwise, we risk students experiencing significant cognitive dissonance that can lead to confusion, anger, or, even worse, apathy.

Just as academia is well served by reaching out to ecovillages as model campuses, ecovillages also need to reach out more to colleges and universities. There are at least four important reasons to build bridges and work together. First, academia is changing. With an increasing internationalization of the curriculum, interest in community partnerships, and recognition of the need for ecological design and interdisciplinary research, universities are beginning to see ecovillages as natural collaborators. For example, the previously mentioned AASHE is a wonderful source for knowledge, inspiration, and networking around these issues within academia. In addition, technological changes such as the internet and distance learning are creating new opportunities for collaboration, such as through an online course on ecovillage design offered in collaboration between Gaia Education and the Open University of Catalonia (Torres 2008).

Second, universities are not going away anytime soon. In the United States, higher education is approximately a $360 billion per year business (Eagan, Kenlry, and Schott 2008). This is not counting the *trillions* of dollars invested in facilities and resources. And universities are where the students are! Over 70 percent of high school graduates in the United States go directly to college (BLS 2010). Nationwide, more than 17 million students are currently enrolled (IES 2006). Worldwide, there are over 150 million college students, and this number continues to rise (Altbach, Reisberg, and Rumbley 2009).

Third, ecovillages need help in order to reach their highest potential. As advanced as ecovillages are in terms of providing campuses for sustainability education, they are still in *kindergarten* in terms of what is truly needed to educate professionals capable of building the institutions and systems required for a sustainable world to be possible. While programs offered through Living Routes and individual ecovillages are a good start, ecovillages need to further collaborate with academia to create "communiversities" where students can spend *years* in ecovillages and other related organizations to gain the background and skills needed to enter the workplace as professionals in fields as diverse as appropriate technology, habitat restoration, sustainable agriculture, group facilitation, holistic health, ecological design, and green building.

The fourth and most important reason for ecovillages to reach out to academia is that college-age students represent a powerful leverage point in the world's "Great Turning toward a more Ecological Age," as Joanna Macy refers to it (1998: 17). Many talk about members of the college population as "emerging adults" in that they are mature enough to ask the big questions yet also open to radical alternatives and new life directions. Emerging adults are key to the dissemination of emerging paradigms, and the world desperately needs leaders who are able to think—and act—outside of the box. Building bridges between ecovillages and academia is literally building bridges to a more sustainable future.

References

AASHE. n.d. "Sustainability Tracking Assessment and Rating System." http://stars.aashe.org (accessed 5 December 2010).

Altbach, Philip, Liz Reisberg, and Laura Rumbley. 2009. "Trends in Global Higher Education: Tracking an Academic Revolution." *A Report Prepared for the UNESCO 2009 World Conference on Higher Education.* Paris: UNESCO.

Buechner, Frederick. 1973. *Wishful Thinking*. New York: Harper One.

Bureau of Labor Statistics (BLS). 2010. "College Enrollment and Work Activity of 2009 High School Graduates." *Economic News Release,* 27 April.

Costanza, Robert. n.d. "The Role of Universities in Creating a Sustainable and Desirable Future." Portland State University Sustainable Solution. http://www.pdx.edu/sustainability/robert-costanza (accessed 7 April 2010).

Dawson, Jonathan. 2007. "Scottish Community Scores Lowest Ecological Footprint Ever Recorded." Findhorn Foundation press release, 18 April, p. 1.

Eagan, David, Julian Kenlry, and Justin Schott. 2008. *Higher Education in a Warming World: The Business Case for Climate Leadership on Campus.* Reston, VA: National Wildlife Federation.

Gaia Education. n.d. "Gaia Education at the Cutting Edge of Sustainability." http://www.gaiaeducation.org (accessed 5 December 2010).

Gilman, Robert. 1991. "The Eco-village Challenge." *In Context* 29 (Summer): 10–17.

Gladwell, Malcolm. 2002. *The Tipping Point: How Little Things Can Make a Big Difference.* New York: Back Bay.

Global Ecovillage Network (GEN). n.d. "Global Ecovillage Network: Connecting Communities for a Better World." http://gen.ecovillage.org (accessed 5 December 2010).

Haley, Jay. 1972. "Critical Overview of Present Status of Family Interaction Research." In *Family Interaction: A Dialogue Between Researchers and Family Therapists,* ed. James. L. Framo. New York: Springer.

Heinberg, Richard. 2004. *Power Down: Options and Actions for a Post-Carbon World.* Gabriola Island, Canada: New Society.

Living Routes. n.d. "Living Routes: Study Abroad in Sustainable Communities." http://www.LivingRoutes.org (accessed 5 December 2010).

Macy, Joanna. 1998. *Coming Back to Life: Practices to Reconnect Our Lives, Our World.* Gabriola Island, Canada: New Society.

May, Rollo. 1975. "Opening Remarks." Session one of the Association for Humanistic Psychology Theory conference, Tucson, AZ, 4 April.

Meadows, Donella. 1991. *Global Citizen.* Washington DC: Island Press.

Monani, Salma. 2009. "An Interview with Julian Agyeman: Just Sustainability and Ecopedagogy." *Green Theory and Praxis: The Journal of Ecopedagogy* 2 (1): 51–68.

Muir, John. 1911. *My First Summer in the Sierra.* New York: Houghton Mifflin.

Nhat Hanh, Thich. 2008. "The Fertile Soil of Sangha." *Tricycle Magazine* (Summer): 13.

Orr, David. 1994. *Earth In Mind.* Washington DC: Island Press.

Tinsley, Stephen, and Heather George. 2006. "Ecological Footprint of the Findhorn Foundation and Community." Forres, Scotland: Sustainable Development Research Centre.

Torres, Anna. 2008. "Ecovillages and Responsible Tourism, Towards a Culture of Sustainability." *Reports of Universitat Oberta de Catalunya (UOC).* Barcelona: Universitat Oberta de Catalunya.

Transition Network. n.d. http://www.transitionnetwork.org (accessed 5 December 2010).

Underwood, Anne. 2007. "The Green Campus." *Newsweek Magazine,* 20–27 August, 60–66.

World Wildlife Fund (WWF). 2010. *Living Planet Report 2010: Biodiversity, Biocapacity, and Development.* Gland, Switzerland: WWF.

Chapter Sixteen

Ecovillages and Capitalism

Creating Sustainable Communities within an Unsustainable Context

Ted Baker

Introduction

In the preface to his 1999 edition of *History, Power, Ideology,* Donald Donham laments the fact that the economic boom of the 1990s was "apparently not conducive to critical social analysis" (xi). Commenting on the consequences of this observation, he pointed to a dearth of engagement with Marxist thought in contemporary anthropological discussions. However, while discussing this phenomenon with a seasoned colleague, he was offered an answer that proved to be prophetic: "Wait until the next stock market crash" (Donham 1999: xi). The global economic crash Donham's colleague dryly predicted occurred nearly ten years later, bringing with it a shaking of the faith in global capitalism and a consequent renewal of interest in Marx and what he had to say about this economic system. While it may be too soon to tell how much impact this most recent economic trough will have on the often rocky relationship between anthropology and anti-capitalist thought, the title of Patterson's (2009) most recent book *Karl Marx, Anthropologist* is suggestive. It would seem that Donham's pining for a re-engagement with Marx and other anti-capitalist thinkers within anthropological circles has arrived.

Another (wider) circle within which anti-capitalist thought has been gaining ground is the community of scholars and activists concerned with the accelerating pace of climate change and ecological collapse. Many are beginning to make explicit connections between the degradation of the biosphere and the expansion of the global capitalist economy, coming to the conclusion that "[i]t's capitalism or a habitable planet—you can't have both."[1] Here the notion of sustainability is central, not only in critiquing the capitalist requirement of perpetual growth but also in exploring alternatives. Sustainable modes of living and being are thus becoming increasingly important to understand, and ecovillages represent a particular grassroots version of this trend.

However, while there has been an increase in anti-capitalist literature stemming from the recognition of environmental and ecological collapse, and an increasing interest in the phenomenon of ecovillages (Bang 2005; Christian 2003; Dawson 2006; Jackson and Svensson 2002; Walker 2005), there has not been much of an attempt to combine the two. This chapter thus represents an attempt to do just that by asking some very basic questions: How are we to conceive of the relationship between ecovillages (and other intentional communities) and the capitalist context they exist within? More specifically, what are the tensions and contradictions engendered by the attempt to construct sustainable communities (ecovillages) within an unsustainable context (capitalism)? I begin with a summary of the unsustainable nature of capitalism and an ethnographic example from recent fieldwork conducted within Whole Village, an ecovillage in southwestern Ontario, Canada; followed by a brief analysis of a key text utilized by the members of this ecovillage in planning for their future. I then proceed to a more theoretical examination of the relationship between ecovillages and capitalism, suggesting that recent developments in anti-capitalist literature may help us better conceptualize this relationship.

Capitalism is Unsustainable

It goes without saying that a proper understanding of any particular intentional community or ecovillage requires an appreciation of the societal context within which they are embedded. As will be shown, attempting to conceptualize any phenomenon without taking into consideration the surrounding cultural matrix risks misunderstanding and flawed conclusions. In this particular case, trying to understand the dynamics within a Canadian ecovillage requires an appreciation of the dominant organizing system within the North American framework that is the culture of capitalism.[2]

Even if you do not swim in Marxist, anarchist, socialist, or communist waters or associate with anti-capitalists in general, you would be hard-pressed to find anyone with knowledge of how capitalism works who would argue that it is a sustainable system. Even those who celebrate the capitalist ethos recognize that there are some unfortunate societal and environmental consequences—they just assume advanced technology and free market mechanisms will take care of the more egregious problems.

In a wide-ranging book examining the global problems that capitalism generates, Richard Robbins locates the source of these problems in the requirement of perpetual growth:

> [T]he prime directive of the culture of capitalism is that it must maintain economic growth. People must buy, produce, invest, and profit more this year than the last and more next year than this. Failure to maintain growth would threaten the economic, social, and political foundations and stability of our entire society. People would be unable to repay debts, banks would fail, millions would lose their jobs, and millions of businesses would go bankrupt, to name only a few of the obvious consequences. (2008: 4–5)

If the logic and requirement of capitalism is perpetual growth, then the obvious conclusion, given a finite planet with limited resources, is that such a system is unsustainable.[3]

While concluding that the necessity of never-ending expansion is unsustainable within the context of a finite world may seem obvious, less apparent is how this translates into the sociocultural realm. If capitalism is unsustainable at the material and ecological level, does this mean that it is also unsustainable at the social level? In other words, are the social relations (based on separation, alienation, competition, and hierarchy) that constitute the culture of capitalism likewise unsustainable?

According to anti-capitalists, the answer is yes. Capitalism, based upon a division of labor between a minority who make the decisions and a majority who carry them out, by nature generates conflict and provokes antagonism. When people are denied their humanity they tend to rebel (although by no means is this inevitable), be it outright revolution or insurrection, or more subtle forms of resistance such as foot-dragging, gossip, or sabotage—what James Scott (1985) labels "everyday forms of resistance." In fact, this is what led Marx and other anti-capitalists to the conclusion that capitalism carries within it the seeds of its own destruction. In other words, it is unsustainable because it will eventually collapse under the weight of the conflict it generates.

So if the culture of capitalism is untenable at several basic levels, then what happens when people decide to experiment with organizations and communities that reject these kinds of unsustainable relations and practices? What happens when a group of people try to create a sustainable community within an unsustainable context?

Whole Village

In the summer of 2007 I decided to visit Whole Village, the first self-proclaimed ecovillage in Ontario, Canada, in order to explore the possibility of conducting a year of ethnographic fieldwork there. Located in the rolling hills of Caledon, Whole Village is a relatively young and fairly small ecovillage that began to take shape at the turn of the millennium. The occasion was a monthly "work bee" held by the community to encourage friends, family, and interested strangers to experience a day of shared work and a potluck lunch.

Once I passed the environmentally sensitive wetlands that hug the western edge of the property and the arching trees that block the view from the main road, the first thing that stood out as I drove down the kilometer-long gravel driveway was the sprawling, buttermilk yellow, one-story eco-residence called Greenhaven that was built to house the members of this young ecovillage. The gravel parking lot out front was filled with cars, and as I pulled into an empty spot I could see a figure pushing a wheelbarrow toward the massive aging barn and red-bricked farmhouse that dominates the northern landscape to the north of Greenhaven. The juxtaposition between the brand-new, 15,000-square-foot state-of-the-art eco-building that I was approaching and the more traditional farmhouse across the lane was stark, and symbolized the considerable difference between this contemporary version of ecovillage living and earlier versions of "back-to-the-land" communal living that are consistently referenced in mainstream discussions of collective living arrangements.

After passing through the foyer—where numerous pairs of shoes and boots lined the wall and a faint hint of barnyard permeated the air (brought in by the boots of those who regularly tended to the flock of chickens and several milking cows)—I entered the common kitchen, where both residents and visitors were milling about trading stories and introducing themselves. Soon everyone was called into the main living room, the most heavily used common area in Greenhaven, to find a seat on one of the several couches and chairs that were placed in a semicircle around the masonry heater/fireplace. One of the Whole Village community members explained how the day would proceed. First everyone was to introduce themselves, and then the jobs that were available would be explained.

Since I had no idea who lived there and who was visiting, one of the patterns that shaped Whole Village was not clear until after the introductions. Those who were full members and owned a suite at Whole Village were predominantly older, retired, or nearing retirement. Most were professionals. Most of those visiting, or temporarily staying there, were younger and starting their careers. As will be seen below, this pattern was a dominant theme within Whole Village—not only due to the recognition by many that in order to survive they needed to attract younger families, but also because it tended to be a fault line along which many contentious issues would either emerge or be amplified.

Once everyone picked a job they felt they could contribute to, we headed outside to begin working. Among the small group of people I was working with was a fellow visitor who had moved to Canada after living on an Israeli kibbutz for almost ten years. I was immediately drawn to this gruff character due to my own fascination with the kibbutz communities that had initially drawn me to the study of communitarian movements. We were working on creating a brick pathway leading from one of the external doorways of Greenhaven, and I decided to strike up a conversation. I asked him what he thought of Whole Village. He stopped shoveling, placed both hands on top of the shovel for support, and snorted with contempt. He was extremely critical of Whole Village, and said that their fate was sealed. According to this ex-communitarian, their project was too expensive, and nobody in their right mind would fork out that much money to join something that was a constant struggle. While his experience with intentional communities was significant, after spending a couple hours working on the pathway I began to realize that he was critical about everything. The gravel under the bricks was not packed right, the height of the doorframe was too high, and the bricks were the wrong kind. I began to get the sense that any way except his way was mistaken and doomed, so I took his initial attack on the prospects for Whole Village's survival with a grain of salt. But, as I was to discover, there was some truth to his grumbling. Most people who came to Whole Village interested in ecovillage living but who later decided not to join explained that their decision, in part, came down to one of financial considerations. They felt they could not contribute to the community in a sufficient manner while also trying to work a full-time job.

There are several reasons why living at Whole Village is not cheap. The most obvious reason is the amount of land (over 190 acres of rolling hills, fertile fields, a wetland, sugar bush, and pond) and the buildings situated on it (the barn, farmhouse, and two sheds, as well as Greenhaven). Those who join are expected to contribute to the cost of the land as well as the cost of their suite. However, there are other more specific reasons. First of all, during the building of Greenhaven they embraced advanced, and expensive, green technology (such as radiant floor heating and a living roof) to maintain a certain standard of living with minimal impact on the environment.[4] Secondly, throughout the process of creating the community (particularly during the building of Greenhaven), there was a high reliance on experts, professionals, and consultants (largely due to the requirements of municipal zoning regulations and building codes).[5] Thirdly, while they are not close enough to a major population center to be within reasonable commuting distance (thus making it more appealing to prospective members), they are not far enough away to reduce the cost of land significantly.[6] Lastly, in the final stages of the search for property there was a last-minute switch in location, leading to a significant exodus of members (related to the third reason), leaving fewer people to share the financial burden.

The External Shaping the Internal

While preparing for fieldwork and researching different intentional communities, I repeatedly encountered the assertion that "living in community" was usually rewarding but always challenging. Communitarians were typically the first to admit that living in community was not a "walk in the park." But it was not until I was actually immersed in the day-to-day experience of living within one of these communities that this recognition was propelled beyond simple intellectual acknowledgement. Living communally was indeed hard. It was at times very rewarding and intensely gratifying, but there were also times when it all seemed overwhelming. There were reasons for this, which did not really crystallize for me until after spending the first few months living at Whole Village and unraveling the dynamics of this particular community.

The first flashpoint of conflict proved to be instructive. Within a few weeks after moving in it was apparent that there was a significant divide between some who felt they were doing all the work—and thus being taken advantage of—and others who felt they were unsuccessfully trying to juggle responsibilities unrelated to community life as well as the numerous projects the community had set for itself, and were thus feeling judged as irresponsible. Interestingly, people from both sides often described feeling overwhelmed, close to "burning out." Since I was struggling to play the objective anthropologist, trying to remain neutral and avoid taking sides (especially given the small and intimate nature of the group), I offered to mediate several meetings between the two sides. What transpired was not only instructive for this particular community, but also for the wider consideration of attempts to achieve sustainable goals within an unsustainable context.

Being an ecovillage, Whole Village has set for itself several goals that require large amounts of time, labor, and capital to achieve. On top of the financial investment required to become a member (which is comparable to the average cost one could expect in purchasing an individual home in southern Ontario), this amounts to a considerable drain on the time and resources that the community can afford. As Jonathan Dawson points out, ecovillages are still largely marginal, citizen-driven initiatives with very little, if any, support from the wider society. They "have very limited access to official sources of funding and tend to be largely dependent on private resources," and thus "many great ideas for projects in ecovillages never see the light of day, or fail to achieve their full potential, due to a lack of finance" (2006: 71).

While Whole Village has set itself goals of land stewardship (restoring the land that had been severely abused by the previous cattle farm, planting thousands of trees, protecting and managing the wetland as well as the maple bush), self-sufficiency (growing their own organic food, cutting firewood for fuel, researching and constructing alternative energy sources), demonstration and outreach (conference workshops, hosting numerous visitors, monthly orientation days, and "work bees"), and numerous meetings (monthly "meetings of the round" and various committee meetings, as well as weekly "check-ins") that operate according to the notoriously time-consuming method of consensus decision making, there are simply not enough bodies to do the work. Due to the economic reality of living there, those who are retired and whose pensions or savings are financing their life at Whole Village are the ones doing much of the work the community has set for itself, while those who are younger or near retirement spend their days either working outside the community (to earn the wages necessary to live there) or attending to other responsibilities and work unrelated to community goals (postsecondary education and homeschooling children).[7]

This dynamic alone has led to resentment on both sides, and statements from the notes I took while facilitating the first meeting illustrate these sentiments.[8] One mother who was homeschooling three children expressed her desire to contribute more, but felt her hands were tied by other responsibilities: "I'd love to do more work but I have limited energy, and little, simple jobs are a big deal for me … I feel like I'm being judged and that I'm not doing enough." Another younger woman who was pursuing a graduate degree felt that even though the community recognized that her academic responsibilities meant that she could not contribute as much, there was still an atmosphere of unacknowledged expectations that she was not meeting. Moreover, the more she felt judged (even if this judgment was unspoken—and she admitted the possibility that this was "all in her head"), the less she felt like contributing—a dynamic that she likened to a "downward spiral."

The negative feelings around this issue were echoed by the other side of the debate, the retired group, who were taking on many of the responsibilities the community had set for itself and stating similar feelings of resentment. One member claimed that she was frustrated that there were a handful of people doing the majority of the work, and that this work was unappreciated: "People take it for granted what I do … I just want to remind everyone that what I do isn't just mine—the group has decided this." Another member echoed this sentiment: "Why do I bother [to do the work] when no one else seems to care … I feel like a nagging mother and I don't want to feel like this."

Several members have observed that this dynamic is unsustainable, but what is important to note is the lack of blame being attributed to wider societal dynamics. This is understandable. When dealing with what can be an emotionally charged atmosphere the tendency is to lay blame on the living, breathing individuals across the table instead of pointing a finger at wider social, political, and economic processes. This makes sense from the middle of the maelstrom, where the bearers of these wider dynamics are people you know well and share a history with. While this is an extremely truncated version of the complexity of this particular dynamic (with an unfortunate emphasis on conflict that ignores and simplifies much), it should be obvious that this contentious situation was not solely a result of incompatible personalities or internal dynamics. Surely the unsustainable external context (capitalism) is at least in part to blame for what seems to be an unsustainable situation.

Why Do Communities Fail? What Is to Blame?

When the people of Whole Village encountered significant conflict and disagreement, one text they constantly referred to was Diana Leafe Christian's *Creating A Life Together: Practical Tools to Grow Ecovillages and Intentional Communities* (2003). A prolific writer, public speaker, and consultant for the ecovillage movement and former editor of the *Communities* magazine (a quarterly published by the Fellowship for Intentional Communities) for fourteen years, Christian is considered one of the foremost authorities on ecovillages. *Creating a Life Together* has been hailed as the bible for those looking to create intentional communities, and at Whole Village Christian's book could possibly be called the key text of the community (at least while I was there), to the point that it was suggested that different passages from the book be read at every monthly "Meeting of the Round." Not everyone read it and not everyone celebrated it, but it was repeatedly sourced when issues came up that required an experienced communitarian perspective.

In the beginning of the book Christian addresses a troubling fact: probably 90 percent of all aspiring ecovillages and intentional communities never make it. She thus "wanted to know about the successful ten percent, those groups that actually created their communities. What did they do right?" (Christian 2003: xv). The question is an old one, but Christian's take on it is instructive. After years of interviewing fellow communitarians "and hearing their stories of community break-up, heartbreak, and even lawsuits" she began to see a pattern: most fail due to what she calls "structural" conflict—which she describes as "problems that arise when founders don't explicitly put certain processes in place or make certain important decisions at the outset, creating one or more omissions in their organizational structure." Failure to do so eventually leads to "built-in structural problems [that] seem to function like time bombs," and when they go off they have a tendency to trigger "a great deal of interpersonal conflict … making the initial structural conflict much worse" (Christian 2003: 7).

However, Christian's argument seems to play down wider societal forces, suggesting that the large majority of ecovillages fail due to a lack of foresight on the part of the founders. She outlines six "crucial elements" that she believes need to be addressed in order to avoid planting these "time bombs," and while the six elements are sound advice, the overarching suggestion is that 90 percent of ecovillages fail due to the deficiencies of bad planning. In other words, the source of failure being proposed is internal.

While Christian alludes to the external context throughout the book, the implications of her main argument suggests that what is important is internal, a position that sounds suspiciously close to blaming the victim. However, a closer reading suggests that her main thesis that the fundamental problem is internal may be premature, illustrated by an interesting conversation she had with the project managers of an emerging community in North Carolina. Nestled in this story is an observation by the two project managers that "probably 95 percent of the major variables involved in a forming community *are not in the founders' control*—land value and availability, banks' lending policies, and city or county zoning regulations" (Christian 2003: 17, emphasis added).

This suggests that Christian's argument that communitarians generally have themselves to blame for the failure of a community to materialize or survive is misplaced. While these two project managers are not discussing the reasons for the failure of communities, they *are* suggesting that 95 percent of how the community is structured and shaped is due to external factors that are not under the control of the community. Is it not therefore possible to argue that a good chunk of the conflict experienced by ecovillages is due to the influence of these external forces? Is it possible that there are other external sources of "structural conflict" or latent "time bombs" that can make ecovillages unsustainable? After all, the factors these community founders are citing—lending policies of financial institutions, property values, and zoning regulations—can be linked directly to capitalist processes and dynamics.

So if the culture of capitalism plays a significant role in the (un)sustainability of ecovillages, is there a better way to conceptualize the relationship between ecovillages and the capitalist context within which they are embedded?

An Old and Bitter Debate Resurrected

Before exploring the possibility of a better conceptualization of the relationship between ecovillages and capitalism (which amounts to a reversal of the line of investigation from the external's impact on the internal to the internal's impact on the external), I need to address the limited amount of literature that has already been generated by this connection. Over the course of two issues of *The International Journal of Inclusive Democracy,* there was a debate over the significance of the ecovillage movement, ignited by a critic of ecovillages who also happened to be a previous member of an Australian ecovillage (Garden 2006a, 2006b; Fotopoulos 2006; Velissaris 2006; Trainer 2006). This actually represented a sequel to an earlier debate between Ted Trainer and Takis Fotopoulos that took place within the pages of the journal *Democracy & Nature* (Trainer 2000, 2002; Fotopoulos 2000, 2002).

While I do not have the space to go into detail regarding the complexity of the arguments offered, what is important to note about this debate is that when we foreground capitalism in the analysis of ecovillages we stumble into a veritable hornets' nest among anti-capitalists, an old and often vitriolic debate within the Left. Emerging in the mid-nineteenth century when Marx and Engels sought to distance their "scientific" brand of socialism from the increasing popularity of what they termed "utopian" socialism, this divide has continued to this day, manifesting itself in the debate over the significance of ecovillages as models for radical change. While both sides would agree on the enormous impact the capitalist context has upon the creation and survival of intentional communities, the source of the divide turns upon the notion of intentional or "utopian" communities as a strategy for undermining and eventually replacing capitalism. Marx condemned anarchists and utopian communitarians alike for embodying a form of "bourgeois" socialism that ignored proper historical analysis. For Marx it was not the "the task of the revolutionary to come up with blueprints for a future society and then try to bring them into being, or, indeed, to try to imagine details of the future society at all" (Graeber 2007: 114).

Trainer, representing a contemporary version of this reviled utopian socialism, suggests that the ecovillage movement, while extremely problematic and contradictory, represents the only viable strategy within a global context of highly unsustainable practices that create rampant consumerism and impending environmental collapse. Fotopoulos completely disagrees, arguing that the ecovillage movement is nothing but an expanded version of bourgeois "life-style strategies" riddled with "all sorts of irrational elements" (Fotopoulos 2006).

While I would agree with Fotopoulos's assessment of the difficulties ecovillages face regarding the capitalist context, his adherence to the Marxist-Leninist assertion that we need to destroy capitalism (via some form of taking state power) before we start building alternatives is problematic. Trainer picks up on this point when he argues that any radical movement for change "cannot be led by vanguard parties," since there "is no value in capturing state power. What's more, it will not be about fighting against capitalism … [T]he way we will defeat it is by ignoring it to death, by turning away from it and building those many bits of the alternative that we could easily build right now" (Trainer 2006). Trainer's comment is interesting in that it seems to be picking up on recent anti-capitalist thought (particularly anarchist and "autonomist" Marxist threads) that has been gaining ground in not only the analysis of capitalist dynamics but also strategies to overcome them.[9]

Take, for example, a recent incarnation of this argument put forward by John Holloway, an Irish Marxist economist, in his publication *Change the World Without Taking Power: The Meaning of Revolution Today*. Briefly stated, his main thrust for writing the book is to suggest that "[t]he world cannot be changed through the state. Both theoretical reflection and a whole century of bad experience tell us so" (2005a: 19). If we are serious about changing the world for the better, then we need to avoid using the state to change society: "This means taking as one's direct and immediate point of reference not the taking of state power, nor even the building of a movement, but, rather, the creation and making explicit of … the social relations for which we are struggling" (Holloway 2005b: 272).[10]

Or take the work of Michael Hardt and Antonio Negri, perhaps the most recognizable theorists to bring autonomist ideas to the English-speaking world through their trilogy *Empire* (2000), *Multitude* (2004), and *Commonwealth* (2009). For Hardt and Negri, the "refusal of work and authority, or really the refusal of voluntary servitude, is the beginning of liberatory politics" (2000: 204). Within the context of empire, battles "might well be won through subtraction and defection" (Hardt and Negri 2000: 212). In other words, the political power of refusal stems from the ability to subtract participation within systems and relationships of domination. Rather than a frontal assault on centralized power and global capital, they argue that freedom can only be attained through an evacuation of its base. However, they are also quick to point out that this desertion and refusal is only a beginning: "The refusal in itself is empty.… Our lines of flight, our exodus must be constituent and create a real alternative. Beyond the simple refusal, or as part of that refusal, we need also to construct a new mode of life and above all a new community" (Hardt and Negri 2000: 204).

This autonomist notion of "revolutionary exodus" or what has also been called "engaged withdrawal" is picked up by David Graeber, an anarchist anthropologist, in his exploration and interrogation of the notion of revolution and revolutionary action: "Revolutionary action does not necessarily have to aim to topple governments. Attempts to create autonomous communities in the face of power (using Castoriadis' definition here: ones that constitute themselves, collectively make their own rules or principles of operation, and continually reexamine them), would, for instance, be almost by definition revolutionary acts" (Graeber 2004: 45).

What is noteworthy about this return to theorizing revolutionary action and radical social change along autonomist and anarchist lines, despite their calls for new kinds of communities and social relations, is a lack of engagement with, and consideration of, actually existing intentional communities and ecovillages. However, one Canadian sociologist has made this connection explicit, suggesting that not only is this concept of engaged withdrawal or exodus the "most pressing challenge faced by radical theoretical practice today," but it is also perhaps best represented (in North America at least) by "intentional communities and back-to-the-land movements" (Day 2005: 209).

Conclusion: The Drive Toward Self-Determination

Whether it is the observations of visitors to Whole Village, the ruminations of actual members of the ecovillage, or the authoritative statements of commentators on the wider ecovillage movement, the overwhelming tendency is to blame internal dynamics for the tensions and conflict that ecovillages and intentional communities inevitably encounter. While cursory attention is paid to wider societal dynamics, forces, and processes, the general (often hidden) assumption is the same: communitarians have themselves to blame for the problems they experience. The unsustainable nature of these communal initiatives is attributed to incompatible personalities, interpersonal conflict, and structural "time bombs." Unacknowledged is the surrounding unsustainable context, the global capitalist reality. The point is not to go to the other extreme and assume that the wider context is fully to blame for these internal rifts, but rather to take account of and acknowledge the often significant impact wider dynamics have upon the internal workings of ecovillages such as Whole Village. Recognizing this impact can not only provide a much more complex and nuanced picture, but it can also help prevent an escalation of the internal blame game that can easily spiral out of control within a community. More importantly, foregrounding the relationship between ecovillages and the capitalist context within which they operate propels the discussion into a reconceptualization of the creation and maintenance of ecovillages as "revolutionary action." In other words, in our investigation of how the external (the culture of capitalism) shapes the internal, we stumble upon subterranean anti-capitalist arguments that suggest this line of inquiry may be directionally misplaced—that we should perhaps be investigating how the internal shapes the external, how the actions, logics, and relations utilized by communitarians in the formation and maintenance of ecovillages and intentional communities represent a refusal and replacement (however minute, partial, and contradictory) of the logics and relations required by the culture of capitalism.

Of course many, particularly those enamored with Marxist-Leninist strategies for radical change, and even many communitarians themselves, would see this assertion as bordering on the absurd—but within a context that amounts to a prevention and preemptive strike on any form of collective self-determination, such a statement might not be as outlandish as it may seem. Regardless of their differences, anti-capitalists of all stripes conceptualize capitalism as a voracious process that is increasingly global and penetrating everyday life with its destructive and alienating logics and relations. However, as Holloway points out, this process can never be complete: "The world is full of fissures … [and] cracks in capitalist domination" (2005a: 220). Furthermore, sometimes these fissures and cracks can be so tiny and seemingly insignificant that "not even the rebels perceive their own rebelliousness" (Holloway 2005a: 220).

Yet while these fissures and cracks in the capitalist façade are always "contradictory because they are rooted in the antagonisms of capitalist society" and thus "easy to criticize, easy to make fun of," what is important to note is "not their present limitations but the direction of their movement" (Holloway 2005a: 220). And this movement is the movement of, or drive toward, self-determination. Holloway points out that capital "in all its forms, is the negation of self-determination" and therefore "the assertion of self-determination necessarily means moving against capitalism." While he is not talking specifically about intentional communities, it is not much of a stretch to suggest such a connection. This is perhaps the lesson to be drawn from ecovillages and intentional communities more generally: while they may not be explicitly anti-capitalist (although some are)—their assertion of self-determination, however limited and contradictory, however easy to ridicule and dismiss, represents a refusal of determination by others, and thus a refusal of the culture of capitalism.

If anti-capitalists seem to be converging around the rejection of the Marxist-Leninist notion that radical change can only be achieved through the state (either through reform or revolution), then it would seem imperative to explore and understand experiments and projects like Whole Village that avoid this quest for power. If radical change will come through the fissures and cracks in the capitalist system that Holloway mentions, then we need to focus attention on how these fissures emerge, the struggles and contradictions they encounter while trying to exist within a capitalist context, and how they can be supported and expanded.

Notes

1. This is the title of a discussion piece in a February 2006 issue of *The Guardian* by Robert Newman. For similar arguments, see *Ecosocialism or Barbarism* (Kelly and Malone 2006), *Ecology Against Capitalism* (Foster 2002), or *The Enemy of Nature: The End of Capitalism or the End of the World?* (Kovel 2002).
2. Like Macfarlane (1987) and Robbins (2008), I use the term "culture of capitalism" to signal an anthropological approach to understanding capitalism as much more than simply an economic system. Of course such an understanding is by no means a recent development, Marx himself having conceptualized capitalism as a total system (even if the economic was seen as somehow primary).
3. One of my favorite bumper stickers sums it up nicely: "Perpetual growth is the philosophy of a cancer cell."
4. The problem with using new "green" technology is that it is usually in an experimental stage, and, as Whole Village has discovered, prone to breaking down or malfunctioning. Furthermore, finding the experts knowledgeable enough to fix them can also be expensive and time-consuming.
5. This is a familiar dilemma for ecovillages. For example, the Findhorn Foundation in Scotland, determined to set up three windmills to produce renewable energy for the community, had to go through the same regulatory process that a developer of a wind farm would have to go through. Incredibly, the actual process of gaining permission to erect the windmills ended up costing them more than the purchase, transport, and installation of the alternative energy sources (Dawson 2006: 68). In discussions with members of Whole Village, I found out that the costs associated with lawyers, professionals, experts, and consultants had cost them an enormous amount of money, thus pushing up the cost of membership. Of course, failing to do so could result in hefty fines and the forced removal or destruction of any illegally raised buildings or structures—something very hard to avoid for a community devoted to demonstrating an alternative model of living (and thus constantly in the public eye).
6. As Dawson (2006: 68) points out, people trying to establish ecovillages in countries in the North have had to deal with sharply rising land prices, largely due to "macro-economic policies" (i.e., capitalist dynamics driven by property markets and speculation). Christian also points out that "since the mid-1980s, the cost of land and housing has skyrocketed relative to most people's assets

and earning power" (2003: xix). While these comments suggest a direct connection, neither relates this constraint on the creation of ecovillages to the wider capitalist context.

7. The exception to this rule are the numerous volunteers and WWOOFers (participants in the World Wide Opportunities on Organic Farms program), who are generally younger but whose room and board are covered in exchange for their labor.
8. The transcribed statements are from a meeting that took place on 6 January 2008. Individual names have been avoided due to the wishes of the community.
9. David Graeber argues that the autonomist tradition "has come to be probably the dominant strain" of Marxism in the last few years (Graeber 2007: 115).
10. Many dismiss his thesis—changing the world without using the state—as infantile and defeatist. For example, in an interview with two rather famous "Bolshies" (one an ex-member of the now-defunct Mexican Communist Party and the other a venerable journalist for a Cuban news agency), Holloway's argument is described as "treasonous" and his book is even accused of being financed by the CIA (Ross 2005).

References

Bang, Jan Martin. 2005. *Ecovillages: A Practical Guide to Sustainable Communities.* Gabriola Island, Canada: New Society.

Christian, Diana Leafe. 2003. *Creating a Life Together: Practical Tools to Grow Ecovillages and Intentional Communities.* Gabriola Island, Canada: New Society.

Dawson, Jonathan. 2006. *Ecovillages: New Frontiers for Sustainability.* White River Junction, VT: Chelsea Green.

Day, Richard J. F. 2005. *Gramsci is Dead: Anarchist Currents in the Newest Social Movements.* London: Pluto Press.

Donham, Donald L. 1999. *History, Power, Ideology: Central Issues in Marxism and Anthropology.* Berkeley: University of California Press.

Foster, John Bellamy. 2002. *Ecology Against Capitalism.* New York: Monthly Review Press.

Fotopoulos, Takis. 2000. "The Limitations of Life-style Strategies: The Ecovillage 'Movement' is NOT the Way Towards a New Democratic Society." *Democracy & Nature* 6 (2): 287–308.

———. 2002. "The Transition to an Alternative Society: The Ecovillage Movement, the Simpler Way and the Inclusive Democracy Project." *Democracy & Nature* 8 (1): 150–57.

———. 2006. "Is the Eco-village Movement a Solution or Part of the Problem?" *The International Journal of Inclusive Democracy* 2 (3). Available at: http://www.inclusivedemocracy.org/journal/vol2/vol2_no3_Takis_eco_village.htm

Garden, Mary. 2006a. "Leaving Utopia." *The International Journal of Inclusive Democracy* 2 (2). Available at: http://www.inclusivedemocracy.org/journal/vol2/vol2_no2_Garden.htm.

———. 2006b. "The Eco-village Movement: Divorced from Reality." *The International Journal of Inclusive Democracy* 2 (3). Available at: http://www.inclusivedemocracy.org/journal/vol2/vol2_no3_Garden_eco_village.htm.

Graeber, David. 2004. *Fragments of an Anarchist Anthropology.* Chicago: Prickly Paradigm Press.

———. 2007. *Possibilities: Essays on Hierarchy, Rebellion, and Desire.* Oakland, CA: AK Press.

Hardt, Michael, and Antonio Negri. 2000. *Empire.* Cambridge, MA: Harvard University Press.

———. 2004. *Multitude: War and Democracy in the Age of Empire.* New York: Penguin Press.

———. 2009. *Commonwealth.* Cambridge, MA: Belknap Press.

Holloway, John. 2005a. *Change the World Without Taking Power: The Meaning of Revolution Today.* 2nd ed. Sterling, VA: Pluto Press.

———. 2005b. "No." *Historical Materialism* 13 (4): 265–84.

Jackson, Hildur, and Karen Svensson. 2002. *Ecovillage Living: Restoring the Earth and Her People.* Foxhole, UK: Green Books.

Kelly, Jane, and Sheila Malone, eds. 2006. *Ecosocialism or Barbarism.* London: IMG Publications.

Kovel, Joel. 2002. *The Enemy of Nature: The End of Capitalism or the End of the World?* New York: Zed Books.

Macfarlane, Alan. 1987. *The Culture of Capitalism.* Oxford: Blackwell.

Newman, Robert. 2006. "It's Capitalism or a Habitable Planet—You Can't Have Both." *The Guardian,* 2 February, 33.

Patterson, Thomas C. 2009. *Karl Marx, Anthropologist.* New York: Berg.

Robbins, Richard H. 2008. *Global Problems and the Culture of Capitalism.* 4th ed. Boston: Pearson.

Ross, John. 2005. "A Visit With John Holloway: How to Change the World Without Taking Power." *Counterpunch,* 2–3 April. http://www.counterpunch.org/ross04022005.html (accessed 31 January 2007).

Scott, James C. 1985. *Weapons of the Weak: Everyday Forms of Peasant Resistance.* New Haven, CT: Yale University Press.

Trainer, Ted. 2000. "Where Are We, Where Do We Want to be, How Do We Get There?" *Democracy & Nature* 6 (2): 267–86.

———. 2002. "Debating the significance of the Global Eco-village Movement: A Reply to Takis Fotopoulos." *Democracy & Nature* 8 (1): 143–49.

———. 2006. "On Eco-villages and the Transition." *The International Journal of Inclusive Democracy* 2 (3). Available at: http://www.inclusivedemocracy.org/journal/vol2/vol2_no3_Trainer_eco-villages.htm.

Velissaris, Teo. 2006. "Reaching Systemic Change: Some Brief Remarks on Mary Garden's 'Leaving Utopia'" *The International Journal of Inclusive Democracy* 2 (2). Available at: http://www.inclusivedemocracy.org/journal/vol2/vol2_no2_Teo_remarks_leaving_utopia.htm.

Walker, Liz. 2005. *Ecovillage at Ithaca: Pioneering a Sustainable Culture.* Gabriola Island, Canada: New Society.

Further Readings on Ecovillages

Christian, Diana Leafe. 2003. *Creating a Life Together: Practical Tools to Grow Ecovillages and Intentional Communities.* Gabriola Island, Canada: New Society.

Dawson, Jonathan. 2006. *Ecovillages: New Frontiers for Sustainability.* Schumacher Briefing 12. Totnes, UK: Green Books.

Fellowship of Intentional Community. 2010. *Communities Directory: A Guide to Cooperative Living.* Rutledge, MO: Fellowship of Intentional Community.

Fotopoulos, Takis. 2000. "The Limitations of Life-style Strategies: The Ecovillage "Movement" is NOT the Way Towards a New Democratic Society." *Democracy & Nature* 6 (2): 287–308.

———. 2002. "The Transition to an Alternative Society: The Ecovillage Movement, the Simpler Way and the Inclusive Democracy Project." *Democracy & Nature* 8 (1): 150–57.

———. 2006. "Is the Eco-village Movement a Solution or Part of the Problem?" *The International Journal of Inclusive Democracy* 2 (3).

Gilman, Robert. 1991. "The Eco-Village Challenge." *In Context* 29. http://www.context.org/ICLIB/IC29/Gilman1.thm.

Hopkins, Rob. 2008. *The Transition Handbook: From Oil Dependency to Local Resilience.* Totnes, UK: Green Books.

Jackson, Hildur, and Karen Svensson, eds. 2002. *Ecovillage Living: Restoring the Earth and Her People.* Totnes, UK: Green Books.

Kasper, Debbie Van Schyndel. 2008. "Redefining Community in the Ecovillage." *Human Ecology Review* 15 (1): 12–24.

Kirby, Andy. 2003. "Redefining Social and Environmental Relations at the Ecovillage at Ithaca: A Case Study." *Journal of Environmental Psychology* 23: 323–32.

Lockyer, Joshua. 2008. "From Earthships to Strawbales: Sustainable Housing in Ecovillages." Photo essay. *Anthropology News* 49 (9): 20.

———. 2010a. "Intentional Community Carbon Reduction and Climate Change Action: From Ecovillages to Transition Towns." In *Low Carbon Communities: Imaginative Approaches to Combating Climate Change Locally,* ed. Michael Peters, Shane Fudge, and Tim Jackson. Cheltenham, UK: Edward Elgar Publishing.

———. 2010b. "Intentional Communities and Sustainability." *Communal Societies* 30 (1): 17–30.

Trainer, Ted. 2000. "Where Are We, Where Do We Want to be, How Do We Get There?" *Democracy & Nature* 6 (2): 267–86.

———. 2002. "Debating the Significance of the Global Eco-village Movement: A Reply to Takis Fotopoulos." *Democracy & Nature* 8 (1): 143–49.

———. 2006. "On Eco-villages and the Transition." *The International Journal of Inclusive Democracy* 2 (3).

Walker, Liz. 2005. *Ecovillage at Ithaca: Pioneering a Sustainable Culture.* Gabriola Island, Canada: New Society.

Notes on Contributors

Guntra A. Aistara, PhD (University of Michigan, 2008), specializes in environmental anthropology. She is currently assistant professor at the Central European University in Budapest, Hungary, and previously worked at the UN-mandated University for Peace in Costa Rica. She is also a cofounder and board member of the Latvian Permaculture Association. She is currently working on a book entitled *Placing Diversity* about small organic farmers' struggles to create and maintain rural spaces as particular places and sources of diversity in the midst of globalization.

Steven M. Alexander, MS, is a PhD candidate in the Department of Environment and Resource Studies at the University of Waterloo and an associate of the Resilience Design Group at Antioch University New England. As former assistant director of the Adirondack Semester, he spent three years working closely with students, faculty, and staff while personally engaging in the process of *reinhabitation.* Trained as a geologist, natural historian, and educator, Steve has worked with students in a variety of bioregions, including the Colorado Plateau, Adirondacks/Northern Forest, and the Greater Yellowstone Geo-ecosystem. He has taught and developed both curriculum and programs for several nonprofits and educational institutions, including the National Outdoor Leadership School, Teton Science Schools, and Wild Rockies Field Institute.

Beatriz Arjona is an environmental biologist by training. Since 2000, she has been dedicated to ecovillage living, cofounding the Ecoaldea Montaña Mágica, the Proyecto Permacultural Amandaris, and the Ecoaldea Aldeafeliz, while also conducting workshops on related themes. She is the director of Change the World-Colombia, co-organizer of Renace Colombia – The Colombian Ecovillage Network, and a member of the organizing committee of the annual gathering of Colombian ecovillages.

Ted Baker is a PhD candidate in social anthropology at York University in Toronto, Ontario. He is currently juggling the responsibilities of being a parent, writing a dissertation, and teaching courses in anthropology, environmentalism, and First Nations studies. He is also involved with a grassroots network doing solidarity work with the Six Nations of the Grand River.

Ron Berezan has been exploring and promoting new possibilities for growing food in urban areas ever since his first "accidental" food garden as a young university student. Since 2003, Ron has operated *The Urban Farmer,* an organic gardening, edible landscaping, and permaculture design service (www.theurbanfarmer.ca). He is writing his first book, tentatively titled *Down the Garden Path: Cultivating Hope for the Ecological Age.* Ron is a member of the Society of Organic Urban Land Care Professionals (SOUL) and holds a master's degree in ecological theology from St. Stephen's College in Edmonton. He now lives in Powell River, British Columbia.

Peter Berg founded the Planet Drum Foundation in 1973 and was its director for thirty-five years. He was a noted ecologist, author, and speaker. Mr. Berg is acknowledged as the originator of the terms *bioregion* and *reinhabitation* to describe land areas in terms of their interdependent plant, animal, and human life. Peter Berg authored a number of books, including *Discovering Your Life-Place: A First Bioregional Workbook* (1995, Planet Drum Books), *A Green City Program for the San Francisco Bay Area and Beyond* (1989, Planet Drum Books; republished 1990, Wingbow Press), *Figures of Regulation: Guides for Re-balancing Society with the Biosphere* (1981, Planet Drum Books), and *Reinhabiting a Separate Country: A Bioregional Anthology of Northern California* (1978, Planet Drum Books).

Brian J. Burke received his PhD from the University of Arizona's School of Anthropology and is currently a member of the Coweeta Listening Project at the University of Georgia. Before beginning his doctoral research on the construction of barter and alternative currency systems in Medellín, Colombia where he encountered Beatriz Arjona and the Colombian Ecovillage Network, he spent a year working on agroecology, permaculture, and ecovillage projects in Central and South America. He has also conducted research on Latino migrant communities in the United States, urban ecology projects on the U.S.-Mexico border, farming cooperatives in Paraguay, and indigenous cooperatives and fair trade in Brazil.

Brian C. Campbell, associate professor of anthropology at the University of Central Arkansas, received his PhD from the University of Georgia's Environmental and Ecological Anthropology Program. His research and service project, Conserving Arkansas's Agricultural Heritage, focuses on agrobiodiversity conservation in Arkansas (and in the Missouri Ozarks) through seed banks, campus and community gardens, and the establishment of public seed exchanges.

Jonathan Dawson is a sustainability educator, author, and activist, currently working as head of economics at Schumacher College in the UK. Until recently, he was resident in the Findhorn Foundation in Scotland and was President of the Global Ecovillage Network. He also works as an advisor on local economic development for a range of governmental agencies and NGOs in Africa.

Katy Fox, PhD, is a social anthropologist and has researched the impacts of EU agriculture policy on the lives of subsistence farmers in Romania. Her follow-up research in Romania brought to the fore environmental questions, and she has since worked with permaculturists and movements defending the livelihood rights of small farmers. She recently moved back to her native Luxembourg and set up CELL, the Centre for Ecological Learning Luxembourg, a laboratory for transitional and permaculture ethics and practice.

Daniel Greenberg has studied and directed community-based educational programs for over fifteen years. He visited and corresponded with over two hundred US intentional communities for his PhD dissertation on children and education in community, and later spent a year at the Findhorn Foundation in Scotland working with children and families there. He is the founding director of Living Routes, which develops accredited ecovillage-based education programs that promote sustainable community development. He lives at the Sirius Community in Shutesbury, Massachusetts.

Randolph Haluza-DeLay, PhD, is associate professor in sociology at The King's University College in Edmonton, Alberta. He is coeditor of the anthology *Speaking for Ourselves: Environmental Justice in Canada* (University of British Columbia Press, 2009), and has written over thirty journal articles, research reports, and book chapters. His book *How the World's Religions are Responding to Climate Change* will be out late in 2013. For the last five years he has been engaged with the various components of local environmental movements and social justice groups. The permaculture network is one aspect of this research and personal engagement.

Baylor Johnson, PhD, is associate professor of philosophy at St. Lawrence University. From 2004 to 2010 he was the director of Outdoor Studies and the Adirondack Semester. He was the principle architect of St. Lawrence's

Outdoor Program and initiatives to incorporate the power of outdoor and experiential education into liberal arts teaching at the university. This initiative led to creation of the Adirondack Semester and the Outdoor Studies minor.

Todd LeVasseur, PhD, is visiting assistant professor in the Religious Studies Department at the College of Charleston, South Carolina, where he also teaches in the Environmental Studies Program. His research interests include studying the emerging phenomenon he labels "religious agrarianism"; religious responses to the emerging climate crisis; and how religious teachings and practices influence environmental values, politics, and behaviors and vice versa.

Joshua Lockyer, PhD, is assistant professor of anthropology at Arkansas Tech University. He spent the last ten plus years working with, conducting research on, teaching about, and drawing inspiration from bioregionalists, permaculturalists, and ecovillagers, especially in the southeastern and Midwestern United States and Europe. His current projects include creating long-term, collaborative, multidisciplinary research and education partnerships with intentional communities in his bioregion and developing a bioregionally focused undergraduate environmental anthropology curriculum at Arkansas Tech University.

James J. Parsons, PhD, was professor and chair of the Department of Geography at the University of California, Berkeley, past president of the Pacific Coast Geographers, and past president of the Association of American Geographers.

Jenny Pickerill, PhD, is a reader in human geography at Leicester University. She has published three books and more than twenty academic articles. Her work focuses on a variety of solutions to environmental problems—instigated through creative activism, environmental justice projects, diverse approaches to transition, and green building. Her most recent project explores the possibilities and implications of affordable eco-housing and is chronicled on her Green Building Blog at http://naturalbuild.wordpress.com.

Aili Pyhälä, postdoctoral researcher at the Ethnoecology Laboratory, Autonomous University of Barcelona, Spain, is a socio-environmental scientist with a background both in the natural and social sciences. She has many years of experience working in developing countries around the world, particularly with rural and indigenous populations, but also as part of ecological and biodiversity related research. An expert in permaculture design, ecovillage design, and ecological footprinting, she continues to focus her efforts on bridging the gap between human and environmental rights issues at the grassroots level and science and decision-making at the policy level, while addressing broader issues concerning development policy and global responsibility.

Bob Randall, PhD, in retirement, continues to teach vegetable and fruit gardening classes, permaculture, and is active in committees of three horticultural education organizations. Since retirement, he taught for a year in the Rice University Ecology Department, was treasurer of the Continental Bioregional Congress, and keynoted conferences in Atlanta and Philadelphia. Bob was Urban Harvest's founding executive director for fourteen years and taught anthropology for twenty years. His University of California–Berkeley doctoral fieldwork was in the southern Philippines and his Binghamton University master's work was on Sahelan salt trade.

James R. Veteto, PhD, is assistant professor and director of The Laboratory of Environmental Anthropology and The Southern Seed Legacy at The University of North Texas. He has worked with local and indigenous communities in southern Appalachia, the Ozarks, and the Sierra Madre Occidental Mountains of northwest Mexico. His work has focused specifically on comparative agrobiodiversity inventories, farmer decision making, conservation strategies, and ecotopian countercultural movements in mountain ecosystems. Before returning to academia, Veteto ran several organic farms and gardens, experimenting in permaculture design and intentional sustainable community living.

Index

Page numbers in italics refer to illustrations.
Page numbers in boldface refer to definitions.
The letter "t" indicates a table. The letter "n" indicates a note. The letter "m" indicates a map.

www.ingramcontent.com/pod-product-compliance
Lightning Source LLC
Chambersburg PA
CBHW060024030426
42334CB00019B/2175
* 9 7 8 1 7 8 2 3 8 9 0 5 7 *